The Dark Side of the Force

The central tradition of mainline economics deals with only one way of making a living, namely, producing useful goods and services. But there is another way of getting ahead: through conflict or the "dark side," that is, by attempting to appropriate what others have produced. Appropriation struggles include military aggression and resistance and also nonmilitary activities such as litigation, strikes and lockouts, takeover contests, and family quarrels. This volume brings the analysis of conflict into the mainstream of economics. Part One explores the causes, conduct, and consequences of conflict as an economic activity. Part Two delves more deeply into the evolutionary sources of our capacities, physical and mental, for both conflict and cooperation. The introductory chapter of the volume, which demonstrates that the force of self-interest has both a bright side and a dark side, was the author's 1993 Presidential Address to the Western Economic Association. Other chapters provide economic models of conflict, historical discussions, experimental tests, and applications to topics in political science and law.

Jack Hirshleifer has served on the faculty of the Department of Economics at the University of California, Los Angeles, since 1960. He was employed as an economist at the RAND Corporation from 1949 to 1955 and taught at the University of Chicago Graduate School of Business from 1955 to 1960. Professor Hirshleifer is a Fellow of the American Academy of Arts and Sciences, a Distinguished Fellow of the American Economic Association, and a Fellow of the Econometric Society. He has served as Vice President of the American Economic Association and in 1993 was elected President of the Western Economic Association. He is a member of the Editorial Boards of the *Journal of Economic Behavior and Organization* and the *Journal of Bioeconomics*.

Professor Hirshleifer's fields of specialization have included water supply and resource economics, capital theory, applied theory of the firm, uncertainty and information, political economy, bioeconomics, and conflict theory. In the last area his work has emphasized the largely unrecognized parallels among the many manifestations of conflict, among them warfare, crime, litigation, strikes and lockouts, redistributive politics, and business takeover contests.

Jack Hirshleifer's previous books include *The Analytics of Uncertainty and Information* (coauthored with John G. Riley, Cambridge University Press, 1992); *Time, Uncertainty, and Information* (1989); *Economic Behavior in Adversity* (1987); *Price Theory and Applications*, 6th edition (coauthored with David Hirshleifer, 1998); and *Investment, Interest, and Capital* (1970).

Praise for *The Dark Side of the Force*

"The second major way of making a living – the appropriation of goods produced by others – has hardly been examined within mainstream economics, even though it could be argued that empirically it is at least as important as production. The former Soviet Union and many developing countries, for example, are largely poor because of the difficulty they have controlling appropriation. Jack Hirshleifer is the first and most eminent economist to have made a sustained effort to understand this second way of making a living. Over the past twenty years he has published a series of articles that has spawned a growing literature within economics and is having an impact beyond economics. This excellent book makes this work more easily accessible. Not only scholars and students in economics but also policy makers and other social scientists will have much to gain from reading it."

– Stergios Skaperdas, *University of California, Irvine*

"Most economists conveniently ignore the fact that all economic and political transactions take place in the shadow of conflict. Jack Hirshleifer is prominent among those who do not, and this timely book collects some of his seminal contributions."

– Karl Warneryd, *Stockholm School of Economics*

The Dark Side of the Force

Economic Foundations of Conflict Theory

JACK HIRSHLEIFER

University of California, Los Angeles

CAMBRIDGE
UNIVERSITY PRESS

PUBLISHED BY THE PRESS SYNDICATE OF THE UNIVERSITY OF CAMBRIDGE
The Pitt Building, Trumpington Street, Cambridge, United Kingdom

CAMBRIDGE UNIVERSITY PRESS
The Edinburgh Building, Cambridge CB2 2RU, UK
40 West 20th Street, New York, NY 10011-4211, USA
10 Stamford Road, Oakleigh, VIC 3166, Australia
Ruiz de Alarcón 13, 28014 Madrid, Spain
Dock House, The Waterfront, Cape Town 8001, South Africa

http://www.cambridge.org

First published 2001

Printed in the United Kingdom

Typeface Times New Roman 11/13 pt.   *System* LATEX 2_ε [TB]

A catalog record for this book is available from the British Library.

Library of Congress Cataloging in Publication Data
Hirshleifer, Jack.
The dark side of the force : economic foundations of conflict theory / Jack Hirshleifer.
p.   cm.
Includes bibliographical references and index.
ISBN 0-521-80412-4 – ISBN 0-521-00917-0 (pb.)
1. Evolutionary economics.   2. Social conflict – Economic aspects.
3. War – Economic aspects.   4. Labor disputes.   5. Competition.   6. Negotiation – Economic
aspects.   7. Cooperativeness – Economic aspects.   8. Economic history.   I. Title: Economic
foundations of conflict theory.   II. Title.
HB97.3.H57   2001
330 – dc21   00-066708

ISBN 0 521 80412 4 hardback
ISBN 0 521 00917 0 paperback

Contents

v

Preface

I am grateful to the publishers for making these previously published articles available in the present volume.

A collection of mine on a related topic, *Economic Behaviour in Adversity*, was published in 1987 by the University of Chicago Press and Wheatsheaf Books. The essays reprinted here do not overlap with the earlier book, with one partial exception: the present volume contains a brief extract from the article "Evolutionary Models in Economics and Law: Cooperation versus Conflict Strategies" (1982), whose full text appeared in the 1987 book.

The 1987 monograph was divided into two sections. The first part consisted of historical studies of great social disasters together with discussions of policy options for dealing with such shattering events. The second part contained several of my early efforts to model the processes of cooperation and conflict that constitute the subject matter of this volume.

In the introduction to the 1987 book, I indicated that economic behavior in conditions of disaster and conflict is "a momentous topic that as yet has been only barely explored by economists." In the intervening years progress has been made, as evidenced by the articles reproduced here and the works of the many other authors cited therein.

The articles in this volume are reproduced as originally published apart from correction of misprints and minor errors. The one exception, as indicated above, is that only an extract has been reproduced from the article "Evolutionary Models in Economics and Law: Cooperation versus Conflict Strategies" (1982).

I am happy to express appreciation to the several coauthors who have kindly granted permission to reproduce the jointly composed articles that appear in this volume. I also thank David Hirshleifer for his invaluable assistance throughout and Scott Parris of Cambridge University Press for many constructive suggestions.

Introduction

The efforts of men are utilized in two different ways: they are directed to the production or transformation of economic goods, or else to the appropriation of goods produced by others.

[Vilfredo Pareto]

In racing for a prize, there are two main ways to win: running faster yourself, or tripping up your opponent. Or suppose you are engaged in a cooperative enterprise with others, possibly within a business firm. Again there are a range of options: you can concentrate on becoming more productive on behalf of the firm as a whole, or else upon grabbing a bigger share for yourself. In the realm of politics, Mary Lease, an agrarian rabble-rouser of the 1890s, put it this way: "Kansas farmers should raise less corn and raise more hell."

Correspondingly, there are two main methods of making a living. The first aims at producing useful goods and services for exchange with other producers. Alternatively, you might try to appropriate a larger slice of whatever is being produced. Think of these as *the way of production and exchange* versus *the way of predation and conflict*. Each way of making a living has an associated technology: there is the familiar *technology of production*, but also a *technology of struggle*. There is one set of techniques for tilling the land, and quite a different set of techniques for capturing land and defending it against intruders.

The way of conflict does not necessarily involve violence. Among the usually nonviolent forms of contests are strikes and lockouts (industrial conflict) and lawsuits (legal conflict). Then there are back-biting maneuvers for advancement on the promotion ladder, and family squabbles ranging from the trivial to the deadly serious. In the world of business a firm might find ways of sabotaging competing enterprises without actually assassinating their executives. Nevertheless, although not all

1

struggles involve violence, warfare serves as a convenient metaphor for strife and contention generally.

The way of production and exchange enlarges the social total of wealth. *The way of predation and conflict* merely redistributes that total (less whatever is dissipated in the struggle). In a world requiring defense against aggressors, even decisionmakers otherwise inclined to be pacific have to balance on the margin between these two strategies. And in fact all choices take place in the shadow of conflict. What a nation can achieve by diplomacy depends largely upon what would happen in the event of war. Deciding whether to plant a crop or build a factory will be influenced by ability to protect your investment against invasions, by enemies foreign or domestic. (Including the efforts of adversaries operating under color of law, such as tax collectors and class-action attorneys.)

Corresponding to the two strategies for making a living there are, in principle, two main branches of economics. Traditional economics has been almost exclusively devoted to one of these branches, the way of production and exchange. But the way of conflict and predation is equally "economic." It responds to the omnipresent fact of scarcity, there is scope for rational choice on the level of the decision-making agent, and decentralized choices interact to bring about a societal equilibrium. Mainline economics has not totally ignored conflictual activities: topics such as crime, litigation, labor-management struggles, rent-seeking contests, redistributive politics, and so forth have received a certain amount of attention. But these investigations have not been woven into the central fabric of economic thought. It is as if international trade, industrial organization, public finance, labor economics, and all the other traditional subdivisions of economic theory had developed as separate fields with no recognition of their common foundation in the microeconomics of production and exchange. A failing of exactly this type has occurred here. The first aim of conflict analysis in economics is therefore to provide an underlying theory of struggle that will be applicable to all the specific topical areas such as warfare, litigation, strikes and lockouts, crime, power politics, and family quarrels. Ultimately, a unified economic theory should allow for *both* of the two main forms of social interaction: on the one hand exchange and contract, and on the other hand struggle and contention.

Here are some illustrative questions – some obvious, some perhaps less so – upon which the articles reprinted here shed light:

1. What governs the intensity of struggle and the associated wastage of resources? When do contenders such as individuals, tribes,

and nations "fight" (literally in the case of warfare, or metaphorically in contexts like political campaigns and litigation) rather than come to an agreed settlement? Do interpersonal sympathy, greater wealth, improved productive opportunities, and increased economic interdependence conduce to peaceful settlement? What happens as conflict technology becomes more destructive? When the contestants are more equally matched, does conflict become more likely?

2. Who wins, and by how much? As determinants of conflictual outcomes, how important are disparities of wealth endowments, comparative advantages in production versus combat, differences in time-preferences or in risk-aversion, and so forth? For example, other things being equal, does conflict tend to improve the position of the initially better endowed side? That is, will the rich become richer and the poor poorer?

3. Is conflict usually or always a mistake on the part of one side or the other, so that better information will tend to promote peaceful settlement?

4. What are threats and promises? Why should they ever be believed? When are they likely to be effective? Conversely, when is "appeasement" likely to work?

Although I have complained about the relative lack of attention to conflictual competition, this volume is not the first to have addressed the topic. For one thing, just about every important social scientist has had something valuable to say about the contest for wealth and advantage. Adam Smith's *The Wealth of Nations* (1776) has dozens of references to war and perhaps hundreds to political quarrels, exploitative taxation, and the like. But Smith and other classic authors never pushed toward systematic analysis of the way of conflict. By the time of Alfred Marshall the central tendency of economic thought had narrowed drastically. War does not even appear in the index of Marshall's *Principles of Economics* (1920). In contrast, standing apart from the central tradition, Karl Marx in *Das Kapital* (1867) placed struggle – the class struggle in particular – at the center of human social activity. However incoherent his effort may have been from a scientific standpoint, Marx at least perceived the analytic gap that modern conflict theory has attempted to fill.

A few pioneering volumes have led the way. Schelling (1960) addressed topics such as threats and deterrence, especially with regard to national strategic policy. Boulding (1962) is wider-ranging, emphasizing the problem of *viability*: the circumstances in which a party to conflict can guarantee its own survival against opposed force. Tullock (1974) was perhaps the first to employ standard analytic building blocks such as preference functions and opportunity sets for dealing with conflict interactions. Of these volumes only Schelling's is at all well known and still in print. More recent monographs, once again hardly well known, include Bernholz (1985), dealing with power balances in international systems, and Usher (1992), who studied the viability of forms of government from despotism to liberal democracy.

Individual journal articles are of course far too numerous to cite extensively here. Two early contributions stand out, however. Bush and Mayer (1974) described a "natural equilibrium" generated by decision makers' competing predatory efforts ("stealing" from one another). Skogh and Stuart (1982) is more fully developed and was apparently the first to model both offense and defense in contesting for income. More recent years have seen a modest boom in analytic treatments of conflict interactions, warranting publication of several valuable edited collections of journal articles, among them Isard and Anderton (1992), Hartley and Sandler (1995), and Garfinkel and Skaperdas (1996). These contributions have addressed a wide range of topics, including – to name but a few – the sources of between-group and within-group conflicts, the conditions leading to compromise and settlement, the technology of warfare and other forms of struggle, the consequences of balances and imbalances of power, and the formation of coalitions and alliances.

This extremely condensed review of the literature undoubtedly displays parochial professional bias. Political scientists also, at least in recent years, have been generating analytic models of warfare and contests for power. (Some such studies are cited in the chapters in this volume.) And a few relevant writings in sociology are analytical in a way that economists would recognize. Even closer to economics – though this fact is largely unknown on both sides – is the work of evolutionary biologists and anthropologists on topics such as predator–prey interactions, contests for territory and dominance, and the power gradient within hierarchical social groups. I will only cite one truly remarkable early contribution, Robert H. MacArthur's *Geographical Ecology* (1972) (especially Chapter 2, "The Machinery of Competition and Predation"). That study developed, among other things, an evolutionary general-equilibrium model of contentious competition (for example, between predators and prey).

I will mention here several continuing themes:

1. Conflict theory shares with exchange theory the central analytic paradigms of *optimization* on the individual level of analysis and societal *equilibrium* on the aggregate level. Features like preference functions, competition, increasing and decreasing returns, and so forth play comparable roles in both branches of economic theorizing.
2. The key difference is that the social interactions dealt with in exchange theory are a source of *mutual* advantage, whereas in conflict theory any advantage gained by one party must come at the expense of its rival or rivals.
3. Any settlement or compromise arrived at, and even the process of exchange itself, takes place in the shadow of the potential conflict lurking in the background.
4. Human society, although of course unique in many ways, nevertheless exists within bounds established by Nature, which, through the evolutionary process, has fashioned important aspects of our morphology, biochemistry, and psychology and behavioral inclinations as well.

Many of these themes are illustrated in the opening essay, one that bears the same title as the book as a whole: "The Dark Side of the Force" (my 1993 Presidential Address to the Western Economic Association). The articles grouped in Part One fall under the general heading *Causes, Consequences, and Conduct of Conflict*. The selections in Part Two, under the heading *Evolutionary Approaches to Conflict and its Resolution*, show how modern evolutionary theory bears upon topics such as the development of law and social ethics and the viability of reciprocity strategies. Finally, the concluding article, "The Expanding Domain of Economics," addresses the imperial pretensions of economics to constitute a universal social science.

REFERENCES

Bernholz, Peter. 1985. *The International Game of Power*. Berlin: Mouton Publishers.
Boulding, Kenneth E. 1962. *Conflict and Defense*. New York: Harper & Brothers.
Bush, Winston C., and Lawrence S. Mayer. 1974. "Some Implications of Anarchy for the Distribution of Property," *Journal of Economic Theory*, 8:401–12.

Garfinkel, Michelle R., and Stergios Skaperdas (eds.). 1996. *The Political Economy of Conflict and Appropriation*. New York: Cambridge University Press.

Hartley, Keith, and Todd Sandler (eds.). 1995. *Handbook of Defense Economics*, v. 1. Amsterdam: Elsevier.

Isard, Walter, and Charles H. Anderton (eds.). 1992. *Economics of Arms Reduction and the Peace Process*. Amsterdam: North-Holland.

MacArthur, Robert H. 1972. *Geographical Ecology*. Princeton, NJ: Princeton University Press.

Marshall, Alfred. 1920. *Principles of Economics*, 8th ed., London: Macmillan and Co., Ltd.

Marx, Karl. 1867. *Das Kapital*, v. 1.

Schelling, Thomas C. 1960. *The Strategy of Conflict*. London: Oxford University Press.

Skogh, Goran, and Charles Stuart. 1982. "A Contractarian Theory of Property Rights and Crime," *Scandinavian Journal of Economics*, 84(1):27–40.

Smith, Adam 1776 [1937]. *The Wealth of Nations*. New York: Modern Library.

Tullock, Gordon. 1974. *The Social Dilemma*. Blacksburg, VA: University Publications.

Usher, Dan. 1992. *The Welfare Economics of Markets, Voting, and Predation*. Ann Arbor, MI: University of Michigan Press.

1

The Dark Side of the Force

Western Economic Association International 1993
Presidential Address

Jack Hirshleifer*

Background of this Chapter

The force referred to here is the pressure of self-interest. But can self-interest have a dark side? Isn't it dark all over? No, there is a bright side as well as a dark side. As Adam Smith famously explained, self-interest often impels a person to serve others. An employee can prosper by being a productive worker, a businessperson by selling desirable products at reasonable prices. Yet sometimes one can succeed – materially, though certainly not morally – by attacking competitors, stealing from one's employer, or defrauding one's customers. Mainline economics has been so concerned to convey the important though partial truth about the possible beneficence of self-interest as to almost forget there is still the dark side.

This 1993 Presidential Address to the Western Economic Association was an attempt to restore the analytic balance: to convince economists that not only the sunny side but also the dark side of self-interest contribute to shaping individual behavior and the forms of human societies. The article was published in *Economic Inquiry*, the flagship journal of the Western Economic Association.

... [T]he age of chivalry is gone. That of sophisters, economists, and calculators, has succeeded: and the glory of Europe is extinguished for ever.[1]

Edmund Burke wrote that accusation against our profession back in the year 1790. Yet, 200 years later, it seems we economists and sophisters have still not managed to extirpate chivalry and generosity. In an

* Professor of Economics, University of California, Los Angeles. This is a slightly expanded version of the Presidential Address delivered at the annual meeting of the Western Economic Association on June 22, 1993 under the title *Cooperation, Conflict, and All That*. (Reprinted from J. Hirshleifer, "The Dark Side of the Force," *Economic Inquiry*, Vol. 32, 1–10, Copyright © 1994, with permission from Oxford University Press.)
[1] Quoted in James [1984, p. 63].

article in the current issue of the *Journal of Economic Perspectives*[2] that received extensive journalistic coverage,[3] the authors reviewed the notorious evidence that people perversely persist in contributing to charities and public goods. And violating the self-interest postulate again, in Prisoners' Dilemma experiments most subjects choose COOPERATE rather than DEFECT. However, one walk of life stands out as an embarrassing exception. Who is it who turn out to be almost as selfish as economic theory makes out? The answer: only economists and their students! Thus, like Socrates, we economists are convicted not only of untruth but of corrupting the young.

Nevertheless, I am among those who remain skeptical about the significance of self-reported contributions to charity, or about behavior in hypothetical or small-stakes Prisoners' Dilemma experiments. My guess is that economists are not more selfish, but only more *acceptant* of human selfishness as a fact of life.

There's an updated proverb from Ecclesiastes:

The race is not always to the swift, or the battle to the strong – but that's the way to bet.

Similarly, unselfishness certainly exists, but don't bet on it.

With regard to the power of love and chivalry as organizing principles of social life, as usual Adam Smith said it best:

In civilized society [man] stands at all times in need of the co-operation and assistance of great multitudes, while his whole life is scarce sufficient to gain the friendship of a few persons.[4]

Love and friendship may sustain cooperation among a few partners, but the elaborate division of labor essential for modern life has to rely on the force of self-interest. Pushing this point to an extreme, Hayek has contended that only when people *learned* to be selfish, learned to overcome their innate instincts toward communal sharing, did it become possible to make the transition from primitive society to free civilized life. Adapting his words slightly:

These habits [of generosity] had to be shed . . . to make the transition to the . . . open society possible. . . . [The] mores [of the market economy] involve withholding from the known needy neighbours what they might require, in order to serve the unknown needs of thousands of unknown others.[5]

---

[2] Frank, Gilovich, and Regan [1993].

[3] See *The Economist*, 29 May 1993, p. 71.

[4] Smith [1937 (1776), p. 14]. See the excellent discussion of Smith's views on this topic in Coase [1976].

[5] Hayek [1979, Epilogue].

So, Hayek would claim, economists aren't corrupting the young by teaching them selfishness – we're civilizing them!

But my point today is different. I want to argue that our profession has on the whole taken not too harsh but rather too benign a view of the human enterprise. Recognizing the force of self-interest, the mainline Marshallian tradition has nevertheless almost entirely overlooked what I will call *the dark side of the force* – to wit: crime, war, and politics. That's like telling the story of Luke Skywalker and Obe Wan Ben Kenobe without mentioning Darth Vader.

"Crime," "war," "politics" – the words do not even appear in the index to Marshall's *Principles of Economics*.[6] Or take the characteristically flat and prosaic way Marshall defines economics on p. 1 of the *Principles*:

... ECONOMICS is a study of mankind in the ordinary business of life; it examines that part of individual and social action which is most closely connected with the attainment and with the use of the material requisites of well-being.

So, for Marshall, economics is bean-counting. Boring, boring, boring. The title page of the *Principles* carries the famous epigraph: "*Natura non facit saltum*" – Nature doesn't make leaps. What Marshall really meant was: "No excitement please, we're English here."[7]

By way of contrast, consider Vilfredo Pareto:

The efforts of men are utilized in two different ways: they are directed to the production or transformation of economic goods, or else to the appropriation of goods produced by others.[8]

The rhetoric isn't too thrilling, I admit; perhaps something was lost in the translation. But the thought is more vigorous. Pareto is saying, sure, you can produce goods for the purpose of mutually beneficial exchange with other parties – OK, that's Marshall's "ordinary business." But there's another way to get rich: you can grab goods that someone else has produced. *Appropriating, grabbing, confiscating* what you want – and, on the flip side, *defending, protecting, sequestering* what you already have – that's economic activity too.

Take television. Cops chase robbers, victims are stalked by hitmen (or should I say hitpersons?), posses cut off rustlers at the pass, plaintiffs sue

---

[6] Marshall [1920].

[7] I hasten to add that Marshall's personal concerns went beyond this straightjacket definition. From many asides in the *Principles* and elsewhere, we know that his interests extended to questions like non-pecuniary motivations and the molding of human character. But, evidently, he regarded such matters as outside the scope of scientific economics.

[8] Quoted in James [1984, p. 160].

defendants, exorcists cast spells against vampires. What is all this but *muscular economics*? Robbers, rustlers, hitpersons, litigants – they're all trying to make a living. Even vampires are making economic choices: sucking blood is presumably the cost-effective way of meeting their unusual nutritional needs.

The balance between these modes of economic activity – the one leading to greater aggregate wealth, and the other to conflict over who gets the wealth – provides the main story line of human history. Following my teacher Joseph Schumpeter I remind you that Karl Marx, though a flop as an economist, did appreciate the importance of the dark side, the conflict option. But Marx's vision was distorted by his preconceived idea that all kinds of conflict, including wars among nations and even the battle of the sexes, could be squeezed into the ill-fitting mold of the class struggle:

The history of all . . . society is the history of class struggles.[9]

This one-dimensional outlook led him to what in principle he deplored, fatuous utopianism, in fantasizing that moderation of the class struggle would bring on universal peace:

In proportion as the antagonism between classes within the nation vanishes, the hostility of one nation to another will come to an end.[10]

Marx had this totally wrong: the truth is the reverse. That in-group amity rises and falls in proportion to external menace, and vice versa, is a practically universal truth.[11]

Niccolo Machiavelli saw matters more clearly:

It is not gold, but good soldiers that insure success . . . for it is impossible that good soldiers should not be able to procure gold.[12]

This is Machiavelli's version of the golden rule: *he who gets to rule, will get the gold.*

Human history is a record of the tension between the way of Niccolo Machiavelli and what might be called the way of Ronald Coase. According to Coase's Theorem, people will never pass up an opportunity to cooperate by means of mutually advantageous exchange. What might be called Machiavelli's Theorem says that no one will ever pass up an

---

[9] Quoted in Bartlett [1968, p. 686].
[10] Quoted in Bartlett [1968, p. 687].
[11] An excellent discussion appears in Ardrey [1966, Ch. 8].
[12] Quoted by Gilbert [1941, p. 15].

opportunity to gain a one-sided advantage by exploiting another party. Machiavelli's Theorem standing alone is only a partial truth, but so is Coase's Theorem standing alone. Our textbooks need to deal with both modes of economic activity. They should be saying that decision-makers will strike an optimal balance between the way of Coase and the way of Machiavelli – between the way of production combined with mutually advantgeous exchange, and the dark-side way of confiscation, exploitation, and conflict.

Crime, war, and politics have received some coverage from economists, it is true, but in the past only as specialized and rather esoteric topics. More recently, under the heading of "rent-seeking," the struggle for resource control is coming to be recognized as a central issue. But rent-seeking, in its usual connotation of maneuvering for licenses and monopoly privileges, is to *conflict* as milkwater is to blood, sweat, and tears. The appropriative struggle can also take more energetic forms, for example strikes and lockouts, bank robbery, revolutionary warfare, and international confrontations. In short, the dark side is no mere out-lying peninsula but rather an entire intellectual continent on the map of economic activity.

(As we come to explore this continent, economists will encounter a number of native tribes – historians, sociologists, psychologists, philosophers, etc. – who, in their various intellectually primitive ways, have preceded us in reconnoitering the dark side of human activity. Once we economists get involved, quite properly we'll of course be brushing aside these a-theoretical aborigines.)[13]

I now offer two propositions about cooperation and conflict. First: *cooperation, with a few obvious exceptions, occurs only in the shadow of conflict.* Only if we understand threats and struggles can we properly appreciate how, why, and when mutually advantageous exchange – between husband and wife, between capital and labor, between nation and nation – can take place. In litigation, for example, it is fear of trial, with its attendant costs and uncertainties, that impels plaintiff and defendant toward negotiated settlement. And, furthermore, the perceived chances for victory at trial shape the specific terms of settlement.[14]

---

[13] A side note to my good friends and honored colleagues in other disciplines. How do I reconcile these comments with the undoubted fine work, in conflict analysis and other areas, being produced by anthropologists, political scientists, psychologists, and so forth? The answer is simple. When these researchers do good work, they're doing economics!

[14] See Cooter, Marks, and Mnookin [1982].

With regard to international conflict, I shall paraphrase Carl von Clausewitz:

For achieving the political aims that are the end of war, the decision by arms is what cash settlement is in trade.[15]

Trade can be conducted without cash settlement, but the ability to make cash settlement ultimately constrains what trades a merchant can engage in. Similarly, Clausewitz is saying, a state remains influential in peacetime only owing to the damage it could inflict in the event of war.

But, you may say, what of the social arrangements, laws, and judicial systems that humans have devised to temper the power struggle? That brings me to my second proposition: *when people cooperate, it is generally a conspiracy for aggression against others (or, at least, is a response to such aggression).*

A nation whose institutions favor Coasian cooperation, Marshall's "ordinary" business activity, will grow wealthy. But, Adam Smith told us:

An industrious, and upon that account a wealthy nation, is of all nations the most likely to be attacked...[16]

If the gains from group aggression are big enough, invaders can get their act together. Sigmund Freud said:

It is always possible to bind together a considerable number of people...so long as there are other people left over to receive the manifestations of their aggressiveness.[17]

And on the defensive side, invasion cements the unity and fighting power of the group attacked.

The bottom line is that nations with wealth-enhancing laws and institutions will not be able to enjoy the fruits thereof unless, when challenged, they can put up a tough fight. And the same holds for political parties, clubs, families, and business firms.

---

[15] Without violating Clausewitz's meaning, I have conflated here two separate quotations:

For political aims are the end and war is the means...

and:

The decision by arms is for all operations in war, great and small, what cash settlement is in trade.

See Rothfels [1941, p. 104–105].

[16] Smith, *The Wealth of Nations* [1937 (1776), p. 659].

[17] Quoted in Tripp [1970, p. 668].

In what follows I will present some more detailed thoughts on the dark side of economic activity, under four headings: (1) the *sources* of conflict, (2) the *technology* of conflict, (3) the *modelling* of conflict interactions, and (4) the *consequences* of conflict.

SOURCES OF CONFLICT

Underlying the trade-off between the way of Ronald Coase and the way of Niccolo Machiavelli are the contending parties' *opportunities, preferences*, and *perceptions*.

Opportunities

Economists can safely predict that decision-makers will lean in the direction of conflict or lean in the direction of cooperative production and exchange, whichever is more profitable on the margin. Productive complementarity favors the exchange option: nations that trade more fight less (Polachek [1980]). Also, since men and women complement one another we see men fighting other men, more frequently and more intensely, than they fight women. At the opposite extreme, recall the Western movie where the villain says to the marshal: "I got nothin' against you, Wyatt Earp, but this town ain't big enough for the two of us." No complementarity there: it's a constant-sum situation, and moviegoers can count on seeing a shootout. Still, generally speaking, adversaries always share *some* mutual interest, if only in reducing the intensity of the struggle.

The law often regulates conflict. Strikes and lockouts are not supposed to involve physical violence. In the world of commerce, merchants are allowed to compete by offering lower prices, not by arson and sabotage. And in judicial proceedings, trial by lawyers has supplanted trial by combat. In olden times a claimant's rights would be upheld by a champion at sword and lance. Now litigants are represented by attorneys – that is, by champions at lies, sophistry, and obfuscation. (Is this an improvement? If time permitted I'm sure I could convince you that replacing trial by combat with trial by lawyers was a ghastly mistake. Ask yourself, which sort of champion is more likely to be found fighting on the side of the just cause: Sir Lancelot or Melvin Belli?)

Even more important than limiting the scope and methods of conflict, the law generally stands ready to enforce agreed settlements. But note the word "enforce": *regulation* of conflict can be achieved only if the regulator has the power to inflict even heavier damage.

I wish I had time to address another domain of sabotage and combat: the promotion ladder or tenure track, otherwise known as the rat race.

But I have to move on, taking the time only for a remark or two about the other elements underlying the choice between settlement and conflict: *preferences* and *perceptions*.

Preferences

Whereas opposed interests (mutually inconsistent opportunity sets) can generate conflict even among entirely "rational" parties, there are also seemingly "irrational" factors: hatred, xenophobia, or uncontrollable anger. These sentiments and passions have presumably evolved under the force of natural selection (Hirshleifer [1987], Frank [1988]). The Darwinian rationale for strong group identification and its converse, xenophobia (however dysfunctional they may seem in modern environments), is evident enough:

A tribe including many members who, from possessing in a high degree the spirit of patriotism, fidelity, obedience, courage, and sympathy, were always ready to aid one another, and to sacrifice themselves for the common good, would be victorious over most other tribes . . .[18]

And:

Envy or hatred seems also to be a highly persistent feeling, perhaps more so than any other that can be named. . . . It seems to be the complement or the converse of the true social instinct.[19]

Even uncontrollable anger can serve a useful role. A predisposition to anger signals "Don't tread on me," a warning that often serves to deter challenges.

Perceptions

Granted that decision-makers are always balancing between the two ways of making a living, the Coasian way and the Machiavellian way, no one can ever actually *know* what the relative costs and benefits of the two options truly are. People have to act on the basis of perceptions. As a broad generalization, uncertainty on the conflict side swamps that on the side of cooperation. ("War is the province of chance" – Clausewitz.)[20] Blainey [1973] goes so far as to claim that war would never occur save for over-optimistic perceptions. He regards war as a kind of school. As soon as the weaker side truly learns its lesson, it will submit and the war

[18] Darwin, *The Descent of Man*, p. 500.
[19] Darwin, *The Descent of Man*, p. 483.
[20] Quoted in Tripp [1970, p. 682].

must come to an end. There's something to this, but Wittman [1979] has pointed out that events like defeat in battle, which convince one party it truly is weaker and thus incline it more toward peace, make the opponent more confident and thus insistent upon more extreme terms. So reduced uncertainty about the outcome of struggle need not necessarily promote peace.

THE TECHNOLOGY OF CONFLICT

In dealing with productive technology, economists do not concern themselves with the design of pipes, girders, beams, engines, or transistors – these matters lie in the province of engineers and technicians. And the proper employment of technology is the task of the businessman. Our job is to analyze what might be called the *macro-technology* of production: are there increasing or decreasing returns to scale, are labor and capital complements or substitutes, and so forth.

When it comes to the *technology of conflict*, the situation is very similar. Guns, bombs, missiles, etc. are designed by technical experts, while their proper employment is the responsibility of military leaders. And even in non-military conflicts, there are players with corresponding roles. Politicians hire speech-writers and media consultants to design optimal strategies of campaign lies and propaganda; litigants hire attorneys to concoct clever ways of hoodwinking judges and juries. These practitioners are, in effect, the engineers and entrepreneurs of the conflict industry. But, owing to the default of the economists, a huge intellectual gap has remained: very little has ever been said about the *macro-technology* of conflict. Yet increasing versus decreasing returns, economies of scale and scope, complementarity of labor and capital are as applicable in the conflict domain as in the productive domain.

One illustration. Starting in the fifteenth century, cannon replaced catapults and trebuchets as siege weapons; as personal armament, the musket supplanted bow and arrow. One's first impression might be that the newer weapons were unambiguously superior, technically speaking. The correct answer is by no means so simple; it involves comparative costs, increasing returns, and complementarity. Cannon allowed *industrial* skills in the factory and workshop to substitute for scarcer *battlefield* skills. And economies of scale in cannon manufacture gave kings a cost advantage over petty lords and barons. As for muskets, they were so inaccurate that, until the rifle came along, a man with a firearm was no match for a trained archer. In the musket's favor were, once again, economies of scale in industrial production and, even more important, the opportunity to combine capital with less-skilled labor. It took years of practice and indeed a whole way of life to make an effective bowman. But a week of drill sufficed for training a musketeer to shoot off his weapon in the general direction of the foe.[21]

In analyzing the macro-technology of conflict, one would like to have plausible functional forms analogous to the Cobb–Douglas or CES formulas of production theory. These functions would describe how "inputs" of fighting efforts on the two sides generate "outputs" in the form of victory or defeat. Two canonical families of such "Contest Success Functions" have been described.[22] In the one family, the outcome depends upon the *ratio* of the fighting efforts, in the other family upon the *difference*. The ratio form is applicable when clashes take place under theoretically ideal conditions such as a uniform battlefield, full information, and absence of fatigue. The difference form applies in the more realistic case where what Clausewitz called *friction*[23] plays a role: where there are sanctuaries and refuges, information is imperfect, and even the victor is subject to disorganization and exhaustion. And while I have been using military metaphors and examples, analogous statements can be made about the "technology" for translating fighting efforts into victory even in non-military struggles like lawsuits or political campaigns.

Somewhat analogous to rapidly diminishing returns in production would be low *decisiveness* in conflict activity. A superior force is by definition always at an advantage, but how much of an advantage? Sometimes a small edge can have drastic consequences. In the Punic Wars the opponents were very nearly matched, and conceivably the outcome might have gone either way. But the balance having tilted toward Rome, the outcome was decisive in the most total sense: Carthage was razed to the ground. The Franco-Prussian War of 1870 was far less decisive. Despite clear Prussian victory on the battlefield, France had only to pay an indemnity and surrender two provinces. Less than fifty years later, a turn of the tide reversed this outcome.

When decisiveness is low the parties are more likely to choose peace – or, at any rate, to reduce the intensity of struggle. In domestic politics, constitutional protections for minorities reduce the decisiveness of majority supremacy. If election defeat doesn't entail deprivation of life

---

[21] For differing views on this history see Batchelder and Freudenberger [1983], Parker [1988], and Anderson [1992].
[22] Hirshleifer [1989].
[23] See the discussion in Rothfels [1941, p. 103].

and property, people need not be excessively concerned about or invest as much effort in political campaigns.[24]

Economic conflict theory helps explain a major paradox of modern politics. We are so used to seeing wealth redistributed from the rich to the poor that it no longer seems surprising. Yet the half of the population above the median wealth surely has more political strength than the half below the median. How can the lower half gain at the expense of the upper half, i.e, the weak defeat the strong in the redistributive struggle? The main answer – note that I set aside sheer generosity on the part of the rich – is that the poor have a *comparative advantage* in conflict as opposed to production (Hirshleifer [1991]). Or looking at it from the other point of view, when it comes to appropriative struggles the rich constitute an attractive target while the poor do not. Think of this as the four P's: *populist politics are profitable for the poor*. And more generally, when the decisiveness of political conflict is not too great, groups finding themselves poorer than before will typically become politically more bellicose, while newly enriched groups become more pacific and accommodating. When the textile industry is doing well, it concentrates on doing business. When times are hard, it sends delegations to Washington instead.

In military contests similarly, sometimes the weaker side unexpectedly "wins" – at least in the relative sense of improving upon its initial position. The Vietnam War is an evident instance. Once again, this is most likely to occur when the decisiveness of conflict is low. In Vietnam, topography and international relations combined to make for low decisiveness. (The U.S. of course owned nuclear weapons that could have been totally decisive, but diplomatic considerations precluded their use.)

On the other hand, if the decisiveness parameter is sufficiently high, i.e., if a preponderance of force makes an enormous difference for the outcome, the advantage tilts heavily to the stronger side. This corresponds to a "natural monopoly" in the conflict industry, leading very likely to a struggle to the death – as between Rome and Carthage, or Czarists versus Bolsheviks in revolutionary Russia.

Many other aspects of conflict technology cry out for investigation, for example when does the offense have the advantage and when the

---

[24] Commentators and publicists often deplore the low voter turnout in American election. For the reasons gives above, this should be taken as a sign of a healthy polity.

defense, and what are the roles of geographical distance and terrain? But I must move on to my next major topic.

MODELLING CONFLICT AND ITS OUTCOME

To some extent this will be familiar ground. Conflict interactions, like all economic interactions, involve equations of *optimization* on the decision-making level and of *equilibrium* on the society-wide level. But just as we have different models in standard theory depending upon the intended application to international trade or industrial organization or income distribution, differing "stylized facts" serve to shape the models appropriate for various domains of conflict theory. In *labor–management relations* both factors are essential for production, so a strong community of interests works to moderate the struggle. *Litigation* is closer to a constant-sum game. Yet litigation is far from total war, for one thing thanks to the exclusion of direct violence, for another because of limited stakes: at issue are only the specific rights or damages claimed.[25]

In contrast with standard theory, conflict theory can only rarely use the "large numbers – perfect competition" simplification. We almost always are dealing with small numbers à la Cournot, Stackelberg, etc. The question then becomes, essentially: who fights whom, and how hard?

I want to propose here a distinction between two elemental "atoms of conflict" – the horizontal and the vertical. In horizontal conflict, while one party might be stronger than the other, strategically they are on a level, making the *Cournot* solution applicable. Vertical or hierarchical conflict, in contrast, involves a superior and inferior. The parties are no longer strategically on a level; the superordinate player is one able to issue a credible threat and/or promise as to how he will respond to the subordinate's behavior.[26]

By combining these "atoms," various molecular configurations can be visualized. The Prisoners' Dilemma is a triangular pattern in which a single superior seeks to defeat or exploit two potentially allied subordinates, the issue being whether the subordinates can get together to frustrate the superordinate.[27] Or conceivably, the triangle might be inverted with two

---

[25] Recent changes in tort law allowing punitive or exemplary penalties, beyond actual damages incurred, have evidently tended to increase the prevalence and intensity of litigation struggles. As a secondary implication, as the stakes grow larger we would expect to see the stronger or richer side winning a larger fraction of the contests.

[26] See Thompson and Faith [1981].

[27] For an analysis of the three-person Prisoners' Dilemma see Stephens [1992].

allied superiors cooperating yet competing in the attempt to exploit an inferior. I believe that exploration of these patterns would shed considerable light upon the various types of alliances[28] formed by individuals, groups, and nations. But once again, I must break off to say just a few words about my final topic.

THE CONSEQUENCES OF CONFLICT

Possibly starting with the alleged extermination of the Neanderthals by modern Homo sapiens, the main outlines of human geography and history have been shaped by the interaction of the productive versus conflictual modes of economic activity. The sizes and shapes of nations are determined by increasing and decreasing returns to geographical extension, as influenced by military and productive technology.[29] As already suggested, the introduction of cannon into siege warfare favored larger over smaller political units, hence led to a sharp reduction in the number of independent principalities from the fifteenth century on. Or, to mention one other example, starting about the same time the combination of cannon and all-weather sailing vessels made possible the imperial expansion of the European powers to America, Africa, and Asia.

Looking within, the state is traditionally defined as having an effective monopoly of force within defined borders. But this monopoly is always threatened by coups, subversion, and disorders.[30] Modern developments in transportation and communication have tended to favor increased centralization on both military and productive grounds. Militarily, were it not for the railroad the South would surely have won its independence in the American Civil War. But then, perhaps, the productive advantages of a larger trade area would have led to ultimate reunification at some later date after the demise of slavery. To cite only one other development, in recent years cheap handguns have made the exercise of force within nations more "democratic," so to speak, with largely unwelcome consequences.

I will close with some remarks on the implications of the conflict option for the very fabric of human nature. The possible evolutionary function of hatred, anger, and xenophobia has already been mentioned. On the physical side, the human species exhibits considerable sexual

---

[28] See Conybeare, Murdoch, and Sandler [1993].
[29] See Friedman [1977] and Wittman [1991].
[30] Usher [1989] provides an interesting economic analysis.

dimorphism: on average, males are bigger and stronger than females. This is not because big men are more productive – everyone knows that women have always done most of the work. No, big and strong males have evolved in order to fight other big and strong males. And, returning to the psychological side, male bonding (Tiger [1969]) is, at least plausibly, a response to increasing returns to group size in combat. And finally, the hypertrophy of the human brain has been, though not without controversy, attributed to the advantages of cleverness and guile in combat, politics, and social intrigue.

The Greek philosopher Heraclitus is supposed to have said: "War is the father of all things." A more accurate statement, which surprisingly enough is also more politically correct, would be: "War is the father of all things, and peace is the mother." Or, to make Edmund Burke's amends for his previously quoted harsh thought about economists, I can cite him here in a more palatable vein:

. . . every human benefit and enjoyment, every virtue, and every prudent act, is founded on compromise and barter.[31]

Thus, in recognizing the role of conflict we must not go overboard in the other direction. All aspects of human life are responses not to conflict alone, but to the interaction of the *two* great life-strategy options: on the one hand production and exchange, on the other hand appropriation and defense against appropriation. Economics has done a good job in dealing with the way of Ronald Coase; what we need now is an equally subtle and structured analysis of the *dark side*: the way of Niccolo Machiavelli.

REFERENCES

Anderson, Gary M. "Cannon, Castles, and Capitalism: The Invention of Gunpowder and the Rise of the West." *Defence Economics* 3, 1992, 147–60.
Ardrey, Robert. *The Territorial Imperative*. New York: Atheneum, 1968.
Bartlett, John. *Familiar Quotations*, 14th ed., edited by Emily Morison Beck. Boston: Little, Brown and Co., 1968.
Batchelder, Ronald W., and Herman Freudenberger. "On the Rational Origins of the Modern Centralized State." *Explorations in Economic History* 20(1), 1983, 1–13.
Blainey, Geoffrey. *The Causes of War*. New York: Free Press, 1973.
Coase, R. H. "Adam Smith's View of Man." *Journal of Law and Economics* 19(3), 1976, 529–45.

---

[31] Quoted in James [1984, p. 86].

Conybeare, John A. C., James C. Murdoch, and Todd Sandler. "Alternative Collective-goods Models of Military Alliances: Theory and Empirics." *Economic Inquiry* 32, 1994, 525–42.

Cooter, Robert, Stephen Marks, and Robert Mnookin. "Bargaining in the Shadow of the Law," *Journal of Legal Studies* 11, June 1982, 225–51.

Darwin, Charles. The Descent of Man and Selection in Relation to Sex," in *The Origin of Species and The Descent of Man* (jointly bound, n.d.), New York: Random House, Inc., The Modern Library.

Earle, Edward Mead, ed. *Makers of Modern Strategy*. Princeton, NJ: Princeton University Press, 1941.

Frank, Robert. *Passions within Reason: The Strategic Role of the Emotions*, New York; W. W. Norton & Co., 1988.

Frank, Robert, Thomas Gilovich, and Dennis T. Regan. "Does Studying Economics Inhibit Cooperation?" *Journal of Economic Perspectives* 7(2), 1993, 159–71.

Friedman, David. "A Theory of the Size and Shape of Nations." *Journal of Political Economy* 85(1), 1977, 59–77.

Gilbert, Felix. "Machiavelli: The Renaissance of the Art of War, in *Makers of Modern Strategy*, edited by E. M. Earle. Princeton, N.J.: Princeton University Press, 1941, Ch. 1.

Hayek, Friedrich A. *Law, Legislation and Liberty*, vol. 3: *The Political Order of a Free People*. Chicago: University of Chicago Press, 1979.

Hirshleifer, Jack. "Economics from a Biological Viewpoint. *Journal of Law and Economics* 20, 1977, 1–52.

————. "On the Emotions as Guarantors of Threats and Promises," in *The Latest on the Best*, edited by John Dupré. Cambridge MA: MIT Press, 1987, 307–26.

————. "Conflict and Rent-Seeking Success Functions: Ratio vs. Difference Models of Relative Success. *Public Choice* 63, November 1989, 101–12.

————. "The Paradox of Power." *Economics and Politics* 3, 1991, 177–200.

James, Simon. *A Dictionary of Economic Quotations*, 2nd ed. Totowa, N.J.: Rowman and Allanheld, 1984.

Marshall, Alfred. *Principles of Economics*, 8th ed. London: Macmillan and Co, Ltd., 1920.

Parker, Geoffrey. *The Military Revolution: Military Innovation and the Rise of the West, 1500–1800*. Cambridge: Cambridge University Press, 1988.

Polachek, Solomon W. "Conflict and Trade." *Journal of Conflict Resolution* 24, March 1980, 55–78.

Rothfels, Hans. "Clausewitz," in *Makers of Modern Strategy*, edited by E. M. Earle. Princeton, N.J.: Princeton University Press, 1941, Ch. 5.

Smith, Adam. *The Wealth of Nations* (1776), Modern Library edition. New York: Random House, Inc., 1937.

Stephens, Glenn. "Putting Nature Back into the State of Nature." Ph.D. dissertation, University of California, Los Angeles, 1992.

Thompson, Earl A., and Roger L. Faith. "A Pure Theory of Strategic Behavior and Social Institutions." *American Economic Review* 71(3), 1981, 366–80.

Tiger, Lionel. *Men in Groups*. New York: Random House, 1969.

Tripp, Rhoda Thomas. *The International Thesaurus of Quotations*. New York: Harper and Row Publishers, 1970.

Usher, Dan. "The Dynastic Cycle and the Stationary State." *American Economic Review* 79(5), 1989, 1031–44.

Wittman, Donald. "How a War Ends: A Rational Model Approach." *Journal of Conflict Resolution* 23, December 1979, 732–63.

_____. "Nations and States: Mergers and Acquisitions: Dissolutions and Divorce." *American Economic Review*, Papers and Proceedings, May 1991, 126–29.

PART ONE

CAUSES, CONSEQUENCES, AND CONDUCT
OF CONFLICT

2

The Bioeconomic Causes of War

Jack Hirshleifer

Background of this Chapter

From earliest times philosophers and social thinkers have asked: Why do men, tribes, and nations fight? This chapter shows how the standard categories of economic thought – interpersonal preferences, opportunities, and perceptions – proximately determine the choice between conflict and cooperation. Yet, on a deeper level, why do our attitudes, the opportunities we face, and our perceptions of others take the form they do? The article explores the biological roots of these motivations and circumstances, ties them to the history of human conflict and contention, and considers prospects for the future.

The article appeared in *Managerial and Decision Economics,* a British management journal, as part of a special issue on the topic of conflict.

Abstract

Wars are fought not only for material goals but for intangible ends such as honor and prestige. In biological terms the ultimate functional motives for fighting are food and sex, the essential elements of reproductive success. Like many other animals, humans seek food and sex directly, but also indirectly via dominance and prestige. In modern times the direct food and sex motives for warfare have waned. But, although largely disconnected from reproductive success, intangible goals such as prestige, dominance, and respect – amplified by the 'affiliative instinct' – remain with us as continuing causes of war.

On August 3, 1914 Sir Edward Grey, the British Foreign Minister, asked the House of Commons to approve an ultimatum to Germany:

I ask the House from the point of view of British interests to consider what may be at stake. If France is beaten to her knees... if Belgium fell under the same dominating influence... if, in a crisis like this, we run away from these

*Reprinted from J. Hirshleifer, "The Bioeconomic causes of war," *Managerial and Decisions Economics*, Vol. 19, 457–66, Copyright © 1998, with permission from John Wiley & Sons Limited.

obligations of honor and interest. . . we should, I believe, sacrifice our respect and good name and reputation before the world and should not escape the most serious and grave economic consequences.[1]

Notice the allusions both to *material goals* ('British interests', 'economic consequences') and *intangible considerations* ('honor', 'respect', 'good name').

And on the German side, earlier in 1914 Chancellor von Bethmann Hollweg declared:

. . . every day Germany sees its population growing by leaps and bounds; its navy, its trade and industry are making unparalleled developments. . . it is forced to expand somehow or other; it has not yet found that 'place in the sun' which is its due.[2]

Here again, at least an undertone suggests an intangible factor. 'Place in the sun' connotes a desire for respect and esteem apart from material assets like territory.

Turning to a different era, the redoubtable Genghis Khan (1167–1227) is supposed to have said:

The greatest pleasure is to vanquish your enemies, to chase them before you, to rob them of their wealth, to see their near and dear bathed in tears, to ride their horses and sleep on the white bellies of their wives and daughters.[3]

Genghis Khan was hardly indifferent to material goals, but his tone rather suggests that an intangible – glorying in the humiliation of others – was his primary motivation.

Or consider World War II. For Germany, *lebensraum* was a material goal. But Adolf Hitler's psychic drives, which became translated into German national policy, centered around sheer malevolence, mainly on racial lines. The Nazi extermination program was pursued even at the expense of Germany's chances of victory.

As the *final causes* of human actions, the sources of our preferences and goals, whether material or intangible, are usually regarded as outside the analytic boundaries of mainline economics. For traditional economics, preferences are exogenous brute facts, coming from outer space so to speak. It is at this point that bioeconomics steps in to rescue and complete economic thought. The premise of bioeconomics is that our preferences have themselves evolved to serve economic functions in a

[1] Quoted in Tuchman (1962).
[2] Quoted in Kagan (1995).
[3] Royle (1989).

very broad sense: those preferences were selected that promoted survival in a world of scarcity and competition.

But I am getting ahead of my story a bit. I first want to analyse the *contingent causes* of peace or war, that is, the proximate reasons for choosing the war option or the peace option, given any particular set of final goals.

MATERIAL GOALS AND THE CONTINGENT CAUSES OF WAR AND PEACE

To highlight the contingent causes leading to the choice of the war option or the peace option, I start with the simplest possible assumption about final goals: that the contending parties are strictly self-interested and materialistic, aiming solely to maximize own-income. Also, following the main analytic tradition of economics, I will be assuming rational behavior on each side.

In Figure 2.1 each point represents the incomes attained by the two contenders – call them Red and Blue. Blue's income I_B is scaled along the horizontal axis: Blue wants to attain a position as far to the right as possible. (His indifference curves are vertical lines.) Red's income I_R is scaled along the vertical axis: Red wants to attain a position as high up as possible. (Her indifference curves are horizontal lines.) The curve QQ is the upper bound of the *settlement opportunity set* – the range of peaceful outcomes achievable if war can be avoided. P_B is Blue's estimate of the outcome of war, and P_R is Red's estimate. As shown in the diagram, by assumption here the estimates are in agreement, defining a unique *perception point* $P_B = P_R$. The shaded *Potential Settlement Region* (PSR) shows the set of possible peaceful arrangements that both sides perceive as yielding a better outcome than war.

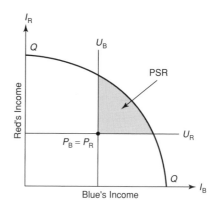

Figure 2.1. Potential Settlement Region (PSR): moderate complementarity, agreed perceptions.

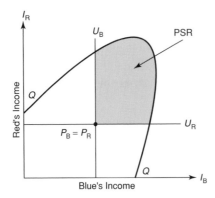

Figure 2.2. Potential Settlement Region (PSR): strong complementarity, agreed perceptions.

Since war is costly, under strictly materialist motivations *a Potential Settlement Region always exists* – assuming the parties correctly assess the opportunity set QQ and the outcome of war (perception point). To that extent, peace always has the edge on war.

A number of influences can affect the magnitude of the Potential Settlement Region, or even its existence. These influences can operate via *opportunities, perceptions,* or *preferences.*

Figure 2.2 illustrates the effect of changed opportunities. In comparison with Figure 2.1, here the QQ locus displays a stronger degree of productive complementarity. If the parties can only agree, they now have much more to gain: the PSR is larger.

It is at least a plausible presumption that, *the larger the PSR, the better the prospects for settlement.* If so, since trade enlarges the income opportunities associated with peace,[4] we would expect the extent of trading to be inversely associated with fighting. There is a problem of the direction of causation here: rather than trade leading to peace, it may be that peace leads to trade. Still, subject to this and other statistical cavils, the empirical results of Polachek (1992) and Mansfield (1994) do broadly support the contention.

Turning to *diverging perceptions,* neither the outcome of war nor the true shape of the peaceful opportunity boundary QQ can ever be fully known. However, the result of war is likely to be even more in doubt than the consequences of peace: "War is the province of uncertainty"

---

[4] Trade implies the existence of more than one commodity, whereas the diagrams here deal with a single 'income' good. However, the vertical and horizontal axes of Figures 2.1 and 2.2 can be re-interpreted as representing suitable *index numbers* of real income defined over a number of goods.

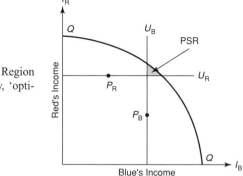

Figure 2.3. Potential Settlement Region (PSR): moderate complementarity, 'optimistic' perceptions.

(Clausewitz).[5] So I will simplify by postulating that doubt attaches *only* to the location of the perception point, that is, to the incomes attainable on each side in the aftermath, were war to occur.

In Figure 2.3, the perception point has now split into two: P_R for Red and P_B for Blue. By assumption here each side is *relatively optimistic* about its prospects: P_R lies to the northwest of P_B. In the situation pictured, Red will not accept any settlement to the south of the horizontal line through P_R, while Blue will refuse any settlement to the west of the vertical through P_B. So, we see, *relative optimism about the outcome of war shrinks the Potential Settlement Region* (shaded area). In fact, a slightly greater degree of relative optimism on either side could have eliminated the PSR entirely.[6]

Relative optimism is related to, though not quite the same as *over-confidence*. The former compares the contenders' beliefs with one another; the latter compares their beliefs with the actual truth. As shown in Figure 2.3, owing to relative optimism Red's perception point P_R lies to the northwest of Blue's P_B, thus reducing the prospects for peace. Over-confidence would do the same, also shrinking the Potential Settlement Region but in a different way – moving the perception point or points outward from the origin.

There is reason to believe that over-confidence is very widely characteristic of human nature. Thus, Adam Smith:

The overweening conceit which the greater part of men have of their own abilities, is an ancient evil remarked by the philosophers and moralists of all ages. (*Wealth of Nations*, Smith, 1776 (1937), p. 107))

[5] Quoted in Shafritz (1990).
[6] For optimism as a contributing cause of litigation see Gould (1973).

And modern psychologists have produced a great deal of evidence to much the same effect.[7]

Such errors of belief lie at the heart of Blainey's *The Causes of War* (Blainey, 1973). On Blainey's view, going to war is rather like going to school. Countries make war because one or both sides needs a lesson. In the course of the conflict, at least one side learns the sad truth (that it is not as strong as it thought, or that the costs are greater than expected) and so eventually becomes willing to settle. Thus, eventually peace becomes possible, or at any rate more possible than before.[8]

Figures 2.1–2.3 displayed merely neutral interpersonal preferences. Let us now consider *benevolence or malevolence* – 'wishing well' or 'wishing ill' to one's opponent. Although interpersonal preferences are intangibles in a sense, assume to begin with that each side wishes well or wishes ill only in terms of material income. A benevolent person would sacrifice some own-income to enrich other parties; a malevolent person would sacrifice some own-income to impoverish others. (At a later point I will be looking into the bioeconomic sources of 'well-wishing' or 'ill-wishing.')

Figure 2.4 reflects mutual *benevolence*. Instead of Blue being concerned solely with maximizing his own income, and Red solely with maximizing her own income, each now attaches positive utility to the other's material well-being. The utility indifference curves, which under the strict self-interest assumption were horizontal lines for Red and vertical lines for Blue, now have the familiar 'convex' shapes. As can be seen in the diagram, mutual benevolence enlarges the Potential Settlement Region.

In contrast, Figure 2.5 pictures mutual *malevolence*: each side is willing to incur a material sacrifice to reduce the other's income. In consequence, the indifference curves now have positive slope. Mutual malevolence compresses the Potential Settlement Region, though not necessarily to the point of eliminating it entirely. (If the contingent

---

[7] For example, Fischoff *et al.* (1977). A bioeconomic interpretation of over-confidence is offered in Waldman (1994).

[8] Blainey's argument is not entirely sound, however. Wittman (1979) points out that while defeat in battle may incline the loser toward peace, the same events are likely to make the opponent more confident than before. Thus the *position* of the PSR – the range of mutually advantageous settlements – could shift, without necessarily increasing the *magnitude* of the PSR. Sparta, after losing the battle of Cyzicus in 410 BCE, offered peace to Athens on very moderate terms, and did so once again after the battle of Arginusae in 406. But the over-confident Athenians rejected both offers, only to be hopelessly defeated and forced to surrender in 404 BCE.

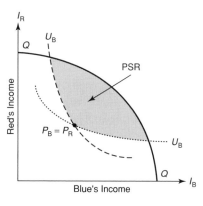

Figure 2.4. Potential Settlement Region (PSR): moderate complementarity, agreed perceptions, benevolent preferences.

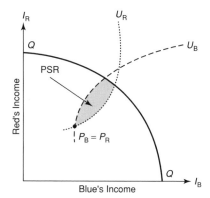

Figure 2.5. Potential Settlement Region (PSR): moderate complementarity, agreed perceptions, malevolent preferences.

circumstances are otherwise sufficiently favorable, even intrinsically hostile parties may find it advisable to come to and abide by a settlement. Hence the aphorism – a dangerous one, yet sometimes a valid reminder: "You don't make peace with your friends but with your enemies.")

A variety of asymmetric patterns are also possible, for example, where one side is benevolent and the other neutral or malevolent.

FINAL CAUSES: THE BIOECONOMIC SOURCES OF BENEVOLENCE/MALEVOLENCE

So far I have taken the *final causes* – the ends or goals that lead people to choose war and peace – as given. But where do these benevolent or malevolent desires stem from? And how are they balanced against the more direct appetite for material income?

To start with a familiar point, sociobiologists emphasize the role of *kinship* in determining attitudes toward others. Animals and humans tend to be benevolent primarily to their own offspring, and after that to more distant relatives. Sociobiological reasoning suggests that benevolence reflects the proportion of shared genes: you share half your genes with your sibling, a quarter with a half-sib, an eighth with a cousin, etc.

In its simplest version, Hamilton's Rule (Hamilton, 1964) states that, other things equal, evolutionary selection will lead a Donor organism D to aid a Recipient organism R if the *cost–benefit ratio* c_D/b_R is less than their *relatedness* r_{DR}:

$$c_D/b_R < r_{DR} \qquad (1)$$

Here cost c_D and benefit b_R are measured in increments to the 'fitness' (i.e., reproductive survival) of Donor and Recipient, respectively. The biological logic is that the gene for helping is (so to speak) indifferent between the survival of its own host or the survival of an identical copy in the body of a related organism – where relatedness measures the chance of the latter occurring. So although the genes are still selfish, the organism will now display a degree of altruism to kin.

Most discussions emphasize only the positive aspects of the kinship factor, but kinship may provide a basis for malevolence as well. To see this, let us first generalize the helping/hurting rule (1).[9] Donor D will be motivated to take any action on the margin for which:

$$\sum_i r_{iD} c_i < \sum_j r_{jD} b_j \qquad (2)$$

where i is an index running over all the *losers* from Donor's action whereas j is an index running over all the *gainers*. (Donor will count himself, with a relatedness of unity, on whichever side of the inequality is appropriate.)

In terms of the categorization above, costs and benefits referred to *opportunities*; only relatedness was the direct source of interpersonal *preferences*. Under the rationality assumption of the previous section, a choosing individual would keep opportunities and preferences quite separate in applying inequality (1) or (2). But natural selection, in shaping the psyches of humans and other organisms, may not have always made such a sharp distinction. If certain aspects of the opportunities have occurred normally and repeatedly in the ancestral environment, Mother Nature may have 'hard-wired' attitudes regarding them into preferences rather than relying upon organisms making rational fitness calculations.

[9] See Hamilton (1970), West Eberhard (1975).

As usual, Adam Smith said it best:

> Thus self-preservation, and the propagation of the species, are the great ends which nature seems to have proposed in the formation of all animals. . . . But. . . it has not been entrusted to the slow and uncertain determinations of our reason, to find out the proper means of bringing them about. Nature has directed us. . . by original and immediate instincts. Hunger, thirst, the passion which unites the two sexes, the love of pleasure, and the dread of pain, prompt us to apply those means for their own sakes, and without any consideration of their tendency to those beneficent ends which the great Director of nature intended to produce by them. (*Theory of Moral Sentiments*, Smith, 1759 (1969), p. 152.)

Indeed, we hardly attribute rationality at all to non-human organisms. Puppies tend to be friendly to humans, but not out of calculated choice. Rather, since humans over evolutionary time were more likely to feed affectionate puppies, natural selection ingrained affectionate attitudes into the genetic heritage of domesticated dogs. (In this case deliberate artificial breeding by humans very likely also played a role.) As for humans, a number of innate likes and dislikes have been identified that are similarly correlated with the results of favorable or unfavorable experiences in the course of evolutionary time. On the negative side are phobias or instinctive aversions, for example to snakes, certain insects, and to potentially threatening strangers. On the positive side are likings for dogs, cats, young children, and so forth.

Returning to sources of malevolence, a major determinant of the costs and benefits associated with helping/hurting actions is the intensity of competition. At the extreme, what might be called *absolute competition*[10] is defined by the condition:

$$\sum_i c_i = \sum_j b_j. \tag{3}$$

That is, the individuals concerned are playing in a constant-sum game.

In two-party absolute competition the ratio c_i/b_j is necessarily unity; in such an environment we would not expect to observe favorable attitudes even toward the closest of kin. (Since no-one can be closer to you than you are yourself.) Among birds, extreme sibling hostility sometimes evolves where within-nest competition is severe, and possible human analogs come to mind.

Let us rewrite the generalized helping/hurting rule (2) in the following form, where $\bar{r}$ is the *average* relatedness of members of the population

---

[10] The discussion here is adapted in part from Hirshleifer (1978).

to Donor:

$$\textstyle\sum_i c_i(r_{iD} - \bar{r}) < \sum_j b_j(r_{jD} - \bar{r}).^{11} \tag{4}$$

So, under absolute competition, it is not simple relatedness but *relatedness greater or less than the average in the population* that serves as the factor weighting costs and benefits. Paraphrasing Hamilton (1970): "Anyone is your enemy who is less closely related to you than the average in the population". Thus, a degree of xenophobia rather than mere indifference toward strangers is indicated.

Chagnon (1983) describes how inter-group hostility in a present-day primitive society responds to the influence of kinship. The Yanomamo are dispersed into separate small villages consisting essentially of extended families, continually at war with one another. For various reasons a village may sometimes grow in population, a process that inevitably reduces average relatedness. Predictably, internal squabbling tends to increase, and the village ultimately splits up along kinship lines – often to the accompaniment of violence.

That biological relatedness is a dominant factor in *primitive* fighting seems plausible enough. But can kinship ties have any bearing for modern warfare? You are only related by 1/8 to your first cousin, and beyond that relatedness falls off rapidly toward zero. So human groups even of very moderate size consist essentially of non-kin. The British soldiers who fought at Omdurman (1898) were quantitatively about as closely related to the fuzzy-wuzzies as they were to Queen Victoria. For all practical purposes, they were not related at all.[12]

However, what serves much the same integrative function as kinship, from ancient to modern times human beings have possessed an *affiliative instinct*: a readiness to divide the world between 'us' and 'them.' Even where kinship is not a factor, cultural influences may lead us to identify our affiliation-group on the basis of shared social class, native language, or even more arbitrary criteria. Affiliations based upon religion, for instance in the Moslem conquests starting in the 10th century,

---

[11] Using (2) and (3) above leads to:

$$\textstyle\sum_i r_{iD}c_i - \bar{r}\sum_i c_i < \sum_j r_{jD}b_j - \bar{r}\sum_j b_j.$$

Inequality (4) follows immediately.

[12] On the other hand, condition (2) might be satisfied if a potential Donor is in a position to help a great many beneficiaries at once, even though no single one of them is a very close relative (West Eberhard, 1975). This consideration may explain the self-sacrificial actions of religious martyrs and military heroes.

in the Christian crusades that followed them, in the Thirty Years War in Germany and so on down to modern times in the Near East, have been immensely important in the history of warfare. And I hardly need say anything about the importance of patriotism, that is, affiliation defined in terms of nationality. Remarkably, even when the assignment of individuals to groups is quite arbitrary, and known to be so, strong group identification commonly emerges (Sherif and Sherif, 1964).

The bonding that stems from the affiliative instinct can elicit extreme self-sacrificial behavior, as when a soldier throws himself on a live grenade to save his comrades. It can also spread over huge communities, so that citizens of great and highly diverse nations like the United States are likely to be as patriotic and self-sacrificial as citizens of tiny states like Andorra or Luxembourg. As a secondary point, though bonding does easily extend beyond biological relatedness, it almost always draws support from what may be called *fictive kinship*. Members of one's affiliation-group may be referred to as brothers and sisters, and the group leader as the father of his people.

'INTANGIBLE' FINAL GOALS: MOTIVES VERSUS FUNCTIONS

So far I have limited the discussion to 'materialist' final ends. Individuals certainly do seek material benefits for themselves, for kin, and more generally for fellow-members of an affiliation-group. But what of *nonmaterial* motives like honor or pride or the desire for dominance? People evidently care about such things, care enough to kill or be killed. Can they be worked into the picture in some analytically useful way? I think the answer is yes, but doing so requires going back – way back – to fundamentals.

In interpreting human behavior we usually think in terms of psychological *motives* like greed or envy or revenge. But in dealing with animals, we typically look for explanations in terms of *biological functions*. We do not say that lions attack antelopes out of hatred or dislike, but for a solid functional reason: getting food. Male lions also battle one another for females, and here the functional aim is again obvious: achieving sexual access. Food and sex are both sought for the same ultimate evolutionary reason: over the generations, those lions able to eat better and mate better left more descendants. Essentially the same holds for other observed types of animal conflict, for example battles over territory or for pecking-order dominance. Territory is a source of food and shelter, and contributes to sexual access as well. (Since females prefer to mate with territorial proprietors.) Similarly for dominance battles:

winners gain better access to food and other material resources, and also to the opposite sex.

If we were to shift our thinking and terminology back from functions to motives, what would we say about animal fighting? Since lions attack antelopes for food, I suppose we would class that as a material or 'economic' motive. Would the quest for sexual access then be 'non-economic'? Perhaps, but when it comes to achieving the functional end of reproductive success, the two are on an equal footing.

Similarly, seeking territory might be classified as a material end, and seeking dominance over others as non-materialistic. But once again the two are quite on a par. Territory and dominance are intermediate goals that, at one remove, provide the food and sexual access which more directly determine reproductive success.

So why then do we speak of *motives* in dealing with humans and of evolutionary *functions* in dealing with animals? Referring back to the Adam Smith quotation just above, Nature, distrusting 'the slow and uncertain determinations' of reason, has provided animals with *instincts* or *drives* that impel them to behaviors effective for acquiring food and mates. And, Smith also suggested, humans are not so very different.

In short, Mother Nature did not trust humans to figure out the means of winning out in the evolutionary struggle. Instead she gave us – just as she gave the animals – 'original and immediate instincts' for food, sex, and so forth that pay off in terms of reproductive success.

Functionally speaking, we have seen, lions fight for food and sex. What of humans? As functional aims of primitive human conflict, Chagnon (1983) emphasizes female capture while Harris (1984) makes resource capture primary. Manson and Wrangham (1991) found that, of 25 primitive human foraging societies where functional causes could be determined, acquiring *resources* was the purpose in 15 instances and acquiring *women* in ten. Allowing for multiple causation, Keeley (1996) provides a tabulation showing that 'economic' factors (booty, land, poaching, slaves) were reported as contributing to 70% of wars among American Indian societies, women to 58%, and 'personal' factors (prestige, trophies, visions) to 36%.[13] (But, as argued above, these 'personal' factors may also have been connected to the quest for reproductive success.)

In *The Descent of Man and Selection in Relation to Sex* (Darwin, 1871), Darwin distinguished two main mechanisms of sexual selection:

---

[13] Keeley (1996) (p. 201).

male combat and female choice. Males can leave more descendants by fighting off other males, or by attracting the favorable attention of females. Military exploits have aspects of both. On the male combat side, by defeating external enemies the warrior protects the females of his own group and may win access to those of the enemy group. In addition, the reputation earned in battle may also discourage internal rivals from challenging him. And to the extent that females have a choice, the honor and glory gained by military exploits demonstrate his possession of 'good genes.' That Yanomamo men who have killed enemies in battle do produce more offspring has been demonstrated by Chagnon (1983).[14]

To summarize at this point: Mother Nature has instilled within us a complex structure of motivations and impulses selected on the basis of effectiveness in promoting reproductive success. As the foundation, the hunger and sex drives conduce directly to this end. Beyond these a variety of ingrained inclinations indirectly lead to the same ends. Most important are the related goals of dominance/prestige/respect, all being status considerations that promote access to food and sex. In a somewhat different category is the previously described affiliative instinct: individuals in tightly knit groups can more effectively take advantage of returns to scale in contending for ultimate biological goals.[15]

LOOKING TOWARD MODERN TIMES

In comparison with primitive social groups, modern societies unite huge numbers of individuals in pursuit of common ends. The kinship barrier that kept primitive groups small has somehow been overcome; individuals have become *citizens*, largely independent of relatedness. Diamond

[14] Thanks to the intellectual advance wrought by sociobiology, it is now evident that the 'classic' pre-sociobiology text of Turney-High on primitive war (Turney-High, 1971) fundamentally misconceives the phenomenon. Turney-High hardly noticed any biological function, indeed any function at all, for primitive warfare. He minimized the significance of material resource-capture, and the female-capture aspect appears to have escaped his attention entirely. Accordingly, he was inclined to describe primitive war as "stupid" or "childish", aimed at goals he regarded as whimsical or ephemeral, for example prestige. Turney-High never recognized that a warrior who sacrifices material booty for a psycho-social end like prestige need not be stupidly giving up something real for a mere dream or fantasy.

[15] These do not exhaust the list of possible ingrained predispositions that might be relevant for warfare. To cite only one more, humans appear to have an *acquisitiveness* instinct that motivates struggle for possessions over and above apparent material needs. Such a trait may substitute for consciously thinking ahead so as to provide for a rainy day. And accumulated possessions may also provide a very readable signal of strength or ability, useful for (among other things) attracting mates.

(1997) argues that the key step was 'religion,' which he defines as an ideology that manipulates group members to become peaceful and obedient internally, and suicidally brave when it comes to external warfare. Speaking more generally and less cynically, advanced societies have somehow hit upon ways to trigger the affiliative instinct by cues such as a shared faith or language or way of life, or common deference to a charismatic leader.

But does that mean that food and sex, the basic bioeconomic motivations for warfare, are no longer relevant? Once we leave the relatively egalitarian realm of primitive societies, it becomes increasingly important to distinguish the purposes of *leaders* from the aims of ordinary citizens. Nevertheless, when it comes to food and other material ends the difference may not be very great. Generals get the biggest share of any booty available, but ordinary soldiers get something too.

Sex is trickier. At least up to ancient times, even in 'civilized' warfare it was common to slaughter all the males but retain the females alive. (For illustrative instances see *Deuteronomy* 20: 12 – 14, or consider the fate of Troy as described in *The Iliad*.) But over the years the sex motive for war does seem to have receded in importance. One possible reason: leaders of large societies have less incentive to capture women from outside, simply because the internal opportunities may suffice! In ancient times leaders of early civilized societies had very favorable mating opportunities even apart from war (Betzig, 1993), and more recent examples also spring to mind.

Of the two routes to reproductive success – sexual access and acquisition of resources – few would claim that the quest for sexual access plays more than the most minor role in explaining modern warfare. And improving technology, the enlarged scope of internal and external trade, and growth of wealth have surely made the peaceful economic process of production and exchange an increasingly attractive alternative to violent aggression as a way of acquiring resources. Nevertheless, 'economic' – that is, materialist – explanations for war surely retain some validity.

One commonly cited material cause of war, based squarely upon biological function, is Malthusian population pressure. Colinvaux (1980) maintains that human history may be said to have begun when technological ingenuity in production of food and other goods allows populations to multiply within the same territorial area. But ultimately a limit is reached, at which point an attempt may be made to invade the niche-space of other populations. The German demand for *lebensraum* appears to be a case in point.

Of course, the driving force here is not literal starvation. Rather, modern populations have conventional notions of an acceptable living standard. Also, though this may be quite recent, the expectation nowadays is that the standard should be rising over time. With these qualifications, Malthusian pressures (the *lebensraum* motive) may possibly still continue to play a very considerable role.

Still, on the whole, what we are seeing in modern times is a kind of *revolt from reproductive success*. Sex is still sought, but it has been largely disconnected from fertility. Food is still sought, but its nutritional function plays only a minor role. Power and dominance are still sought, though often yielding not very much in the way of sex and food and even less in terms of reproductive success (see, e.g., Vining, 1986).

The waning of the biological stakes should, one might have anticipated, have been accompanied by a reduction in the intensity and lethality of warfare. Indeed, such a trend appeared for a while to be occurring in the modern era, only to be reversed by the great wars in the first half of the 20th century. That change of direction may have been due to the increased deadliness and 'overkill' tendency of weaponry. Arguably, warfare in the last quarter of this century has been moving the other way, thanks to precision munitions and the increasing predominance of military skill over mere mass.

SUMMARY AND CONCLUDING REMARKS

The final causes of war are the same as the causes of peace. War and peace are alternative strategic options for achieving the same ends. It is the contingent causes – mainly, opportunities and perceptions – that determine the actual choices made.

Starting with the final causes, although the direct drive for reproductive success has less saliency in the modern era, nevertheless the elements in our psychic makeup that conduce to warfare are outgrowths of our biological heritage. Mother Nature has given us drives that promoted reproductive success over the long course of evolutionary time. The most fundamental of these are the sex and hunger drives, which translate directly into desires for mates and for resources. Benevolence toward kin and malevolence toward non-kin also have direct biological significance. At a further remove are psychological instincts or drives that conduce to sexual access or resource acquisition, in particular the closely grouped ends of honor/respect/glory/prestige.

However, these motivations concern individual behavior, whereas the wars of modern interest concern large human aggregations. Under the impulse of the affiliative instinct, fellow group members become one's fictive kin. Although readiness to form such groups is biological, the actual partition lines – the ways that people define 'us' versus 'them' – are culturally determined. Group identifications in terms of language and religion and class and personal loyalties have all been historically important, but warfare in modern times has mainly been associated with nationality: itself a somewhat amorphous category, but one evidently capable of motivating human beings to great heights of within-group self-sacrifice and equally extreme depths of depravity toward out-groups.

So what is the overall answer as to the bioeconomic causes of war in modern times? For reasons I have partially explained earlier, the biological stakes of warfare have been dwindling. Wars are no longer aimed at sexual access, and even resources are more importantly valued as symbols – Chancellor Bethmann's 'a place in the sun' – rather than for actual material benefits. True, some nations will always be expanding in population and industry, others falling behind. A growing nation is likely to feel entitled to a larger fraction of the world's resources, which the status quo powers will be reluctant to concede. But, I suggest, were it not for the symbolic or prestige aspect, disputes over resources would be solvable without recourse to war.

Turning to the contingent causes, I summarized these under the headings of opportunities and perceptions. As for the influence of *perceptions*, that is, relative optimism and/or over-confidence about the outcome of conflict, little seems to have changed. War has always been the province of uncertainty, and the outcome does not seem to have become more predictable than it ever was. With regard to *opportunities*, so far as material ends are concerned the reasons for going to war are diminishing. The costs of war, even for the winners, have risen (and for nuclear wars, the costs have become unbearable even to contemplate). Meanwhile, the possible gains from war have shrunk in comparison with the benefits of peaceful trade. Yet the *symbolic* objects of war – honor, prestige, glory – remain as scarce as ever, since they constitute a zero-sum game. So wars, when they occur, are increasingly likely to turn upon perceived aspirations for 'a place in the sun.'

To end on a somewhat encouraging note, I referred earlier to the rather cynical contention in Diamond (1997) that ideologies and religions were invented mainly to make societies fight better against outsiders. But there are also universalistic ideologies and religions. Now that we are somewhat freed from the imperatives of striving for reproductive success, these more pacific ideologies are less handicapped in the competition for influence over how humans think and act.

REFERENCES

L.L. Betzig (1993). Sex, succession, and stratification in the first six civilizations. In *Social Stratification and Socioeconomic Inequality* (edited by L. Ellis), New York: Praeger, pp. 37–74.

G. Blainey (1973). *The Causes of War*, New York: The Free Press.

N.A. Chagnon (1983). *Yanomamo: The Fierce People*, 3rd edn, New York: Holt, Rinehart and Winston.

P. Colinvaux (1980). *The Fates of Nations*, New York: Simon and Schuster.

C. Darwin (1871). *The Descent of Man and Selection in Relation to Sex*, London: J. Murray.

J. Diamond (1997). *Guns, Germs, and Steel*, New York: W. W. Norton & Co.

B. Fischoff, P. Slovic, and S. Lichtenstein (1977). Knowing with certainty: The appropriateness of extreme confidence. *Journal of Experimental Psychology*, 3, 552–64.

J.P. Gould (1973). The economics of legal conflicts. *Journal of Legal Studies*, 2, 279–300.

W.D. Hamilton (1964). The genetical evolution of social behavior, I. *Journal of Theoretical Biology*, 7, 1–17.

W.D. Hamilton (1970). Selfish and spiteful behaviour in an evolutionary model. *Nature*, 228, 1218–20.

M. Harris (1984). A cultural materialist theory of band and village warfare: The Yanomamo test. In *Warfare, Culture, and Environment* (edited by R.B. Ferguson), New York: Academic Press), pp. 111–40.

J. Hirshleifer (1978). Natural economy versus political economy. *Journal of Social and Biological Structures*, 1, 319–37.

D. Kagan (1995). *On the Origins of War and the Preservation of Peace*, New York: Doubleday.

L.H. Keeley (1996). *War Before Civilization*, New York: Oxford University Press.

E.D. Mansfield (1994). *Power, Trade, and War*, Princeton, NJ: Princeton University Press.

J.H. Manson and R. W. Wrangham (1991). Intergroup aggression in chimpanzees and humans. *Current Anthropology*, 32, 369–90.

S.W. Polachek (1992). Conflict and trade: An economic approach to political international interactions. In *Economics of Arms Reduction and the Peace Process* (edited by W. Isard and C. H. Anderton), Amsterdam: North-Holland, pp. 89–120.

T. Royle (1989). *A Dictionary of Military Quotations*, New York: Simon and Schuster.

J.M. Shafritz (1990). *Words on War*, New York: Prentice Hall.

M. Sherif and C. W. Sherif (1964). *Reference Groups: Exploration into Conformity and Deviation of Adolescents*, New York: Harper and Row.

A. Smith (1759 [1969]). *The Theory of Moral Sentiments*, Indianapolis: Liberty Classics.

A. Smith (1776 [1937]). *The Wealth of Nations*, New York: Modern Library.

B.W. Tuchman (1962). *The Guns of August*, New York: Macmillan.

H.H. Turney-High (1971). *Primitive War*, 2nd edn, Columbia, SC: University of South Carolina Press.

D.R. Vining (1986). Social versus reproductive success: The central theoretical problem of human sociobiology. *Behavioral and Brain Sciences*, 9, 167–216.

M. Waldman (1994). Systematic errors and the theory of natural selection. *American Economic Review*, 84, 482–97.

M.J. West Eberhard (1975). The evolution of social behavior by kin selection. *Quarterly Review of Biology*, 50, 1–33.

D. Wittman (1979). How a war ends. *Journal of Conflict Resolution*, 23, 743–63.

3

The Paradox of Power*

Jack Hirshleifer

Background of this Chapter

What is the paradox of power? It is the seemingly puzzling observation that poorer or weaker contenders often gain from conflict, at the expense of richer or stronger opponents. The article shows why, in a conflict-driven society, it is *not* generally true that "the rich get richer and the poor poorer," though that sometimes does indeed happen. More generally, the battle is not always to the strong. The reason is that in a wide range of circumstances it pays the smaller or weaker contender *to fight harder*.

In the belief that economics journals might regard the topic as outside their domain, I first submitted this paper to a major political science journal. And when that failed, to a second political science journal. In each case the reception was markedly hostile. A newer and less established journal with an interdisciplinary emphasis, *Economics and Politics*, did accept it.

This article has been reprinted in a volume edited by Gianluca Fiorentini and Stefano Zamagni (1999, *The Economics of Corruption and Illegal Markets*, v. 2, Cheltenham, UK: Edward Elgar Publishing Co.).

Abstract

In power struggles, the strong might be expected to grow ever stronger and the weak weaker still. But in actuality, poorer or smaller combatants often end up improving their position relative to richer or larger ones. This is the paradox of power. The explanation is that initially poorer contenders are rationally motivated to fight harder, to invest relatively more in conflictual activity. Only when the decisiveness of conflict is sufficiently high does the richer side gain relatively in terms of achieved income. Among other things, the paradox of power explains political redistributions of income from the rich to the poor.

*February 1990, revised June 1991. This is a considerably revised version of my paper. *The Dimensions of Power as Illustrated by a Steady-state Model of Conflict*. The RAND Corporation, N-2889-PCT (July 1989), reporting on research supported in part by the Pew Charitable Trusts. For helpful assistance and comments I thank Robert Ayanian, Ting Fang Chiang, Malcolm Fisher, David Henderson, Gregory Hildebrandt, David A. Hirshleifer, Jay Y. C. Jen, Jacob A. Stockfisch, Katchen Terasawa, and Murray Wolfson. (Reprinted from J. Hirshleifer, "The Paradox of Power," *Economics and Politics*, Vol. 3, 177–200, Copyright © 1991, with permission from Blackwell Publishers.)

In conflictual interactions (broadly interpreted to include not only hot and cold wars but also lawsuits, strikes and lockouts, redistributive politics, and even family rivalries) we might ordinarily expect the strong to grow ever stronger and the weak weaker. Nevertheless, surprisingly often, initially weaker or poorer contenders end up gaining on initially stronger or wealthier opponents. This is the paradox of power.[1]

In wars, smaller or poorer nations have often fought much larger ones to a standstill, the recent Vietnam conflict being but one instance. As a more general historical phenomenon, from earliest times poor nomadic tribes have successfully preyed upon more affluent cities and empires. Turning to the modern political redistributive struggle, although in democratic states the wealthy would normally be presumed to have more political power than the poor, we almost always observe income being transferred from upper to lower fractiles of the wealth distribution.[2] As another contemporary example, the farmers, although steadily diminishing in numbers and therefore in voting strength have nevertheless been winning ever-increasing subsidies and benefits. Some analysts have even pointed to a paradoxical "Law of the Few" as a general characteristic of majoritarian politics.[3]

On the other hand, history is replete with examples to the opposite effect, where the strong have exploited the weak. Over the centuries the Jews of Europe, certainly a weaker group in political and military terms, were repeatedly despoiled of their wealth – at times by rulers, at times by the masses, often by both. In despotic societies, tyrants commonly drain the wealth of their subjects.[4] And on occasions too numerous to cite in detail, more powerful nations or tribes have subjugated weaker neighbors.

---

[1] "Power" here is taken to mean the ability to achieve one's ends in the face of rivals. For an interpretation of the traditional literature on power from an economic point of view, see Bartlett (1989, Ch. 1–2).

[2] In 1976 the lowest-income quintile of U.S. families initially received only 0.3% of aggregate family income but redistribution through the tax-transfer system raised their share to 7.2%. Correspondingly, the highest quintile began with 50.2% of aggregate family income but ended up with 41.4% after taxes and transfers (Browning and Browning (1979), pp. 203–205). Such redistribution is evidently not simply a matter of relative numbers, i.e., of masses of the poor at the bottom of the pyramid outvoting a few rich at the top. In fact, since on average the wealthy have larger family sizes, the highest-income quintile of families comprises a larger number of people than the lowest quintile.

[3] The law of the few suggests, for example, that as the numbers of the elderly continue to grow, their political power will decrease – so that redistributive benefits to the aged will tend to fall rather than rise (McKenzie [1990]).

[4] "In Rwanda . . . the masses of the people were peasants who were forced to contribute goods and services to the support of a vast and complex political administration.

The key to the paradox of power is a surprisingly simple economic point, yet one that has been inadequately appreciated. While wealth certainly provides the wherewithal for successfully exploiting a poorer opponent, *the initially disadvantaged group is typically rationally motivated to fight harder.*[5] Or, put the other way, non-conflictual or cooperative strategies tend to be relatively more rewarding for the better-endowed side.

In the analysis here, it is postulated that the stakes are limited: one side cannot totally exterminate or enslave the other. Constitutional rules, for example, normally prevent redistributive politics from going on to total confiscation. Industrial, legal, and family conflicts are evidently also subject to strict limits. And even in warfare, one side – owing possibly to technological limitations, to the presence of third parties, or to moral restraints – might not aim at total destruction of its opponent. Bounds upon what can be done in the way of conflict increase the attractiveness of cooperative techniques for achieving one's goals.

War and peace, or more generally conflict and settlement, are usually regarded as mutually exclusive. Rival nations are said to be at war or else at peace; a trade union may call a strike or else sign a collective-bargaining contract; a lawsuit may be settled or litigated in court. But it will be convenient here to employ a paradigm in which the choice is not between "going to war" and "making peace." Instead, the parties choose a steady-state strategy along a continuum ranging between the extremes of struggle and accommodation. To some extent this is a matter of perspective. At any single moment, members of a labor union are either on strike or at work. Taking the long view, however, we can regard the union as having adopted a strategy of going on strike a certain proportion of the time. Similarly, a primitive tribe may be observed to alternate between peace and war with its neighbors, but over the long run its actions can be interpreted as a chosen division of effort between productive exploitation of its own territory versus appropriative struggles with other tribes.

Apart from the central issue of the relative success achieved by richer versus poorer contenders, the analysis will also cast light upon questions

---

... Although they are said to have gloried in their subjugation, which is a matter in doubt, they received little beyond the minimum reallocations in return for almost the entirety of their production over and above what was needed for their own bare subsistence." – Codere (1968), p. 242. And see also the Biblical tale of Naboth's vineyard (1 Kings 21).

[5] Only two-party interactions are considered here. This assumption rules out cases in which a small group might gain disproportionate power by being able to swing the outcome between two larger contenders.

such as:

(1) Will progress in productive technology promote cooperation? As the returns from productive investments improve, will the rival contestants tend to shift their resource allocations more toward producing or more toward fighting?
(2) What about corresponding progress in the technology of conflict?
(3) As economies become more intertwined so that trade linkages across boundaries become stronger, will international conflict decrease?[6] In the first decade of the twentieth century, increasingly close productive ties among the national economics of Europe led to a widespread belief that large-scale war had become out of the question.[7] The first World War dashed these hopes. Since we are now seeing a revival of such beliefs,[8] it will be important to understand why productive complementarity is less effective a force for peace than might initially have been anticipated.

MODELLING CONFLICTUAL EQUILIBRIUM

Just as there is a general equilibrium of a market economy, there is also an equilibrium outcome when rivals may also compete by conflict and struggle. The analytical elements of such an equilibrium include:

The contenders and their intentions: I abstract here from the within-group incentive problem and assume that decision-makers on each side make collectively rational choices aimed solely at maximizing group income.

Capabilities: Each side has resources that can be utilized for productive activity or conflictual activity. In accordance with the limited-stakes assumption, the underlying resources themselves are supposed invulnerable to destruction or capture. Only the income generated by productive use of resources is at issue.

Technology: In parallel with the familiar *technology of production* that translates productive efforts into income, there is a *technology of conflict* that translates commitments of resources to struggle into distributive success.

Rules of the game and solution concept: In competition through struggle, the equilibrium may depend upon the sequence of moves, the

---

[6] On this see, for example, Polachek (1980).
[7] Angell (1911).
[8] See, for example, Mueller (1989).

informational assumptions, whether or not threats are permitted, and so forth. I will be assuming that the Cournot solution concept is applicable.[9]

Two broad, almost self-evident generalizations apply to mixed interactions in which the parties are simultaneously cooperating yet competing with one another: (i) The resources devoted to productive activity mainly determine the aggregate income available. (ii) The contenders' relative commitments to conflictual activity mainly determine how the aggregate income will be distributed between them.

The equation system reflecting these considerations has four classes of logical elements.

First, each side $i = 1, 2$ must divide its exogenously given resources R_i between productive effort E_i and fighting effort F_i:

$$E_1 + F_1 = R_1$$
$$E_2 + F_2 = R_2$$
Resource Partition Equations (1)

Second, the productive technology is summarized by an Aggregate Production Function (APF) showing how the productive efforts E_1 and E_2 combine to determine income I – the social total available for division between the two parties. A convenient form for our purposes is:

$$I = A\left(E_1^{1/s} + E_2^{1/s}\right)^s$$
Aggregate Production Function (2)

This type of production function is characterized by constant returns to scale and constant elasticity of substitution. Parameter A is a *total productivity index*: as the overall yields of the resource inputs rise over time, owing to technical progress, A increases. Parameter s, which plays a crucial role in the analysis, is a *complementarity index*: as nations become more closely and synergistically linked by international trade, for example, s rises. As can be seen in Figure 3.1, higher values of s are reflected in increasingly convex curvature of the productive isoquants. At the lower limit, when $s = 1$, the APF takes on a linear (additive) form.[10]

The third element, the Contest Success Function (CSF), summarizes the technology of conflict – whose inputs are the fighting efforts F_1 and

---

[9] I have considered Stackelberg and hierarchical solution concepts elsewhere (Hirshleifer (1998)).

[10] Values of s below 1 have the unacceptable implication that the marginal products of productive input are increasing throughout.

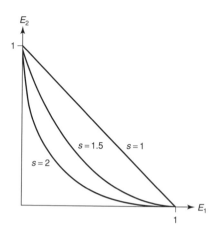

Figure 3.1. Unit isoquants of the Aggregate Production Function (APF), for different values of the complementarity parameter *s*.

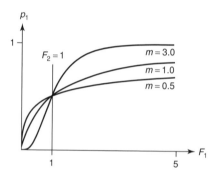

Figure 3.2. The Contest Success Function (CSF), for different values of the mass effect parameter *m*.

F_2, and whose outputs are the distributive shares p_1 and p_2 (where of course $p_1 + p_2 = 1$).

There are significantly different ways of formulating the Contest Success Function.[11] However, for analytical tractability I will assume here that the outcome of the struggle depends only upon the *ratio* of the parties' conflictual efforts F_1 and F_2, indexed by a single *mass effect parameter m*:[12]

$$p_1 = F_1^m / \left(F_1^m + F_2^m \right)$$
$$p_2 = F_2^m / \left(F_1^m + F_2^m \right)$$

Contest Success Functions   (3)

---

[11] I have explored elsewhere some of the implications of making fighting success a function of the *numerical difference* between the commitments (Hirshleifer (1988, 1989)). It is also possible, for example, to adjust the equations so as to make one side militarily more effective than the other (see for example Grossman (1991)) or to make defense less costly than offense.

[12] See Tullock (1980).

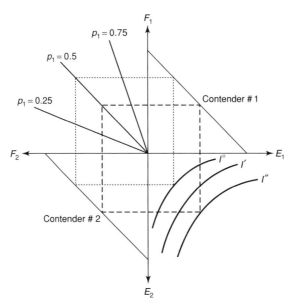

Figure 3.3. Productive technology determines income I while conflict technology determines fractional share p_1.

As illustrated in Figure 3.2, the mass effect parameter m scales the *decisiveness of conflict*, that is, the degree to which a superior input ratio F_1/F_2 translates into a superior proportionate success ratio p_1/p_2.

Finally, there are Income Distribution Equations defining the achieved income levels I_1 and I_2:

$$I_1 = p_1 I$$
$$I_2 = p_2 I$$

Income Distribution Equations (4)

Equations (3) and (4) together imply that all income falls into a common pool available for capture by either side. More generally, the contenders might also have opportunities for generating invulnerable[13] income, but this consideration is set aside here.

The equation system (1) through (4) is illustrated by the four-way diagram of Figure 3.3. The upper-right quadrant shows the range of

---

[13] In a model allowing for some fraction of invulnerable income, each side would be deciding among three rather than only two options: resources R_i could be allocated to conflictual effort, to productive effort that generates contestable income I, or to productive effort yielding invulnerable income. More generally still, income on either side could be scaled along a vulnerability dimension: for example, crops grown along a country's borders are more vulnerable to capture than production taking place in the interior.

contender #1's choices between productive effort E_1 and conflictual effort F_1, within his initial resource endowment R_1. The diagonally opposite quadrant shows the corresponding options for contender #2. The upper-left quadrant shows how the respective fighting efforts F_1 and F_2 determine p_1, the share of aggregate income won by #1, where of course $p_2 \equiv 1 - p_1$. (The p_1 contours are straight lines emerging from the origin, which follows from the assumption stated above that the distributive shares are functions only of the ratio F_1/F_2.) Finally, the lower-right quadrant shows how the productive efforts E_1 and E_2 combine to generate different overall totals of income I.

The dashed rectangle in Figure 3.3 illustrates one possible outcome of the postulated interaction: for given initial choices E_1, F_1 on the part of decision-maker #1 and E_2, F_2 on the part of #2, the productive activity levels E_1 and E_2 determine aggregate income I while the conflictual commitments F_1 and F_2 determine the respective shares p_1 and p_2. The dotted rectangle shows what happens when the two sides choose instead to devote more effort to fighting. As drawn here, the increases in F_1 and F_2 have cancelled one another out so that p_1 and p_2 remain unchanged. Thus, the only effect of *symmetrically* increased fighting efforts may be to reduce the amount of income available to be divided.

REACTION CURVES AND COURNOT EQUILIBRIUM

On the assumption that the underlying strategic situation justifies the Cournot solution concept, the Reaction Curves RC_1 and RC_2 show each side's optimal fighting effort given the corresponding choice on the part of the opponent. The Cournot solution occurs at the intersection where each party's decision is a best response to the opponent's action.

Decision-maker #1's optimizing problem can be expressed:

$$\text{Max } I_1 = p_1(F_1|F_2) \times I(E_1|E_2) \text{ subject to } E_1 + F_1 = R_1 \quad (5)$$

and similarly for side #2. Using equations (2) and (3), by standard constrained-optimization techniques we can solve for the Reaction Curves RC_1 and RC_2:

$$\frac{F_1 E_1^{(1 \cdot s)/s}}{F_2^m} = \frac{m\left(E_1^{1/s} + E_2^{1/s}\right)}{F_1^m + F_2^m}$$

$$\text{Reaction Curves} \quad (6)$$

$$\frac{F_2 E_2^{(1 \cdot s)/s}}{F_1^m} = \frac{m\left(E_1^{1/s} + E_2^{1/s}\right)}{F_1^m + F_2^m}$$

Note that the parameter A of the Aggregate Production Function has cancelled out and does not enter into the Reaction Curve equations at all. Thus, responding to a question raised in the introduction, *an increase in overall economic productivity leaves the proportionate allocation of resources between producing and fighting unchanged.* Intuitively, an increase in A raises the marginal profitability of productive activity and of conflictual activity in the same proportion (see below).

These equations are simultaneously valid only when both sides' choices are in the interior range, with $F_1 < R_1$. It can be shown that for any $s > 1$ (that is, except for the limiting case $s = 1$ where productive complementarity is absent), only interior solutions exist. While there is no convenient general analytical solution, in the special case where $m = 1$ and the resource endowments are equal (that is, when $R_1 = R_2$), for any s the equilibrium is simply:

$$F_1 = F_2 = E_1 = E_2 = (R_1 + R_2)/4$$

$$\text{Symmetrical Cournot solution} \quad (m = 1) \qquad (7)$$

Here, exactly half of the available resources are dissipated in mutually wasteful fighting effort. (As will be seen, higher values of m lead to still greater dissipation of resources, lower values to lesser dissipation.)

To begin with, it will be of interest to consider the limiting case where productive complementarity is absent ($s = 1$). While a corner solution is then possible, the solution will nevertheless always be in the interior whenever the parties' endowments are symmetrical so that equation (7) applies. In Figure 3.4, the parameters are set at $A = m = s = 1$. The RC_1^o and RC_2^o Reaction Curves in the diagram apply for equal initial resources, specifically $R_1 = R_2 = 100$. The interior intersection of the Reaction Curves is the Cournot equilibrium,[14] as summarized in Numerical Example 1.

Numerical Example 1: With resources $(R_1, R_2) = (100, 100)$ and assuming parameter values $A = s = m = 1$, equation (7) indicates that exactly half the resources on each side are dissipated in conflict: $(F_1, F_2) = (50, 50)$. The remaining resources on each side are put to productive

[14] The Reaction Curves also appear to intersect at $F_1 = F_2 = 0$, but the zero – zero intersection is not a Cournot equilibrium. If (say) player #1 chooses $F_1 = 0$, then player #2 would rationally respond by setting F_2 equal to any small positive magnitude, since doing so discontinuously improves his fighting success from 50% to 100%. Thus, strictly speaking, the Reaction Curves are defined only over the open interval that does *not* include the singular point at the origin.

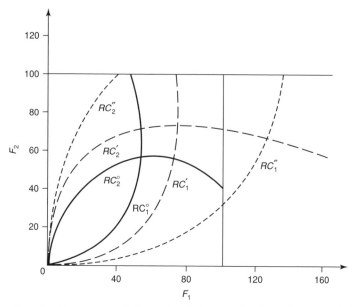

Figure 3.4. Reaction curves and Cournot equilibrium – interior and corner solutions.

use: $(E_1, E_2) = (50, 50)$. These generate an aggregate income $I = 100$, which is then equally divided between the contenders: $(I_1, I_2) = (50, 50)$.

RESOURCE DISPARITIES AND INCOME: THE PARADOX OF POWER

The paradox of power (POP) emerges when a preponderant resource ratio $R_1/R_2 > 1$ is not reflected in a correspondingly large achieved income ratio I_1/I_2. I shall be examining "strong" versus "weak" forms of the paradox:

POP (strong form): In mixed conflict – cooperation interactions, the contending parties will end up with exactly identical incomes ($I_1/I_2 = 1$) regardless of the initial resource distribution.

POP (strong form): In mixed conflict – cooperation interactions, the final distribution of income will have lesser dispersion than the initial distribution of resources. Thus, assuming #1 is the better-endowed side: $R_1/R_2 > I_1/I_2 > 1$.

Considering once again the limiting case where $s = 1$ (where there is no complementarity between the productive activities on the two sides), the Reaction Curve equations (6) reduce to:

$$\frac{F_1}{F_2^m} = \frac{m(E_1 + E_2)}{F_1^m + F_2^m}$$

Reaction Curves ($s = 1$) (6a)

$$\frac{F_2}{F_1^m} = \frac{m(E_1 + E_2)}{F_1^m + F_2^m}$$

Of course, these equations are valid only for interior solutions. On this assumption, at equilibrium we must have $F_1 = F_2$. Thus, regardless of initial resource disparities, so long as the solution remains in the interior, the equilibrium fighting efforts will always be exactly equal. This implies, of course, equal incomes $I_1 = I_2$ – the *strong form of* the *POP applies.*

In Figure 3.4, under the same parameter assumptions, the *dashed* curves RC_1' and RC_2' represent a situation where #1's resources R_1 have doubled in size while #2's are held constant. Despite this asymmetry, at the intersection of the RC_1' and RC_2' curves the fighting efforts F_1 and F_2 – though both larger than before – remain equal to one another! It follows, of course, that the richer party must now be devoting absolutely and relatively more resources to productive effort.

Numerical Example 2: With $A = m = s = 1$ as before, let the initial resources be $(R_1, R_2) = (200, 100)$. At the Cournot equilibrium, once again half of the social aggregate of resources is dissipated in conflictual effort: $(F_1, F_2) = (75, 75)$. The wealthier side devotes more effort to production so that $(E_1, E_2) = (125, 25)$. Nevertheless, the equality of F_1 and F_2 dictates that the final incomes must also be equal: $(I_1, I_2) = (75, 75)$.

An intuitive interpretation is as follows. With an increase in his endowment, contender #1 (he) will surely want to spend more on each of the two types of activity: his E_1 and F_1 will both be greater. Knowing this, side #2 (she) then has both offensive and defensive incentives to shift toward spending *more* than before on fighting (choosing a larger F_2), and therefore less on production (E_2 must be smaller). Her offensive incentive for making F_2 larger is that, E_1 being greater, there is more social income available to be seized. Her defensive incentive is that, F_1 being greater, she has to make F_2 larger even if only to maintain her previous level of income.

The key to the paradox of power is that, when a contender's resources are small relative to the opponent's, *the marginal yield of fighting activity is higher to begin with than the marginal yield of productive activity.*

This is transparently easy to see for the special case of $m = s = 1$. Then, supposing that #2 is the poorer-endowed side, differentiation of $I_2 = p_2 I$ leads to:

$$\frac{\partial I_2}{\partial E_2} = \frac{AF_2}{F_1 + F_2} \quad \text{and} \quad \frac{\partial I_2}{\partial F_2} = \frac{AF_1(E_1 + E_2)}{(F_1 + F_2)^2} \tag{8}$$

When R_2 is very small then of course E_2 and F_2 must be small as well. As both E_2 and F_2 go toward zero, the partial derivative $\partial I_2/\partial E_2$ (the marginal payoff of productive activity) also goes to zero, while the partial derivative $\partial I_2/\partial F_2$ (the marginal payoff of fighting effort) remains positive. Thus, as R_2 approaches zero, the poorer side will find that any productive expenditure E_2 will largely be wasted, since the wealthier opponent will be capturing almost all of whatever is produced. But any positive F_2, however small, will win some share of the enlarged total product available.

Conflict is therefore a relatively more attractive option for the poorer side.[15] Fighting effort permits you to "tax" the opponent's production, while your own production is "taxed" by his fighting effort. When your rival is richer it becomes relatively more profitable to tax him (to capture part of his larger production) and relatively more burdensome to be taxed by him (to devote effort to production which will be largely captured by him anyway). Thus rational behavior in a conflict interaction, under the assumptions here, is for the poorer side to specialize more in fighting, the richer side more in production.

What about the possibility of corner solutions? In the special case of $s = 1$, there will be some critical resource ratio $R_1/R_2 = \rho^*$ at which the poorer side has already devoted *all* of its resources to fighting (has become a pure predator, so to speak). It can be shown that the critical ratio, beyond which the poorer side will be forced to a corner solution, is given by:

$$\rho^* = R_1/R_2 = (2 + m)/m \tag{9}$$

Resource ratios more extreme than ρ^* lead to corner solutions where the Reaction Curve for the poorer side (#2, say) reduces simply to $F_2 = R_2$. At corner solutions, since the fighting efforts are no longer equal, the *strong form of the POP* cannot hold. Nevertheless, the *weak*

---

[15] Compare Becker ((1983), p. 385): "Politically successful groups tend to be small relative to the size of the groups taxed to pay their subsidies". However, as will be noted below, Becker employs an entirely different line of reasoning to arrive at this result.

form of the POP may apply – that is, attained incomes, while no longer exactly equalized, could remain less unequal than the initial resource endowments. In Figure 3.4 the dotted Reaction Curves RC_1^o and RC_2^o illustrate such a case, where #1's resources have doubled again relative to #2's. These Reaction Curves intersect at a corner equilibrium for #2.

Numerical Example 3: Let the resource endowments be $(R_1, R_2) = (400,100)$. It can be verified that, for the assumed parameter values $A = m = s = 1$, the critical resource ratio ρ^* is 3. Since $R_1/R_2 = 4$, side #2 will have to devote all its resources to fighting ($F_2 = 100$). The solution is $(F_1, F_2) = (123.6,100)$. The better-endowed side now obtains a larger proportionate share $(p_1, p_2) = (0.553,0.447)$ and higher level of income $(I_1, I_2) = (152.8,123.6)$. Nevertheless, the attained income ratio $I_1/I_2 = 1.236$ is considerably smaller than the resource ratio $R_1/R_2 = 4$.

Another point of interest: within any given resource total $R_1 + R_2$, corner equilibria involve less overall wastage of resources in fighting.

Figure 3.5 provides a more general picture of how incomes respond to the resource ratio, given the parameter values $A = m = s = 1$. (Henceforth, the total productivity index A of the Aggregate Production Function will always be assumed equal to unity.) In the diagrams here, #2 is always the poorer side with resources arbitrarily fixed at $R_2 = 1$. We have seen that the absolute allocations F_1 and F_2 to fighting effort are equal in the interior range, up to the critical resource ratio $R_1/R_2 = \rho^* = 3$. Figure 3.5(a) shows how this is reflected in the *proportionate* allocations, the curve F_2/R_2 rising in this range for the poorer side while F_1/R_1 is declining for the richer side. (Of course, the equal *absolute* allocations imply $p_1 = p_2$ in this range.) Once the critical ratio $\rho^* = 3$ is exceeded, for the poorer side $F_2/R_2 = 1$. So #1's fractional share p_1 begins to rise steadily relative to p_2, even though the optimal F_1/R_1 for the richer side continues to decline. Correspondingly, Figure 3.5(b) shows that the achieved incomes I_1 and I_2 remain exactly equal in the range of interior solutions before the critical ratio is reached. Only in the range of corner solutions does the better-endowed side achieve an income advantage. (In Figure 3.5(b) the curve labelled I is the aggregate income produced, while $\bar{I}$ represents the ideal level of aggregate income that could be generated if no resources were devoted to fighting effort on either side.)

Summarizing, for the parameter values $m = s = 1$ *the strong form* of the paradox of power (POP) continues to hold so long as the resource ratio is only moderately unequal, so that the equilibrium falls within the

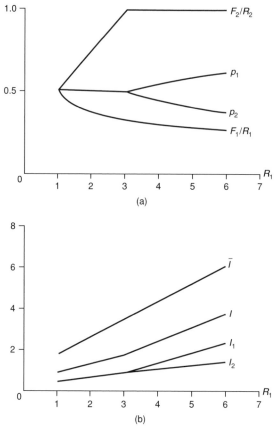

Figure 3.5. Proportionate allocations to fighting, fractional shares, and achieved incomes – $m = 1, s = 1$.

interior-solution range. When the resource asymmetry becomes sufficiently great, the parties enter a corner-solution range where only *the weak form* of the POP applies.

However, as already indicated $s = 1$ is a limiting case. In social interactions we normally expect to observe a certain degree of productive complementarity. Nations at war with one another can, alternatively or even at the same time, also benefit from trade that leads to an improved international division of labor.[16] This is of course even clearer

---

[16] War may or may not be accompanied by a total cessation of trade between the contending sides. "Cold" wars, where only minor actual combats take place, are of course quite consistent with ongoing trade. And substantial trade across the lines sometimes occurs even in quite hot wars, a notable example being the American Civil War.

in industrial relations, where labor and capital are productively vital to one another even as the two sides struggle over shares of the firm's revenues.

As the complementarity index s rises, for either contender the marginal payoff of productive effort E_i will rise in comparison with the marginal payoff of fighting effort F_i. Thus, as s increases we might be inclined to anticipate "an era of better feeling" in which each side redirects its activities so as to devote more effort to increasing the size of the pie, and less to grabbing a bigger slice. However, the actual outcome is somewhat more complex.

Figure 3.6 is the analog of Figure 3.5, except that the productive complementarity parameter is set at $s = 1.25$ in place of $s = 1$. As already indicated, there are no corner solutions whenever $s > 1$. Apart from the smoothing due to this change, the broad picture is similar to the previous diagram. Of course, the potential income $\bar{I}$, the actual aggregate income I, and the achieved incomes on each side are all larger than before. However, closer comparison of the F_i / R_i curves reveals that while the poorer side is tilting somewhat away from fighting, the wealthier side shifts a bit in the opposite direction. The consequence is a greater vertical spread between p_1 and p_2. In other words, while productive complementarity provides absolute benefits to both sides, it operates comparatively in favor of the wealthier side. Not only is there more income to fight over, but since the poorer side is now holding back somewhat from fighting, the wealthier side will find it relatively easier to obtain a larger share. Nevertheless, it remains true that $I_1/I_2 < R_1/R_2$. So, given that the mass effect parameter m (measuring the decisiveness of conflict) is set at $m = 1$, *the weak form of the paradox of power continues to apply* – even when a greater degree of complementarity is postulated.

Numerical Example 4: Under the conditions of Numerical Example 2, with initial resources $(R_1, R_2) = (200, 100)$ and $A = m = s = 1$, the solution was in the range of interior equilibria, with $(F_1, F_2) = (75, 75)$, $(p_1, p_1) = (0.5, 0.5)$, and incomes $(I_1, I_2) = (75, 75)$ – i.e., the strong form of the POP applied. Holding all conditions the same except for an increase in s to 1.25, at the new equilibrium the fighting efforts become $(F_1, F_2) = (77.1, 67.5)$. The proportionate shares change somewhat in favor of the better-endowed side to $(p_1, p_2) = (0.533, 0.467)$ and similarly for the attained incomes $(I_1, I_2) = (94.9, 83.1)$. Increased

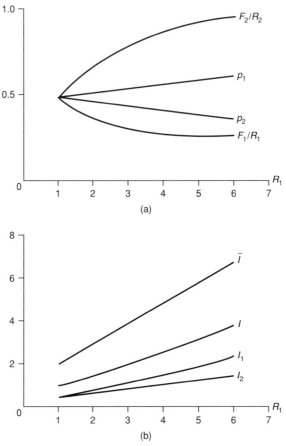

Figure 3.6. Proportionate allocations to fighting, fractional shares, and achieved incomes – $m = 1$, $s = 1.25$.

productive complementarity benefits both sides, but differentially favors the wealthier contender. Nevertheless, $I_1/I_2 = 1.42$ remains less than $R_1/R_2 = 2$: the weak form of the POP applies.

Thus, responding to the second numbered question in the introductory section, the numerical simulation suggests that a higher degree of productive complementarity (such as might result from increased international trade and greater integration of national economics over time) does tend to induce some net reorientation of resources away from fighting. Actually, the better-endowed side fights somewhat more, but the poorer side's fighting effort falls by a larger amount. But owing to these countervailing influences, the overall effect is not as great as might be expected. And the increased value of the complementarity parameter confers a somewhat greater absolute and relative benefit upon the better-endowed side.

WHEN CONFLICT BECOMES MORE DECISIVE

This section considers the implications of improvements in conflict technology. Specifically, what happens when the mass effect parameter m in equation (3) rises? That is, when the "decisiveness" of conflict increases, meaning that any given preponderance of fighting effort F_1/F_2 will be reflected in a disproportionately larger ratio of the achieved success proportions $p_1/p_2 = I_1/I_2$?

In Figure 3.7, which corresponds to the limiting $s = 1$ case, the solid curves (for p_1 and p_2 in the upper panel, and I_1 and I_2 in the lower panel) are repeated from Figure 3.5 (based on $m = 1$) while the dashed curves show the solution values for a higher mass effect parameter ($m = 2$). Notably, as m increases *both* sides are motivated to invest more than before in fighting effort. Consequently, the poorer side #2 hits its boundary constraint $F_2 = R_2$ earlier; the range of interior solutions applies here only up to $\rho^* = 2$. Beyond this point, as the dashed curves in Figure 3.7(a) show, p_1 rises dramatically relative to p_2, meaning that the *improvement in fighting technology operates strongly in favor of the better-endowed side*. Correspondingly, Figure 3.7(b) shows that, despite the greater diversions from productive efforts on both sides, over a considerable range the better-endowed side does not only relatively but even absolutely better than before.

Numerical Example 5: In Numerical Example 3, with $s = 1$ and initial resources $(R_1, R_2) = (400, 100)$ the solution was in the region of corner equilibria, with fighting efforts $(F_1, F_2) = (123.6, 100)$, income shares $(p_1, p_2) = (0.553, 0.447)$, and incomes $(I_1, I_2) = (152.8, 123.6)$. When $m = 2$ so that fighting becomes more decisive, the less well-endowed side #2 can do nothing about it, being already at a corner optimum. So F_2 remains at 100, but side #1 can now advantageously increase its F_1. The new solution values are $(F_1, F_2) = (151.3, 100)$, $(p_1, p_2) = (0.696, 0.304)$, and $(I_1, I_2) = (173.1, 75.6)$. So, in comparison with Numerical Example 3, the increase in the mass effect parameter has

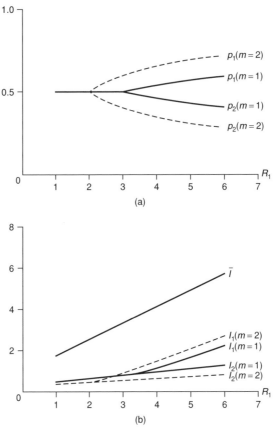

Figure 3.7. When fighting becomes more decisive: $m = 2$ versus $m = 1$ (for $s = 1$).

substantially reduced aggregate income I but considerably improved the outcome for the better-endowed side. Nevertheless, the weak form of the POP still holds here: $p_1/p_2 = I_1/I_2$ equals 2.288, considerably less than the resource ratio $R_1/R_2 = 4$.

A change in conflict technology that raises the mass effect parameter m, so as to make conflict more decisive than before, provides a widened opportunity for the better-endowed side. A richer contestant, evidently, will be more able to afford the large investments in fighting effort needed to take advantage of the enhanced decisiveness of conflict. But, the question is, in equilibrium will a better-endowed contender actually find it optimal to utilize this opportunity to the extent of reversing the paradox of power? In other words, can greater decisiveness of conflict ever outweigh the previously emphasized proposition – that the poorer side does

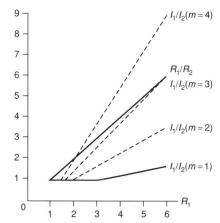

Figure 3.8. Income ratio versus resource ratio, varying m (for $s = 1$).

relatively better ($I_1/I_2 < R_1/R_2$) in mixed cooperative – conflictual situations, because it has more to gain and less to lose by fighting rather than producing?

In the numerical example just above, with $s = 1$ and given the resource ratio $R_1/R_2 = 4$, an increase in the mass effect parameter from $m = 1$ to $m = 2$ was not sufficient to overcome the paradox of power. However, the more general picture provided in Figure 3.8 suggests a different result. With the complementarity index set at $s = 1$, the diagram shows curves picturing the income ratios I_1/I_2 as a function of the resource ratio R_1/R_2, for levels of m ranging from $m = 1$ to $m = 4$. As can be seen, there is an initial range along each of the I_1/I_2 curves where $I_1/I_2 = 1$, that is, where the strong form of POP applies. Beyond the critical resource ratio $R_1/R_2 = \rho^*$ for each such curve, there is a range of corner solutions where I_1/I_2 rises above unity.

The picture suggests, and carrying out the simulations over a larger range of resource ratios confirms, that for $m = 1$ and $m = 2$ the POP will always hold, at least in its weak form. But for $m = 3$ it begins to look as if the POP might be violated for sufficiently large resource ratios, and the curve for $m = 4$ conclusively establishes that such a violation may well occur – that is, that I_1/I_2 may exceed R_1/R_2. Figure 3.9, the corresponding diagram for $s = 1.25$, reveals a similar picture, though without any initial range where $I_1/I_2 = 1$.

Numerical Example 6: Given $s = 1$ and resources $(R_1, R_2) =$ (400, 100), in the previous Example we saw that, for $m = 2$, the income ratio I_1/I_2 equalled 2.288, less than the resource ratio $R_1/R_2 = 4$. Now

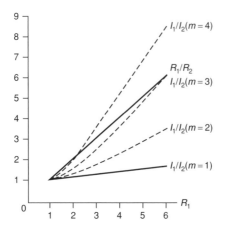

Figure 3.9. Income ratio versus resource ratio, varying m (for $s = 1.25$).

setting $m = 4$, the corner equilibrium has fighting efforts $(F_1, F_2) = (152.9, 100)$, success fractions $(p_1, p_2) = (0.845, 0.145)$, and achieved incomes $(208.9, 38.2)$. So I_1/I_2 now equals 5.465, which *exceeds* the resource ratio $R_1/R_2 = 4$.

If the model of this paper had implied that the paradox of power (at least in its weak form) is *universally* applicable, it would have proved too much. For history reveals that although the less well-endowed side often does surprisingly well in conflict situations, nevertheless the strong and rich do often succeed in exploiting the weak and poor. What this paper does is to explain when we can expect to observe each type of outcome – sometimes the poor doing relatively better, sometimes the rich. The balance of relative advantage is the result of two countervailing factors. On the one hand, poorer contenders have a comparative advantage, so to speak, in fighting. That is, they are motivated to devote relatively more effort to conflictual as opposed to productive effort. But on the other hand, when the decisiveness of conflict is large (that is, when a preponderance of fighting effort has a disproportionate effect upon the outcome of conflict), the better-endowed side is better placed to take advantage of this fact.

What are the circumstances that make fighting more or less decisive? According to Lanchester [1916], under "ancient" conditions fighting was man-for-man, so the larger army could not bring all its forces to bear – hence military strength was linear in the forces committed ($m = 1$). Under "modern" conditions, long-range weapons allow concentration of fire, making strength proportional to the square of the forces engaged ($m = 2$). Turning away from military to political contests within nations, in democratic politics a high m corresponds to "majority tyranny." Put the other way, winning a majority is less *decisive* to the extent that checks and balances, civil rights, and other constitutional provisions limit a dominant faction's ability to use the machinery of government for oppression of minorities. Thus, requiring super-majority approval for crucial actions like amending the U.S. constitution limits the decisiveness of ordinary majority control. The consequence, very likely intended by the Founding Fathers, is that all factions have a reduced incentive to escalate the domestic political struggle.

DISCUSSION AND SUMMARY

The analysis here dealt with struggles over a common pool of income. The parties' opposed interests as to division of the pool lead them to engage in conflictual activity, but they are also motivated to engage in productive activity with the aim of making the social total of income as large as possible. The chosen levels of these two activities determine the outcome of a steady-state process in which contenders divide their efforts between productive activity and appropriative struggle.

Management and labor, for example, ordinarily cooperate in production while struggling over the factor shares. The same applies for contests taking place within families or clubs: individual members may want to do as well as possible for themselves, but still must take care not to totally subvert the common goals. We can think of such struggles as conducted under constitutional rules limiting the stakes at issue. Specifically, it was assumed here that the resource bases of the competitors are invulnerable: only *income* is in contention. Thus, within the firm, workers do not ordinarily try to seize the factory or machinery, nor does management aim at enslaving the employees (although under abnormal or revolutionary conditions, such escalation has been known to occur).

Conflicts among tribes or nations are perhaps more likely to take the form of intensified struggles for resources. Nevertheless, nations and tribes still have a common interest in furthering trade and avoiding destructive warfare. Domestic politics of the familiar type fit the model rather well: taxation may be used to redistribute income, but there are constitutional protections against massive seizures of property. (Once again, however, revolutionary circumstances sometimes occur in which the redistribution game is played for higher stakes.)

Substantively, the main theme of the analysis concerned the *paradox of power* – the observation that, in many though not all conflictual contexts, the relatively less well-endowed side improves its position compared with its better-endowed rival. As a leading example, in modern political redistributive struggles the rich end up transferring income to the poor. The underlying explanation derives from a comparison of the marginal payoffs of productive versus conflictual activities, which reveals that the less well-endowed side has a comparative advantage in fighting, the richer side in producing. Appropriative effort allows you to place a tax upon your opponent's productive effort, and it is more profitable to tax a rich opponent than a poor one. When the paradox of power is applicable, the conflict process, while dissipating income in aggregate, also tends to bring about a more equal distribution of whatever income remains.

However, it would be absurd to claim that the paradox of power holds universally – that, in mixed conflictual-cooperative interactions poorer contenders always gain relative to their richer opponents. In war and politics both, sometimes the rich do get richer and the poor poorer. The analysis here revealed that the comparative advantage of the poor in conflictual processes can be overcome when the *decisiveness* of conflict is sufficiently great, that is, when a given ratio of fighting efforts is very disproportionately effective in determining the outcome of conflict. High decisiveness operates to the advantage of better-endowed parties, who are always able to invest more heavily in fighting should it be profitable to do so. Over past centuries military technology, it appears, has tended in the direction of greater decisiveness, which roughly translates into an advantage of the offense over the defense. This factor helps explain the extinction of so many smaller states in the modern era. When it comes to the more limited contests that take place within nation-states (class struggles) or firms (labor-management conflicts) or families (sibling and generational rivalries), no such tendency is evident and the paradox of power does seem mainly to hold.

The paradox of power aside, among the other results of interest are:

1. Generalized progress in productive technology, though of benefit to both sides, has essentially no effect upon the parties' *proportionate* allocations of resources between conflict and production. Fighting activity and productive activity tend to increase more or less in parallel.

2. Greater productive complementarity between the parties (as might result from increased international trade) does tend to induce some shift of resources away from conflictual activity, but the effect

need not be large. In addition, the better-endowed side reaps a disproportionate share of the benefit.

3. Apart from their tendency to favor the better-endowed side, improvements in the technology of conflict cause all contenders to tilt in the direction of greater conflictual activity. Since the increased fighting efforts largely cancel one another out, the net effect is typically a substantial social loss.

As in all attempts to model complex phenomena, a variety of simplifying assumptions were employed here. To comment briefly on a few of these: (i) Only two-party interactions were examined, ruling out issues like alliances and the balance of power.[17] (ii) Full information was assumed throughout, so that factors like deception have been set aside.[18] (iii) The simplified mathematical form of the Contest Success Function does not allow for differences between offensive and defensive weapons, between ground and naval forces, between battle-seeking and Fabian tactics, and so on.[19] (iv) The steady-state assumption rules out issues involving timing, such as arms races, economic growth, or (on a smaller time-scale) signalling resolve through successive escalation.[20] (v) In the model here, all income falls into a common pool available for capture. More generally, each side might have some income secure from capture, and in fact would be making an optimizing choice between resources devoted in that way versus resources generating income in a common pool. (vi) The underlying *resources* on each side were assumed invulnerable to seizure. (vii) Apart from opportunity costs in the form of foregone production, fighting was assumed nondestructive. (vii) The effects of distance and other geographical factors were not considered. (viii) The Nash–Cournot solution concept was employed; no allowance was made for Stackelberg leadership or for the use of threats and promises.

Even when generalized in the various ways suggested by the list above, the steady-state model will remain inappropriate for the analysis of conflicts dominated by single overwhelming or irreversible events like a Pearl Harbor attack. In the military domain it is more applicable to protracted cold wars or to continuing low-level combats like those between

---

[17] There is of course a vast literature on these questions. I shall cite here only Blainey (1973) and Bernholz (1985).

[18] On this see, for example, Tullock (1974, Ch. 10) and Brams (1977).

[19] See footnote 11 above.

[20] See, for example, Intriligator [1975], Wolfson [1985], and Garfinkel [1990].

city-dwellers and nomads in early times, or among the small states of pre-imperial China (as described in Sun Tze's *The Art of War*). Outside the military domain, it is particularly relevant for analyzing the ongoing cooperative-conflictual processes we observe in capital – labor relations, in politics, and within families.

I will expand briefly on only one application, political redistribution of income. In modern politics, at least, redistribution is overwhelmingly from the rich to the poor. This might seem surprising. After all, starting from their initial resource advantage the rich could, it appears, make themselves richer still by appropriating what others have produced. And on the other hand, if a presently poor group is powerful enough to achieve redistribution in its own favor, why stop at equality when it can go on further and expropriate the rich?

Several explanations have been put forward, among them: (1) altruism on the one side and envy on the other imply essentially unanimous support for equalization, but not for reversal of the positions of rich and poor; (2) the deadweight costs of the transfer process set limits upon how far any beneficiary group can advantageously push for redistribution.[21] The alternative explanation offered here is the paradox of power. Since the marginal payoff of conflictual effort (i.e., of redistributive political activity) tends to be higher for the less well-endowed side, *popularist politics are profitable for the poor*.

As a further implication, any exogenous change in relative wealths will motivate newly deprived groups to shift their energies toward redistributive politics. When tuition fees rise, college students will organize demonstrations; if disaster strikes, impacted areas demand assistance from government; when the business cycle trends downward, industries seek tariff protection; and in times of low agricultural prices, Kansas farmers "raise less corn and raise more hell." Since the newly enriched groups will be shifting their energies more toward production, the political equilibrium changes. So government will lean against the wind[22] to moderate the impact of *losses*, even when suffered by individuals who are by no means *poor*. After a Bel-Air fire, affluent householders are made eligible for Federal disaster relief; when car sales fall, wealthy shareholders of Ford and GM are permitted to share the benefits of import quotas upon Japanese autos.

---

[21] This is the factor playing the key role in Becker [1983].
[22] Hirshleifer [1976].

REFERENCES

Angell, Norman, 1911, *The Great Illusion*, New York: G. P. Putnam's Sons.
Bartlett, Randall, 1989, *Economics and Power*, Cambridge: Cambridge University Press.
Becker, Gary S., 1983, "A theory of competition among pressure groups for political influence." *Quarterly Journal of Economics*, 98, 370–400.
Bernholz, Peter, 1985, *The International Game of Power*, Berlin: Mouton Publishers.
Blainey, Geoffrey, 1973, *The Causes of War*, New York: The Free Press.
Brams, Steven J., 1977, "Deception in 2 × 2 Games." *Journal of Peace Science*, 2, 171–203.
Browning, Edgar K. and Jacquelene M. Browning, 1979, *Public Finance and the Price System*, New York: Macmillan.
Codere, Helen, 1968, "Exchange and display," in David L. Sills, ed., *International Encyclopedia of the Social Sciences*, The Macmillan Company and The Free Press, 5, 239–245.
Garfinkel, Michelle R., 1990, "Arming as a strategic investment in a cooperative equilibrium." *American Economic Review*, 80, 50–68.
Grossman, Herschel I., 1991, "A general equilibrium model of insurrections." *American Economic Review*, 81, 912–921.
Hirshleifer, Jack, 1976, "Toward a more general theory of regulation: comment." *Journal of Law and Economics*, 19, 241–244.
Hirshleifer, Jack, 1988, "The analytics of continuing conflict." *Synthese*, 76, 201–233.
Hirshleifer, Jack, 1989, "Conflict and rent-seeking success functions: ratio vs. difference models of relative success." *Public Choice*, 63, 101–112.
Intriligator, Michael D., 1975, "Strategic considerations in the Richardson model of arms races." *Journal of Political Economy*, 83, 339–353.
Lanchester, Frederick William, 1916, *Aircraft in Warfare: The Dawn of the Fourth Arm*, London: Constable. Extract reprinted in James R. Newman, ed., 1956, *The World of Mathematics*, New York: Simon and Schuster, 4, 2138–2157.
McKenzie, Richard B., 1990, *The retreat of the elderly welfare state*, Center for the Study of American Business, Washington University—St. Louis.
Mueller, John, 1989, *Retreat from Doomsday: The Obsolescence of Major War*, New York: Basic Books.
Polachek, Solomon William, 1980, "Conflict and trade." *Journal of Conflict Resolution*, 24, 55–80.
Tullock, Gordon, 1974, *The Social Dilemma*, Blacksburg VA: University Publications.
Tullock, Gordon, 1980, "Efficient rent seeking," in J. M. Buchanan, R. D. Tollison, and G. Tullock, eds., *Toward a Theory of the Rent-Seeking Society*, College Station TX: Texas A&M Univ. Press.
Wolfson, Murray, 1985, "Notes on economic warfare." *Conflict Management and Peace Science*, 8, 1–19.

4

Do the Rich Get Richer and the Poor Poorer?

Experimental Tests of a Model of Power

*Yvonne Durham, Jack Hirshleifer, and Vernon L. Smith**

Background of this Chapter

Theories may be accepted simply because they are consistent with observation, with what we can see happening in the world. But a more
stringent test is the method of experiment. Scientific experiments subject
hypothesized explanations to rigorous testing, by controlling for extra-
neous variables. Experimental investigation is generally more difficult
in the social sciences than in the physical sciences, or in the life sciences
when the latter deal with beings below the human level. Nevertheless, the
method of experiment has become increasingly influential within economics. At the forefront of this line of endeavor has been the Economic
Science Laboratory at the University of Arizona under the leadership of
Professor Vernon L. Smith.

I was fortunate to have the opportunity of helping Professor Smith
and his then-student Yvonne Durham design and analyze an experiment
aimed at subjecting the model of the previous paper – and in particular
the prediction as to when the "paradox of power" would and would not
be observed – to empirical test.

I thank Yvonne Durham and Vernon L. Smith for allowing the reprinting of this jointly authored article.

In a market economy, there is no clear implication as to whether
economic activities will tend to reduce or else to widen initial wealth
disparities. When it comes to political or military struggles, in contrast,
it might be expected that initially stronger or richer contenders would

* Durham: Department of Economics, University of Arkansas, Fayetteville, AR 72703;
Hirshleifer: Department of Economics, UCLA, Los Angeles, CA 90095; Smith, Economic Science Laboratory, University of Arizona, Tucson, AZ 85721. We thank the
two anonymous referees of this Journal for extremely valuable comments and suggestions. (Reprinted from Y. Durham, J. Hirshleifer, and V. L. Smith, "Do the Rich
Get Richer and the Poor Poorer? Experimental Tests of a Model of Power," *American
Economic Review*, Vol. 88, No. 4, 970–83, Copyright ©1998, with permission from
the American Economic Association.)

grow ever stronger and richer still. What has been termed the "Paradox of Power" (POP) (Hirshleifer, 1991) is the observation that very often the reverse occurs: poorer or weaker contestants improve their position relative to richer or stronger opponents. In warfare, small nations have often defeated larger ones, as notably occurred in Vietnam. Or consider political clashes over income redistribution. Although citizens in the upper half of the income spectrum surely have more political strength than those in the lower half, modern governments have systematically been transferring income from the former (stronger) to the latter (weaker) group.[1]

Individuals, groups, or nations – if rational and self-interested – will equalize the marginal returns of two main ways of generating income: (1) production and mutually advantageous exchange, versus (2) "appropriative" efforts designed to redistribute income or capture resources previously controlled by other parties (or to defend against the latter's attempts to do the same). Management and labor jointly generate the aggregate output of the firm, for example, yet at the same time contend with one another over distribution of the proceeds.

As for the Paradox of Power, the theoretical explanation is that initially weaker or poorer contenders are typically motivated *to fight harder*, that is, to devote relatively more effort to appropriative (conflictual) effort. Put another way, the marginal payoff of appropriative effort relative to productive effort is typically greater at low levels of income. (When agricultural prices fell to extraordinarily low levels in the great depression of the 1890's, Kansas farmers were urged by their leaders to "raise less corn and raise more hell.") Looking at it the other way, while the rich may have the capability of exploiting the poor, it might not pay them to do so.

Nevertheless, in some social contexts, initially richer and more powerful contestants do exploit weaker rivals. Affluent aristocracies often use their power to extort even more resources from the lower classes. So the question is, when does and when does not the Paradox of Power hold? In the model, the governing factor is a parameter m reflecting the *decisiveness* of conflictual effort. When decisiveness is low, the rich are content to concentrate upon producing a larger social pie of income even though the poor will be gaining an improved share thereof. But when conflictual preponderance makes a sufficiently weighty difference for achieved income – at the extreme, when the battle is "winner take

---

[1] Edgar K. Browning and Jacquelene M. Browning (1994, pp. 259–61).

all" – the rich cannot afford to let the poor win the contest over distributive shares.

The balance between production and struggle, as two ways of making a living, has been examined in a number of theoretical studies, among them Trygve Haavelmo (1954), Goran Skogh and Charles Stuart (1982), Hirshleifer (1989, 1991), Stergios Skaperdas (1992), and Herschel I. Grossman and Minseong Kim (1994). But how decision makers choose between productive and conflictual activities has not heretofore, so far as we could determine, been addressed experimentally. That was the first object of the study reported in this paper.

A second aim was to consider the degree to which subjects ended up at the theoretical noncooperative Nash solution, as opposed to more cooperative outcomes generating larger income for the group as a whole. In the experimental literature the extent of cooperation has been found to be sensitive to, among other things, the number of iterations of the game and whether partners are held fixed or else varied from round to round. Our experimental investigation was designed to address these questions as well.

The first section below outlines the analytic model. The next section explains our implementation of tests of the model. The third section describes the experimental procedures and outcomes. The last section discusses the results and summarizes.

THE MODEL

Each of two contenders $i = 1, 2$ must divide his/her exogenously given resource endowment R_i between productive effort E_i and appropriative ("fighting") effort F_i:

$$E_1 + F_1 = R_1 \tag{1}$$
$$E_2 + F_2 = R_2.$$

The E_i efforts are inputs to a joint production function. A convenient form for this function, characterized by constant returns to scale and constant elasticity of substitution, is:

$$I = A\big(E_1^{1/s} + E_2^{1/s}\big)^s, \tag{2}$$

where A is an index of total productivity and s is an index of complementarity between E_1 and E_2.[2] However, for utmost simplicity here we have

---

[2] To allow for differential productivity, E_1 and E_2 could be multiplied by productive "efficiency coefficients" e_1 and e_2. We do not explore this kind of asymmetry here.

assumed $A = s = 1$, so that (2) reduces to the simple additive equation:

$$I = E_1 + E_2. \tag{2a}$$

Thus, the parties can cooperate by combining their productive efforts so as to generate a common pool of income available to the two of them jointly. But the respective shares p_1 and p_2 (where $p_1 + p_2 = 1$) are determined in a conflictual process. In particular, the Contest Success Function (CSF) takes the fighting efforts F_i as inputs, yielding the distributive shares as outputs:

$$\begin{aligned} p_1 &= F_1^m / \left(F_1^m + F_2^m \right) \\ p_2 &= F_2^m / \left(F_1^m + F_2^m \right). \end{aligned} \tag{3}$$

Here m is a "decisiveness parameter" controlling the mapping of the input ratio F_1 / F_2 into the success ratio p_1 / p_2. For $m \leq 1$ the CSF is characterized by diminishing marginal returns as F_1 increases with given F_2, or vice versa. However, for $m > 1$ there will be an initial range of increasing returns before diminishing marginal returns set in.[3,4]

As a simplifying assumption, we postulate that conflict is nondestructive, i.e., there is no "battle damage." Choosing fighting activity over productive activity involves some opportunity loss of potential output, but the struggle does not itself damage the resource base or otherwise reduce the aggregate of income attainable.

Finally, the incomes accruing to the contestants are:

$$\begin{aligned} I_1 &= p_1 I \\ I_2 &= p_2 I. \end{aligned} \tag{4}$$

For each level of fighting effort by contender 2, there is a corresponding optimal effort for contender 1 (and vice versa). Thus, 1's optimization problem is to choose $F_1 \geq 0$ so as to solve:

$$\text{Max } I_1 = p_1(F_1 | F_2) \times I(E_1 | E_2)$$

$$\text{subject to } E_1 + F_1 = R_1$$

and similarly for side 2.

---

[3] To allow for possible differences in conflictual ability, the inputs F_1 and F_2 could be multiplied by "fighting efficiency coefficients" f_1 and f_2. This type of asymmetry is also ruled out here.

[4] Alternative possible forms of what are called here Contest Success Functions are discussed in Gordon Tullock (1980), Avinash Dixit (1987), Hirshleifer (1989), and Skaperdas (1996).

Assuming neither party's resource constraint is binding, and using the simplified production function (2a), the Nash–Cournot reaction functions are:

$$\frac{F_1}{F_2^m} = \frac{m(E_1 + E_2)}{F_1^m + F_2^m}$$

$$\frac{F_2}{F_1^m} = \frac{m(E_1 + E_2)}{F_1^m + F_2^m}. \tag{5}$$

The right-hand sides being identical, $F_1 = F_2$ is always a solution of these equations. That is, the reaction curves intersect along the 45-degree line between the F_1 and F_2 axes. In fact, this is the sole intersection in the positive quadrant.

If however the boundary constraint is binding for the poorer side (which we always take to be contender 2), the second equation would be replaced by:

$$F_2 = R_2. \tag{5a}$$

In that case, at equilibrium F_1 and F_2 are in general unequal, but the intersection of the reaction functions still determines the Nash–Cournot equilibrium values of the fighting efforts.

As indicated above, the experiments were intended in part to challenge a number of specific predictions derived from the model. In particular:

(i) *Fighting Intensities.* – As the decisiveness parameter m exogenously increases, it pays both sides to "fight harder," i.e., the equilibrium fighting efforts F_i will rise. (Implying, of course, that the ultimate achieved incomes I_i must fall.)

(ii) *Conflict as an Equalizing Process (Paradox of Power), Strong vs. Weak Form.* – For sufficiently low values of the decisiveness parameter m, disparities in achieved income will – owing to the Paradox of Power – be smaller than the initial disparities in resource endowments. Letting contender 1 be the initially better-endowed side:

$$R_1/R_2 > I_1/I_2 \geq 1. \tag{6}$$

When the *equality* on the right holds (i.e., when the achieved incomes of the initially richer and initially poorer sides end up exactly equal) we have the "strong form" of the Paradox of Power. As already noted, for any interior solution (that is, when the poorer side does not run into its resource constraint) we must have $F_1 = F_2$, so that the strong form of the paradox necessarily applies.[5] It can be shown that there will be interior solutions up to some critical value ρ of the resource ratio:

$$\rho = (2 + m)/m. \tag{7}$$

Thus specifically, in our experiments employing the low value $m = 1$ for the decisiveness parameter, the prediction is that the strong form of the POP will hold for low resource ratios, specifically for $R_1/R_2 \leq 3$. For resource ratios larger than $\rho = 3$, only the weak form, i.e., the strict *inequality* on the right of equation (6), is predicted.

(iii) *Conflict as an Inequality-Aggravating Process.* – The model also indicates that for sufficiently high values of the decisiveness coefficient m and the resource ratio R_1/R_2, the Paradox of Power will *not* apply. The rich would get richer and the poor poorer. Specifically, for our experiments using the high decisiveness coefficient $m = 4$, the critical value τ of the resource ratio for this condition is approximately 2.18.[6] Also, from (7), when $m = 4$ the critical ρ separating the weak from the strong forms of the Paradox of Power equals 1.5. Thus in our experiments using the low resource ratio $25/15 = 1.67$ we expect the weak form of the Paradox of Power to hold , since 1.67 lies between ρ and τ. However, for the experiments with $R_1/R_2 = 32/8 = 4 > \tau = 2.18$, the prediction is that the initially better-endowed party will improve its relative position compared to the less well-endowed side:

$$I_1/I_2 = (F_1/F_2)^m > R_1/R_2. \tag{8}$$

IMPLEMENTING TESTS OF THE MODEL

Certain game-theoretic and implementational concerns are also addressed in our experimental test of the above model. In the strict game-theoretic sense, the noncooperative equilibrium is about strangers who meet once, interact strategically in their self-interest, and will never meet

---

[5] This result can come about only using the simplified production function (2a), where the productive complementarity coefficient is set at $s = 1$. For the more general CES production function (2), with $s > 1$, at equilibrium only the weak form of the paradox holds.

[6] The value of τ was obtained by finding the resource ratio at which the condition $I_1/I_2 = R_1/R_2$ was met for $m = 4$.

again. Such conditions control for repeated-game effects, since the antagonists have no history or future. Yet in many contexts individuals interact in repeated games, where they can signal, punish, and build reputations. In the particularly simple version where the one-shot game is iterated with the same payoffs each round, we have a supergame. The study of such games has been motivated by the intuition or "folk theorem" that repetition makes cooperation possible (Jean-François Mertens, 1987). But formal theorems to this effect for finite horizons have not been forthcoming, and interest has settled on experimental studies of both single-play games and supergames, and on variations in the protocol for matching players in repeat play.

Kevin A. McCabe et al. (1996) studied a class of extensive-form games in which the parties move sequentially in a series of rounds. In any round the first-mover can forward signal the desire to cooperate, but the other player can defect. In one game the first player can punish such defections. In the other he/she has no such recourse. If pairs are matched at random for each play in a repeated sequence of unknown length, subjects gradually learn to cooperate when the punishment option is available; when this option is not available they tend to play noncooperatively. If instead the same pairs remain matched for the entire length of the supergame, they tend to achieve cooperation whether or not the opportunity for direct punishment or defection is available.

Consequently, in addition to testing the substantive predictions associated with the Paradox of Power, we will be addressing some of these issues that have arisen in the experimental and game-theoretic traditions. Specifically, we will be comparing the results of experiments in which the partners are randomly varied in each round with experiments in which the partners are fixed throughout the supergame. As suggested by the preceding discussion, we anticipate that the condition of fixed partners will favor somewhat more cooperative behavior. However, we will be implementing a normal-form game (simultaneous choice of strategies presented in a payoff matrix each round) rather than an extensive-form game (sequential choice by the players each round). McCabe and Smith (1997) show that the extensive form favors cooperation relative to the normal form of two theoretically "equivalent" games. This is because cooperative intentions can be signalled by one player and the second player can reciprocate (not defect) within the same round. Hence, the normal form of the experiments reported below is expected to make cooperation (i.e., reduced levels of fighting) difficult even in repeat interactions.

EXPERIMENTAL PROCEDURES AND OUTCOMES

Experimental Design

We conducted 24 experiments using a total of 278 subjects. No subject participated in more than one experiment. There were six bargaining pairs in each experiment, except for a few cases with only four or five pairs. Each experiment involved repeated play, the payoffs being constant in each round. Within each round, each subject pair chose simultaneously a (row, column) in a matrix displaying the payoffs of each. Subjects were not informed how many rounds would take place; in fact, in each experiment there were 16 or 17 rounds before termination. Subjects were recruited for two-hour sessions but the experiments took much less time, making credible the condition of an unknown horizon.[7]

In every round each subject allocated his/her initial endowment of tokens between an "Investment Account" (IA) and a "Rationing Account" (RA). (We deliberately avoided using any terminology suggestive of "fighting.")[8] Tokens contributed to the IA corresponded to productive effort E_i in the theoretical model: the paired IA contributions generated an aggregate pool of income (in the form of "experimental pesos") in accordance with equation (2a) above. Funds put into the RA corresponded to fighting effort F_i and determined the respective distributive shares p_1 and p_2 in accordance with equations (3). For simplicity, only integer choices were permitted. (More precisely, each subject could allocate, within his/her resource constraint, amounts in integral hundreds of tokens to invest in the IA – the remainder, of course, going into the RA.) The totals of pesos ultimately achieved were converted into actual dollars at the end of the experiment, so subjects had a substantial motivation to make well-calculated choices. (The payoffs ranged from $0.25 to $75.25, not including the $5 fee for showing up. The average payoff was $17.66.)

To challenge the implications of the model, we manipulated the resource endowments R_1 and R_2 and also the decisiveness coefficient m. Four experiments were run with each of the three endowment vectors $(R_1, R_2) = (20, 20), (25, 15)$, and $(32, 8)$ – the first series using a low value $m = 1$ of the decisiveness parameter, and the next using a high value $m = 4$. Thus there were 24 experiments in all.

---

[7] In McCabe et al. (1996) this technique was found to be effective in leading to cooperation, even on the "last" repetition.

[8] Copies of the instructions are available upon request.

Table 4.1. Treatments

Endowments		Number of Experiments (Number of Subjects)*		
(R_1, R_2)	Decisiveness (m)	Variable Pairing	Fixed Pairing	Totals
20, 20	1	2 (24)	2 (24)	4 (48)
25, 15	1	2 (24)	2 (24)	4 (48)
32, 8	1	2 (22)	2 (24)	4 (46)
20, 20	4	2 (22)	2 (22)	4 (44)
25, 15	4	2 (20)	2 (24)	4 (44)
32, 8	4	2 (24)	2 (24)	4 (48)
	TOTALS	12 (136)	12 (142)	24 (278)

*Owing to some recruiting problems, a few experiments were run using only eight or ten subjects (four or five pairs). Each experiment was run for either 16 or 17 rounds.

Also, in view of the McCabe et al. (1996) result that cooperation is promoted by repeated play with the same partners, each group of four experiments was further subdivided into alternative matching protocols. In the first ("varying partners") protocol, partners were randomly changed each round. Under the second ("fixed partners") protocol, subjects were randomly paired at the beginning of the experiment but played repeatedly with the same partner throughout.

Overall there were eight experiments under each of the three endowment conditions. Four of the eight involved varying partners, and four fixed partners. There was an analogous subdivision between experiments conducted using $m = 1$ and using $m = 4$. The upshot is that there were exactly two experiments for each of the 12 sets of experimental conditions or "treatments." The treatment design is summarized in Table 4.1.

Results – Nash versus Cooperative Solutions

The theoretical model described in the previous section derived the Nash–Cournot noncooperative equilibrium. However, the experimental literature has intensively investigated conditions under which subjects might arrive at a more cooperative outcome. This is the first issue addressed:

H_o : the null hypothesis is that $(F_1, F_2) = (C_1, C_2)$

H_a : the alternative hypothesis is that $(F_1, F_2) = (N_1, N_2)$.

Here the N_i signify the respective fighting efforts F_i under the Nash solution, while the C_i are the fighting efforts under the Cooperative solution.

Table 4.2. Experimental Results

Treatment Parameters			Nash Solution				Average Results (Sixteenth Observations)		
Experiment no.	m	Pairing	R_1, R_2	R_1/R_2	N_1, N_2	N_1/N_2	F_1, F_2	F_1/F_2	I_1/I_2
1	1	V	20, 20	1	10, 10	1	7.83, 6.83	1.15	1.15
2	1	V	20, 20	1	10, 10	1	8, 9	0.89	0.89
3	1	F	20, 20	1	10, 10	1	8.67, 6.67	1.30	1.30
4	1	F	20, 20	1	10, 10	1	4, 5	0.8	0.8
5	1	V	25, 15	1.67	10, 10	1	10.83, 8.5	1.27	1.27
6	1	V	25, 15	1.67	10, 10	1	9, 9.17	0.98	0.98
7	1	F	25, 15	1.67	10, 10	1	10.17, 9	1.13	1.13
8	1	F	25, 15	1.67	10, 10	1	7.67, 6.83	1.12	1.12
9	1	V	32, 8	4	10, 8	1.25	11.83, 7.67	1.54	1.54
10	1	V	32, 8	4	10, 8	1.25	10.33, 7.5	1.38	1.38
11	1	F	32, 8	4	10, 8	1.25	5.17, 3.17	1.63	1.63
12	1	F	32, 8	4	10, 8	1.25	5.4, 4.6	1.17	1.17
13	4	V	20, 20	1	16, 16	1	10.33, 12.83	0.81	0.42
14	4	V	20, 20	1	16, 16	1	14.67, 15.33	0.96	0.84
15	4	F	20, 20	1	16, 16	1	11.67, 13.83	0.84	0.51
16	4	F	20, 20	1	16, 16	1	10, 9.2	1.09	1.40
17	4	V	25, 15	1.67	16, 15	1.07	15.5, 11.83	1.31	2.95
18	4	V	25, 15	1.67	16, 15	1.07	16.5, 12.5	1.32	3.04
19	4	F	25, 15	1.67	16, 15	1.07	16.17, 13.83	1.17	1.87
20	4	F	25, 15	1.67	16, 15	1.07	13.5, 12.33	1.10	1.44
21	4	V	32, 8	4	12, 8	1.5	11.67, 7.33	1.59	6.42
22	4	V	32, 8	4	12, 8	1.5	11.67, 7	1.67	7.72
23	4	F	32, 8	4	12, 8	1.5	10.5, 7.5	1.4	3.84
24	4	F	32, 8	4	12, 8	1.5	11, 4.67	2.36	30.76

The theoretical Nash solution is generated by the intersection of the reaction functions of equations (5) above for an interior outcome – or in the case of a boundary outcome (where the poorer contender 2's resource constraint is binding), substituting (5a) for the second equation in (5). The Cooperative solution was defined as $(C_1, C_2) = (1, 1)$. That is, each side devotes the minimal allowable positive amount to fighting effort.[9] Table 4.2 is a summary that allows a comparison between the Nash equilibrium and the *average* of the six (or, in a few cases, four

---

[9] In equations (3), the relative shares p_1 and p_2 are indeterminate when $F_1 = F_2 = 0$. To remedy the indeterminacy, the Profit Table in the Instructions provided for zero payoff to a player whenever he or she put zero into the RA, i.e., whenever $F_i = 0$ was chosen. So the cooperative combination maximizing the aggregate payoff, under the integer constraint, is $(C_1, C_2) = (1, 1)$.

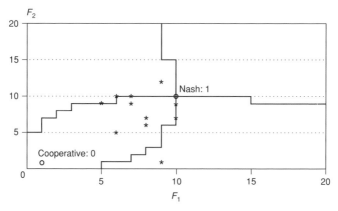

Figure 4.1. Experiments A1 and B1 $(R_1, R_2) = (20, 20); m = 1;$ Varying partners.

or five) observations on round 16 in each of the 24 experiments. Note that almost all the contesting pairs' choices are much closer to the Nash prediction than to the Cooperative (1, 1), but are biased on the low side of Nash.

As an illustration, Figure 4.1 depicts the first two of the 24 experiments. Each * symbol plots the fighting efforts F_1 and F_2 chosen by one of the 12 bargaining pairs in the sixteenth (the last or next-to-last) round. Also shown are the reaction (step) functions, the computed Nash non-cooperative equilibrium at the intersection of these functions, and the postulated Cooperative solution at (1, 1). At a glance, the observations tend to fall between the Nash and the Cooperative solutions, but much nearer to the former. This was in fact typical; error deviations from Nash tended to the Cooperative side.

We used the likelihood ratio to test the alternative Nash hypothesis H_a against the cooperative null hypothesis H_o.[10] It was assumed that the observations for the "fighting efforts" F_i are normally distributed, with mean $\mu = C$ under H_o or mean $\mu = N$ under H_a, and variance

---

[10] Computing the likelihood ratio allows the analysis to include Bayesian updating of prior beliefs as well as traditional significance tests. We consider both avenues, with similar results. The likelihood ratio is particularly convenient for Bayesian conversion of *prior beliefs p′* into *posterior beliefs p″* in light of the experimental evidence. The relevant version of Bayes' Theorem is:

$$\frac{p_o''}{p_a''} = \frac{\text{Likelihood of evidence under } H_o}{\text{Likelihood of evidence under } H_a} \times \frac{p_o'}{p_a'}.$$

$V = S^2$ (the sample variance).[11] Then for any given treatment the likelihood ratio is:

$$\lambda = \frac{\exp\left[-\frac{1}{2S^2}\Sigma_{t,i}(F_{it} - C)^2\right]}{\exp\left[-\frac{1}{2S^2}\Sigma_{t,i}(F_{it} - N)^2\right]} \tag{9a}$$

$$= \exp\left\{\frac{1}{2S^2}\left[2\Sigma_{t,i}(F_{it}(C - N) + Tn(N^2 - C^2)\right]\right\}.$$

$$\ln \lambda = Tn\bar{F}(C - N)/S^2 + (N^2 - C^2)(Tn/2S^2). \tag{9b}$$

Here the t subscript indexes the rounds from 1 to T, while the i subscript indexes the individual pair observations from 1 to n.

A $\lambda < 1$ would indicate that, for this particular treatment, the observed choices had a higher probability of occurring under the alternative (Nash) hypothesis than under the null (Cooperative) hypothesis. The 12 rows of Table 4.3 list the λ's for all the treatments, expressed for convenience in terms of logs (the log-likelihood ratios) as in (9b). Positive entries in the table represent results favoring the null hypothesis while negative entries favor the alternative hypothesis.

The columns toward the left of Table 4.3 identify the conditions for each of the 12 treatments. The remaining columns show the results for "All Rounds" and also for the "Sixteenth Round" (that is, the last or next-to-last round) separately. [For the "Sixteenth Round" columns, equations (9a) and (9b) are modified by simply dropping the indexing over t.] From the statistical point of view, the "All Rounds" reports provide a larger sample size (though not independent) and thus are less influenced by random fluctuations. On the other hand, the "Sixteenth Round" reports are more likely to isolate the mature behavior of the experimental subjects. Finally, F_1 refers to the subject having the larger, and F_2 the smaller, resource endowment. (In the equal-endowment cases, the assignment of F_1 versus F_2 was random.)

The results summarized in Tables 4.2 and 4.3 overwhelmingly support the Nash as opposed to the Cooperative solution. In Table 4.3 the predominantly negative values of the log-likelihood ratios (46 of the 48 tabulated entries) correspond of course to likelihood ratios less than

---

[11] As a technical qualification, a strict Bayesian would want to deal with the fact that the true normal variance V is unknown. In principle one ought to specify prior beliefs about the variance and deal with it as a "nuisance parameter." However, we have taken the liberty of simply employing the observed sample variance S^2 for V. Doing so provides an enormous computational saving without substantially affecting the results.

Table 4.3. Log-Likelihood Ratios, Nash Versus Cooperative Solution*

Treatment Parameters and Matching Protocol				All Rounds ($T \cdot n = 198$) Types		Sixteenth Round ($n = 12$) Types	
R_1	R_2	m	Pairing	F_1	F_2	F_1	F_2
20	20	1	V	−873	−654	−87	−30
20	20	1	F	−545	−169	−3.8	−0.7§
25	15	1	V	−939	−1302	−31	−133
25	15	1	F	−262	−218	−20	−23
32	8	1	V	−879	−2583	−31	−111
32	8	1	F	−123	−73	0.8§	8.5*
20	20	4	V	−1260	−1376	−114	−78
20	20	4	F	−68	−92	−6.3	−10
25	15	4	V	−1475	−541	−1001	−115
25	15	4	F	−860	−796	−48	−69
32	8	4	V	−2756	−1643	−1008	−114
32	8	4	F	−373	−332	−43	−23

*B. W. Lindgren (1962), for example, derives a most powerful test (among the class of tests where α errors are not smaller, none has a larger power $1 - \beta$ for a simple H_o against a simple H_a using the likelihood ratio. The best critical region is $\lambda = N_o(x)/N_a(x) < K$, where $N(x)$ is the normal density evaluated for H_o or H_a, and K is a constant chosen to set the Type I error (α) at the desired level. H_o is then rejected in favor of H_a if $\lambda < K$.

Setting $\alpha = 0.001$, K_E for each experimental treatment E was computed from the following [for the Sixteenth Round case, $T = 1$ in (9)]:

$$\text{PROB}_{\mu = C = 1}(\bar{F}_E > K_E) = 1 - N\left(\frac{K_E - C}{S_E/\sqrt{n}}\right) = 0.001,$$

where $\bar{F}_E$ is the sample mean level of observed fighting, and S_E^2 is the variance across all n pairs in treatment E. The results from this likelihood ratio test allow us to reject the hypothesis $\mu = C = 1$ (cooperation) in all cases except for the * entry. The entries marked § indicate cases where cooperation is rejected in favor of Nash, but when H_o and H_a are interchanged so that cooperation becomes the null hypothesis, Nash is rejected in favor of cooperation. This illustrates the inherent ambiguity of "classical tests": the outcome need not be independent of which hypothesis is chosen as the null!

unity in equation (9a) above.[12] Using a likelihood ratio test, 45 of the 48 entries in Table 4.3 unambiguously – at significance level $\alpha = 0.005$ – imply rejecting the Cooperative hypothesis in favor of Nash. Only 1 of the 48 (the single entry marked *) unambiguously does the reverse. For the remaining two entries marked §, significance testing using $\alpha = 0.001$

---

[12] Under a Bayesian interpretation, any observer, regardless of prior beliefs, should revise those beliefs so as to attach greater confidence to the Nash hypothesis.

indicates that whichever hypothesis is taken to be the null is rejected in favor of the other![13]

Apart from the generally negative signs for the log λ's, two features of Table 4.3 stand out. First, in all 24 possible comparisons the log-likelihood ratios for the "Sixteenth Round" columns are somewhat less negative than in the corresponding "All Rounds" columns. This is in part the consequence of smaller sample size, but that is evidently not the entire story – since the only two instances of positive values both fall under the "Sixteenth Round" headings. So, for these cases there is the suggestion that participants were "learning to cooperate" by the sixteenth round of interaction. Second, again for all 24 comparisons, the results under the "fixed partners" (F) condition are noticeably less negative than the corresponding "varying partners" (V) results. Since the "fixed partners" condition facilitates the development of mutual understanding, we examine the dynamics of their interaction below for evidence of best-response moves.

It is particularly significant that the only exceptions to the observed tendency to converge to near the Nash equilibrium occur under the treatment in which the Nash equilibrium lies at the boundary of the constraint set for one of the bargainers. As shown in Smith and James M. Walker (1993), in such cases any deviation or slippage from the predicted outcome is necessarily biased, and changes in variance will change the mean. We should also note that, with fixed partners, if bargainers deviate from Nash, either to signal cooperation or to punish failures to reciprocate, a bargainer whose Nash outcome is on a boundary can signal cooperation without constraint, but punishment is asymmetrically restricted.

We can quantify the average percent deviations in the direction of cooperation by defining "slippage fractions" S_1 and S_2:

$$S_i \equiv \frac{N_i - F_i}{N_i - C_i}. \tag{10}$$

In Table 4.4, a positive number in the two right-hand columns indicates slippage in the direction of cooperation. A negative number indicates slippage in the direction of conflict beyond that called for by the Nash solution. As expected, the positive numbers far outweigh the

---

[13] In Bayesian terms, for these two cases the likelihoods are about equal under the null and alternative hypotheses, so no great revision of prior beliefs is indicated. The evidence, while improbable either way, is not much more improbable under one hypothesis than under the other.

Table 4.4. Slippage Toward Cooperation

Treatment Parameters						Nash Solution	Average Results		Average Slippage*	
Experiment no.	m	Pairing	R_1, R_2	R_1/R_2	N_1, N_2	F_1	F_2	S_1	S_2
1	1	V	20, 20	1	10, 10	7.83	6.83	0.24	0.35
2	1	V	20, 20	1	10, 10	8	9	0.22	0.11
3	1	F	20, 20	1	10, 10	8.67	6.67	0.15	0.37
4	1	F	20, 20	1	10, 10	4	5	0.67	0.56
5	1	V	25, 15	1.67	10, 10	10.83	8.5	−0.09	0.17
6	1	V	25, 15	1.67	10, 10	9	9.17	0.11	0.09
7	1	F	25, 15	1.67	10, 10	10.17	9	−0.02	0.11
8	1	F	25, 15	1.67	10, 10	7.67	6.83	0.26	0.41
9	1	V	32, 8	4	10, 8	11.83	7.67	−0.20	0.05
10	1	V	32, 8	4	10, 8	10.33	7.5	−0.04	0.07
11	1	F	32, 8	4	10, 8	5.17	3.17	0.54	0.69
12	1	F	32, 8	4	10, 8	5.4	4.6	0.51	0.46
13	4	V	20, 20	1	16, 16	10.33	12.83	0.38	0.21
14	4	V	20, 20	1	16, 16	14.67	15.33	0.09	0.04
15	4	F	20, 20	1	16, 16	11.67	13.83	0.29	0.15
16	4	F	20, 20	1	16, 16	10	9.2	0.40	0.45
17	4	V	25, 15	1.67	16, 15	15.5	11.83	0.33	0.23
18	4	V	25, 15	1.67	16, 15	16.5	12.5	−0.03	0.18
19	4	F	25, 15	1.67	16, 15	16.17	13.83	−0.01	0.08
20	4	F	25, 15	1.67	16, 15	13.5	12.33	0.17	0.19
21	4	V	32, 8	4	12, 8	11.67	7.33	0.03	0.10
22	4	V	32, 8	4	12, 8	11.67	7	0.03	0.40
23	4	F	32, 8	4	12, 8	10.5	7.5	0.14	0.07
24	4	F	32, 8	4	12, 8	11	4.67	0.09	0.48

*$S_i = (N_i - F_i)/(N_i - C)$.

negative numbers, and the positive numbers predominate more under the "fixed partners" (F) condition. Finally, there is a noticeable *positive correlation* between the S_1 and S_2 numbers on each row of the table: when one subject behaves cooperatively, his/her partner is likely to do so as well. Once again, as expected, this positive correlation holds particularly for the "fixed partners" condition. And in addition, it holds noticeably more strongly for the cases with equal resource endowments $(R_1, R_2) = (20, 20)$.

Dynamics of Interactions for Fixed Partners

A fuller treatment of how individual pairs interact requires analysis of their interactive choices over time. If each player in period t chooses a profit-maximizing strategy based on the other player's choice in period

$t-1$ (a shortsighted best-reply strategy) then they will converge to Nash. In fact subjects' choices may have some inertia, and may involve cooperative signalling. One way of modelling these dynamic interactions, and obtaining a measure of the propensity to choose best replies, is to estimate the following equation for F_{it} (the fighting effort chosen by subject i in period t):

$$F_{it} = (1 - \delta_i)F_{it-1} + \delta_i F_{it}^* + \varepsilon_{it} \qquad (11)$$
$$= F_{it}^* + (1 - \delta_i)\left(F_{it-1} - F_{it}^*\right) + \varepsilon_{it},$$

where F_{it}^* is the best reply in period t to i's choice of strategy in period $t-1$. In this myopic Cournot dynamic, the deterministic component of F_{it} is distributed between an adaptive weight element δ related to i's current best reply F_{it}^* (to the opponent's previous-round choice) and an inertial element $1 - \delta$ related to i's previous choice F_{it-1}. Or, in the second form of (11) the choice of F_{it} can be interpreted as a best reply, plus an imperfect adaptive adjustment based on the error difference between last period's choice F_{it-1} and this period's best reply. Figure 4.2 provides a histogram of the frequency distribution of 140 individual estimates of δ_i over all decision trials for each i. Overwhelmingly, the individual δ_i (and therefore the $1 - \delta_i$) values are in the unit interval indicating some weight being given to i's previous choice and some to i's best reply. They are also overwhelmingly significantly different from zero. Note that over half the subjects exhibit values of $(1 - \delta_i)$ of at least 0.5, indicating considerable weight being attached to correcting the error

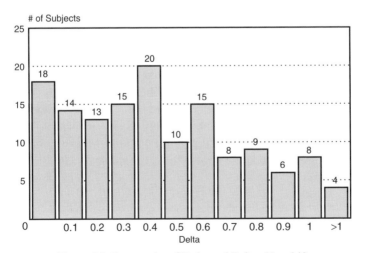

Figure 4.2. Frequencies of Estimated Deltas $N = 140$.

deviation $F_{it-1} - F_{it}^*$. For the fixed-pairs condition the data substantially support the adaptive best-response Cournot dynamic.

Results – The Paradox of Power

The experiments tested a number of specific predictions of the analytic model.

> *Prediction 1:* Higher values of the decisiveness parameter m will lead to larger fighting efforts on both sides.

So the fighting efforts F_1 and F_2 should both be greater at the higher decisiveness level $m = 4$ than at $m = 1$. The upper half of Table 4.2 shows the results for $m = 1$, and the lower half for $m = 4$. There are 48 comparisons, of which a remarkable 45 are in the direction predicted.

> *Prediction 2a:* At the low value $m = 1$ for the decisiveness parameter, the initially poorer side will always end up improving its position.

At $m = 1$, the attained income ratio I_1/I_2 (which for $m = 1$ simply equals the ratio of fighting efforts F_1/F_2) should exceed the resource ratio R_1/R_2. The requirement of unequal initial endowments limits the relevant data to rows 5 through 12 of Table 4.2. Here all eight of the eight comparisons showed the predicted relative improvement – that is, $I_1/I_2 < R_1/R_2$ – and almost always by quite a wide margin.

> *Prediction 2b:* For $m = 1$ the poorer side should attain approximate equality of income (strong form of the POP) for initial resource ratios $R_1/R_2 < 3$, but only some relative improvement ($1 < I_1/I_2 < R_1/R_2$) for larger resource ratios (weak form of the POP).

Looking once again only at the unequal endowments cases, rows 5 through 12 of Table 4.2, the average of the tabulated results is $I_1/I_2 = 1.125$, on the high side of the predicted $I_1/I_2 = 1$. By way of comparison, for rows 9 through 12 where only the weak form $I_1/I_2 > 1$ is predicted, the average outcome is $I_1/I_2 = 1.43$. So, at least *relatively*, the predicted comparison of the strong-form versus weak-form predictions is supported.

> *Prediction 2c:* At the high value $m = 4$ for the decisiveness coefficient, the Paradox of Power should continue to hold (in its weak form) for $\rho < R_1/R_2 < \tau$, where $\rho = 1.5$ and $\tau = 2.18$. But for higher resource ratios the richer side should end up actually improving on

its relative position. That is, in this range $I_1/I_2 = (F_1/F_2)^4$ should exceed R_1/R_2.

For the unequal-endowments rows 17 through 20 of Table 4.2, the resource ratio is $R_1/R_2 = 25/15 = 1.67$, lying between ρ and τ. So the Paradox of Power is predicted in these cases. However, for rows 21 through 24 the resource ratio is $R_1/R_2 = 32/8 = 4 > 2.18 = \tau$, so we expect the rich to become richer still.

Taking up the latter group first, three of the four cases support the prediction $I_1/I_2 = (F_1/F_2)^4 > 4$. In fact, the average of the observed results was a much higher $I_1/I_2 = 12.19$. Turning to the first group, however, all four cases violate the prediction! Quantitatively, the predicted Nash outcome $(N_1, N_2) = (16, 15)$ implies $I_1/I_2 = (16/15)^4 = 1.29 < 1.67$, while the average of the observed results was $I_1/I_2 = 2.32 > 1.67$.

DISCUSSION AND SUMMARY

This experimental investigation deals with a mixed-incentive, iterated-play, bilateral interaction. In each of some 16 rounds, paired individuals had to strike a balance between production and appropriation: more explicitly, between investing resources in joint production versus engaging in a distributive struggle over the respective shares.

We tested two main kinds of predictions:

(1) The first group dealt with issues common to much of the game-theoretic and experimental literature. Of these, the major question was the degree to which the experimental outcomes approximated the noncooperative Nash solution, as opposed to a more cooperative outcome generating a larger income for the group as a whole. We also compared protocols with randomly varying partners each round as opposed to fixed partners over the entire sequence of play.

(2) The second group of predictions dealt with inferences from the specific model of conflict in Hirshleifer (1991), and specifically those associated with the Paradox of Power. The paradox is that, in many situations, an initially poorer side will end up gaining in relative position in comparison with an initially richer and thus stronger opponent.

With regard to the first group of predictions, the experimental observations overwhelmingly supported the Nash as opposed to the Cooperative solution. However, while the Nash solution is much better supported in a dichotomous comparison between the two, the experimental results typically displayed some degree of slippage in the direction of cooperation. The convergence toward Nash was weaker under the fixed partners as opposed to the varying partners protocol, and also was weaker in the mature (sixteenth round) choices than the overall behavior. Together with an observed tendency toward positive correlation of the deviations from the Nash equilibrium, these results are consistent with a "learning to cooperate" interpretation. Fixed partners over multiple rounds of interaction favor the development of mutual understanding relative to varying partners. Still, we must reemphasize, overall the results were dominated by noncooperative (Nash) behavior. A dynamic analysis of fixed partner interaction predominantly supported a Cournot myopic adaptive best-reply strategy in which subjects' choices were best replies to their opponent's previous choice, but with a positive correction for error in anticipating that previous best reply. This dynamic helps to explain the convergence tendencies to Nash.

With regard to the underlying conflict model, the central prediction (Prediction 1) was that larger fighting efforts would be observed for higher values of the "decisiveness coefficient" m – a parameter that indicates the degree to which the fighting efforts as inputs determine the relative shares of incomes attained. Prediction 1 was overwhelmingly confirmed: in 45 of 48 comparisons, when fighting became a more decisive determinant of relative income shares, both sides invested more in the struggle.

The evidence was more mixed regarding when the Paradox of Power – that the poorer side would improve its relative position – would hold. For the experiments employing a low value $m = 1$ for the decisiveness coefficient, Prediction 2a was that at least the "weak form" of the paradox should always hold, that is, that $I_1/I_2 > R_1/R_2$. In fact eight of eight possible comparisons confirmed Prediction 2a. Prediction 2b was more stringent, specifying that for the four cases where the initial resource ratio was sufficiently low the "strong form" should hold: $I_1 = I_2$. The observed average income ratio for these cases was $I_1/I_2 = 1.125$, not very far from the prediction.

For the high value $m = 4$ of the decisiveness coefficient, Prediction 2c was that the Paradox of Power would hold in its weak form for the low-resource ratio $R_1/R_2 = 1.67$, but should be violated for the high resource ratio $R_1/R_2 = 4$. The latter part of this prediction was substantially confirmed. For an already high resource ratio it was predicted that the rich would get richer, and in fact they did so. But they also did so for the 1.67:1 resource ratio where, according to the theory, the poor should instead have improved their position. From the point of view of the theoretical prediction, the richer contestants might be fighting too hard, or the poorer not hard enough. Inspection of lines 17–20 of Table 4.4 indicates that the rich are on average close to $F_1 = 16$, the predicted amount of resources devoted to fighting, but the poor are falling short of the predicted $F_2 = 15$. However, there is a boundary problem here: the Nash prediction for the poorer side would require them to devote 100 percent of their resources ($R_2 = 15$) to fighting. Thus, any error whatsoever on their part must necessarily lead to a deficiency of fighting effort, which at least partially rationalizes the "anomalous" result found.

To sum up: in this experimental context our results support the Nash as opposed to the Cooperative solution, though with some degree of slippage in the direction of the latter. And the theoretical predictions as to when the Paradox of Power – that an initially weaker party will improve its position relative to a stronger opponent – will or will not be observed, are also broadly supported.

REFERENCES

Browning, Edgar K. and Browning, Jacquelene M. *Public finance and the price system*, 4th Ed. Englewood Cliffs, NJ: Prentice Hall, 1994.

Dixit, Avinash. "Strategic Behavior in Contests." *American Economic Review*, December 1987, *77*(5), pp. 891–98.

Grossman, Herschel I. and Kim, Minseong. "Swords or Plowshares? A Theory of the Security of Claims to Property." *Journal of Political Economy*, December 1995, *103*(6), pp. 1275–88.

Haavelmo, Trygve. *A study in the theory of economic evolution.* Amsterdam: North-Holland, 1954.

Hirshleifer, Jack. "Conflict and Rent-Seeking Success Functions: Ratio vs. Difference Models of Relative Success." *Public Choice*, November 1989, *63*(2), pp. 101–12.

———. "The Paradox of Power." *Economics and Politics*, November 1991, *3*(3), pp. 177–200.

Lindgren, B. W. *Statistical theory.* New York: Macmillan, 1962.

McCabe, Kevin A.; Rassenti, Stephen J., and Smith, Vernon L. "Game Theory and Reciprocity in Some Extensive Form Experimental Games." *Proceedings of the National Academy of Sciences*, November 12, 1996, *93*(23), pp. 13421–28.

McCabe, Kevin and Smith, Vernon. "Intentionality Detection and Mindreading: Why Game Form Matters." Unpublished manuscript, Economic Science Laboratory, University of Arizona, May 1997.

Mertens, Jean-François. "Repeated Games," in John Eatwell, Murray Milgate, and Peter Newman, eds., *The new Palgrave: A dictionary of economics.* London: MacMillan, 1987, pp. 151–53.

Skaperdas, Stergios. "Cooperation, Conflict, and Power in the Absence of Property Rights." *American Economic Review*, September 1992, *82*(4), pp. 720–39.

———. "Contest Success Functions." *Economic Theory*, February 1996, *7*(2), pp. 283–90.

Skogh, Goran and Stuart, Charles. "A Contractarian Theory of Property Rights and Crime." *Scandinavian Journal of Economics*, 1982, *84*(1), pp. 27–40.

Smith, Vernon L. and Walker, James M. "Monetary Rewards and Decision Cost in Experimental Economics." *Economic Inquiry*, April 1993, *31*(2), pp. 245–61.

Tullock, Gordon. "Efficient Rent Seeking," in James M. Buchanan, Robert D. Tollison, and Gordon Tullock, eds., *Toward a theory of the rent-seeking society*. College Station, TX: Texas A&M University Press, 1980, pp. 97–112.

5

Conflict and Rent-Seeking Success Functions

Ratio vs. Difference Models of Relative Success*

Jack Hirshleifer

Background of this Chapter

Just as there is a technology of production, there is a technology of conflict and struggle. The key to the latter is the Conflict Success Function (CSF). The CSF is a mathematical relation whose inputs are the fighting efforts of the combatants on each side and whose output is a division of the prize between them – in extreme cases, total victory for one side and defeat for the other. This article proposes two especially simple analytic forms for the CSF. In the first, relative success depends upon the *ratio* of the fighting inputs; in the second, the outcome depends upon their *difference*. The article then examines real-world conditions under which one or the other form of the CSF is likely to be applicable.

Various aspects of Conflict Success Functions (sometimes termed Contest Success Functions) have been investigated by, among others, Stergios Skaperdas (1996, "Contest Success Functions," *Economic Theory* 7: 283–90) and Hugh Neary (1997, "Equilibrium Structure in an Economic Model of Conflict," *Economic Inquiry*, 35: 480–95).

Abstract

The rent-seeking competitions studied by economists fall within a much broader category of conflict interactions that also includes military combats, election campaigns, industrial disputes, lawsuits, and sibling rivalries. In the rent-seeking literature, each party's success p_i (which can be interpreted either as the probability of victory or as the proportion of the prize won) has usually been taken to be a function of the ratio of the respective resource commitments. Alternatively, however, p_i may instead be a function of the difference between the parties' commitments to the contest. The Contest Success Function (CSF) for the difference form is a logistic curve in which, as is consistent with military experience, increasing returns apply up to an

---

* In preparing successive drafts of this paper I have benefited from suggestions and comments from Michele Boldrin, Avinash Dixit, Arye L. Hillman, David Hirshleifer, Eric S. Maskin, David Levine, Eric Rasmusen, John G. Riley, Russell Roberts, and Leo K. Simon. (Reprinted from J. Hirshleifer, "Conflict and Rent-Seeking Success Functions: Ratio vs. Difference Models of Relative Success," *Public Choice*, Vol. 63, 101–112, Copyright © 1989, with permission from The Locke Institute.)

inflection point at equal resource commitments. A crucial flaw of the traditional ratio model is that neither one-sided submission nor two-sided peace between the parties can ever occur as a Cournot equilibrium. In contrast, both of these outcomes are entirely consistent with a model in which success is a function of the difference *between the parties' resource commitments.*

INTRODUCTION

Following the seminal contributions of Gordon Tullock (1967, 1980), a number of papers[1] have explored various aspects of rent-seeking competitions. In such contests, each of N players invests effort $C_i (i = 1, \ldots, N)$ in the hope of gaining a prize of value V. Existing analyses have mainly explored the nature of equilibrium with varying numbers of contestants, the central issue addressed being whether or not under- or over-dissipation of rents will occur.

The fundamental notion of competitions in which relative success is a function of the parties' respective resource commitments applies far beyond the rent-seeking context. Military combats, election campaigns, industrial struggles (strikes and lockouts), legal conflicts (lawsuits), and even rivalries among siblings or between spouses within the family all fall under this heading. Owing perhaps to failure to perceive these wider implications, the papers in the rent-seeking literature generally do not adopt a *general-equilibrium* approach which would make explicit provision for the alternative productive or consumptive uses of resources employed in rent-seeking competitions. Also, what is very important, a general-equilibrium model would typically make the value of the prize an endogenous variable rather than an exogenously given parameter. I have attempted to provide such a general-equilibrium analysis in Hirshleifer (1988).

This note has a more limited aim, however. My main purpose is to point out that Tullock's basic equation for success in rent-seeking competition represents only one of two canonical families of possibilities, the second and at least equally interesting family having been totally ignored in the existing literature. Specifically, in Tullock's formula each party's success is a function of the *ratios* of the respective efforts or inputs C_i. As will be shown, a number of significantly different results are obtained when, alternatively, relative success is determined by the

---

[1] See, e.g., Hillman and Katz (1984), Corcoran and Karels (1985), Higgins, Shughart and Tollison (1985), Appelbaum and Katz (1986), Allard (1988), Hillman and Samet (1987).

differences among the inputs. I will also be allowing for possibly different prize valuations $V_i \neq V_j$.[2]

CONTEST SUCCESS FUNCTIONS

For $N = 2$ players, in Tullock's basic model the proportionate outcomes p_i depend in a simple way upon the contest inputs or efforts C_i:

$$p_1/p_2 = (C_1/C_2)^m \tag{1}$$

Here each p_i may be interpreted either as the party's respective *probability of success* in a discrete either-or competition or else as the *proportionate share* of the prize won in a continuous-outcome contest. Since $p_1 + p_2 = 1$, equation (1) is equivalent to:

$$p_i = \frac{C_1^m}{C_1^m + C_2^m} \tag{2}$$

For given C_2, this may be called the Contest Success Function (CSF) for player #1; the CSF for the other player is defined correspondingly. (I have implicitly been assuming that the two sides' resources have equal effectiveness in the contest. More generally, it would be possible to adjust each side's C_i by an effectiveness coefficient; this straightforward generalization will be omitted here.)

The effect of the "mass effect parameter" m upon the shape of player #1's Contest Success Function is displayed in Figure 5.1, in which player #2's resource input has been arbitrarily fixed at $C_2 = 100$. Regardless of the level of m, we see that $p_1 = p_2 = .5$ when $C_1 = C_2$. If $m \leq 1$, diminishing returns to competitive effort hold throughout. But for $m > 1$, an initial range of increasing returns exists instead. More specifically, taking the second derivative in the usual way, the inflection point along the CSF of player #1 is determined by the condition:

$$\frac{C_1}{C_2} = \left(\frac{m-1}{m+1}\right)^{1/m} \tag{3a}$$

or, equivalently,

$$p_1 = (m-1)/2m \tag{3b}$$

---

[2] A recent paper of Hillman and Riley (1988) makes use of still another family of contest payoff functions, in which – in contrast with the sharing rules analyzed here – the entire prize, as in an auction, goes to the high bidder. Their paper also allows for differing prize valuations.

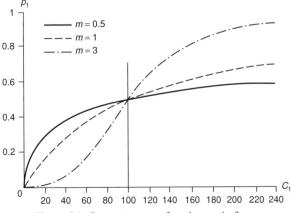

Figure 5.1. Contest success function: ratio form.

Since m cannot meaningfully be zero or negative we see that, for given C_2, there is a point of inflection in the positive range of C_1 only if $m > 1$.[3]

While it is often plausible to assume that contest power is a function of the *ratio* of the forces or efforts committed, this is by no means the only possibly valid functional relation. Nor are all the implications of the ratio form always reasonable. One implication, for example, is that a side investing zero effort must lose everything so long as the opponent commits any finite amount of resources at all, however small, to the struggle. When, alternatively, the outcome is assumed to be a function of the *difference* between the two sides' efforts, a player can have some chance or share of success even without committing resources to the contest. In struggles between nations, for example, one side may surrender rather than resist. While the hope may sometimes be to appease the aggressor, it might make sense to surrender to a totally unappeasable opponent if the submitting nation does not expect to lose absolutely everything by giving up the struggle. And this is reasonable, since in general it will be costly for the victor, even in the absence of resistance, to locate and extract all the possible spoils.

---

[3] In the standard Lanchester equations of military combat (Lanchester, 1916 (1956); Brackney, 1959), the outcome is also assumed to depend upon the *ratio* of the forces committed. But for Lanchester the battle result is always fully deterministic, in the sense that the side with larger forces (adjusted for fighting effectiveness) is 100% certain to win. This makes the CSF a step function, which jumps from $p_1 = 0$ to $p_1 = 1$ when $C_1 = C_2$. So Lanchester's formula can be regarded as the limiting case of equation (2) as the mass effect parameter m goes to infinity. The same holds also for the auction-style payoffs in Hillman and Riley (1988).

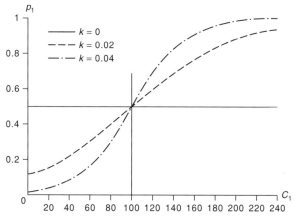

Figure 5.2. Contest success function: difference (logistic) form.

There is one other factor to consider, namely, the location of the inflection point of the CSF. When it comes to military interactions, "God is on the side of the larger battalions." There is an enormous gain when your side's forces increase from just a little smaller than the enemy's to just a little larger.[4] This implies that the range of increasing returns to player #1's commitment C_1 extends up to $C_1 = C_2$, or equivalently up to $p_1 = p_2$.[5] But, we have seen, when the ratio form of the CSF is used, increasing returns, if present at all (that is, if $m > 1$), can only hold up to some $C_1 < C_2$.

Postulating that contest success depends upon the *difference* between the resource commitments, the required conditions – that $C_1 = 0$ need not imply $p_1 = 0$, and that the inflection point occurs at $C_1 = C_2$ – are met by the *logistic* family of curves:

$$p_1 = \frac{1}{1 + \exp\{k(C_2 - C_1)\}} \qquad (4)$$

where p_2 is defined correspondingly. (As is logically required, $p_1 + p_2 = 1$.) In particular, when $C_1 = 0$ player #1 still retains a share of success $p_1 = 1/(1 + \exp\{kC_2\})$. Figure 5.2 shows several CSF curves for

---

[4] As seen in the previous footnote, the Lanchester equations of combat take this to the extreme. The larger force is 100% certain of victory; the smaller force has no chance at all.

[5] Compare T. N. Dupuy's study of diminishing returns in combat interactions between Allied and German forces in World War II (Dupuy, 1987: Ch. 11). Dupuy's curves generally show the inflection point displaced slightly from the "equal forces, equal success" point, owing (on his interpretation) to the superior unit effectiveness of the German army.

varying k, where k is the "mass effect parameter" applicable to the logistic function.

In a military context we might expect the *ratio form* of the Contest Success Function to be applicable when clashes take place under close to "idealized" conditions such as: an undifferentiated battlefield, full information, and unflagging weapons effectiveness. In contrast, the *difference form* tends to apply where there are sanctuaries and refuges, where information is imperfect, and where the victorious player is subject to fatigue and distraction. Given such "imperfections of the combat market," the defeated side need not lose absolutely everything. (For the sake of concreteness I have been using military metaphors and examples, but analogous statements can evidently be made about non-military struggles – e.g., lawsuits or political campaigns or rent-seeking competitions.)

The generalization of equation (2) for any number of players N was provided in Tullock's initial paper. For the ith contestant, the probability of success becomes:

$$p_i = \frac{C_i^m}{C_1^m + C_2^m + \cdots + C_N^m} = \frac{C_i^m}{\Sigma_j C_j^m} \tag{5}$$

Of course, the p_i's sum to unity.

Employing the difference (logistic) form instead, the corresponding generalization of equation (4) is:

$$p_i = \frac{\exp\{kC_i\}}{\Sigma_j \exp\{kC_j\}} \tag{6}$$

It is evident from the form of the last fraction on the right that, as required, the sum of these p_i's will also be unity.[6]

To illustrate, if $N = 3$ and $i = 1$, equation (6) becomes:

$$p_1 = \frac{1}{1 + \exp\{k(C_2 - C_1)\} + \exp\{k(C_3 - C_1)\}} \tag{6a}$$

Both (5) and (6) fall within the more general category of *logit* functions.[7]

---

[6] I thank David Levine and Michele Boldrin who independently discovered this generalization of the logistic Contest Success Function.

[7] The definition of the logit in this context is:

$$p_i = \frac{f(C_i)}{\Sigma_j f(C_j)}$$

Using only the general properties of logit functions, Dixit (1987) obtained some important qualitative results for "strategic" (non-Nash) behavior in asymmetrical contests.

SYMMETRICAL NASH – COURNOT EQUILIBRIUM

As has been mentioned, when the ratio form of the CSF applies each side will surely always commit some resources to the contest. If peace is defined by the condition $C_1 = C_2 = 0$, then peace can never occur as a Cournot equilibrium under the traditional ratio model!

The demonstration is simple. Side #1 will be seeking to maximize its "profit":

$$Y_1 = V p_1 - C_1 \tag{7}$$

where V is the given value of the prize and p_1 is determined as in equation (2). A similar equation holds of course for player #2. Suppose momentarily it were the case that $C_1 = C_2 = 0$, the parties sharing the prize equally without fighting. Then, assuming only that $V > 0$, under the Cournot assumption either player would be motivated to defect, since even the smallest finite commitment of resources makes the defector's relative success jump from 50% to 100%. In effect, the marginal profitability of i's contest contribution is infinite when $C_i = 0$.

In contrast, when the logistic Contest Success Function applies, two-sided peace may easily hold as a stable Cournot solution. Since the player who defects from $C_1 = C_2 = 0$ does not get the benefit of a discrete jump from 50% to 100% success, there is a finite marginal gain to be balanced against the marginal cost of contest effort.[8]

Numerical Example 1: Player #1 seeks to maximize his profit as in equation (7), with p_1 defined by the logistic CSF equation (4) above. If $C_2 = 0$, then finding the derivative in the usual way leads to:

$$\frac{k \exp\{-kC_1\}}{(1 + \exp\{-kC_1\})^2} = \frac{1}{V}$$

For $C_1 = 0$ to be a solution, we must have $V = 4/k$. By symmetry, an analogous equation will hold for player #2. So if, for example, $k = .04$ and $V = 100$, then (as claimed) $C_1 = C_2 = 0$ will indeed be a Cournot equilibrium. In this equilibrium $p_1 = p_2 = .5$ so that the parties each have profit of 50.

ASYMMETRICAL EQUILIBRIUM

What about the possibility of *one-sided submission* rather than two-sided peace? This means that player #1 (say) chooses, $C_1 > 0$ while player #2 sets $C_2 = 0$. For such an outcome, some kind of asymmetry must be

---

[8] For the analogous result in a general-equilibrium context, see Hirshleifer (1988, Part B).

introduced – in the parties' valuations of the prize, in the effectiveness of their respective contest efforts, or possibly in the costs of such efforts. But regardless of any such asymmetries, under the ratio model one-sided submission as a Cournot equilibrium can no more occur than could two-sided peace!

We need look only at asymmetries due to inequalities in valuations of the prize. Specifically, suppose $V_1 > V_2$, suggesting that there might be a Cournot equilibrium with $C_1 > 0$ while $C_2 = 0$. Using the profit equation (7) for player #1, and equation (2) for the Contest Success Function in ratio form, the first-order condition is:

$$\frac{\partial Y_1}{\partial C_1} = \frac{V_1 m C_1^{m-1}\left(C_2^m\right)}{\left(C_1^m + C_2^m\right)^2} - 1 = 0 \tag{8}$$

Evidently, whenever $C_2 = 0$ the marginal profit of contest effort to player #1 is always negative. So under the ratio form of the CSF, it will never be possible to have an asymmetrical contest outcome with one party having zero and the other having positive commitment of resources.

For the difference form (logistic CSF), however, the asymmetrical outcomes are quite different. First of all, taking the partial derivatives of the respective Contest Success Functions leads to:

$$\frac{\partial p_1}{\partial C_1} = \frac{k \exp\{k(C_1 + C_2)\}}{(\exp\{kC_1\} + \exp\{kC_2\})^2} = \frac{\partial p_2}{\partial C_2} \tag{9}$$

This possibly surprising proposition states that at any pair of C_1, C_2 choices, the partial derivatives (the "marginal products" of the respective contest efforts) are always the same for both sides. It follows immediately that, if the valuations V_1 and V_2 are unequal, it is impossible to simultaneously satisfy (as the respective first-order conditions for a profit maximum would require):

$$\frac{\partial p_1}{\partial C_1} = 1/V_1 \quad \text{and} \quad \frac{\partial p_2}{\partial C_2} = 1/V_2 \tag{10}$$

Thus, when the difference form of the CSF applies, there cannot be an *interior* asymmetrical Nash–Cournot solution. (Whereas, we have just seen, using the ratio form there cannot be a *corner* asymmetrical solution.)

This impossibility theorem for the difference form is somewhat too strong, since it is an artifact of the assumption implicit in equation (7) that the Marginal Cost of contest effort is constant. If the Marginal Cost

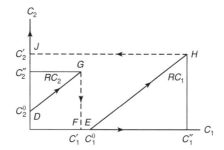

Figure 5.3. Logistic reaction curves: Strong asymmetry.

of contest effort is rising, equations (10) might be satisfied so as to permit an interior Nash–Cournot equilibrium. More generally, with rising Marginal Cost there could be either a corner or an interior asymmetrical solution, depending upon the numerical parameters and the exact functional form.[9]

Assuming for simplicity that Marginal Cost is constant as in equation (7), the Reaction Curves RC_1 and RC_2 associated with the logistic CSF are parallel straight lines of 45° slope, up to a point of discontinuity. More specifically, in the continuous range the Reaction Curve equations are:[10]

$$C_1 = C_2 + A_1, \text{ where } A_1 = (2/k)\cosh^{-1}\{.5\,\mathrm{sqrt}(kV_1)\}$$
$$C_2 = C_1 + A_2, \text{ where } A_2 = (2/k)\cosh^{-1}\{.5\,\mathrm{sqrt}(kV_2)\} \qquad (11)$$

The discontinuities fall into three distinct patterns – depending upon the relative positions of the points C_i^0, C_i', and C_i'' as sketched in Figures 5.3 through 5.5 – each leading to a particular class of Cournot solution.

The pattern of Reaction Curves RC_1 and RC_2 pictured in Figure 5.3 represents the "strong asymmetry" case, which stems from a relatively

---

[9] Dixit (1987) appears to assume, incorrectly, that all logit functions do lead to an interior Nash–Cournot asymmetrical equilibrium.

[10] Player #1 maximizes $Y_1 = p_1 V_1 - C_1$ where p_1 is given by:

$$p_1 = 1/(1 + \exp\{k(C_2 - C_1)\}) \equiv 1/D \text{ (writing } D \text{ for the denominator)}$$

For given C_2, the first-order condition $dY_1/dC_1 = 0$ is:

$$V_1(dp_1/dC_1) \equiv kV_1 \exp\{k(C_2 - C_1)\}/D^2 = 1$$

Rearranging and taking square roots leads to:

$$\mathrm{sqrt}(kV_1) = \exp\{(-k/2)(C_2 - C_1)\} + \exp\{(k/2)(C_2 - C_1)\}$$

Since $\cosh x \equiv .5\{\exp(x) + \exp(-x)\} \equiv \cosh(-x)$, we can write:

$$.5\,\mathrm{sqrt}(kV_1) = \cosh\{-(k/2)(C_2 - C_1)\} \equiv \cosh\{(k/2)(C_2 - C_1)\}$$

Thus: $(k/2)(C_2 - C_1) = \cosh^{-1}\{.5\,\mathrm{sqrt}(kV_1)\}$.

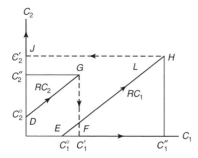

Figure 5.4. Logistic reaction curves: moderate asymmetry.

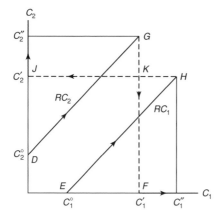

Figure 5.5. Logistic reaction curves: symmetry or near-symmetry.

large difference $V_1 - V_2$ between the parties' valuations of the prize. Here RC_2, the Reaction Curve for the lower-valuing player, rises as C_1 increases – but only up to point G where the opponent's effort has reached a certain critical value C_1'. At G, player #2's optimum drops off discretely to $C_2 = 0$ (point F), and of course remains at zero for all higher values of C_1. (The explanation is that, given a logistic CSF, the lower-valuing player can always take home *some* profit by investing zero effort. Hence doing so always remains a viable alternative, and eventually becomes more advantageous than trying to keep up with very large contest efforts on the part of his higher-valuing opponent.) If, as in Figure 5.3, $C_1' < C_1^0$ – that is, point F is to the left of point E, the latter being the point where the higher-valuing player's Reaction Curve RC_1 intercepts the horizontal axis – then the Nash – Cournot equilibrium is at E, where $(C_1, C_2) = (C_1^0, 0)$. It is easy to verify that, at point E, each player's effort is a *best response* to the opponent's choice. This solution represents one-sided submission: the lower-valuing player has abandoned the struggle.

Numerical Example 2: Once again each player seeks to maximize his profit $Y_i = V p_i - C_i$, where p_i is defined by equation (4) above. Let the required asymmetry be in the valuations of the prize, where specifically $V_1 = 400$ and $V_2 = 100$. Assuming $k = .04$, the Reaction Curves are as pictured in Figure 5.3, with $C_1^0 = A_1 = 65.848$ and $C_2^0 = A_2 = 0$. If the higher-valuing player #1 takes $C_2 = 0$ as given, his profit-maximizing solution C_1 equals $A_1 = 65.848$ (point E). Turning to player #2, with $C_1 = 65.848$ taken as given the profit-maximizing[11] C_2 is indeed $C_2 = 0$.

The expectations on each side as to the other party's behavior being mutually consistent, this is a Cournot equilibrium. The associated shares are $p_1 = .933$ and $p_2 = .067$, and the profits are $Y_1 = 307.4$ and $Y_2 = 6.699$. Note that the higher-valuing player does *disproportionately* better: not only is his prize worth more, but he fights harder for it.

Figure 5.4 illustrates a "moderate asymmetry" pattern. Here, the difference between V_1 and V_2 being smaller, point E (the horizontal intercept of RC_1) lies to the left of point F (at the discontinuity along RC_2). In consequence, point E, where player #2 unilaterally submits, is no longer a Cournot equilibrium. (That is, player #2 will no longer choose $C_2 = 0$ as his best response to player #1's choice of $C_1 = C_1^0 = A_1$.) As the prize valuations V_1 and V_2 approach equality, finally, the "symmetrical or near-symmetrical" pattern of Figure 5.5 is obtained. Here also, it will be evident, unilateral submission will not occur. The actual solutions for both the Figure 5.4 and the Figure 5.5 patterns involve mixed strategies on one or both sides,[12] but the specifics of these solutions are not of immediate concern to us.

As the next step, it would be natural to ask whether the ratio versus the difference forms of the Contest Success Function lead to correspondingly different outcomes in terms of the Stackelberg or other asymmetrical solution concepts. I will not, however, be pursuing these implications here.

CONCLUSION

In analyzing rent-seeking or other conflict competitions, models allowing relative success to respond continuously to changes in contest commitments have heretofore assumed that success must be a function of the

---

[11] As suggested by the preceding discussion, this optimum is not at a smooth maximum (zero first derivative). Instead, player #2's profit function has a negative first derivative throughout, leading him to cut back effort until the limit of zero is reached.

[12] The key feature guaranteeing existence of a Nash–Cournot equilibrium is that the payoff functions are continuous, even though the Reaction Curves have discontinuities. See Debreu (1952) and Glicksberg (1952). I thank Eric S. Maskin for this point.

ratio of the parties' resource commitments. However, this assumption is inconsistent with the observation that two-sided peace or one-sided submission do sometimes occur in the world. When relative success is postulated to stem instead from the *numerical difference* between the respective contest inputs, a Contest Success Function taking the form of a logistic equation is derived. Two-sided peaceful outcomes emerge in Cournot equilibrium when the "mass effect parameter" of the logistic CSF curve is sufficiently low. One-sided submission can also occur when there is a large disparity between the parties' valuation of the prize. As these valuations approach equality, the logistic CSF leads to mixed-strategy Cournot equilibria.

REFERENCES

Allard, R.J. (1988). Rent-seeking with non-identical players. *Public Choice* 57: 3–14.

Appelbaum, E. and Katz, E. (1986). Transfer seeking and avoidance: On the full costs of rent-seeking. *Public Choice* 48: 175–181.

Brackney, H. (1959). The dynamics of military combat. *Operations Research* 7: 30–44.

Corcoran, W.J. and Karels, G.V. (1985). Rent-seeking behavior in the long run. *Public Choice* 46: 227–246.

Debreu, G. (1952). A social equilibrium existence theorem. *Proceedings of the National Academy of Science* 38: 886–893.

Dixit, A. (1987). Strategic behavior in contests. *American Economic Review* 77 (December): 891–898.

Dupuy, T.N. (1987). *Understanding war: History and theory of combat.* New York: Paragon House Publishers.

Glicksberg, I.L. (1952). A further generalization of the Kakutani Fixed Point Theorem with applications to Nash equilibrium points. *Proceedings of the American Mathematical Society* 38: 170–174.

Higgins, R.S., Shughart, W.F. and Tollison, R.F. (1985). Free entry and efficient rent-seeking. *Public Choice* 46: 247–258.

Hillman, A.L. and Katz, E. (1984). Risk averse rent-seekers and the social cost of monopoly power. *Economic Journal* 94: 104–110.

Hillman, A.L. and Riley, J.G. (1988). *Politically contestable rents and transfers.* UCLA Economics Dept. Working Paper #452 (rev. March 1988).

Hillman, A.L. and Samet, D. (1987). Dissipation of rents and revenues in small numbers contests. *Public Choice* 54: 63–82.

Hirshleifer, J. (1988). The analytics of continuing conflict. *Synthese* 76: 201–233.

Lanchester, F.W. (1916). *Aircraft in warfare: The dawn of the fourth arm.* Constable. (1956) Extract reprinted in James R. Newman (Ed.), *The world of mathematics* 4: 2138–2157. New York: Simon & Schuster.

Tullock, G. (1967). The welfare costs of tariffs, monopolies, and theft. *Western Economic Journal* 5: 224–232.
Tullock, G. (1980). Efficient rent-seeking. In J.M. Buchanan, R.D. Tollison and G. Tullock (Eds.), *Toward a theory of the rent-seeking society*, 97–112. College Station: Texas A&M University Press.

6

Anarchy and Its Breakdown

Jack Hirshleifer

Background of this Chapter

How can anarchy "break down"? The explanation is that, as defined here, anarchy is not mere chaos. True, under anarchy there is no central authority. Control over resources is maintained only by self-defense, not by law. Nevertheless, such a social order may have structure and predictability.

Anarchy and Its Breakdown can be regarded as a successor to *The Paradox of Power* (Chap. 3). In "Paradox" the resources available to contenders were assumed safe from appropriation; only the jointly produced income was at stake. In the course of ordinary industrial conflict within the business firm, for example, management does not attempt to enslave the workers, nor do the latter aim to take over the enterprise. But here the underlying resources themselves are in contention, as when nations fight for territorial gain. Raising the stakes in this way makes stability harder to attain. Thus, it becomes somewhat more likely that the rich will get richer and the poor poorer, the powerful more powerful and the weak weaker still. Once again, the Conflict Success Function – the technology of conflict – is crucial for determining the outcome. The historical sections of the article show (among other things) how changing military technology, which has tended to make weapons superiority more decisive over time, mainly explains why the number of independently viable states and principalities has declined steadily over recent centuries.

The article has previously been reprinted in a volume edited by Michelle R. Garfinkel and Stergios Skaperdas (1996, *The Political Economy of Conflict and Appropriation*, Cambridge, UK: Cambridge University Press).

* For helpful comments I thank Jeffrey Frieden, David Hirshleifer, Jay Y. C. Jen, John Pezzey, Alan Rogers, Stergios Skaperdas. Charles Stuart, Earl Thompson, Dan Usher, Michael Waldman, Don Wittman, and Murray Wolfson, as well as two anonymous referees of this journal. (Reprinted from J. Hirshleifer, "Anarchy and Its Breakdown," *Journal of Political Economy*, Vol. 103, No. 1, 27–52, Copyright © 1995, The University of Chicago.)

Abstract

Anarchy, defined as a system in which participants can seize and defend resources without regulation from above, is not chaos but rather a spontaneous order. However, anarchy is fragile and may dissolve either into formless "amorphy" or into a more organized system such as hierarchy. Under anarchy, each contestant balances between productive exploitation of the current resource base and fighting to acquire or defend resources. Anarchy is sustainable only when there are strongly diminishing returns to fighting effort (the "decisiveness parameter" is sufficiently low) and incomes exceed the viability minimum. These considerations explain many features of animal and human conflict.

What do the following have in common? (1) international struggles for control of the globe's resources, (2) gang warfare in Prohibition-era Chicago, (3) miners versus claim jumpers in the California gold rush, (4) animal territoriality, and (5) male elephant seals who fight to sequester "harems" of females. Answer: They are all anarchic situations.

Anarchy is not chaos. At least potentially, anarchic relationships can constitute a stable system. But not all environments are capable of sustaining an anarchic order. Anarchy can break down, to be replaced by another pattern of relationships.

Anarchy is a natural economy (Ghiselin 1978), or spontaneous order in the sense of Hayek (1979). Various forms of spontaneous order emerge from resource competition among animals, among them territoriality and dominance relationships (as surveyed in Wilson [1975, chaps. 11–13]). As for humans, while associations ranging from primitive tribes to modern nation-states are all governed internally by some form of law, their external relations with one another remain mainly anarchic. Yet intertribal or international systems also have their regularities and systematic analyzable patterns (see, e.g., Waltz 1959; Snyder and Diesing 1977; Bernholz 1985).

The term "anarchy" in ordinary usage conflates two rather different situations that the biological literature carefully distinguishes: "scramble" versus "interference" competition (Nicholson 1954) or, in an alternative terminology, "exploitation" versus "resource defense" (Krebs and Davies 1987, p. 93). Under scramble competition, which might be termed *amorphy*[1] (absence of form), resources are not sequestered but consumed on the move. In the open sea, for example, resources are so fugitive that fish do not attempt to defend territories. Jean-Jacques Rousseau evidently had amorphy in mind when he described man in the

---

[1] Not a new coinage on my part: *The Shorter Oxford Dictionary* (3d ed., 1955) cites a use by Jonathan Swift in 1704.

state of nature as "wandering up and down the forests, without industry, without speech, without home, an equal stranger to war and to all ties, neither standing in need of his fellow-creatures nor having any desire to hurt them" (1950, p. 230).

Although amorphic competition poses a number of interesting modeling issues, the present analysis is limited to environments in which durable resources such as land territories or movable capital goods are captured and defended by individuals or by groups. (I shall generally treat *groups* as unitary actors that have somehow managed to resolve the internal collective-action problem.) So, as defined here, anarchy is a social arrangement in which contenders struggle to conquer and defend durable resources, without effective regulation by either higher authorities or social pressures.[2]

Given the possibility of sequestering resources, anarchic competitors have to divide their efforts between two main types of activities: (1) productively exploiting the assets currently controlled and (2) seizing and defending a resource base. Correspondingly, there are two separate technologies: a *technology of production* and a *technology of appropriation, conflict, and struggle* (Hirshleifer 1991*b*). There are ways of tilling the land, and quite a different set of ways of capturing land and securing it against intruders.

While I shall be using military terminology such as "capturing" and "fighting," they are to be understood as metaphors. Falling also into the category of interference struggles are political campaigns, rent-seeking maneuvers for licenses and monopoly privileges (Tullock 1967), commercial efforts to raise rivals' costs (Salop and Scheffman 1983), strikes and lockouts, and litigation – all being conflictual activities that need not involve actual violence.

A decision maker's chosen balance between productive and conflictual efforts may be influenced in the peaceful direction by an element of productive complementarity. Management and labor, since they need one another, are less motivated to engage in destructive struggles within the firm. Similarly, mutual interdependence within the polity may moderate

---

[2] Since regulation can vary from total to zero effectiveness, anarchy is typically a matter of degree. In gold rush California the U.S. Army, though decimated by desertion to the goldfields, did maintain a limited presence (Sherman [1885] 1990, chaps. 2–3). And during the bootlegging wars in Prohibition-era Chicago (Allsop 1968), the local police, while notoriously corrupt, were still a factor. In fact, an element of anarchy persists even in the most normal of times: law and order being imperfect, some provision for self-defense of person and property is almost always advisable.

international, regional, and other interest group conflicts.[3] Exchange relationships, in particular, increase mutual interdependence and thus partially harmonize diverging interests. But I shall be assuming here a starker environment in which productive opportunities are entirely disjoint and the exchange option is excluded, so that competitors have to fight, or at least be prepared to fight, if they are to acquire or retain resources.[4]

The economic theory of conflict, like economic modeling generally, involves two analytical steps: (i) *Optimization:* Each competitor chooses a preferred balance of productive effort versus conflictual effort. (ii) *Equilibrium:* On the social level, the separate optimizing decisions interact to determine levels of production and the extent of fighting activity, together with the distribution of product among the claimants. While the economic literature on conflict theory remains relatively sparse, in recent years a number of models employing such an analytical structure have been offered. But, as far as I know, none of these earlier writings has analyzed the viability of anarchy as a spontaneous social order.[5]

Among the specific issues to be considered here are the following.

1. *When is there a stable anarchic solution?* – Under what conditions can two or more anarchic contestants retain viable shares of the socially available resources in equilibrium? Or put the other way, in what circumstances does the anarchic system "break down" in favor of amorphy on the one hand or, alternatively, in favor of tyranny or some other form of social control?

---

[3] For analyses of conflict as moderated by a cooperative element in production, see Hirshleifer (1988) and Skaperdas (1992).

[4] Fighting is of course Pareto-inefficient. All parties could always benefit from an agreed peaceful resolution, but under anarchy there is no superior authority to enforce any such agreement. (In some cases *threats* may suffice to deter conflict, but that possibility is not modeled here.)

[5] I shall briefly review some related analytical contributions: (1) In Bush and Mayer (1974), production is costless (manna-like), but competitors may also *steal*, generating a "natural equilibrium." (2) Skogh and Stuart (1982) allowed for three types of activities: production, transfers (i.e., stealing, or offensive activity), and protection against transfers (defensive activity). (3) Usher (1989) modeled an alternation between despotism and anarchy. In anarchy there are two professions: farmers and bandits. The possible anarchic equilibria include a mixed population of farmers and bandits, an all-farmer outcome, and a (nonviable) all-bandit outcome. (4) Closest to the present paper in terms of modeling approach are Hirshleifer (1988, 1991*a*), Skaperdas (1992), and Grossman and Kim (1994). However, in these articles agents have inalienable resource endowments or, at most, only a one-time reallocation is allowed. In contrast, the *continuing* struggle for resource endowments is the central phenomenon addressed in the present paper.

2. *Equilibrium allocations of effort.* – In a stable anarchic equilibrium, what fractions of resources will be devoted to fighting? What levels of incomes will be attained?
3. *Numbers.* – If the number of contenders N is exogenously given, how are the equilibrium fighting efforts and attained levels of income affected as N changes? Alternatively, if N is endogenous, how many contenders can survive?
4. *Technology and comparative advantage.* – How do the outcomes respond to parametric variations, one-sided or two-sided, in the technology of production or in the technology of struggle?
5. *Strategic position.* – How do the outcomes respond to positional asymmetries, for example where one side is a Stackelberg leader?

The analysis here employs standard (though possibly still highly arguable!) economic postulates such as rationality, self-interested motivations, and diminishing returns. Certain other assumptions are designed to achieve analytical simplicity in ways familiar to economists; for example, only steady-state solutions are considered. But to push ahead I have also at times made more special modeling choices, for example, about the conflict technology. Whenever possible I shall try to flag the results of such "nongeneric" assumptions and discuss the analytical implications.

For the simplest symmetric case of two competitors ($N = 2$), the first section describes the conditions for a stable anarchic equilibrium. The next section analyzes the optimizing decision and final outcomes. The third section considers both exogenous and endogenous variation in the number of contenders N, and the fourth section examines the consequences of various types of asymmetries between the rival parties. The fifth section relates the analysis to important features of animal and human conflict. The penultimate section summarizes the results and limitations. The final section asks "After anarchy, what?"

STABILITY OF CONFLICT EQUILIBRIUM ($N = 2$)

Each of two rival claimants aims solely to maximize own income. Neither benevolent nor malevolent preferences play a role, nor is there any taste for leisure or other non-income-generating activity.

At any moment of time, each contender $i = 1, 2$ divides his or her current resource availability R_i between *productive effort* E_i (designed to extract income from resources currently controlled) and *fighting effort* F_i (aimed at acquiring new resources at the expense of competitors, or repelling them as they attempt to do the same):[6]

$$R_i = a_i E_i + b_i F_i. \tag{1}$$

The aggregate resource base, $R \equiv R_1 + R_2$, is assumed constant and independent of the parties' actions.[7] The a_i and b_i can be interpreted as unit conversion costs (assumed constant) of transforming resources into productive effort or into fighting effort, respectively. In a military metaphor, b_i is a *logistics cost coefficient* quantifying the resource burden per fighting unit supported. Similarly, a_i, the *production cost coefficient*, measures the resources required to maintain a worker or machine in civilian production.[8] In the decades preceding the American Civil War, inventions such as the steamboat and railroad sharply reduced a_i (since workers could be fed and machines built more cheaply) and also b_i (since supplies could more easily be delivered to fighting troops). In consequence, vastly larger armies were able to take the field in the Civil War than in the Revolutionary War or the War of 1812.

It will sometimes be more convenient to deal with the corresponding "intensities" e_i and f_i:

$$e_i \equiv \frac{E_i}{R_i}, \ f_i \equiv \frac{F_i}{R_i}. \tag{2}$$

The e_i and f_i will be the crucial decision variables on each side, subject of course to:

$$a_i e_i + b_i f_i = 1. \tag{3}$$

Under the assumption of steady-state conditions, each side makes an optimal once-and-for-all choice of e_i and f_i.[9]

---

[6] I do not distinguish here between offensive and defensive activities. On this see Skogh and Stuart (1982) and Grossman and Kim (1994).

[7] This crucial assumption – implying that fighting, while a diversion of resources, is nondestructive – will be discussed further in the last section.

[8] Taking a_i and b_i as constants implies a constant marginal rate of substitution between productive effort and fighting effort. Diminishing returns enter at another stage: the translation of productive effort E_i into income and of fighting effort F_i into contest success.

[9] More generally, instead of a once-and-for-all choice of f_i and the implied e_i, side i's choice could vary with the level of resources on hand. For example, it might pay to devote a larger fraction of resources to fighting when one is poor and a smaller fraction when rich (Hirshleifer 1991a). However, finding the optimal function $f_i(R_i)$ as a best reply to the opponent's corresponding $f_j(R_j)$, and vice versa, poses a fearsome analytic problem that I do not attempt to address here.

The steady-state fighting intensity f_i can allow for time averaging. A tribe choosing an f_i such that half its resources are devoted to fighting need not have half its human and material capital engaged in war night and day, season in and season out. More likely, the tribe as a whole will be alternating between periods of war and periods of peace. Similarly, although a labor union may alternate between periods of strike and periods of work, its long-term strategy could be interpreted as choice of a steady-state average fighting intensity f_i.

With income to side i symbolized as Y_i, let the production function take the simple form:

$$\text{Production function: } Y_i = E_i^h = (e_i R_i)^h. \tag{4}$$

Resource control is achieved only by fighting, the outcome being the *success fractions* p_1 and p_2 (where of course $p_1 + p_2 = 1$). Thus:

$$\text{Resource partition equation: } R_i = p_i R. \tag{5}$$

The technology of conflict is summarized by the Contest Success Function (CSF), which in the form employed here determines the success ratio p_1/p_2 as a function of the ratio of the fighting efforts F_1/F_2 and (what plays a crucial role in the analysis) a *decisiveness parameter* $m > 0$:[10]

$$\text{Contest Success Function: } \frac{p_1}{p_2} = \left(\frac{F_1}{F_2}\right)^m \tag{6a}$$

or, equivalently:

$$p_1 = \frac{F_1^m}{F_1^m + F_2^m},$$
$$p_2 = \frac{F_2^m}{F_1^m + F_2^m}. \tag{6b}$$

Figure 6.1 illustrates how, with F_2 held fixed, the success fraction p_1 responds to changes in fighting effort F_1. Evidently, the sensitivity of p_1 to F_1 grows as the decisiveness parameter m increases.

In military struggles, low m corresponds to the defense having the upper hand. On the western front in World War I, entrenchment plus the machine gun made for very low decisiveness m. Throughout 1914–18,

---

[10] This form of the CSF, in which the success fractions are determined by the *ratio* of the fighting efforts, was proposed in Tullock (1980). If instead the outcome were to depend on the *difference* between the fighting efforts, the CSF would be a logistic function (Hirshleifer 1988). The question of the appropriate form for the CSF will arise again below.

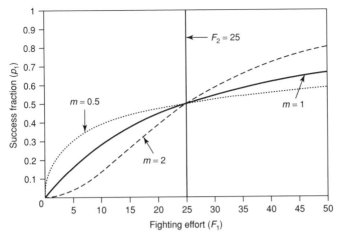

Figure 6.1. Contest Success Function (CSF).

attacks with even very large force superiority rarely succeeded in doing more than move the front lines back a few miles, at enormous cost in men and materiel. But in World War II the combination of airplanes, tanks, and mechanized infantry allowed the offense to concentrate fire-power more rapidly than the defense, thus intensifying the effect of force superiority.[11] On the other hand, high decisiveness on the battlefield does not necessarily translate into correspondingly high decisiveness in a war as a whole. In 1870, Prussia won complete battlefield supremacy over France. But whereas Rome had razed Carthage to the ground, Prussia settled for very moderate peace terms: France had only to pay an indemnity and surrender the frontier provinces of Alsace and Lorraine. Prussian moderation was presumably due, in part at least, to fear of a guerrilla resistance against which its battlefield supremacy would be much less decisive.

The decisiveness factor is by no means limited to strictly military struggles. In democratic constitutions, features such as separation of powers and bills of rights reduce the decisiveness of majority supremacy, thereby tending to moderate the intensity of factional struggles. If the political system were winner take all, decisiveness m would be very high and all politics would be a fight to the death.[12]

---

[11] Of course, differences in *ability to employ* newer technologies are also often crucial, as demonstrated in the German victory over France in 1940. (This and other asymmetries will be addressed in the section on the three types of asymmetries.)

[12] "Constitutions that are observed and last for a long time are those that reduce the stakes of political battles" (Przeworski 1991, p. 36).

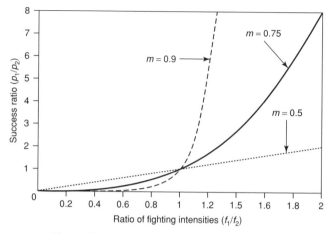

Figure 6.2. Fighting intensities and success ratio.

From (5) and (6a):

$$\frac{R_1}{R_2} = \left(\frac{F_1}{F_2}\right)^m = \frac{(f_1 R_1)^m}{(f_2 R_2)^m}.$$

This reduces to:

$$f_1^m R_1^{m-1} = f_2^m R_2^{m-1}. \tag{7a}$$

So, finally:

$$\text{Equilibrium success ratio (steady state):} \quad \frac{p_1}{p_2} = \left(\frac{f_1}{f_2}\right)^{m/(1-m)}. \tag{7b}$$

Equations (7a) and (7b) describe the logically required steady-state relationships between the parties' chosen fighting intensities f_i and the equilibrium success ratio p_1/p_2 or resource ratio R_1/R_2. Figure 6.2 plots different values of m. Note that as $m \to 1$, the curve approaches a limiting step function such that $p_1/p_2 = 0$ for all $f_1 < f_2$ and jumps to $p_1/p_2 = \infty$ for $f_1 > f_2$. Without explicit proof, it will be evident that *for an interior stable equilibrium, the decisiveness parameter must lie in the range* $0 < m < 1$.

The preceding discussion has brought out one way in which anarchy could break down: an excessively large decisiveness parameter m leads to dynamic instability, that is, movement toward a corner solution (see numerical example 1 in the Appendix). A second source of breakdown is *income inadequacy*. Suppose that some minimum income y is required to sustain life for an individual actor or for a group to preserve its institutional integrity. Then anarchy cannot be stable if the equilibrium of the dynamic process implies income $Y_i < y$ for either contender. The following result summarizes this discussion.

RESULT 1. The conditions for sustainability of a two-party anarchic system include (i) a sufficiently low decisiveness parameter m and (ii) sufficiently high attained incomes Y_i:

$$\text{Condition for dynamic stability: } m < 1$$
$$\text{Condition for viability: } Y_i \geq y, i = 1, 2. \tag{8}$$

Note that these are *necessary*, not sufficient, conditions for anarchy to be sustained. As will be seen below, anarchy may be fragile even when the conditions are satisfied.

OPTIMIZATION AND EQUILIBRIUM IN SYMMETRICAL CONFLICT ($N = 2$)

Figure 6.2 did not illustrate the *solution* of the anarchic system for $N = 2$ but only the relations that must hold, in equilibrium, among the dependent variables R_1 and R_2 and the decision variables f_1 and f_2. The actual solution involves optimizing behavior on each side. Under the traditional Cournot assumption, each contender i chooses between steady-state e_i and f_i on the assumption that the opponent's corresponding choices will remain unchanged. In the maximization of income Y_i, a larger fighting effort f_i captures more resources or territory whereas a larger productive effort e_i generates more income from the territory controlled. Thus player 1's optimal f_1 is given by:

$$\max Y_1 = E_1^h = (e_1 R_1)^h = (e_1 R p_1)^h = \left(\frac{e_1 R f_1^M}{f_1^M + f_2^M} \right)^h \tag{9}$$

subject to $a_1 e_1 + b_1 f_1 = 1$, and defining for compactness $M \equiv m/(1 - m)$.

Straightforward steps then generate player 1's reaction curve RC_1, showing his optimal f_1 as the opponent varies her f_2.[13] A corresponding

---

[13] The first-order conditions, where λ is the Lagrangian multiplier, are:

$$h(e_1 p_1 R)^{h-1} \frac{R f_1^M}{f_1^M + f_2^M} - \lambda a_1 = 0$$

and

$$h(e_1 p_1 R)^{h-1} \frac{e_1 R M f_1^{M-1} f_2^M}{\left(f_1^M + f_2^M \right)^2} - \lambda b_1 = 0.$$

Routine steps lead to eq. (10a), the reaction curve for player 1.

analysis leads the opponent to her reaction curve RC_2:

$$\text{reaction curve } RC_1: \frac{f_1^M}{f_2^M} = \frac{M}{b_1 f_1} - (M+1) \tag{10a}$$

and

$$\text{reaction curve } RC_2: \frac{f_2^M}{f_1^M} = \frac{M}{b_2 f_2} - (M+1). \tag{10b}$$

The reaction curve for player i, RC_i, depends only on the decisiveness parameter m and on the decision maker's own logistics cost coefficient b_i. From the analytical form of the equations, and as illustrated in Figure 6.3, the reaction curves have positive slopes throughout. Thus, if player 1 chooses higher f_1, it pays player 2 to respond with higher f_2. And note that, as required for stability, in the neighborhood of equilibrium the matching is less than one for one.

Equations (10a) and (10b) may be solved for f_1 and f_2, thus determining the equilibrium of the entire system. Unfortunately, there is no convenient general analytic solution. However, this section deals with the *symmetric* case in which $a_1 = a_2 = a$ and $b_1 = b_2 = b$. Hence $f_1 = f_2$ at equilibrium, and (10a) and (10b) reduce to:

Symmetrical conflict equilibrium ($N = 2$):

$$f_1 = f_2 = \frac{M}{b(M+2)} = \frac{m}{b(2-m)}. \tag{11}$$

Symmetrical solutions for $b = 1$ are illustrated by the intersections of the paired RC_1 and RC_2 curves in Figure 6.3. If $m = {}^1/_2$, the inner pair of curves apply and the solution is $f_1 = f_2 = .333$. With a higher

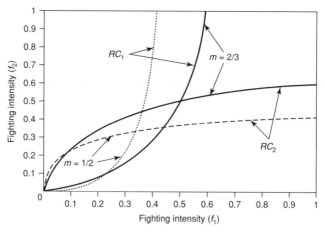

Figure 6.3. Reaction curves ($m = {}^1/_2$ and $m = {}^2/_3$).

decisiveness parameter $m = \frac{2}{3}$, the intersection occurs at $f_1 = f_2 = .5$. The results below follow from the form of equation (11).

RESULT 2. When the conditions for dynamic stability and viability both hold, in symmetrical conflict larger values of the *decisiveness parameter m* imply higher equilibrium fighting intensities f_1 and f_2 and thus higher fighting levels F_1 and F_2. And similarly, the lower the common value b of the *logistics cost coefficient*, the greater the equilibrium f_i and F_i.

For the underlying intuition recall that, as m increase, any given disparity between the fighting efforts F_1 and F_2 comes to have an increasingly powerful effect on the partition of resources. So as m grows, each side is motivated to "try harder" – to choose a higher fighting intensity f_i than before. And similarly for the logistics cost coefficient: a reduction in b makes fighting effort cheaper, and hence more of it comes to be generated on each side.

What is possibly disturbing, equation (11) implies that f_i cannot be zero in equilibrium. There can never be total peace in the sense of devoting zero resources to conflict. This is a "nongeneric" result, since there are alternate forms of the CSF that could be consistent with total peace (Hirshleifer 1988; Skaperdas 1992). On the other hand, the implication might be regarded as quite realistic in many or most anarchic contexts.

Since $p_1 = p_2 = \frac{1}{2}$ in the symmetrical conflict situation, direct substitutions lead to the equilibrium per capita incomes:

$$Y_i \equiv (e_i \, p_i \, R)^h = \left[\frac{1-m}{a(2-m)} R \right]^h. \tag{12}$$

RESULT 3. In the symmetrical conflict situation, when the conditions for dynamic stability and viability both hold, the incomes achieved (i) *rise* in response to increase in aggregate resource availability R and the productivity parameter h, but (ii) *fall* in response to increases in the decisiveness parameter m and the production cost coefficient a.[14] (See also numerical example 2 in the Appendix.)

---

[14] A possibly puzzling feature of eq. (12) is that, although a lower logistics cost coefficient b was shown above as increasing the fighting efforts f_i, the ultimate incomes Y_i end up independent of b. The reason is that lower b has two countervailing effects. On the one hand it implies lower e_i – smaller productive efforts on each side. But on the other hand, a smaller b means that the opportunity cost burden of any given f_i is less. That these two effects exactly cancel out is, however, also a "nongeneric" feature of the model and hence is not insisted on here. (Specifically, explorations indicate that the result would not be robust to changes in the form of the CSF that would make it sensitive to the *differences* in the respective fighting efforts.)

NUMBER OF COMPETITORS – EXOGENOUS VS. ENDOGENOUS VARIATION

Exogenously Varying N

Suppose that a fixed number of competitors N engage in a *mêlée* – a Hobbesian struggle of each against all, coalitions being ruled out.[15] The Cournot solution has each contender i choosing a fighting intensity f_i on the assumption that every opponent j will be holding f_j fixed. Generalizing equation (7a) yields:

$$f_1^m R_1^{m-1} = f_2^m R_2^{m-1} = \cdots = f_N^m R_N^{m-1} \tag{13a}$$

or, equivalently:

$$p_1 : p_2 : \cdots : p_N = (f_1 : f_2 : \cdots : f_N)^M. \tag{13b}$$

Once again, for dynamic stability it is necessary to have $M > 0$, that is $m < 1$. Of course, the viability condition $Y_i \geq y$ must also hold.

Contender 1's optimizing problem is:

$$\max Y_1 = (e_1 R_1)^h = (e_1 p_1 R)^h = \left(\frac{e_1 R f_1^M}{f_1^M + f_2^M + \cdots + f_N^M} \right)^h \tag{14}$$

subject to $a_1 e_1 + b_1 f_1 = 1$. The analogue of equation (10a), the generalized reaction curve for the first among N competitors, is:

$$\text{reaction curve } RC_1: \quad \frac{f_1^M}{f_2^M + \cdots + f_N^M} = \frac{M}{b_1 f_1} - (M + 1). \tag{15}$$

And similarly for the other decision makers from contender 2 on.

If we assume symmetrical logistics cost coefficients $b_i = b$ and productive cost coefficients $a_i = a$ and use the fact that in symmetrical equilibrium all the f_i are equal, the solution is:

Symmetrical conflict equilibrium (general N):

$$f_1 = f_2 = \cdots = f_N = \frac{M/b}{M + 1 + [1/(N-1)]} = \frac{m(N-1)}{b(N-m)}. \tag{16}$$

As before, the fractions of resources devoted to fighting increase as the decisiveness parameter m rises and as the logistics cost coefficient b falls. And we see now that these fighting intensities also increase with

---

[15] "During the time men live without a common power to keep them in awe, they are in that condition which is called war; and such a war as is of every man against every man" (Hobbes, *Leviathan*, chap. 13).

larger numbers. That is, as N rises parametrically, each contender has to waste more effort in fighting even to retain his new (reduced) pro rata share. The equilibrium incomes are:

$$Y_i = (e_i p_i R)^h = \left[\frac{1-m}{a(N-m)} R \right]^h, \tag{17}$$

provided as always that $m < 1$ and $Y_i \geq y$.

RESULT 4A. *Parametrically varying N, fixed R.* – Under the assumption that the conditions for sustainability of anarchy hold, with symmetrical production cost coefficients $a_i = a$ and logistics cost coefficients $b_i = b$, if aggregate resources remain fixed, then as N rises exogenously the equilibrium fighting intensities f_i increase. Individual incomes fall as N rises, owing to (i) smaller pro rata resource shares $p_i = 1/N$ and (ii) larger f_i.

It follows immediately that, as N increases, the attained incomes under anarchy are not only smaller *per capita* but smaller *in aggregate*.

Now consider instead a friendlier environment in which the aggregate resource base is not fixed but grows in proportion to the number of claimants. We can imagine that each entrant brings in a resource quantum r, so that $R \equiv Nr$. Evidently, the expanding resource base exactly cancels out the adverse effect of increased N associated with the reduced pro rata share. But the adverse effect of the larger fighting efforts f_i remains. Under this more optimistic assumption the equilibrium incomes become:

$$Y_i = (e_i p_i R)^h = \left[\frac{1-m}{a(N-m)} Nr \right]^h. \tag{18}$$

RESULT 4B. *R and N rising in proportion.* – Even if aggregate resource availability R increases in proportion to numbers N, individual incomes still fall as N rises, owing to the higher equilibrium fighting intensities f_i.

Figure 6.4 illustrates how fighting intensity f_i rises with numbers N, and the implications of that fact for per capita income $Y_i = (e_i p_i R)^h$ under both the more and the less favorable assumptions about the relation of aggregate resources to the number of contenders. (The parameter values for the diagram are as stated in numerical example 3 in the Appendix.)

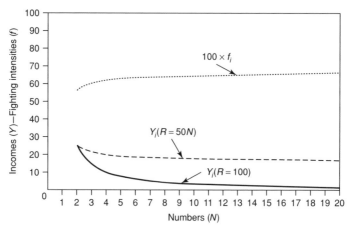

Figure 6.4. Effect of rising numbers (N).

Endogenous N

If population numbers are subject to Malthusian increase/decrease or to immigration/emigration, the equilibrium N will be determined by the viability limit y – a kind of zero-profit condition:

$$\text{Condition for equilibrium } N\colon\ Y_i(N) = y. \tag{19}$$

Once again, the actual viable population will depend on whether aggregate resources R are fixed or alternatively grow in proportion to N. (See numerical example 4 in the Appendix.)

> RESULT 5. If N is endogenously determined, a zero-profit condition will establish the viable number of contestants, the number being of course smaller when aggregate resources remain constant and larger when each added entrant brings in a resource increment.

THREE TYPES OF ASYMMETRIES

So far only symmetrical solutions have been analyzed. In this section three different kinds of asymmetries are considered: cost differences, functional differences, and positional differences.

Cost Differences

A lower production cost coefficient ($a_1 < a_2$) or logistics cost coefficient ($b_1 < b_2$) would of course give side 1 a corresponding advantage. (Since these are absolute comparisons, it is quite possible for one side to have the advantage in both directions at once.)

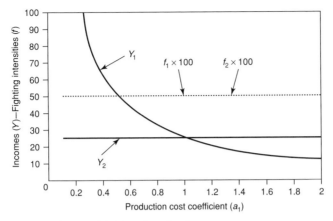

Figure 6.5. Effect of production cost asymmetry.

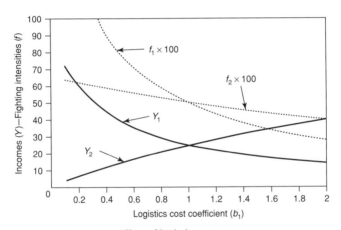

Figure 6.6. Effect of logistics cost asymmetry.

Figure 6.5[16] shows that a reduced production cost coefficient a_1 for player 1 leaves all the equilibrium solutions unchanged except for raising 1's own income Y_1.[17] In contrast, as the logistics cost coefficient b_1 falls in Figure 6.6, contender 1's fighting intensity f_1 and income Y_1 both rise. And, since contender 2 will respond with less than a one for one increase in f_2, she suffers reduced income Y_2.

[16] Figures 6.5–6.8 each represent a large number of simulations using variations of the base case parameters given in numerical example 2.

[17] This also needs to be flagged as one of the "nongeneric" results adverted to in the opening section. The special assumption most implicated here is the total disjunction of the productive efforts on the two sides. Given a degree of productive interaction, a reduction in one side's production cost coefficient a_1 would generally affect the opponent's f_2 and hence redound back on player 1's optimal choice of fighting intensity f_1.

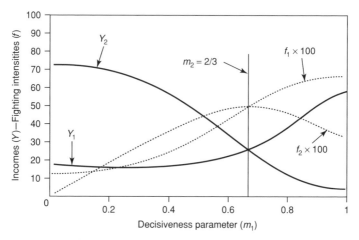

Figure 6.7. Effect of decisiveness asymmetry.

Functional Differences

Equation (4) for the production function postulated a common productivity parameter h. More generally, there could be differing h_i. If $h_1 > h_2$, side 1 has a productive advantage yielding him higher income $Y_1 > Y_2$. (No diagram is provided for this simulation, since – apart from a left-right reversal – such a picture would closely parallel Figure 6.5. That is, a *rise* in h_1, with h_2 held fixed, is very like a *fall* in the productive cost coefficient a_1, with a_2 held fixed.) Similarly, equation (6) could be generalized to allow for differing decisiveness parameters m_i. Figure 6.7 indicates that as m_1 rises, with m_2 held constant, contender 1's optimal f_1 always increases. Contender 2 at first replies with a smaller increase in f_2, but eventually she retreats from the unequal struggle and devotes more effort to production instead.

Positional Differences

Under the Cournot assumption, the parties are symmetrically situated. Among the many possible positional asymmetries, only the Stackelberg situation will be considered here. As first mover, the Stackelberg "leader" chooses a fighting intensity to which the opponent then optimally responds. Ability to move first is often advantageous, for example taking the high ground as a military tactic. But the second mover, able to optimize in the light of the opponent's known choice, always has a countervailing informational advantage. So it is not clear a priori whether, in

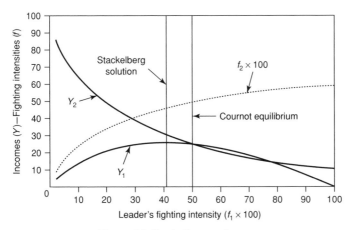

Figure 6.8. Stackelberg optimum.

the present context, a Stackelberg leader can be expected to come out ahead.[18]

Figure 6.8 shows that, in comparisons of the Stackelberg with the Cournot equilibrium, the fighting efforts f_i have become smaller and the incomes Y_i consequently higher on both sides. But note that the follower does better than the leader! Is this a general result? Recall that the reaction curves (see Figure 6.3) have positive slopes throughout. So if player 1 as leader were to choose a smaller-than-Cournot f_1, player 2 would respond with a smaller f_2, implying higher aggregate income for the two together. However, as already pointed out, in the neighborhood of equilibrium the best reply to an increase in the opponent's f_i is always less than one for one. So while the leader gains absolutely, he loses out relatively.[19] In international affairs, for example, suppose that nation 1 were to take the initiative in a disarmament move, reducing f_1 in the hope that nation 2 will reciprocate. The model suggests that only partial reciprocation would occur, leaving the first disarmer at a relative disadvantage.

[18] A Stackelberg leader is quite different from a *hierarchical* leader. The latter is someone who, in order to influence a subordinate's behavior, can issue a credible prior threat or promise as to how he or she will react to the latter's choice. Thus the hierarchical leader is somehow able to *commit in advance to a reaction curve*, in the light of which it is up to the subordinate to make the first action move (see Thompson and Faith 1981; Hirshleifer 1988).

[19] More generally, in an otherwise symmetrical situation with sequential moves, if the reaction curves are positively sloped, the relative advantage always goes to the second mover (Gal-Or 1985).

The Dark Side of the Force

RESULT 6. In the Stackelberg equilibrium, in comparison with the Cournot outcome, both sides' fighting efforts f_i are smaller and incomes Y_i higher. But the follower gains relative to the leader.

DISCUSSION AND APPLICATIONS

The model presented above, while more of a framework of analysis than a tightly specified theory, suggests new ways of understanding diverse yet logically parallel phenomena arising in entirely separate domains. I shall illustrate its bearing for some observed patterns of animal territoriality and human warfare.

Animal Territoriality[20]

The biologists' textbook approach to the problem of territoriality is termed the *economic defense model*. Ecological theorists ask, When does it pay to defend territories, and if it does pay, what are the determinants of territory size and the level of conflict? I shall list only a few points of contact with the previous theoretical development.

(i) If resources are unpredictable or nondefendable, organisms do not appropriate territories but compete by "scrambling"; that is, the social system is amorphy rather than anarchy in the sense of this paper. Territoriality (anarchy) tends to emerge when resources are defendable and predictable, and also dispersed. When resources are predictable and defendable but are geographically concentrated instead, dominance hierarchies tend to replace territoriality. (*Explanation:* Struggles for control of tightly concentrated resources approach "winner-take-all" battles [high decisiveness m]. High m makes anarchy dynamically unstable [from result 1 above], leading to dictatorship by the strongest.)

(ii) In a territorial system, increased population, even if sustainable in terms of the viability limit, reduces per capita territory size (smaller p_i and R_i). Less obviously, larger N raises the intensity of aggressive interactions (higher f_i, from result 4A above). As population pressure increases further, proprietors have to spend so much time fighting intruders that the system eventually breaks down. (Per capita incomes Y_i fall below viability limit y [result 1].) Under these conditions, territoriality is commonly succeeded

[20] This discussion is based mainly on McNaughton and Wolf (1973, chaps. 11–12), Wilson (1975, chap. 12), Morse (1980, chaps. 9–10), and Krebs and Davies (1987, chap. 5).

by a dominance hierarchy in which at least a few stronger animals retain access to the resource (Barash 1977, p. 262).[21]

(iii) While dominance systems lie outside the domain of the present model, the steepness of the hierarchical gradient – the disproportionality between incomes of dominants versus subordinates – tends to be minimized when there are ecological opportunities for subordinates to exit the group and when fighting abilities are not too dissimilar.[22] These conditions correspond to a low value of the decisiveness parameter (small m) and relatively modest decisiveness asymmetry (not too disparate m_i's). Thus, the same qualitative factors that conduce to survival of anarchy also serve to mitigate the exploitive features of dominance systems.

Human Warfare

The model here, with its necessarily severe simplifications, can hardly be expected to "predict" all the subtleties and complications of human social arrangements. Still, it sheds light on some patterns of human social conflict, of which warfare is the most obvious.

Among the Enga tribesmen of New Guinea, at least up to quite recently, warfare was the regular means of redistributing territories (Meggitt 1977). Contrary to assertions that primitive war is largely a ritualized show with few casualties, warfare in New Guinea was a serious matter. Deaths in battle or from wounds accounted for around 35 percent of lifetime mortality among male adults.[23] The factor driving warfare has been increasing population density. (*Explanation*: As Malthusian pressures depress per capita incomes, it comes to a choice between fighting and starving. Yet, owing to low decisiveness m, no single tribe has been able to take over. The anarchic system appears to be stabilized by war casualties that bring per capita incomes Y_i back in line with the viability limit y.)

---

[21] An experiment with Norway rats indicates that if overcrowding becomes extremely severe, even hierarchy can break down in favor of a "pathological" (i.e., amorphic) state (Calhoun 1962).

[22] See Vehrencamp (1983) and, for analogous results in terms of human hierarchical structures, Betzig (1992).

[23] For the Yanomamo tribesmen of South America ("the fierce people"), Chagnon (1988) provides a similar estimate: 30 percent of adult male mortality is the result of violent conflict. An interesting comparison: for Prohibition-era Chicago, Allsop (1968, p. 41) reports 703 gangland fatalities in the course of 14 years. Given the number of active gangster-fighters, the proportion of deaths may not be too dissimilar.

In ancient Greece[24] the persistence of small city-states was associated with relatively indecisive warfare patterns (low m). The phalanx was the dominant tactical formation, missile weapons were largely ineffective, and cavalry almost absent – factors that combined to preclude the deadly pursuit that makes victory truly decisive.

However, with advancing wealth and commerce, sea power became increasingly important. Naval conflict tends of its nature to be militarily more decisive; the stronger force gains command of the seas. Athens, which was the wealthiest state and had a large and skilled navy, reduced many smaller city-states to dependencies within its empire. (*Explanation*: Higher decisiveness m implied higher fighting intensities f_i and thus a smaller number of militarily viable contenders N.) But Athens was ultimately defeated by a countercoalition led by Sparta (Aegospotami, 404 B.C.). Sparta in turn failed to achieve sole hierarchical dominance (Leuctra, 371 B.C.), and a period of shifting alliances followed. (The available conflict technology was characterized by a decisiveness parameter m *too high* for independent city-states to survive without allies, but *not high enough* for a single hegemon to defeat countercoalitions.)

Eventually Macedon gained military predominance (Charonea, 338 B.C.), owing in large part to Philip II's successful integration of cavalry, missile weapons, and siege apparatus with infantry in a disciplined force. (These military innovations led to higher m in land combat. And, of course, Macedon had the asymmetric advantage of being first in the field with them.) In the ensuing conflict between the united Greek forces under Alexander versus the Persian Empire, cavalry (high m) was again crucial to the decisive victory (Gaugamela, 331 B.C.). But none of Alexander's successors was able to achieve sole control. (Owing mainly to the huge land masses involved, conflict decisiveness m was still not high enough for hegemony.) Thus an anarchic system returned in the form of a shifting pattern of three or four successor states, each based on combined sea and land power. This pattern lasted for some 150 years, ending when Rome finally did achieve hegemony in the Mediterranean (Pydna, 168 B.C.). (Rome benefited, it seems, from asymmetrically higher m due more to superior organization than to any special weaponry or tactics.)

A number of other historical periods or episodes also illustrate implications of our model.

---

[24] This discussion is based largely on Fuller (1954, chaps. 1–3), Preston and Wise (1979, chaps. 1–2), and of course Thucydides.

1. *Cannons.* – In the early fifteenth century, the introduction of cannons made it possible to batter down old-style castle walls, ending a long historical period of indecisive siege warfare. A major consequence was a sharp reduction in the number of independent principalities in western Europe. (Higher m implies higher f_i, which implies smaller viable N.)[25] Actually, this *technological* predominance of the offense was only temporary, being shortly reversed by improvements in the art of fortification. But the *economic* effect remained much the same, since their enormous cost put modern fortifications beyond the reach of smaller political units[26] (asymmetrically lower logistic cost coefficient b favoring the larger states, given returns to scale in producing and transporting cannons).

2. *Gang wars.* – In Prohibition-era Chicago, the Capone mob ultimately achieved hegemonic control, owing perhaps to superior ruthlessness as evidenced by the St. Valentine's Day massacre (asymmetrically higher m). As movie and television viewers know, it took decisive intervention by an outside power, the federal government, to put Capone away.

3. *California gold rush.* – In contrast, even though the official organs of law were impotent, no Capone-type hegemony over the "fortyniners" ever developed. Highly dispersed resources (widely separated goldfields in difficult mountainous country) made it difficult for a gang to achieve effective control (low decisiveness m). Another factor, falling outside the model here, is that despite the collective-action problems involved, mining camp communities were surprisingly effective in setting up "social contracts" for resisting invaders (Umbeck 1981).

CONCLUSIONS AND LIMITATIONS

It will be convenient to summarize by responding briefly to the specific questions raised in the Introduction.

1. *When is there a stable anarchic solution?* – An anarchic system, to be sustained, must be *dynamically stable* and *viable*. The former

---

[25] See Batchelder and Freudenberger (1983) and especially Parker (1988, chap. 1). But also compare Anderson (1992).

[26] In 1553 the city of Siena undertook modernization of its fortifications. But the costs were so high that, when attack came, not only were the defense works still incomplete but funds to hire a supporting mercenary army or fleet were lacking. So in 1555 Siena surrendered to Florence and permanently lost its independence (see Parker 1988, p. 12).

condition holds when, most important, the decisiveness of conflict (measured by the parameter m in the model) is sufficiently low; else the most militarily effective contender would become a hegemon. Viability requires sufficiently high income Y_i for survival on the individual level or, in the case of larger contending units, for maintaining group integrity.

2. *Equilibrium allocations of effort.* – In the symmetrical Cournot solution with $N = 2$ contestants, the crucial result is that as the decisiveness parameter m rises, each side is forced to fight harder (f_1 and f_2 both increase). The consequences include reduced incomes on both sides.

3. *Numbers.* – As N grows exogenously, equilibrium fighting intensities f_i rise. With fixed aggregate resources R, per capita incomes Y_i fall for two reasons: first, because each party's pro rata share $p_i = 1/N$ is less and, second, because f_i is higher. That is, a contestant has to fight harder just to obtain a given pro rata share. This second reason continues to apply even in a more generous environment in which resources grow in proportion to N. If N is *endogenous*, the equilibrium number of contenders is determined by the viability condition $Y_i \geq y$; that is, entry occurs up to the point of zero profit.

4. *Technology and comparative advantage.* – An asymmetrical productive improvement (a decrease in the production cost coefficient a_i or an increase in the productivity parameter h_i) increases own-income Y_i but within the model here does not otherwise affect any of the results. (However, I have flagged this as a "nongeneric" result deriving from special features of the model, in particular, the total disjunction of productive opportunities.) On the conflict side, corresponding one-sided improvements (i.e., a reduction in the logistics cost coefficient b_i or an increase in the decisiveness parameter m_i) generally increase own-income while reducing opponent income.

5. *Strategic position.* – The Stackelberg solution, as compared with the symmetric Cournot equilibrium, involves reduced fighting on both sides, but the follower gains relative to the leader. This evidently tends to stabilize the anarchic system. Although all could benefit from the change, each single participant is motivated to hold back and let the opponent become the leader.

The analytic results here depend on a particular way of modeling anarchy that omits many possibly important elements. To mention only a few: (1) Full information was assumed throughout, so that factors such as deception have been set aside (see, e.g., Tullock 1974, chap. 10; Brams 1977). (2) Apart from opportunity costs in the form of foregone production, fighting was assumed nondestructive. (This assumption biases our results in the direction of conflict.)[27] (3) Distance and other geographical factors (see, e.g., Boulding 1962, chaps. 12–13) were not explicitly considered, though they entered implicitly as determinants of the logistics cost and decisiveness parameters. (4) The steady-state assumption rules out issues involving *timing*, such as arms races, economic growth, or (on a smaller time scale) signaling resolve through successive escalation. (5) Finally, I have not attempted to model the problems of group formation and collective action (but see the next section).

The justification for these and other omissions is that one must begin somewhere. The model illustrates a method of analysis. In many contexts, for example, it might be unacceptable to omit the element of collateral damage (qualification 2 above). Still, that effect could be incorporated by means of an adjustment within the general analytical framework.

AFTER ANARCHY, WHAT?

Though this topic lies outside the bounds of the model, the analysis here insistently suggests the following question: Supposing that anarchy does break down, what happens next?

Theoretical considerations, as well as the historical and other applications described above, combine to suggest that anarchic systems are fragile. Anarchy is always liable to "break down" into amorphy or "break up" into organization! First of all, exogenous changes may lead to violation of the necessary conditions of result 1. Military technology (very often, though not always) has moved in the direction of higher decisiveness m, threatening *dynamic stability*. And Malthusian pressures are at work to dilute per capita incomes, threatening *viability*.

But even if the necessary conditions are met, making anarchy in principle sustainable, the system may be undermined by "the urge to merge." Benefits from group formation may include (1) reduced fighting within, (2) complementarities in production, and (3) enhanced ability to fight outsiders. The other side of the coin, the factor hampering mergers, is

---

[27] The model of Grossman and Kim (1994) allows for damage due to fighting. The extent of "collateral damage" has been influenced by two opposed technological trends: greater destructive power and improved aiming precision. In a nonmilitary context, Becker's (1983) analysis of pressure group competition shows how incidental damage to the economy ("deadweight loss") tends to limit the extent of conflict.

the collective-action problem: how to get agreement on a social contract and, even more important, how to enforce it.

It is useful to distinguish *vertical* from *horizontal* social contracts. The vertical alternative, Thomas Hobbes's version, would be represented by arrangements such as hierarchical dominance in the biological realm or dictatorship on the human level. John Locke's version, the horizontal alternative, corresponds to more egalitarian arrangements in either sphere.[28]

Of the two major sources of breakdown – dynamic instability and income inviability – the former is likely to lead to a vertical social contract. An excessively high decisiveness coefficient m implies a range of increasing returns to fighting effort. At the extreme, this may imply a "natural monopoly" in fighting activity; that is, the struggle is likely to end up with all the resources under one party's control. In contrast, the mere fact of low income under anarchy, since it may be the consequence of many different forces, of itself provides no clear indication as to what is likely to happen next.

Owing to closer sympathies, better monitoring of shirkers, and so forth, the collective-action problem is more readily solved in small groups. But these small groups in turn come into anarchic competition at the group level. This of course provides a cascading motivation for unification one level higher up. In modern times this process has led to a sharp reduction in the number of independent states and principalities: in Europe alone, from hundreds or even thousands to around a dozen or two after the unifications of Germany and Italy. Still, there never has been an all-European state. Nor should we assume that the process can go only in the direction of agglomeration, as the fall of the Roman Empire and the recent dissolution of the Soviet Union demonstrate.

The upshot is that, even if anarchy breaks up into organization on one level, anarchic conflict may be sharpened at the higher level. If the clans within a tribe agree on a social contract, peace among the clans may be only the prelude to more violent struggles against other tribes.

APPENDIX: NUMERICAL EXAMPLES

All these numerical examples are connected and can be read together as a running illustration of the model.

---

[28] Chicago gangland history (Allsop 1968) provides nice instances of both arrangements. Johnny Torrio, a "statesman-like" leader, attempted to bring all the gangs together in a Lockian solution with profit sharing and allocation of territories. However, the intransigent South Side O'Donnells resisted confederation. Torrio's more ruthless successor, Al Capone, ultimately succeeded in imposing a vertical Hobbesian solution.

Numerical Example 1

Let the decisiveness parameter be $m = \frac{2}{3}$. Then equations (7a) and (7b) simplify to $p_1/p_2 = R_1/R_2 = (f_1/f_2)^2$. If the total resources available are $R = 100$ and the fighting intensities on each side have been chosen (not necessarily optimally) to be $f_1 = .1$ and $f_2 = .2$, respectively, then $p_1/p_2 = (.1/.2)^2 = \frac{1}{4}$, implying that, in equilibrium, $R_1 = 20$ and $R_2 = 80$.

To illustrate convergence when $m = \frac{2}{3}$, suppose that the initial resource vector is set at $(R_1^o, R_2^o) = (60, 40)$. The first-period conflict outcome is $p_1/p_2 = (6/8)^{2/3} = .825$, implying an end-of-period revised resource allocation $(R_1', R_2') = (45.2, 54.8)$. After one more period of conflict the resource allocation becomes $(R_1'', R_2'') = (35.7, 64.3)$. Evidently, the equilibrium $(R_1, R_2) = (20, 80)$ is being approached asymptotically.

In contrast, for a decisiveness parameter in the range $m > 1$, say $m = 2$, starting from the same initial resource vector $(60, 40)$, the first- and second-period reallocations would be $(36.0, 64.0)$ and $(7.3, 92.7)$. The process rapidly diverges in favor of the side with the higher f_i.

Numerical Example 2

In the previous numerical example the contenders were arbitrarily assumed to have chosen fighting intensities $f_1 = .1$ and $f_2 = .2$, leading to the equilibrium resource distribution $R_1 = 20$ and $R_2 = 80$. But if the parties choose *optimally* instead under the Nash–Cournot assumption, with $m = \frac{2}{3}$ and symmetrical logistics cost coefficients $b_1 = b_2 = b = 1$, from equation (11) the equilibrium choices are $f_1 = f_2 = .5$, implying an equal equilibrium resource division $R_1 = R_2 = 50$. From (12), and with production cost coefficients $a_1 = a_2 = a = 1$ and productivity parameter $h = 1$ (constant returns in production), the associated incomes are $Y_1 = Y_2 = 25$. (In contrast, had no conflict occurred – that is, if the choices had been $f_1 = f_2 = 0$ – the per capita incomes would have been 50 each.)

Numerical Example 3

With aggregate resources $R = 100$ and $N = 2$, equilibrium fighting intensities in the previous example were $f_1 = f_2 = .5$, yielding per capita incomes $Y_1 = Y_2 = 25$. If we use the same parameter values and hold aggregate resources fixed at 100, for $N = 3$ the equilibrium fighting efforts rise to $f_1 = f_2 = .571$ and the per capita incomes fall to $Y_i = 14.3$, approximately. (Note that the *aggregate* income is lower as well.) If, on the other hand, resources were to rise in proportion to numbers – specifically here, if $R \equiv Nr$, where $r = 50$ – then in equilibrium $Y_i = 21.4$, approximately. Thus, even when the resource base expands with N, there is a per capita income loss owing to the larger optimal f_i.

Numerical Example 4

With the same parameter values, for aggregate resources fixed at $R = 100$, suppose that the viability threshold is $y = 4$. From equation (17), the equilibrium incomes are $Y_i = 4$ at $N = 9$. So this fixed resource magnitude will support a population of $N = 9$ competitors. If instead resources expand with population so that $R \equiv 50N$, the situation is much more favorable. In such an environment, equation (19) indicates that an equilibrium population of $N = 9$ could be supported even at a much higher viability threshold $y = 18$.

Numerical Example 5

Under the quantitative assumptions of numerical example 2, the Cournot equilibrium was $f_1 = f_2 = .5$ and $Y_1 = Y_2 = 25$. When the same numerical assumptions are used, side 1 as Stackelberg leader does best by choosing a somewhat lower $f_1 = .41$, approximately, and his income rises slightly to about 25.7. The second mover optimally responds by cutting back her fighting intensity only to about .466, reaping a considerably higher income of around 30.1.

REFERENCES

Allsop, Kenneth. *The Bootleggers: The Story of Chicago's Prohibition Era.* 2d ed. New Rochelle, N.Y.: Arlington, 1968.

Anderson, Gary M. "Cannon, Castles, and Capitalism: The Invention of Gunpowder and the Rise of the West." *Defence Econ.* 3, no. 2 (1992): 147–60.

Barash, David P. *Sociobiology and Behavior.* New York: Elsevier, 1977.

Batchelder, Ronald W., and Freudenberger, Herman H. "On the Rational Origins of the Modern Centralized State." *Explorations Econ. Hist.* 20 (January 1983): 1–13.

Becker, Gary S. "A Theory of Competition among Pressure Groups for Political Influence." *Q.J.E.* 98 (August 1983): 371–400.

Bernholz, Peter. *The International Game of Power: Past, Present, and Future.* Berlin: Mouton, 1985.

Betzig, Laura. "Of Human Bonding: Cooperation or Exploitation." *Soc. Sci. Information* 31, no. 4 (1992): 611–42.

Boulding, Kenneth E. *Conflict and Defense: A General Theory.* New York: Harper, 1962.

Brams, Steven J. "Deception in 2 × 2 Games." *J. Peace Sci.* 2 (Spring 1977): 171–203.

Bush, Winston C., and Mayer, Lawrence S. "Some Implications of Anarchy for the Distribution of Property." *J. Econ. Theory* 8 (August 1974): 401–12.

Calhoun, John B. "Population Density and Social Pathology." *Scientific American* 206 (February 1962): 139–48.

Chagnon, Napoleon A. "Life Histories, Blood Revenge, and Warfare in a Tribal Population." *Science* 239 (February 26, 1988): 985–92.

Fuller, John F. C. *From the Earliest Times to the Battle of Lepanto.* Vol. 1 of *A Military History of the Western World.* New York: Da Capo, 1954.

Gal-Or, Esther. "First Mover and Second Mover Advantages." *Int. Econ. Rev.* 26 (October 1985): 649–53.

Ghiselin, Michael T. "The Economy of the Body." *A.E.R. Papers and Proc.* 68 (May 1978): 233–37.

Grossman, Herschel I., and Kim, Minseong. "A Theory of the Security of Claims to Property." Working Paper no. 94-12. Providence, R.I.: Brown Univ., Dept. Econ., June 1994.

Hayek, Friedrich A. *The Political Order of a Free People.* Vol. 3 of *Law, Legislation and Liberty: A New Statement of the Liberal Principles of Justice and Political Economy.* Chicago: Univ. Chicago Press, 1979.

Hirshleifer, Jack. "The Analytics of Continuing Conflict." *Synthese* 76 (August 1988): 201–33.

———. "The Paradox of Power." *Econ. and Politics* 3 (November 1991): 177–200. (*a*)

———. "The Technology of Conflict as an Economic Activity." *A.E.R. Papers and Proc.* 81 (May 1991): 130–34. (*b*)

Krebs, John R., and Davies, Nicholas B. *An Introduction to Behavioural Ecology.* 2d. ed. Oxford: Blackwell Scientific, 1987.

Meggitt, Mervyn J. *Blood Is Their Argument: War among the Mae Enga Tribesmen of the New Guinea Highlands.* Palo Alto, Calif.: Mayfield, 1977.

McNaughton, Samuel J., and Wolf, Larry L. *General Ecology.* New York: Holt, Rinehart, and Winston, 1973.

Morse, Douglass H. *Behavioral Mechanisms in Ecology.* Cambridge, Mass.: Harvard Univ. Press, 1980.

Nicholson, A. J. "An Outline of the Dynamics of Animal Populations." *Australian J. Zoology* 2 (May 1954): 9–65.

Parker, Geoffrey. *The Military Revolution: Military Innovation and the Rise of the West, 1500–1800.* Cambridge: Cambridge Univ. Press, 1988.

Preston, Richard A., and Wise, Sydney F. *Men in Arms: A History of Warfare and Its Interrelationships with Western Society.* 4th ed. New York: Holt, Rinehart, and Winston, 1979.

Przeworski, Adam. *Democracy and the Market: Political and Economic Reform in Eastern Europe and Latin America.* Cambridge: Cambridge Univ. Press, 1991.

Rousseau, Jean-Jacques. "A Discourse on the Origin of Inequality." In *The Social Contract and Discourses*, translated by G. D. H. Cole. Everyman's Library. New York: Dutton, 1950.

Salop, Steven C., and Scheffman, David T. "Raising Rivals' Costs." *A.E.R. Papers and Proc.* 73 (May 1983): 267–71.

Sherman, William Tecumseh. *Memoirs of General W. T. Sherman.* 2d ed. New York: Appleton, 1885. Reprint. New York: Library of America, 1990.

Skaperdas, Stergios. "Cooperation, Conflict, and Power in the Absence of Property Rights." *A.E.R.* 82 (September 1992): 720–39.

Skogh, Goran, and Stuart, Charles. "A Contractarian Theory of Property Rights and Crime." *Scandinavian J. Econ.* 84, no. 1 (1982): 27–40.

Snyder, Glenn H., and Diesing, Paul. *Conflict among Nations: Bargaining, Decision Making, and System Structure in International Crises.* Princeton, N.J.: Princeton Univ. Press, 1977.

Thompson, Earl A., and Faith, Roger L. "A Pure Theory of Strategic Behavior and Social Institutions." *A.E.R.* 71 (June 1981): 366–80.

Tullock, Gordon. "The Welfare Costs of Tariffs, Monopolies, and Theft." *Western Econ. J.* 5 (June 1967): 224–32.

———. *The Social Dilemma: The Economics of War and Revolution.* Blacksburg, Va.: University Pubs., 1974.

———. "Efficient Rent Seeking." In *Toward a Theory of the Rent-Seeking Society*, edited by James M. Buchanan, Robert D. Tollison, and Gordon Tullock. College Station: Texas A&M Univ. Press, 1980.

Umbeck, John. "Might Makes Rights: A Theory of the Formation and Initial Distribution of Property Rights." *Econ. Inquiry* 19 (January 1981): 38–59.

Usher, Dan. "The Dynastic Cycle and the Stationary State." *A.E.R.* 79 (December 1989): 1031–44.

Vehrencamp, Sandra L. "A Model for the Evolution of Despotic versus Egalitarian Societies." *Animal Behaviour* 31 (August 1983): 667–82.

Waltz, Kenneth N. *Man, the State, and War: A Theoretical Analysis.* New York: Columbia Univ. Press, 1959.

Wilson, Edward O. *Sociobiology: The New Synthesis.* Cambridge, Mass.: Harvard Univ. Press, 1975.

7

Truth, Effort, and the Legal Battle

Jack Hirshleifer and Evan Osborne

Background of this Chapter

Litigation is a form of conflict. The "fighting efforts" on each side – the costs of lawyers, of factual investigation and legal research, and (in some instances) even of bribery – importantly determine the outcome. However, in legal disputes a new feature enters: *truth* may also play a role. Other things being equal, the party whose case is more meritorious is more likely to win. This article shows how fighting efforts and truth interact to determine the equilibrium levels of litigation efforts and the likelihood of a just outcome.

I thank Evan Osborne for allowing reprinting of this jointly authored article.

Abstract

In lawsuits, relative success depends upon two main factors: the true degree of fault and the efforts invested on each side. A proposed Litigation Success Function displays this dependence while satisfying other essential properties. Under two different protocols, Nash–Cournot and Stackelberg, solutions are obtained for the litigation efforts, proportionate success, and values of the lawsuit on each side. Outcomes are evaluated in terms of two normative criteria: (i) achieving "justice" (interpreted as equality between degree of Defendant fault and relative Plaintiff success) and (ii) minimizing aggregate litigation cost. Achievement of these aims is determined by the decisiveness *of litigation effort in comparison with true fault.*

Trials are battles. In consequence, litigation shares certain family traits with wars, strikes, and other human conflicts – violent and nonviolent.

*Reprinted from J. Hirshleifer and E. Osborne, "Truth, Effort, and the Legal Battle," *Public Choice*, forthcoming, Copyright © 2001, with permission from the Locke Institute.

We thank Joannes Mongardini and Qing Wang for assistance with the computations and graphics. Helpful comments have been received from Herschel Grossman, David Hirshleifer, Avery Katz, David Levine, Gary Schwartz, Stergios Skaperdas, journal referees, and seminar participants at George Washington University, UCLA, and the University of California at Irvine.

True, not all lawsuits proceed to trial, just as not all international disputes culminate in war. But the potential "decision at arms" casts its shadow over any settlement negotiations the parties might undertake.[1]

Law and economics scholars have concentrated attention mainly upon the reasons for lawsuits, the likelihood of settlement, and the implications of alternative cost-shifting systems ("English rule" versus "American rule") and attorney payment structures (e.g., hourly rates versus contingent fees). Only quite recently have a few studies appeared that have analyzed the legal battle itself. In the small existing literature, the present paper is most closely related to Braeutigam, Owen, and Panzar (1984), Katz (1988), Hause (1989), Kobayashi and Lott (1996),[2] and Farmer and Pecorino (1999).

We will be generating a model of litigation as conflict, involving optimization on the part of each litigant (how much effort to devote to the contest) and the consequent equilibrium outcome in terms of success achieved and costs incurred. Although there are implications for already well-researched topics such as the likelihood of settlement and the influence of alternative fee structures, we will be concentrating upon other equally important issues that have not received so much attention. Among these are:

1. Does the litigant with the more meritorious case tend to "fight harder," that is, to invest more in litigation effort?
2. Taking the two litigants together, does aggregate effort tend to be greatest when Defendant fault is high, low, or intermediate?
3. Under what circumstances does it pay Defendant to concede or Plaintiff not to bring suit?
4. What characteristics of litigation systems may bias the outcome toward Plaintiff or toward Defendant?
5. What normative criteria should be used to evaluate litigation systems?

FUNDAMENTALS AND APPROACH

The first issue is; Why litigate at all? Going to court is always Pareto-dominated by a range of potential settlements. Furthermore, although in international power struggles and other conflictual contexts negotiated

---

[1] "Pretrial bargaining may be described as a game played in the shadow of the law." – Cooter, Marks, and Mnookin (1982).

[2] Unlike our own and the other studies cited, the Kobayoshi and Lott (1996) analysis runs in terms of criminal rather than civil litigation. For present purposes this difference is inessential.

settlements might not be enforceable, when it comes to lawsuits effective procedures exist for implementing any agreements arrived at. Several explanations for nonsettlement might be offered.

1. The parties might attach differing expected values to the outcome of trial. If each side is relatively optimistic about how well it will do – either because of differences in perceptions of the stakes or of the probabilities of winning – litigation becomes more likely. Our analysis postulates equal stakes. As for beliefs, we assume Plaintiff (P) and Defendant (D) have common knowledge of all the underlying functions and parameters: the actual level of fault, the stakes, the costs of trial, and the structural relationships set forth in the model itself.

2. Failure to settle might also be due to attitudes toward risk. Although normal risk-aversion makes settlement more likely, conceivably one or the other contender might actually be characterized by risk-preference.[3] We rule out this element as well, postulating that both sides are risk-neutral.

3. Scarcely ever considered in the literature, but arguably an important force, is sheer hostility or malevolence: a contender might be willing to sacrifice own-wealth in order to distress the opponent. Or conceivably, he or she might have a taste for belligerence as such. We rule out all these possible explanations and will simply assume (in accordance with most of the existing literature) that each contender aims simply at maximizing his or her own expected income.

So why ever go to trial? Without attempting a full answer, we simply call upon the common observation that negotiation failures ("bargaining impasses") often occur even where differences in beliefs or attitudes toward risk do not appear to be involved.[4] (The difficulty is sometimes attributed to "costs of negotiation," though that is little more than a verbal restatement of the problem.)[5]

---

[3] The roles of optimism and attitudes toward risk were explored in the early analytic works of Landes (1971) and Gould (1973), followed by many other authors.

[4] Whether rational agents "should" always be able to extricate themselves from bargaining impasses remains a subject of debate among game theorists. See, for example, Aumann (1976) and Binmore (1992, 208–209). And of course, real-life humans are not always fully rational.

[5] Even if settlement were ultimately certain, our model could still describe the hypothetical calculations of the contending parties as they estimate minimum terms for agreement.

A second issue is, Who are the decision makers? A litigant and his or her attorney never have perfectly harmonious interests, so a general model of litigation struggles would have to deal with at least four parties: the principals and attorneys on each side. We bypass these agency questions to deal solely with the decisions of two litigants who employ attorneys and other inputs into the legal battle.[6] Thus, there is a single choice variable on each side, the litigation efforts L_P for Plaintiff and L_D for Defendant.

A third modeling issue involves the protocol of interaction and associated solution concept. Although no single paradigm can ever capture the full complexity of a lawsuit, for our purposes three relatively simple solution concepts suggest themselves: (1) Nash–Cournot, (2) Stackelberg, and (3) Threat-and-promise.

1. Nash–Cournot: The protocol underlying the familiar Nash–Cournot solution is symmetrical. Plaintiff and Defendant respectively decide on L_P and L_D in ignorance of the opponent's simultaneous choice. The condition of equilibrium is that each side's selection must be a best reply; neither can gain from a unilateral switch.

2. Stackelberg: One side (the "leader") commits to a level of effort to which the other then makes an optimizing response. For lawsuits, the time sequence of events makes it more plausible for the Plaintiff to be the leader.

3. Threat-and-promise: Here, although the Plaintiff is still the first to choose a level of litigation effort, before he can do so the Defendant is permitted to make a prior commitment aimed at influencing that decision. More specifically, the Defendant commits not to a specified level of litigation effort but to a reaction function. In effect, the Defendant says: "If your opening move is as I desire, I will reward you (promise), but if not I will punish you (threat).[7]

We would not contend that any one of these three elementary protocols is the "correct" way to represent litigation. Social interactions, whether cooperative or conflictual, are almost always too complex to

[6] An attorney engaged on a contingent-fee basis has in effect become a partner of the litigant. This tends to reduce incentive divergences between them, but we are assuming away conflicts of interest to begin with. (Our analysis also disregards possible informational discrepancies between principals and their attorneys.)

[7] Threat-and-promise protocols are examined in Hirshleifer (1988), building in part upon Schelling (1960) and Thompson and Faith (1981).

be captured by any simple model. Most of the related analyses in the literature have employed the symmetrical Nash–Cournot protocol and solution concept.[8] That might be satisfactory in many contexts.[9] However, in the litigation setting an obvious asymmetry exists: there is no lawsuit unless Plaintiff brings it.[10]

The Stackelberg and Threat-and-promise protocols make use of this asymmetry in the different ways described above. In this analysis we start with the Nash–Cournot solution, mainly for purposes of comparison, but our central analysis runs in terms of a slightly generalized Stackelberg protocol with the Plaintiff as leader. (Unfortunately, space and time constraints preclude consideration of Threat-and-promise protocols here.)

BUILDING BLOCKS

The Cost Function

By assumption, Plaintiff's cost C_P depends only upon his own litigation effort L_P, and Defendant's C_D only upon her own litigation effort L_D. Litigation effort is an index of real inputs such as attorney hours, pages of documentation, and so forth, translated into dollars by a cost function $C_i(L_i)$, $i = P, D$. For simplicity here, fixed costs are ruled out, and marginal cost γ is assumed constant, so that,

$$C_i = \gamma L_i. \tag{1}$$

We assume that Plaintiff and Defendant have identical cost functions (since the same lawyers and other inputs to litigation are available for hire by both sides). Each party is assumed to be responsible for its own legal costs regardless of the outcome – the so-called American rule.

---

[8] Kobayashi and Lott (1996), although modeling the (criminal) trial itself as a Nash–Cournot game, allow for a prior "plea bargaining" phase in which the prosecution makes the first move. The analysis in Farmer and Pecorino (1999) is basically Nash–Cournot, but they look into Stackelberg protocols in some instances where there is no Nash–Cournot solution.

[9] The Nash–Cournot solution concept is rather paradoxical. An equilibrium is said to exist if each side's selection is a best response to the opponent's choice. But the Nash protocol requires simultaneity, which means that neither side knows the opponent's choice to which it is supposed to be replying optimally. Implicit therefore is a kind of unmodeled learning and mutual accommodation process which, over time, may converge to the kind of equilibrium described. (See Binmore 1992; Chap. 9.)

[10] Using the symmetrical Nash–Cournot solution concept, Katz (1988; p. 129) says that "the designation of the parties as plaintiff and defendant is arbitrary." In contrast, for the asymmetrical Stackelberg and Threat-and-promise protocols, the Plaintiff–Defendant distinction is essential.

The Value of the Lawsuit

The value of the lawsuit to each side, which for risk-neutral litigants is the mathematical expectation of gain or loss in the event of trial, is defined as:

$$V_i \equiv \pi J_i - C_i, \qquad (2)$$

J_P and J_D are the respective stakes, assumed identical except for sign. (Apart from litigation cost, Plaintiff stands to gain what Defendant loses.) Thus, J_P is positive, and $J_D \equiv -J_P$. (We will sometimes simply write J for $J_P \equiv -J_D$.) Plaintiff's proportionate degree of success is symbolized by π, or, for explicitness, we will sometimes write π_P. Defendant's proportionate success is $\pi_D \equiv 1 - \pi$. It follows that Defendant's value of the lawsuit V_D is always nonpositive. For Plaintiff, V_P might be either positive or negative; if the latter, he will not bring suit at all.

There are two equally valid interpretations of these success measures.

1. $\pi \equiv \pi_P$ could be regarded as a probability, that is, as the likelihood of Plaintiff victory in an all-or-nothing, yes–no situation. The idea is that there is a standard of appropriate behavior or "due care." If Defendant is adjudged to have met the standard, she retains the judgment amount at stake; if not, Plaintiff wins it.
2. Under the alternative "comparative fault" interpretation, the outcome is a proportionate division of the stakes. Here $\pi \equiv \pi_P$ would represent the deterministic fractional share awarded to Plaintiff in response to Defendant's adjudged degree of fault.

Our risk-neutrality assumption makes it unnecessary to choose between these two interpretations. A risk-neutral litigant will be indifferent between a given probability of receiving the entire stake at issue or receiving a corresponding deterministic fractional share.

Fault

Defendant fault (Y) lies in the interval $(0,1)$. $Y = 1$ means that Defendant is totally in the wrong, and $Y = 0$ means that Plaintiff's case is entirely without merit.

In some of the literature on the economics of litigation, it has been assumed that the court will infallibly ascertain the true degree of fault.[11]

---

[11] See, for example, Priest and Klein (1984). More precisely, Priest and Klein assume the court will correctly determine whether the true fault lies to one or the other side of the relevant "decision standard."

The litigants do not themselves know the truth, but the court will correctly discern it. We assume the reverse: the true degree of fault Y is known by both litigants but is not known by the court (whose decision is therefore subject to influence by the litigation efforts on the two sides).[12]

THE LITIGATION SUCCESS FUNCTION (LSF)

The Litigation Success Function (LSF) is the crucial and most novel element of our model. The LSF summarizes the relevant conflict technology.[13] As a kind of analog of the production function in standard economics, "inputs" in the form of litigation efforts L_P and L_D generate "outputs" π_P and π_D denoting Plaintiff and Defendant success.

We now postulate certain features that a satisfactory LSF should display.

1. The achieved success fractions π_P and π_D should depend upon the litigation efforts L_P and L_D and the degree of Defendant fault Y.
2. The LSF should satisfy what has been called the logit property (Dixit 1987). That is, the functions determining the parties' respective prospects of success must be such that π_P and π_D sum to unity.
3. Given equal degrees of fault ($Y = 1 - Y = 0.5$), the outcome at trial should depend only upon the litigation efforts.
4. And, correspondingly, given equal efforts ($L_P = L_D$) the outcome should depend only upon the degree of fault.
5. If Defendant is totally in the wrong (if her fault is $Y = 1$), she should always lose the entire stake – provided only that Plaintiff makes some positive effort $L_P > 0$. And similarly, a Defendant totally without fault ($Y = 0$) should always pay nothing, provided she chooses some $L_D > 0$.

Perhaps the simplest LSF meeting all these criteria can be written in the form:

$$\frac{\pi_P}{\pi_D} = \left(\frac{L_P}{L_D}\right)^{\alpha} \frac{Y}{1-Y}. \tag{3}$$

---

[12] Though it was a criminal rather than civil proceeding, the O.J. Simpson case may be an illuminating instance. Were the defense and prosecution unaware of where the truth lay, whereas the judge and jury were able to discover it? Or were the contenders quite aware of the true guilt or innocence of the accused, whereas the judge and jury were fallible?

[13] The Litigation Success Function is an adaptation of what has been called the "Contest Success Function" in the literature on the economics of conflict (Hirshleifer 1989, Skaperdas 1996).

Or, solving for the respective degrees of success:

$$\pi_P = \frac{L_P^\alpha Y}{L_P^\alpha Y + L_D^\alpha (1 - Y)} \quad \text{and} \quad \pi_D = \frac{L_D^\alpha (1 - Y)}{L_P^\alpha Y + L_D^\alpha (1 - Y)}. \quad (4)$$

Equation (3) shows the outcome of the legal battle as a success ratio. The right-hand side is the product of an effort factor L_P/L_D and a fault factor $Y/(1 - Y)$, the former being weighted by a force exponent α. With this LSF, Plaintiff's proportionate success will exactly reflect Defendant's fault, and thus $\pi_P = Y$, whenever either (i): $L_P = L_D$ (the two sides invest equal efforts), or (ii) $\alpha = 0$ (legal efforts are totally ineffective as compared with "the power of truth" – the underlying merits of the case).

As for effort, the assumption here is that the respective chances of success are a function of the effort ratio L_P/L_D. This is not the only conceivable formulation, but it seems appropriate for our purposes.[14] And similarly for the fault factor $Y/(1 - Y)$ – the relative advantage of having truth on your side.

The force exponent α weights the relative importance of effort versus fault in determining the outcome. Differing judicial systems will be characterized by different values of α. Where judges have broad leeway to instruct juries, the power of advocacy on each side might be correspondingly diminished – α would be relatively low. In contrast, α would be comparatively high if, by law or custom, judges were to limit themselves to procedural issues and refrain from instructing juries on the substantive merits of the case.

It is easy to verify that all the desirable features listed above are satisfied by the LSF of Eqs. (3) and (4).

Various generalizations of this LSF are possible.

1. "Effectiveness coefficients" e_P and e_D could be attached to the decision variables L_P and L_D in equations (3) and (4) to reflect the possibility that one side or the other is more adept in converting legal effort into a successful judicial outcome.

---

[14] Two "canonical" ways of dealing with the effort factor are as a ratio L_P/L_D or as a difference $L_P - L_D$ (Hirshleifer 1989). If the difference form were employed, zero effort would not necessarily entail total loss. In warfare, for example, a nation might capitulate and still retain some of its territory. (The victor might choose not to press its advantage to the limit, even against a nonresisting opponent.) But failing to contest a lawsuit generally leads to an adverse judgment for the full amount.

2. The judicial system might be characterized by a degree of bias, intended or not, in one direction or the other. In American criminal procedure there is a traditional intended bias in favor of defendants, whose guilt must be established "beyond a reasonable doubt."[15] Bias could be modeled by introducing a suitable asymmetry into the form of Eqs. (3) and (4).

3. The force exponent α in Eq. (3) parametrically weights the effort factor L_P/L_D relative to the fault factor $Y/(1 - Y)$, but arguably there should also be a parametrically varying "truth exponent" β attaching to the fault factor as well. Whereas α measures the "decisiveness of effort," β would scale the "decisiveness of truth" in determining the outcome. Allowing both α and β to vary parametrically implies that not only the relative sizes of α and β matter but their absolute magnitudes as well. If α and β were both very low, for example, the success ratio must necessarily end up close to unity: π would remain close to 0.5 regardless of *both* truth and effort.

Apart from the desire for simplicity, we had a particular reason for fixing the β parameter at unity. Doing so gives the LSF an additional attribute we will call proportionality. Proportionality represents a strengthening of the fourth property in our list of features. When efforts are equal ($L_P = L_D$), Plaintiff's proportionate success does not merely "depend upon" Defendant's degree of fault but must actually equal it numerically ($\pi = Y$). (The significance of proportionality will become clear in our discussion of the meaning of 'justice' below.)

In the earlier literature, the analyses of Braeutigam et al. (1984) and Hause (1989) also contain elements analogous to our LSF, in allowing for both effort and fault. But their formulations leave this dependence in quite general and abstract form. Kobayashi and Lott (1996), though without any particular justification, specify a functional form that is closer to ours. Indeed the algebraic example they employ would be identical with our LSF save for one crucial omission: it lacks the force exponent α.

In Katz (1988) the formal analysis once again deals with an abstract and general LSF, but an example is offered almost identical with the LSF

---

[15] A less defensible instance of bias is the tendency of state courts to favor in-state plaintiffs against out-of-state defendants. See Tabarrok and Helland (1999).

of Eqs. (3) and (4).[16] Katz's interpretation diverges somewhat from ours: he emphasizes the informational over the conflictual aspects of lawsuits. Legal efforts take the form of searching for supporting "arguments"; the side producing a sufficient preponderance of arguments becomes the winner. But finding arguments – locating evidence and making valid logical inferences therefrom – are not the only ways to influence judicial outcomes. Litigants and their attorneys can and do use a wide range of other techniques, not excluding deception, bribery, and coercion. Our approach makes litigation more akin to warfare than to information gathering. Valid arguments help one's case, certainly, but seeking them is only one of many routes to victory. Finally, Farmer and Pecorino (1999), once again without any explicit justification, base their analysis upon the LSF of Katz's illustrative example.[17]

In contrast with these earlier contributions, our contention has been that proper modeling of the litigation battle should logically satisfy several highly plausible desiderata, as described in the preceding discussion. These considerations dictate a distinctive formulation of the LSF that will enable us to obtain sharper results.

THE INTERACTION OF EFFORT AND FAULT

Figure 7.1 is a numerical illustration showing how Plaintiff's success π_P varies as his litigation effort L_P in Eq. (4) ranges upward from 0 to 2, with Defendant's effort held fixed at $L_D = 0.5$. (The stakes are normalized throughout at $J_P = -J_D = 1$.) Figure 7.1 (a) pictures a relatively low level of Defendant fault ($Y = 1/3$), and Figure 7.1 (b) a relatively high level ($Y = 2/3$).

As expected, Plaintiff effort L_P always has a positive influence upon the success fraction π_P, as revealed by the positive slopes of all the curves. Within each panel of Figure 7.1, the different curves show the effects of changing the force exponent α. Notice that higher α raises Plaintiff success π in the range $L_P > L_D$ but lowers π when $L_P < L_D$. In other words, α measures the sensitivity of the final outcome to preponderant fighting effort. Between the low-fault and high-fault panels there is a

---

[16] The LSF in Katz's illustrative example might be written $\dfrac{\pi_P}{\pi_D} = \dfrac{(L_P)^{\alpha_P}}{(L_D)^{\alpha_D}} e^M$. (Katz allows the force exponents α_i to differ between Plaintiff and Defendant.) The exponent M is intended to signify the "merits" of Plaintiff's case. Evidently, apart from the different scaling, e^M plays the same role as our fault factor $Y/(1 - Y)$ in Eq. (3).

[17] Farmer and Pecorino (1999) set $\alpha_P = \alpha_D = \alpha$, thus coming even closer to our formulation in Eq. (3).

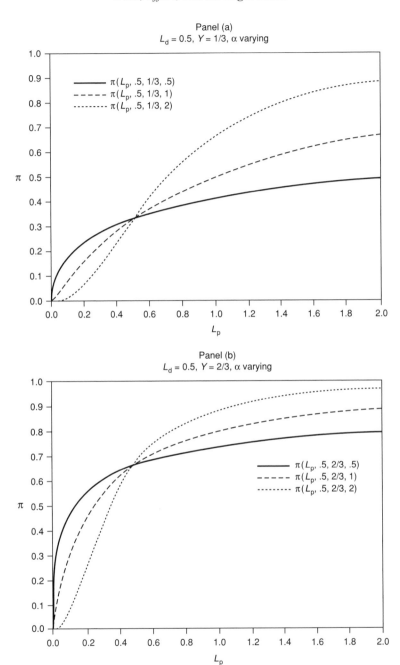

Figure 7.1. Probability of plaintiff success. (a) $L_d = 0.5$, $Y = 1/3$, α varying. (b) $L_d = 0.5$, $Y = 2/3$, α varying.

general upward shift of the whole set of curves: higher levels of fault always raise Plaintiff's prospect of success.

The same parameters affect the marginal products, Plaintiff's $mp_P \equiv d\pi/dL_P$ and Defendant's $mp_D \equiv d(1-\pi)/dL_D \equiv -d\pi/dL_D$. Standard steps lead to

$$mp_D = \frac{\alpha\, L_D^{\alpha-1} L_P^\alpha\, Y(1-Y)}{\left[L_P^\alpha\, Y + L_D^\alpha\,(1-Y)\right]^2}. \tag{5}$$

In Figure 7.2 the two panels show how Defendant's marginal product varies as a function of her effort L_D. In Figure 7.2(a), fault is fixed at the midvalue $Y = 0.5$. For a sufficiently low force exponent ($\alpha \leq 1$), diminishing marginal returns govern throughout, whereas, at higher levels of α, there is an initial range of increasing marginal returns. Figure 7.2(b) illustrates the effect of parametrically changing the degree of fault Y, holding $\alpha = 1$. For a relatively high-fault defendant ($Y = 0.75$), the marginal product of fighting is low to begin with and thereafter declines slowly as effort increases. In contrast, for a relatively low-fault defendant ($Y = 0.25$), mp_D is initially extremely high but falls off rapidly. Intuitively, for such a Defendant relative success approaches 100 percent quite rapidly, so there is not much room for raising it further by increased legal effort.

OPTIMIZATION AND EQUILIBRIUM – NASH–COURNOT SOLUTION

As pointed out in the opening section, most typically in the litigation literature the Nash–Cournot protocol and associated solution concept have been employed. That would be appropriate if the two sides were to make their litigation commitments simultaneously (or, more generally, in ignorance of the opponent's corresponding decision). In contrast, our contention is that the Stackelberg protocol, Plaintiff having the first move, is closer to the normal sequence of decisions.[18] As background, however, this section first takes up Nash–Cournot solutions.[19]

In the symmetrical Nash–Cournot analysis, each side makes a best response to the opponent's chosen level of litigation effort. Under risk-neutrality, the best responses maximize the respective expected values

---

[18] The third protocol mentioned in the first section, Threat-and-promise, is not dealt with here.

[19] But in view of the excellent recent analysis by Farmer and Pecorino (1999), a condensed presentation will suffice.

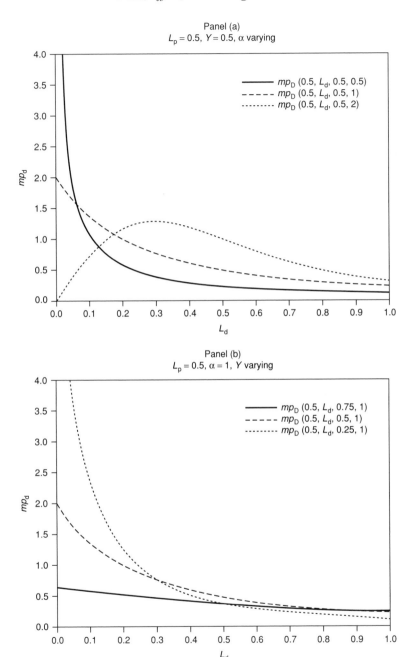

Figure 7.2. Defendant's marginal product. (a) $L_p = 0.5$, $Y = 0.5$, α varying. (b) $L_p = 0.5\,Y$ varying, $\alpha = 1$.

V_P and V_D of the lawsuit:

$$\text{Plaintiff}: \quad \text{Max } V_P \equiv \pi_P J_P - C_P$$
$$(L_P \mid L_D) \tag{6}$$

$$\text{Defendant}: \quad \text{Max } V_D \equiv \pi_D J_D - C_D.$$
$$(L_D \mid L_P)$$

In interior solutions, each litigant would equate his or her value of the marginal product – $J_P \times mp_P$ for Plaintiff and $-J_D \times mp_D$ for Defendant – to the marginal cost γ. This first-order condition generates a pair of Reaction Curves, RC_P and RC_D, whose intersection is the Nash–Cournot solution.[20] (We defer consideration of corner solutions for the moment.)

Owing to the symmetry of the two contenders' situations, it suffices to explore one set of Reaction Curves. Figure 7.3 illustrates Defendant's RC_D, that is, her optimal L_D in response to any given L_P on Plaintiff's part. In Figure 7.3 L_D at first rises in response to increasing Plaintiff effort L_P but then eventually falls off owing to diminishing returns. Figure 7.3(a) shows the effect of varying marginal cost: at higher γ, Defendant's optimal L_D is always smaller for any given L_P. Figure 7.3(b) shows the effect of varying fault Y. When Defendant has a weak case (high Y), her peak L_D occurs when the opponent's L_P is still quite low, whereas with a strong case (low Y) the peak L_D occurs much later. *Explanation:* A Defendant with a weak case will put in a big effort only if Plaintiff is not fighting very hard. But with a strong case it pays a Defendant to remain in contention even when Plaintiff is putting in a big effort.

Making use of Eq. (5) and the corresponding equation for Plaintiff's mp_P, the Nash–Cournot protocol permits an analytic solution for the decision variables L_P and L_D. Given the various assumed symmetries, in particular identical cost functions and equal stakes, the only possible reason for unequal litigation efforts has to do with the level of fault Y. Referring back to Question (1) in our introductory discussion – Does the litigant with the more meritorious case tend to "fight harder"? – the answer is summarized in Proposition 1.

---

[20] Because the mp_i curves are not always monotonic, there may be more than one solution satisfying the first-order conditions. Our simulations show the solution values satisfying both the first-order and second-order conditions for a maximum.

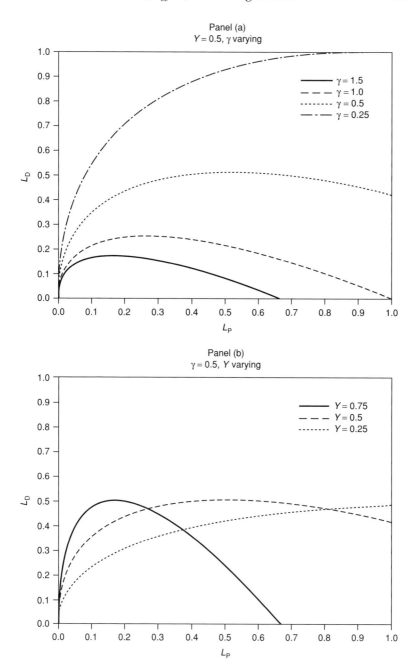

Figure 7.3. Defendant's reaction curves. (a) $Y = 0.5$, γ varying. (b) $\gamma = 0.5$, Y varying.

Proposition 1
Under the Nash–Cournot protocol and our other maintained assumptions, in equilibrium the respective litigation efforts L_P and L_D will always be equal, regardless of the level of fault Y.[21]

It follows immediately from Eq. (4) that:

Corollary:

$$\pi_P = Y.$$

Thus, when the Nash–Cournot protocol is operative, the proportionality property referred to earlier is satisfied at equilibrium.[22]

Using L for the common equilibrium value of $L_P = L_D$, correspondingly simple steps lead to:

Proposition 2
In equilibrium:

$$L = \alpha \frac{J}{\gamma} Y(1 - Y) \qquad (7)^{23}$$

The comparative-static effects of changes in the stakes J, marginal cost γ, force exponent α, and fault Y are clear from the form of Eq. (7). This equation also serves to answer the second question posed in our introductory discussion: Taking the two litigants together, does aggregate

---

[21] The very simple proof starts with the first-order conditions:

$$J \times mp_i = \gamma \quad (i = P, D)$$

Defendant's mp_D is given in Eq. (5), and it is easy to verify that Plaintiff's mp_P is identical except that the exponents of L_P and L_D are interchanged in the numerator. Taking the ratio and cancelling:

$$\frac{mp_P}{mp_D} = \frac{L_D}{L_P}$$

Because in equilibrium both marginal products equal γ/J, it follows that $L_P = L_D$.

[22] Farmer and Pecorino (1999, 275) also arrive at Proposition 1, but their formulation (following Katz 1988) does not lead them to the proportionality result in our Corollary.

[23] In Eq. (5), substituting L for L_P and L_D:

$$mp_D = \frac{\alpha Y(1 - Y)}{L}.$$

Then, solving $J \times mp_D = \gamma$ leads to the equation in the text. Farmer and Pecorino (1999, 275) obtain essentially the same result in their Eq. (6).

effort tend to be greatest when Defendant fault is high, low, or intermediate? From the way $Y(1 - Y)$ enters into Eq. (7), aggregate effort evidently peaks when fault is exactly midway at $Y = 0.5$.[24]

However, recall that we have explored only interior solutions, excluding corner outcomes (in which the optimal L_P, L_D, or both, are zero). One of the main possible sources of corner solutions, fixed costs, has been ruled out for this Nash–Cournot analysis, and we will do the same for the Stackelberg analysis to come. But even with fixed costs set aside, under certain conditions (e.g., if marginal product is rising over an initial range, as occurs for values of the decisiveness parameter $\alpha > 1$), it might be more advantageous for a contestant to concede (set litigation effort at zero) rather than equate the value of the marginal product to marginal cost.[25] Because our analysis of the Nash–Cournot protocol is mainly to provide background for the more novel Stackelberg analysis, and especially because Farmer and Pecorino (1999) have very thoroughly analyzed many of the complexities involved with corner solutions, we will pass over that topic here. But in dealing with the Stackelberg protocol in the sections to come, possible corner solutions will play an important role.[26]

OPTIMIZATION AND EQUILIBRIUM – STACKELBERG SOLUTION

In our version of the Stackelberg protocol, Plaintiff commits first to a level of litigation effort L_P, after which Defendant responds with L_D. Because analytic solutions are not generally obtainable, we will mainly be using numerical simulations to portray the results achieved. One significant extension of the Stackelberg protocol will be considered. Under the standard Stackelberg assumption, the first-mover's commitment is totally irrevocable. But in lawsuits, where Plaintiff is the first-mover, if Defendant ever concedes Plaintiff can usually escape some of the

---

[24] Farmer and Pecorino (1999, 275) obtain an analogous result: effort peaks when, in their notation, $M = 0$.

[25] However, even with an initial range of rising marginal product it is not possible to have a symmetrical corner solution. If side i were to choose $L_i = 0$, then the other contender can win the entire prize by setting its L_j equal to some tiny epsilon. This consideration indicates that, in the absence of interior solutions, a symmetrical Nash equilibrium would involve mixed strategies on both sides.

[26] Farmer and Pecorino (1999) employ the Stackelberg model *only* when the Nash–Cournot protocol would dictate a corner solution. Our contention, in contrast, is that the Stackelberg model might well be appropriate even when the Nash–Cournot analysis leads to an interior solution – if in fact the parties are not making their decisions simultaneously but in sequence.

expenses he would otherwise have been committed to. To capture this idea, our model allows for recovery of some (exogenously fixed) proportion ρ of Plaintiff's initial commitment. (This might correspond to Plaintiff's attorney being paid a retainer up front on the understanding that, if Defendant concedes, some fraction thereof will be refunded.) Of course, setting $\rho = 0$ reduces to the standard Stackelberg model.

Given risk-neutrality, each side will as before simply want to maximize its expected value of the lawsuit. Because Defendant as second-mover knows Plaintiff's L_P, she chooses L_D as a straightforward optimization problem just as in Eq. (6) above.

To allow for corner optima, denote as $\bar{L}_i$ the level of litigant i's effort indicated by the first-order and second-order conditions for an optimum. If at $\bar{L}_D$ Defendant would lose more than J_D by fighting, she does still better by conceding instead.[27] Taking this possibility into account, her best choice of legal effort becomes:

$$L_D = \bar{L}_D, \text{ if } V_D(\bar{L}_D) \geq J_D,$$
$$L_D = 0 \text{ otherwise.} \tag{8}$$

Plaintiff will then choose L_P so as to maximize his value of the lawsuit V_P, subject to Defendant's best response in Eq. (8).

Setting the stakes parameters at $J_P = 1$, $J_D = -1$ and marginal cost at $\gamma = 0.5$, Figure 7.4 illustrates a convenient "base case" in which the force exponent is $\alpha = 1$ and the recovery coefficient is $\rho = 0$. The pictured results are solutions for comparative-static variation of the parameter Y – Defendant fault. In Figure 7.4(a) L_P and L_D are both initially rising functions of Y. Notice that L_D exceeds L_P up to $Y = 0.5$, after which $L_P > L_D$. Thus, in contrast with the Nash–Cournot result obtained above, here the side with a better case fights harder. In absolute terms, once fault exceeds $Y = 0.5$, Defendant effort begins to fall off, whereas Plaintiff effort continues to increase somewhat longer – specifically up to about $Y = 0.67$, at which point Defendant hits her corner solution at $L_D = 0$. From that point on, Plaintiff reduces his L_P as well.[28]

---

[27] Similarly, if $V_P < 0$ at $\bar{L}_P$, Plaintiff would do better not filing the case at all. Under our maintained assumptions, however (in particular, because we rule out fixed costs), it always pays Plaintiff to file within the range of parameter values considered in our simulations.

[28] It might be thought that when Defendant sets $L_D = 0$, Plaintiff should shift to the infinitesimal L_P that would suffice to achieve $\pi_P = 1$. But as Stackelberg leader Plaintiff must move first. He is investing the amount of effort required to *deter* Defendant from choosing a positive L_D.

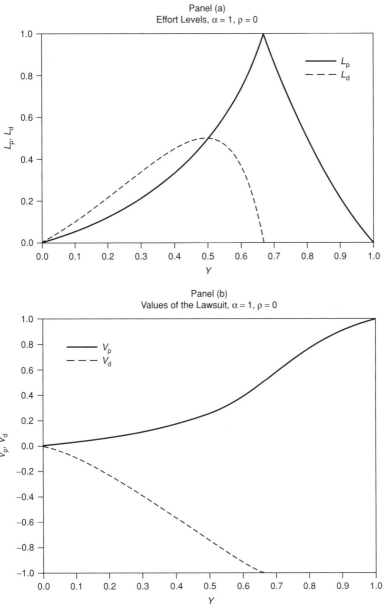

Figure 7.4. Effort levels as functions of fault Y. (a) $\alpha = 1$, $\rho = 0$. (b) Values of the lawsuit as functions of fault Y, $\alpha = 1$, $\rho = 0$.

Figure 7.4(b) shows the corresponding values of the lawsuit V_P and V_D. Notice that when Defendant is at her corner solution (when she chooses $L_D = 0$), is chosen her $V_D = -1$. This is the maximum Defendant can ever lose.

Figure 7.5 illustrates the effect of allowing Plaintiff a nonzero recovery coefficient, specifically $\rho = 0.5$. Because recovery only becomes operative when $L_D = 0$, for low values of fault Y the two panels here are identical with those in Figure 7.4. But when fault reaches about $Y = 0.5$, in Figure 7.5(a) Plaintiff's effort jumps discontinuously to a much higher level ($L_P \approx 2$) – a level that induces Defendant to concede (to set $L_D = 0$). Plaintiff then recovers half the cost of his L_P commitment. Figure 7.5(b) shows the corresponding values of the lawsuit V_P and V_D.

Evidently, when Plaintiff has a good case (when the level of fault Y is high), the prospect of partial recovery benefits him and correspondingly disadvantages Defendant. And if Y is high, with $\rho > 0$, fewer lawsuits will go to trial, because Defendant is more likely to concede. In contrast, when Plaintiff has a poor case (low value of Y), the prospect of recovery will make no difference.

Returning to the zero-recovery ($\rho = 0$) condition, Figure 7.6 shows the effect of a parametric reduction of the force exponent from $\alpha = 1$ to $\alpha = 0.5$. As can be seen, both sides now invest substantially less in litigation effort. Also, L_P being lower, Defendant does not hit her corner solution anywhere within the open interval $0 < Y < 1$, and the respective lawsuit values V_P and V_D are generally higher owing to the reduced fighting efforts.

The lower force exponent makes the outcome for Plaintiff less unfavorable when he has a poor case (low Y) but not quite as advantageous when the case is good (high Y). And similarly for Defendant, the favorable and unfavorable extremes are tempered. *Explanation:* When Plaintiff has a poor case, L_D tends to exceed L_P. But when α is low, the amount of this excess is less; the decisiveness of effort being lower, it does not pay Defendant to overtop Plaintiff's commitment so heavily. Consequently, Plaintiff ends up a bit better off. The reverse of course holds in the range where Plaintiff has a good case (high Y).

Finally, Figure 7.7 illustrates the implications of a high force exponent ($\alpha = 2$) with the recovery coefficient still held at $\rho = 0$. Here the overwhelming feature is how much earlier on the scale of fault, around

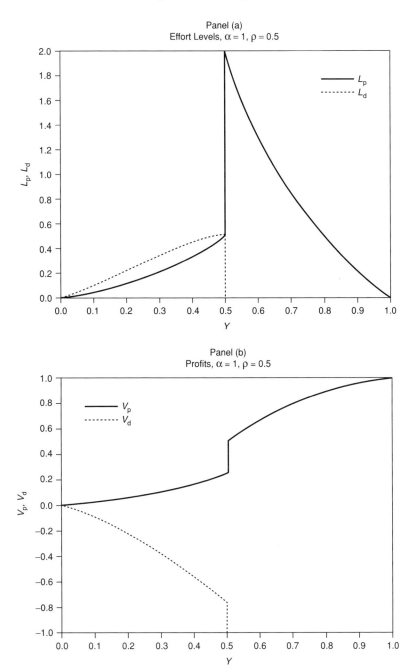

Figure 7.5. Effort levels as function of fault Y. (a) $\alpha = 1$, $\rho = 0.5$. (b) Values of the lawsuit as function of fault Y, $\alpha = 1$, $\rho = 0.5$.

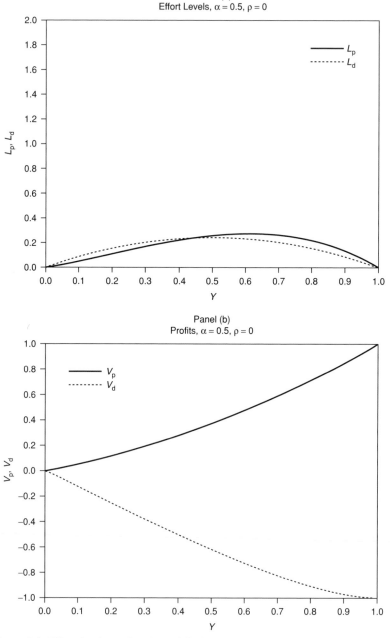

Figure 7.6. Effort levels as function of fault Y (low decisiveness), $\alpha = 0.5$, $\rho = 0$. (b) Values of the lawsuit as function of fault Y (low decisiveness), $\alpha = 0.5$, $\rho = 0$.

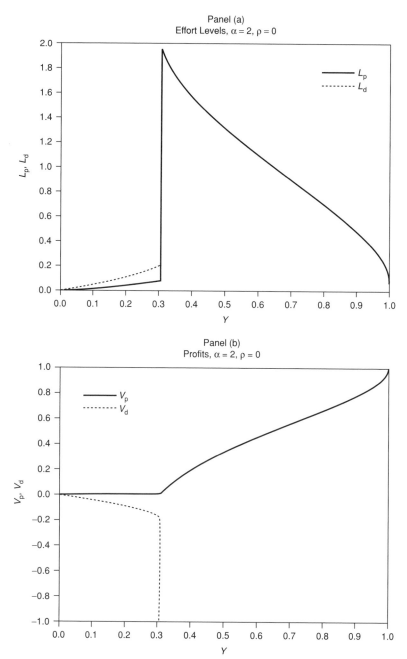

Figure 7.7. Effort levels as function of fault Y (high decisiveness), $\alpha = 2, \rho = 0$.
(b) Values of the lawsuit as function of fault Y (high decisiveness), $\alpha = 2, \rho = 0$.

$Y = 0.3$, the Plaintiff can compel Defendant to concede (to set $L_D = 0$). So long as his case is not too hopeless, by choosing a sufficiently high L_P Plaintiff can make resistance a losing proposition for Defendant. Thus, in this important respect, high α works strongly to the advantage of Plaintiff. Within the interior range, however, the opposite holds: higher α benefits Defendant. Because Defendant moves last, her L_D will exceed Plaintiff's L_P, and the ratio $L_p/L_D > 1$ now has a heavily amplified effect in reducing Plaintiff's success fraction π_P. Also, as a secondary consideration, Plaintiff, knowing this, will tend initially to choose a small L_P, and thus even a high ratio L_D/L_P need not involve Defendant in high legal costs.

'JUSTICE' VERSUS SOCIAL COST

On the subject of normative evaluation, textbooks generally say that social performance ought to be evaluated in terms of efficiency and distributive considerations. Loosely speaking, society wants to maximize the size of the pie and then divide it up fairly.

For calculating the efficiency of legal systems, usually more important than the costs of lawsuits themselves are the effects upon behaviors outside the courtroom. Thinking in terms of auto accidents, a litigation system should aim at offering proper incentives for careful driving. Unfortunately, just what is the appropriate degree of careful driving and how the judicial process might help bring it about are huge and difficult issues. However, arguably at least, the legal standards defining fault Y and determining the stakes J_P and J_D at issue may reflect a social estimate of the rewards and penalties needed.[29] In any case, we can only take account of a limited efficiency criterion here, to wit, minimizing the cost of the litigation process itself.

With respect to distribution effects, mainline economics usually offers no guidance at all. Yet litigation systems clearly employ such a criterion in the concept of 'justice.' What does justice signify? Without attempting to enter into philosophical debate, we will bite the bullet and define a system as 'just' if it meets the condition we have called proportionality:

$$\pi = Y \qquad\qquad (9)$$

According to this criterion, Plaintiff's relative success should equal Defendant's degree of fault. On the comparative-fault interpretation, if

---

[29] For example, to reinforce deterrent effects upon careless driving, the laws may permit or even require punitive damages over and above actual loss suffered.

fault is 50 percent the contenders should split the stakes equally. Or, under the due-care interpretation, each side should have a 50-percent chance of winner-take-all victory.

For the Nash–Cournot protocol, the Corollary to Proposition 1 indicates that at any interior equilibrium the 'justice' condition is exactly met. Because equilibrium litigation efforts are always equal, from Eq. (3) Plaintiff's proportionate success will always equal Defendant's proportionate degree of fault. This does not in general occur in the Stackelberg analysis, and it will be of interest to explore the direction of divergence.

Under the Stackelberg protocol, Figure 7.8(a) shows π_P as a function of Y under various parametric conditions. For any specified set of conditions, the 'justice' condition would be exactly met if the associated curve were to overlie the 45° line exactly (as occurs in interior Nash–Cournot equilibria). As would be expected from our previous discussion of the implications of high versus low values of the force exponent, in Figure 7.8(a) – if one deals for the moment only with the three curves for which the recovery factor is absent ($\rho = 0$) – the curve for $\alpha = 0.5$ lies very close to the 45° line, whereas the curve for $\alpha = 2$ diverges the most.

Note also that $\pi_P(Y)$ almost always lies below the 45° line for $Y < 0.5$ and above the 45° line for $Y > 0.5$. This is consistent with our general result that the side with the better case tends to fight harder. (The only exception in Figure 7.8 is the range of discontinuity along the $\alpha = 2$ curve starting about $Y = 0.3$, the fault level at which Defendant surrenders.) Thus, one might say, under the Stackelberg protocol the reward to merit tends to be excessive. (The effect is smallest for $\alpha = 0.5$, where the decisiveness of legal effort is least.)

Figure 7.8 also illustrates a degree of pro-Plaintiff bias in the range where a high L_P commitment can force a Defendant to surrender entirely. In Figure 7.8(a) this is most evident for the high force exponent ($\alpha = 2$) curve for which Plaintiff can induce surrender starting at a fault level as low as $Y = 0.3$. Allowing for a recovery factor also strongly favors Plaintiff, as can be seen by comparing the with-recovery and without-recovery curves for the intermediate level of the force exponent ($\alpha = 1$).

Figure 7.8(b) indicates that, in line with expectation, aggregate cost $C_P + C_D$ is least when the force exponent is low ($\alpha = 0.5$). Because low α weakens the influence of litigation efforts L_i, neither side wants to invest so heavily in them. Aggregate cost also tends to be minimized at the extremes of very high fault and very low fault, as in the Nash–Cournot

The Dark Side of the Force

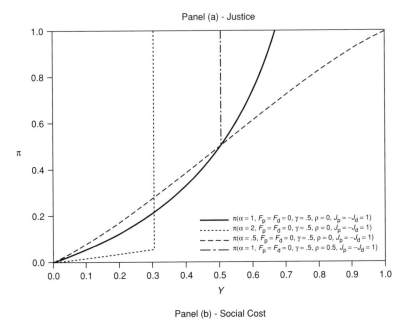

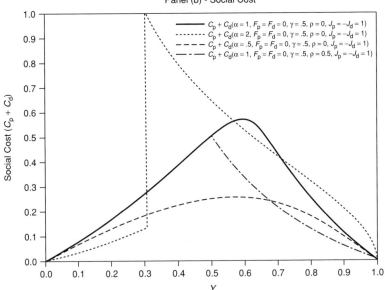

Figure 7.8. (a) Justice. (b) Social cost.

analysis. (A side with a very poor case will not want to spend very much on it. And, knowing this, the opponent need not make a large commitment either.)[30] However, whereas under the Nash–Cournot protocol legal efforts (and therefore aggregate costs) were greatest at $Y = 0.5$ exactly, inspection of Figure 7.8(b) indicates that – if we set aside the curves where maxima occur at points of discontinuity – highest aggregate costs are incurred at fault levels somewhat greater than $Y = 0.5$. This occurs because, although Plaintiff has the more meritorious case for $Y > 0.5$, under the Stackelberg protocol Defendant has the advantage of being able to make a maximizing response to the opponent's commitment. To overcome this handicap, Plaintiff must invest more in litigation effort than would otherwise be ideal. This handicap is attenuated if Plaintiff benefits from a recovery factor $\rho > 0$.

Setting aside the single curve reflecting this recovery factor, a possibly surprising feature of Figure 7.8(b) is that, in the ranges of discontinuity where Defendant concedes, the overall litigation cost does *not* fall immediately to very low levels. In fact, for the $\alpha = 2$ curve, aggregate cost jumps sharply at the discontinuity point. The reason is that in order to induce Defendant to set $L_D = 0$, Plaintiff has to commit to a high L_P.

EMPIRICAL IMPLICATIONS

All sensible models of the litigation process would make many similar predictions: for example that (other things being equal) litigation efforts will be greater the larger the stakes and the smaller the costs; that the size, likelihood, or both of verdicts for the Plaintiff will be positively correlated with Defendant fault; and that the party investing greater litigation effort is more likely to win. However, several testable implications of our analysis are less universal.

Unfortunately, as so often happens, some of the model's parameters and variables are not measurable in any simple direct way. This is notably true of fault[31] Y and of the force exponent α. And the stakes J_i, the costs

[30] This result is analogous to the finding in Priest and Klein (1984) that cases in which true fault is near the legal standard are more likely to be litigated. (We assume that litigation always takes place, but the intensity of litigation effort is greatest toward the middling fault levels that would presumably be in the neighborhood of Priest and Klein's "legal standard.)"

[31] Our model of an imperfect litigation process cannot draw inferences as to fault from data on judgments; in fact, that association would be the central empirical question. However, proxies for fault independent of actual court judgments have been used by, for example, Farber and White (1991) for medical malpractice cases and Wittman (1985) for auto accident liability litigation.

C_i, and the litigation efforts L_i, although somewhat more visible, also raise serious problems of measurement. So we mainly limit ourselves here to describing a few *indirect* implications of the analysis.

Without actually measuring the force exponent α, it is possible to distinguish settings associated with higher or lower α. First, α can plausibly be assumed to be lower for the European inquisitorial system, where lawyers play a distinctly secondary role, than for the Anglo–American adversarial system. And similarly, α is presumably lower in British courts, where judges keep a tight rein upon what litigants and their lawyers are permitted to do, than in American courts. In addition, the force parameter α is presumably lower in courts of appeal, where authentic facts and valid forms of reasoning (the "power of truth") are likely to carry more weight. Finally, because arbitration and other forms of alternative dispute resolution have come into existence mainly owing to complaints about high expenses and long delays in courts of law, it seems at least plausible that they will be characterized by lower α.[32]

For all these comparisons, the model predicts that, other things being equal, litigation efforts L_i on both sides should tend to be smaller in the lower-α type of forum. Although by no means a controlled experiment, a 1989 study by the British accounting firm Tillinghast has reported that gross tort costs are – in terms of percent of GNP – three to nine times as high in the United States as in the other twelve other economically advanced countries surveyed (cited in Litan 1991).[33] A related implication is that appeals should be more prevalent in the United States than the United Kingdom. The presumably higher force exponent α characterizing lower courts means that the "power of truth" is less in those forums, and thus reversible errors are more likely to occur.

Several other possible implications are connected with differences between the Nash–Cournot and Stackelberg protocols. Under Nash–

---

[32] Some consequences of the introduction of lawyers into arbitration proceedings are described in and Block and Stieber (1987) and Ashenfelter and Bloom (1990).

[33] The 1987 Tillinghast estimate cited for the United States is 2.6 percent of GNP, whereas the other countries range from 0.3 percent (Australia) to 0.8 percent (Switzerland). The U.K. figure is 0.5 percent. However, these "gross" tort costs include amounts paid out as judgments, which are of course only transfers. Litan cites Tillinghast as estimating that only about 25 percent of U.S. tort costs are paid out to cover victims' economic losses, leaving some 75 percent of the 2.6 percent U.S. figure as a "net" magnitude comparable to our $C_P + C_D$. Even this reduced U.S. amount remains far higher than the gross tort costs in any of the other countries listed.

Cournot, for interior solutions litigation investments should be greatest for intermediate fault – $Y = 0.5$ – and litigation efforts should always be equal. Under the Stackelberg protocol, aggregate costs $C_P + C_D$ are maximized at somewhat higher fault levels (though in our simulations the shift away from $Y = 0.5$ tended to be only moderate). Also, the Stackelberg protocol requires the first-mover (Plaintiff) to credibly commit. Members of the Plaintiff bar might thus be predicted to be more aggressive and stubborn than attorneys generally.

Finally, one further implication stemming from our Stackelberg simulations is that Plaintiff's ability to commit may often induce even low-fault Defendants to concede. That such "nuisance suits" often succeed is of course widely believed, but a rigorous demonstration would require independent estimates of true fault.[34]

CONCLUDING REMARKS

Although settlement is always Pareto-preferred to litigation, for reasons not modeled here the parties nevertheless fail to come to an agreement. (Or, on an alternative interpretation, the analysis could reflect the hypothetical calculations of litigants as to minimum acceptable terms in an ultimately successful negotiation process.)

Plaintiff's relative success π, under our maintained assumption of risk-neutrality, can be interpreted either as his probability of yes or no victory or as his deterministic share of the stakes at issue, and correspondingly for Defendant's relative success $1 - \pi$. Certain very reasonable criteria lead to a specific form of Litigation Success Function in which the relative degrees of success π, $1 - \pi$ depend upon two ratios: an effort factor L_P/L_D and a fault factor $Y/(1 - Y)$, the former being weighted by a force exponent α. Also involved in the litigants' decisions are the cost functions $C_i(L_i)$, which are here assumed identical for the two sides.

Though starting with the more usual Nash–Cournot solutions for purposes of comparison, we argued that the asymmetrical Stackelberg protocol – Plaintiff moving first – is more appropriate for typical litigation

---

[34] Other authors such as Rosenberg and Shavell (1985) and Bebchuk (1996) have explained successful nuisance suits as being due to differences between the parties in litigation costs or magnitudes of the stakes. Our Stackelberg model, in contrast, predicts that nuisance suits will sometimes be successful even when such differentials are ruled out.

situations. For the Nash–Cournot protocol, on our maintained assumptions as to identical cost functions and numerically equal stakes, and ruling out corner equilibria, we obtained very simple analytic solutions. But the Stackelberg protocol required undertaking a number of simulations. The results were interpreted in terms of two normative criteria: (1) that 'justice' calls for the proportionality property $\pi = Y$, that is, Plaintiff's relative success should equal Defendant's degree of fault, and (2) that the social total of costs, $C_P + C_D$, should be as low as possible. Some of the specific results may be summarized as follows:

1. Under the Nash–Cournot protocol, in any interior equilibrium the litigation efforts L_P and L_D will be equal regardless of the level of fault Y. It follows as a corollary that the 'justice' condition $\pi_P = Y$ is always met; Plaintiff's proportionate success will equal Defendant's proportionate fault. These results almost never exactly hold for the Stackelberg protocol.
2. A low force exponent α always leads to small litigation efforts L_P and L_D. This implies that the 'justice' condition $\pi_P = Y$ is closely approximated, even under the Stackelberg protocol, and also that aggregate costs $C_P + C_D$ are low.
3. The summed costs $C_P + C_D$ are always low toward the extremes of fault (where Y is close to 0 or 1) and are highest for intermediate values of fault.
4. In contrast to the Nash–Cournot result, under the Stackelberg protocol the side with the more meritorious case ordinarily fights harder: merit and effort are complements.
5. For the Stackelberg protocol, again in contrast with Nash–Cournot, "virtue is over-rewarded." Owing to the positive interaction between fault levels and litigation efforts, outcomes tilt disproportionately in favor of the side with the more meritorious case.
6. Under certain conditions the Stackelberg protocol involves a pro-Plaintiff bias: over a range of parameter values, Plaintiff can commit to an L_P sufficiently high to induce even a relatively blameless Defendant to concede.
7. Pro-Plaintiff bias is exacerbated if Plaintiff can recover part of his investment in the event of Defendant surrender.
8. When Defendant concedes, it might have been thought there would at least be a social benefit in the form of reduced litigation cost. This is generally not the case because, in order to induce surrender, Plaintiff must commit to high L_P. Even if partially recovered, the

commitment to high L_P generally outweighs the social cost saving due to lower L_D.

Several possible extensions of the model suggest themselves. It would be particularly important to study protocols of interaction that better approximate the complexities of the negotiation process, for example the Threat-and-promise protocol mentioned earlier. And even within the Nash–Cournot and our version of the Stackelberg protocol it would be of interest to consider the implications of:

1. Varying the absolute and relative magnitudes of the stakes J_P and J_D and the marginal cost parameter γ;
2. Allowing for fixed as well as variable litigation costs;
3. Taking account of the principal-agent interaction between litigant and attorney on each side;
4. Allowing the weights attaching to effort and truth (exponents α and β) to vary independently, that is, not restricting the analysis to Litigation Success Functions meeting the 'proportionality' condition;
5. Weakening the common-knowledge assumptions by, for example, allowing commitment to be interpreted as a (possibly deceptive) signal of the strength of the committing party's case.

Although an exploratory model like ours does not warrant drawing confident inferences about possible legal reforms, at least one normative implication seems very robust, to wit, the adverse implications of a high force exponent α. How might α be reduced? There are at least two possibilities. Judges are presumably more likely than juries to see through the noise of lawyers' clamor, which suggests extending the range of disputes for which nonjury trials are permitted or required. Even for jury trials, the ability of judges to control the proceedings could be expanded. And alternative modes of dispute resolution, particularly those involving self-representation, might in some contexts be encouraged in place of representation by attorneys.

In addition, it is straightforward (as follows from almost all models of litigation) that higher court fees proportioned to the size of the trial (in terms of days spent in the courtroom, pages of documentation, etc.) would reduce the equilibrium levels of litigation efforts. A tax on judgment awards would have similar effects. Of course, cost reduction would have to be weighed against possible adverse effects in terms of the distributive criterion associated with the achievement of 'justice.'

REFERENCES

Ashenfelter, O., and Bloom, D. E. (1990). Lawyers as agents of the devil in a Prisoner's Dilemma game. John M. Olin Program for the Study of Economic Organization and Public Policy, Princeton University.

Aumann, R. J. (1976). Agreeing to disagree. *The Annals of Statistics* 4 (6): 1236–1239.

Bebchuk, L. (1996). A new theory concerning the credibility and success of threats to sue. *Journal of Legal Studies* 25: 1–26.

Binmore, K. (1992). *Fun and Games.* Lexington, MA: D. C. Heath & Co.

Block, R. N., and Stieber, S. (1987). The impact of attorneys and arbitrators on arbitration awards. *Industrial and Labor Relations Review* 40 (4): 543–555.

Braeutigam, R., Owen, B., and Panzar, J. (1984). An economic analysis of alternative fee-shifting systems. *Law and Contemporary Problems* 47 (1): 173–185.

Cooter, R., and Marks, S., with Mnookin, R. (1982). Bargaining in the shadow of the law: A testable model of strategic behavior. *Journal of Legal Studies* 11: 225–251.

Dixit, A. (1987). Strategic behavior in contests. *American Economic Review* 77: 891–898.

Farber, H. S., and White, M. J. (1991). Medical malpractice: An empirical examination of the litigation process. *RAND Journal of Economics* 22: 199–217.

Farmer, A., and Pecorino, P. (1999). Legal expenditures as a rent-seeking game. *Public Choice* 100: 271–288.

Gould, John (1973). The economics of legal conflict. *Journal of Legal Studies* 2: 279–300.

Hause, J. C. (1989). Indemnity, settlement, and litigation, or I'll be suing you. *Journal of Legal Studies* 13: 157–179.

Hirshleifer, J. (1988). The analytics of continuing conflict. *Synthese* 76: 201–234.

Hirshleifer, J. (1989). Conflict and rent-seeking success functions: Ratio vs. difference models of relative success. *Public Choice* 63: 101–112.

Katz, A. (1988). Judicial decisionmaking and litigation expenditure. *International Review of Law and Economics* 8: 127–143.

Kobayashi, B. H., and Lott, J. R., Jr. (1996). In defense of criminal defense expenditures and plea bargaining. *International Review of Law and Economics* 16: 397–416.

Landes, W. M. (1971). An economic analysis of the courts. *Journal of Law and Economics* 11: 61–107.

Litan, R. E. (1991). The liability explosion and American trade performance: Myths and realities. In P. W. Schuck (Ed.), *Tort Law and the Public Interest: Competition, Innovation, and Consumer Welfare.* New York: W. W. Norton.

Priest, G., and Klein, B. (1984). The selection of disputes for litigation. *Journal of Legal Studies* 13:1–55.

Rosenberg, D., and Shavell, S. (1985). A model in which suits are brought for their nuisance value. *International Review of Law and Economics* 5: 3–13.

Schelling, T. C. (1960). *The Strategy of Conflict*. London: Oxford University Press.

Skaperdas, S. (1996). Contest success functions. *Economic Theory* 7: 283–290.

Tabarrok, A., and Helland, E. (1999). Court politics: The political economy of tort awards. *Journal of Law and Economics* 42: 157–188.

Thompson, E. A., and Faith, R. L. (1981). A pure theory of strategic behavior and social institutions. *American Economic Review* 71: 366–380.

Wittman, D. (1985). Is the selection of cases for trial biased? *Journal of Legal Studies* 14: 185–214.

8

Are Equilibrium Strategies Unaffected by Incentives?

Jack Hirshleifer and Eric Rasmusen

Background of this Chapter

This article investigates a rather startling theoretical claim that had appeared in major political science journals. To wit, that a change in penalties can have no effect upon criminals' decisions, or, even more sweepingly, that altering incentives will not modify people's behavior!

Although I suspect this claim may have been put forward somewhat tongue-in-cheek, as a 'devil's advocate' kind of game-theoretic argument, it did receive considerable attention in the political science literature. Despite attempts at refutation by several authors, the source of the error remained subject to dispute. This paper pinpoints where the original argument went astray and provides (I believe) useful insights as to how game theory is properly applied to social policy choices.

I thank Eric Rasmusen for allowing the reprinting of this jointly authored article.

Abstract

In a mixed-strategy Nash equilibrium, changing one player's payoffs affects only the other player's equilibrium strategy mix. This 'Payoff Irrelevance Proposition' (PIP) appears to undercut the main foundations of economic policy analysis since, allegedly, equilibrium behavior will not respond to changes in incentives. We show, in contrast, that: (1) When the policy-maker has the first move in a sequential-move game, the PIP does not hold. (2) Even in a simultaneous-move game, the PIP holds only when the policy space is discrete, and for sufficiently small payoff revisions. Thus, incentives do generally affect behavior in equilibrium.

KEY WORDS • game theory • incentives and payoffs • mixed strategies • the Police Game

* We thank George Tsebelis, Hilmar Doering and two anonymous referees for valuable suggestions and comments. Ting Fang Chiang provided helpful assistance with the diagrams. Eric Rasmusen thanks the Olin Foundation for financial support. [Reprinted from J. Hirshleifer and E. Rasmusen, "Are Equilibrium Strategies Unaffected by Incentives," *Journal of Theoretical Politics*, Vol. 4, No. 3, 353–67, Copyright © 1992, with permission from Sage Publications Ltd.)

At a mixed-strategy Nash equilibrium of a two-person non-cooperative game, changing one player's payoffs affects only the other player's equilibrium strategy mix.[1] A series of papers by George Tsebelis (1989, 1990a,b) uses this well-known theorem to draw startling inferences about policies aimed at deterring undesired actions. Among the assertions are that: (1) in crime control, increasing the size of penalties will not reduce the number of offenses; (2) in international affairs, imposing economic sanctions will not lead the targeted nation to modify its actions; and (3) in hierarchical systems, supervision will not improve the behavior of subordinates. The policy-maker, despite being able to influence the payoffs, supposedly cannot affect the actual equilibrium choice (mixed strategy) of the targeted parties. We call this assertion the Payoff Irrelevance Proposition (PIP).

The PIP, to the extent that it is applicable in some social context, evidently undercuts standard economic reasoning about how behavior might be influenced by policy-makers. In analyzing the trade-off between probability of detection and size of penalties, for example, Becker (1968) and Ehrlich (1973) presumed that incentives do affect the choices of rational criminals; their analyses require drastic revision if sanctions do not affect how criminals behave. More generally, if the PIP applies, the usual arguments for and against policy measures like tariffs, taxes, subsidies and regulations are all gravely weakened.[2] (The PIP does not imply that policy is totally useless, however. If criminal penalties are increased, although the PIP predicts that the amount of crime will not change, the police may be able to economize by investing less effort in enforcing the laws.)

Rising to the challenge, we show that the PIP is applicable only in what are, from a policy point of view, very special and indeed limiting cases. So the foundation of the economic approach to policy – the premise that incentives do affect the equilibrium behavior of impacted parties – is solid after all. While other critics[3] have argued that policy situations ought to be modelled as repeated games or that two-person games are

---

[1] Provided that the changes in the first player's payoffs do not affect the *elements* entering, with non-zero probability, into his strategy mix.

[2] There is a seeming resemblance between the Payoff Irrelevance Proposition and 'rational expectations' theorems (for example, Barro, 1974), on the ineffectiveness of fiscal policy. But the similarity is superficial. The rational expectations argument is that policy is ineffective *because it has been fully anticipated*; strategic uncertainty is not involved. The Payoff Irrelevance Proposition, in contrast, is based upon the nature of the mixed-strategy equilibrium under strategic uncertainty.

[3] See Bianco et al. (1990).

unrealistic, our analysis is based upon the order of moves and the number and range of allowed strategies.

THE POLICE GAME AND THE PAYOFF IRRELEVANCE PROPOSITION (PIP)

In the characteristic situation ("the Police Game") described by Tsebelis, the police are the policy-making authority, choosing between *patrolling* to enforce the law and *not patrolling* (strategies P and NP). The potential criminals choose between *committing* and *not committing* crimes (strategies C and NC). Table 8.1 shows the respective payoffs abstractly. Following Tsebelis's assumptions, for the criminals $c_4 > c_3$ and $c_2 > c_1$, while for the police $p_4 > p_3$ and $p_2 > p_1$. (The criminals will choose C if they know the police are not patrolling, but NC if the police are patrolling; the police will choose P if they anticipate that crimes will be committed, but NP if they do not expect any offenses.) Table 8.2 is a numerical illustration consistent with these specifications, bigger numbers representing more desired outcomes.

This is a discoordination game, with no Nash equilibrium in pure strategies. As the arrows in the tables indicate, one player or the other will want to deviate from any combination of pure strategies. Following standard procedures, the mixed-strategy equilibrium (where θ_c is the probability that criminals use their C strategy and θ_p is similarly the probability that police use their P strategy) is given by:

$$\theta_c = (p_4 - p_3)/(p_2 - p_1 + p_4 - p_3)$$
$$\theta_p = (c_4 - c_3)/(c_2 - c_1 + c_4 - c_3) \tag{1}$$

It is easy to verify that, for the specific numerical matrix of Table 8.2, $\theta_c = \theta_p = 1/2$.

Equations (1) show the Payoff Irrelevance Proposition at work. The probability mixture chosen by the criminals is a function only of the police payoffs, and that of the police is a function only of the criminal

Table 8.1. Payoffs in the 2 × 2 Police Game

		Police	
		NP	*P*
Criminals	*NC*	$c_3, p_4 \quad \leftarrow$	c_2, p_3
		$\downarrow$	$\uparrow$
	C	$c_4, p_1 \quad \rightarrow$	c_1, p_2
		$c_4 > c_3,$	$c_2 > c_1$
		$p_4 > p_3,$	$p_2 > p_1$

**Table 8.2. The 2 × 2 Police Game –
Numerical Example**

		Police		
		NP		*P*
	NC	3, 4	←	2, 3
Criminals		↓		↑
	C	4, 1	→	1, 2

payoffs. If penalties for crime were increased, therefore (that is, if c_1 were reduced), θ_c would remain the same but θ_p would change. The probability of committing crime would be left unchanged in the new equilibrium; only the probability of patrolling would change.

Intuitively, the reasoning underlying the PIP is the following. At the mixed-strategy equilibrium, the criminals are willing to choose randomly between *C* and *NC*, so it must be that their expected payoffs from *C* and *NC* are identical. After a change in the criminals' payoff parameters – say an increase in the penalties for crime – since *C* and *NC* would no longer yield the same expected payoffs, the initial response of the criminals would be to choose one or the other. So, if the overall conditions still dictate a mixed-strategy equilibrium, it must be that the *police* behavior changes suitably. Specifically, the police will change their strategy mix to make the criminal yields from choosing *C* and *NC* once again equal. And in fact the same exact proportions of *C* and *NC* must be restored in order to keep the police indifferent between their strategies *P* and *NP*.

SIMULTANEOUS VERSUS SEQUENTIAL PLAY

The first substantive issue to be addressed is whether the Police Game ought to be modelled as a simultaneous-play or sequential-play game. These terms are to be understood in an informational rather than a calendar-time sense. If the police move first in time but their chosen move remains unknown to the criminals, the two sides are still effectively playing a simultaneous-move game. It is the asymmetric ability of one side to respond to the other's known choice that characterizes the sequential-play game. Put another way, in a simultaneous-move game both sides have to behave strategically, whereas in a sequential-play game only the first-mover is involved in a strategic choice – the last-mover has all the information needed for making a simple optimizing choice.

In the nature of the case, policy-makers like the police in the Police Game have to reason strategically. In deciding whether to allocate more resources to the south end of town than to the north end, the police must rationally ask themselves how potential offenders would respond. If the decision is to patrol the north end more heavily, the criminals, it can usually be anticipated, will become aware of this and shift their depredations to the south end.[4] The criminals, on the other hand, as individually small actors, will normally optimize in a non-strategic way, like "price-takers" in micro-economic theory. An individual offender could not reasonably say to himself, "If I shift to the south end of town, the police will change their planned allocation of effort to come after me there, so I won't derive any advantage." Most criminal activities – from murder and theft to fraud and insider trading – are engaged in by decentralized actors behaving nonstrategically. (As an evident exception, however, if crime were cartelized through a Mafia-type organization, both the police and the criminal planners would have to play strategically.)

Setting this exception aside, the Police Game should normally be analyzed in terms of a sequential-play protocol in which the authorities make the initial move.[5] Applying the usual "subgame-perfect equilibrium" concept, in which the first-mover makes a rational choice on the assumption that the last-mover will also behave rationally, we see in Table 8.1 that the police would choose P if $p_3 > p_1$ and NP if the opposite holds. That is, the police would enforce the law if they prefer the outcome "Patrol, Not commit" over "Not patrol, Commit" – while if their preferences were reversed, they would not patrol. In the specific illustration of Table 8.2 the police have the first of these rankings ($p_3 > p_1$), with the desirable consequence that all crimes are deterred. But given the cost of patrolling this may not always be the case. As an economic choice, the community in general and the police as their representatives routinely tolerate relatively minor crimes such as possession of small amounts of marijuana. For such offenses they may prefer 'Not patrol, Commit' – $p_1 > p_3$.[6]

---

[4] The authorities may well attempt to publicize their actions. One of us recently heard a radio ad of the Chicago Transit Authority advising criminals (truthfully?) that enforcement levels had been increased.

[5] The corresponding assumption, that one firm is the 'leader' in setting output quantity, leads to the (asymmetrical) Stackelberg solution in duopoly theory. The simultaneous-play protocol, that is, the assumption that each firm chooses its output in ignorance of the other's decision, leads to the (symmetrical) Cournot equilibrium.

[6] Instead of the numbers in Table 8.2, for example, the police payoffs could be:

	NP	P
NC	4	1
C	2	3

Here $p_1 = 2$ exceeds $p_3 = 1$.

Whichever way the ordering goes for different types of offenses, the crucial point is that in this sequential-move game[7] the PIP generally fails. Specifically, we saw that under the conditions of Table 8.1 the police would patrol if they prefer the outcome "Patrol, Not commit" over "Not patrol, Commit" – while if their preferences were reversed, they would not enforce the law. It is true, however, that a change in the criminal payoffs will still leave the criminals' optimal responses to the prior police moves unaffected – provided that the payoff changes do not alter the assumed rankings $c_4 > c_3$ and $c_2 > c_1$ which define the Police Game. But if a payoff change were to modify these rankings, as it easily might, then the criminal last-move responses and the police first-move actions will both typically be affected.

This conclusion will be stated as our first listed result:

Result 1

Most often, policy interactions are better modelled as sequential games, not as simultaneous-move games. In such sequential games, the Payoff Irrelevance Proposition does not generally hold. Changes in own-payoffs may affect the choices of the policy-making authorities (who have the first move), of the targeted individuals and groups (who respond non-strategically), or both.

SIMULTANEOUS-PLAY EQUILIBRIUM WITH A STRATEGY CONTINUUM

In the preceding section we indicated that policy-makers normally will be playing a sequential-move rather than a simultaneous-move game with the affected parties. There are, however, a number of important exceptions, among them: (1) if the targeted party or parties are as much of a centrally organized entity as the policy-makers themselves, and (2) if the policy-makers, although having the option of the first move, find it

---

[7] Tsebelis (1989: 83) concedes that, in the Police Game, it is "more realistic" to assume that the police have the first move, so that the conditions for the sequential equilibrium apply. But he incorrectly asserts that the sequential solution will be the *same* as the solution to the simultaneous-play game. His reasoning appears to be based on the premise that the police, although having the first move, would find it advisable to keep their strategy choice secret. This would in effect throw the parties back into the simultaneous-move game, with the same solution as before. But secrecy (giving up the first move) is not *generally* more profitable than making the first move and openly announcing it. In the numerical illustration of Table 8.2, for example, the best sequential play leads to the outcome "Patrol, Not commit" with a payoff to the police of $p_3 = 3$. The simultaneous-play equilibrium $\theta_c = \theta_p = 1/2$ achievable under secrecy has a payoff to the police of only 2 1/2. Thus, in this case, the police would be unwise to sacrifice the advantage of the first move.

more advantageous to act secretly. In this section we are postulating that one or the other of these exceptions applies, so that the simultaneous-move protocol is indeed applicable. Even so, we shall see, the PIP has only a limited range of applicability.

A natural way to approach the simultaneous-move Police Game is to postulate that both police and criminals can choose over a strategy continuum. Instead of the restriction to the discrete options C versus NC on the one side and P versus NP on the other, let criminals choose crime level $0 \leq C \leq 1$ while the police simultaneously choose patrolling level $0 \leq P \leq 1$.

A standard method of solution for games with continuous strategy spaces is to determine the Reaction Curves showing each side's optimal action as a function of the other's choice. The intersection of the Reaction Curves represents the simultaneous-play Nash–Cournot equilibrium. Some simple examples are illuminating.

Example 1: Suppose the payoff functions, for the criminals and police respectively, are:

$$V_c = \alpha_c C - \beta_c C^2/2 - \gamma_c P$$
$$V_p = \alpha_p P - \beta_p P^2/2 - \gamma_p C \qquad (2)$$

where the Greek letters signify positive parameters. Here each side's payoff is a quadratic function of its own level of activity and a negative-linear function of the opponent's level of activity.

The implied Reaction Curves are:[8]

$$RC_c : C = \alpha_c/\beta_c$$
$$RC_p : P = \alpha_p/\beta_p \qquad (3)$$

In this first example, even though the payoff V_c varies negatively with P, the chosen level of crime C is independent of P. Instead, it responds only to the criminals' own payoffs: C increases as the criminals' 'gain parameter' α_c rises and decreases as their 'diminishing returns parameter' β_c rises. Similarly, the patrolling effort P will depend only upon the police 'gain parameter' α_p and 'diminishing returns parameter' β_p. As shown in Figure 8.1, the criminals' Reaction Curve RC_c is the solid horizontal line at $C = \alpha_c/\beta_c$, while the police Reaction Curve RC_p is a vertical line at $P = \alpha_p \beta_p$. The equilibrium is of course at the intersection of the

---

[8] Found by setting the first derivatives $\partial V_c/\partial C$ and $\partial V_p/\partial P$ equal to zero and solving for C and P.

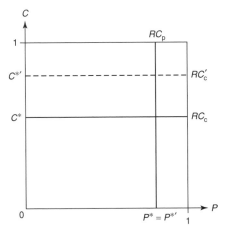

Figure 8.1. Simultaneous-move police game with strategy continuum: effect of increased criminal payoffs when equilibrium strategy choices depend upon own payoff parameters only.

two Reaction Curves, the solution being:

$$C^* = \alpha_c/\beta_c \quad \text{and} \quad P^* = \alpha_p/\beta_p \qquad (4)$$

Now we ask, what if the criminals' payoff parameters were to change? The dashed line in Figure 8.1 shows how the criminals' Reaction Curve RC_c shifts in response to an increase in the ratio α_c/β_c – which of course could be the consequence either of a rise in the 'gain parameter' α_c or a fall in the 'diminishing returns parameter' β_c. Evidently, the criminals' Reaction Curve shifts upward so that the new equilibrium involves a larger amount of criminal activity with unchanged police activity. While this is a special case, it demonstrates that, to the exact contrary of the PIP, in the simultaneous-play game it is perfectly possible to have each side's optimal choice depend solely upon its own payoff parameters and not at all upon the opponents' payoffs.[9]

Nevertheless, that the PIP *might* possibly hold is illustrated by a second example.

Example 2: Suppose the payoff functions, for the criminals and police respectively, are instead:

$$V_c = (\alpha_c - \beta_c P)C - \gamma_c P$$
$$V_p = (-\alpha_p + \beta_p C)P - \gamma_p C \qquad (5)$$

---

[9] The criminals are maximizing V_c with respect to C while the police are maximizing V_p with respect to P. It is easy to see that the first derivative $\partial V_c/\partial C$ does not depend upon P, and similarly $\partial V_p/\partial P$ does not depend upon C.

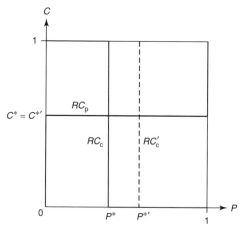

Figure 8.2. Simultaneous-move police game with strategy continuum: effect of increased criminal payoffs when equilibrium strategy choices depend upon opponent's payoff parameters only.

with $\gamma_p > \beta_p$ and all the parameters positive as before. Maximizing each payoff with respect to its control variable leads to the solution:

$$C^* = \alpha_p/\beta_p \quad \text{and} \quad P^* = \alpha_c/\beta_c \qquad (6)$$

Here the equilibrium strategy for each side depends only upon the *opponent's* payoff parameters. Specifically, as shown in Figure 8.2, a rise in α_c or a fall in β_c leads only to an increase in police activity P^*.

It is of interest to remark on several aspects of this second example: (i) The PIP applies here as a pure-strategy equilibrium in a continuous strategy space, rather than as a mixed-strategy equilibrium in a discrete strategy space. (ii) The payoff functions have the undesirable feature of failing to display diminishing returns. The marginal return to police activity, for example, varies with C but remains constant as P increases. (iii) The implications for the respective Reaction Curves, as pictured in Figure 8.2, are rather strange. The police, for example, will respond with $P = 0$ to any $C < C^*$ and with $P = 1$ to any $C > C^*$. So a change in crime level C will, over most of its range, lead to no response at all, but at the critical point $C = \alpha_p/\beta_p$ the tiniest change in C would trigger a total swing in police activity toward one extreme or the other. So the two Reaction Curves would each be a discontinuous step-function, the intersection being at the respective points of discontinuity.

We have seen that it is possible to have payoff functions in which the equilibrium levels of activity depend only on the player's own payoff

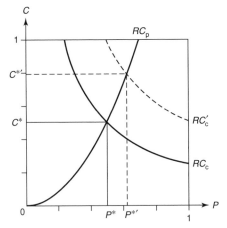

Figure 8.3. Simultaneous-move police game with strategy continuum: effect of increased criminal Payoffs when equilibrium strategy choices depend on both sides' payoff parameters.

parameters (Example 1); or, less plausibly, only upon the opponent's payoff parameters (Example 2). The general and most reasonable case, of course, is where the equilibrium depends upon the payoff parameters *of both sides*. Typically, the Reaction Curves will be sloping as illustrated in Figure 8.3. Consistent with the spirit of the Police Game, the criminals' Reaction Curve RC_c would be negatively sloped: as the police increase patrolling, the criminals prefer a lower level of criminal activity. And, correspondingly, the police Reaction Curve RC_p would be positively sloped: as offenders increase C, the police would prefer a higher level of patrolling.

Example 3: The illustration in Figure 8.3 is based upon the payoff functions:

$$V_c = \alpha_c C - \beta_c P C^2 / 2$$
$$V_p = -\alpha_p P - \beta_p C / P \tag{7}$$

where all the constants are positive as before.

These payoff functions retain the desirable property that the marginal returns, to both the criminals' efforts C and the police efforts P, are always diminishing. The implied Reaction Curves are:

$$RC_c : C = \alpha_c / (\beta_c P)$$
$$RC_p : P = (\beta_p C / \alpha_p)^{1/2} \tag{8}$$

The equilibrium levels of C and P, obtained by solving equations (8) simultaneously, are:

$$C^* = \left(\alpha_c^2 \alpha_p / \beta_c^2 \beta_p\right)^{1/3}$$
$$P^* = (\alpha_c \beta_p / \alpha_p \beta_c)^{1/3} \tag{9}$$

The solid curves in Figure 8.3 correspond to the parameter values $(\alpha_c, \beta_c, \alpha_p, \beta_p) = (1, 4, 2, 1)$. The equilibrium strategy-pair, in pure strategies of course, is then $C^* = P^* = 1/2$. That each party's equilibrium choice does depend upon its own as well as upon the other's payoff parameters is evident from the form of equations (9). If, for example, the criminal 'gain parameter' α_c rises from 1 to 2, the criminals' Reaction Curve RC_c shifts upward as illustrated by the dashed curve in the diagram. At the new solution, $(C^*, P^*) = (.7937, .6300)$. Thus, an increase in criminal payoffs has led to a rise in both the amount of crime and the amount of patrolling. Summarizing:

Result 2

In simultaneous-move games, if the players have continuous strategy spaces there will typically be a pure-strategy equilibrium for which the Payoff Irrelevance Proposition does not generally hold.[10]

The paradoxical PIP result, we can now see, is essentially an artifact due to lumpiness. Rational choice involves trade-offs, and lumpiness of the options available reduces what can be done in the way of trade-offs. Suppose a consumer initially finds apples too expensive to buy, but then the price falls. If the choice is between buying 50 apples or none, such a consumer may still take none – whereas, offered the opportunity of buying single apples, he might buy two or three instead. Similarly, a choice between a discrete C or NC is less susceptible to the influence of payoff changes than a choice over the entire range of options in between.

---

[10] A technical qualification: the Reaction Curves must actually intersect in the interior of the strategy space. If they do not, there may be a corner solution in which players choose extreme behavior that may not alter when parameters change. If electrocuting burglars reduces burglary to zero, then increasing the penalty to boiling in oil will have no effect. Sufficient conditions for an interior intersection are that the strategy sets be compact and convex, and that a player's payoff be quasi-concave in his own strategy (see Rasmusen 1989: 124–5).

SIMULTANEOUS-PLAY EQUILIBRIUM
WITH DISCRETE STRATEGIES

Still under the simultaneous-play protocol, suppose now that while the underlying situation remains the continuous-strategy space as in the figures, for some reason only selected discrete options and not the entire continuum are available to the parties. As can be seen, the case for the PIP is strongest here. It is convenient to state the result first, with the development to follow.

Result 3

The Payoff Irrelevance Proposition may or may not hold for simultaneous-move games if the strategy space is discrete. For it to hold, the payoff changes must be 'sufficiently small' (in a sense to be made precise below).

Let equations (7) continue to represent the payoff functions, as in our previous illustration. But now suppose that the parties can no longer choose C and P over the continuum. Instead, C for the criminals and P for the police must be chosen from the set $\{.2, .4, .6, .8, 1\}$. As can be seen in Figure 8.3, the strategy options .4 and .6 for each side are the 'immediate neighbors' bracketing the (no longer available) continuous-strategy equilibrium choices $C^* = .5 = P^*$. It is a plausible procedure, valid here though unfortunately not universally correct, to consider only these immediate neighbors as candidates for a possible mixed-strategy equilibrium.[11]

Table 8.3 illustrates the entire range of payoffs, while Table 8.4 is a condensation showing only the immediate-neighbor options: $C \in \{.4, .6\}$ and $P \in \{.4, .6\}$.[12] There is no pure-strategy equilibrium for this game. Using equations (1) to find the equilibrium mix of the two

---

[11] More extreme pure strategies might enter into a mixed-strategy equilibrium, even conceivably in place of a 'neighboring' strategy, since the payoff functions might take on any of a wide variety of forms. The payoff functions need not necessarily be monotonic or even bitonic in the C and P variables, and the interaction can be formulated in many different ways.

[12] Table 8.4 is an allowable condensation, since in Table 8.3 all but the .4 and .6 row and column strategies can be ruled out by iterated strict dominance. Specifically: (1) the $P = 1$ and $P = .2$ columns can be deleted as they are dominated by $P = .8$ and $P = .4$ respectively; (2) then the $C = .2$ row is dominated by $C = .4$, and $C = .8$ and $C = 1$ are both dominated by $C = .6$; (3) and finally, the $P = .8$ column is then dominated by $P = .6$. This process leaves only the .4 and .6 strategies on each side.

Table 8.3. The Police Game with Five Discrete Strategies

		Police				
		.2	.4	.6	.8	1
Criminals	.2	.184, −1.4	.168, −1.3	.152, −1.533	.136, −1.85	.12, −2.2
	.4	.336, −2.4	.272, −1.8	.208, −1.867	.144, −2.1	.08, −2.4
	.6	.456, −3.4	.312, −2.3	.168, −2.2	.024, −2.35	−.12, −2.6
	.8	.544, −4.4	.288, −2.8	.032, −2.533	−.244, −2.6	−.48, −2.8
	1	.6, −5.4	.2, −3.3	−.2, −2.867	−.6, −2.85	− 1, −3

**Table 8.4. Strategies of Table 8.3 That are Used
in Equilibrium**

		Police	
		.4	.6
Criminals	.4	.272, −1.8	.208, −1.867
	.6	.312, −2.3	.168, −2.2

**Table 8.5. A Truncated Strategy Set
from Table 8.3**

		Police	
		.4	1
Criminals	.4	.272, −1.8	.08, −2.4
	1	.2, −3.3	−1, −3

neighboring strategies, over the strategy sets $\{.2, .4, .6, .8, 1\}$ the equilibrium mixtures are: for the criminals, $\theta_c = (0, .6, .4, 0, 0)$ and for the police $\theta_p = (0, .5, .5, 0, 0)$.

Thus we have shown by construction that a mixed-strategy equilibrium is *possible* given a discrete strategy space for the Police Game. That a mixed-strategy outcome is not *inevitable* is illustrated in Table 8.5. Here the available strategy options are, by assumption, .4 and 1.0 on each side.[13] In Table 8.5, $C^* = P^* = .4$ is a *pure-strategy* equilibrium.

[13] Whereas Table 8.4 was a condensation of the underlying Table 8.3 showing the strategies entering into the equilibrium mixture on each side, Table 8.5 is quite different. It represents a quite different game where, by assumption, all but the two specified strategies on each side have been disallowed.

Table 8.6. Table 8.3 with Increased Criminal Gain Parameter

		Police				
		.2	.4	.6	.8	1
Criminals	.2	−.384, −1.4	.368, −1.3	.352, −1.533	.336, −1.85	.32, −2.2
	.4	.736, −2.4	.672, −1.8	.608, −1.867	.544, −2.1	.48, −2.4
	.6	1.056, −3.4	.912, −2.3	.768, −2.2	.624, −2.35	.48, −2.6
	.8	1.344, −4.4	1.088, −2.8	.832, −2.533	.576, −2.6	.32, −2.8
	1	1.6, −5.4	1.2, −3.3	.8, −2.867	.4, −2.85	0, −3

These results suggest that there is likely to be a pure-strategy equilibrium when the available choices are asymmetrically placed – one of the strategy-pairs being located close to and the others far away from the pure-strategy equilibrium choices of the underlying continuum. Conversely, when the available choices are more or less evenly distant from the equilibrium of the continuous game, a mixed-strategy equilibrium is likely.[14]

Finally, let us return to the claim that the PIP holds at least within the window of conditions leading to mixed-strategy equilibria. Intuition suggests that if the equilibrium strategy mixture is not to be affected, only payoff changes within a limited range are allowable. More specifically, our previous analysis suggests that for such insensitivity to hold, the payoff parameter variations must be small enough so as not to cause a shift either to a pure-strategy equilibrium or to a mixed equilibrium involving different strategy elements.

Looking at Figure 8.3, the continuous-strategy intersection involving the dashed RC_C curve was generated by a change in the criminals' gain parameter from $\alpha_c = 1$ to $\alpha_c = 2$. Is this change 'sufficiently small' for insensitivity to hold in the discrete-strategy game described above, where the options on each side ranged from .2 to 1 in steps of .2 each? That is, will the criminals' optimal strategy remain the mixture of $C = .4$ and $C = .6$ with probabilities .6 and .4 respectively? Notice that the intersection involving the new RC_C curve no longer lies between .4 and .6, which may lead us to suspect that this parameter change is not 'sufficiently small' to leave the criminals' optimum mix unaffected. And in fact, Table 8.6 – like Table 8.3 but calculated in terms of the criminal 'gain parameter' $\alpha_c = 2$ instead of $\alpha_c = 1$ – reveals that $(C^*, P^*) =$

---

[14] This is only a tendency rather than a strict rule, since (as previously noted) distance as measured in the strategy space need not correlate well with distance in terms of the payoffs.

(.8, .6) is now a pure-strategy equilibrium. That this strategy-pair is a pure-strategy solution is not surprising since it is very close to (.7937, .6300), which was the equilibrium of the corresponding *continuous-strategy* game using the changed α_c parameter.

Thus, we have verified Result 3 by example. In particular, we have shown that, with a discrete strategy space, there may or may not be a mixed-strategy equilibrium. If there is a mixed-strategy equilibrium, then the PIP will be valid only for payoff changes that are 'sufficiently small' in the sense of not affecting the strategies entering into the equilibrium mixture.

CONCLUSION

In discrete two-strategy simultaneous-move games with a mixed-strategy equilibrium, a change in one player's payoffs affects only the other player's equilibrium mix. We call this the PIP. It has been alleged that the PIP vitiates the economic arguments for or against policy initiatives; although policy-makers can alter the payoffs received from alternative strategies, changes in payoffs allegedly do not modify the equilibrium strategy mix of the affected parties. In particular, in the Police Game an increase in penalties will assertedly not affect the criminals' mix between committing and not committing crimes.

In this paper we showed that:

1. Policy-making is ordinarily better modelled not in terms of a simultaneous-move protocol but as a sequential-move game in which the authorities have the first move. Using the standard subgame-perfect equilibrium concept for sequential-move games, the PIP will not generally apply. Changes in incentives on either side will ordinarily affect the equilibrium behavior of the policy-makers themselves and of the individuals or groups they are trying to influence.

2. Even in the simultaneous-move game, if the strategy space is a continuum there will typically be a pure-strategy Nash equilibrium in which changes in payoffs affect the behavior of both sides. Only in very special cases will the PIP hold.

3. The case for the PIP is strongest when, in the simultaneous-move game, the strategy space consists of discrete options. If choices are sufficiently lumpy, a game may have a mixed-strategy equilibrium so that the PIP does apply over a certain range. Specifically, it holds only for payoff changes that are 'sufficiently small' in the sense of not shifting the strategy elements entering into the equilibrium.

We conclude that the PIP is only rarely applicable in actual policy-making situations. Incentives do, almost always, affect behavior in equilibrium.

REFERENCES

Barro, R. J. (1974) "Are Government Bonds Net Wealth?," *Journal of Political Economy* 82:1095–117.

Becker, G. S. (1968) "Crime and Punishment: An Economic Approach," *Journal of Political Economy* 76:169–217.

Bianco, W., P. Ordeshook and G. Tsebelis (1990) "Crime and Punishment: Are One-Shot Two-Person Games Enough?" *American Political Science Review* 84:569–86.

Ehrlich, I. (1973) "Participation in Illegitimate Activities: A Theoretical and Empirical Investigation," *Journal of Political Economy* 81:521–65.

Rasmusen, E. (1989) *Games and Information*. Oxford: Basil Blackwell.

Tsebelis, G. (1989) "The Abuse of Probability in Political Analysis: The Robinson Crusoe Fallacy," *American Political Science Review* 83:77–91.

Tsebelis, G. (1990a) "Are Sanctions Effective?" *Journal of Conflict Resolution* 34:3–28.

Tsebelis, G. (1990b) "Penalty Has No Impact on Crime: A Game-Theoretic Analysis," *Rationality and Society* 2:255–86.

PART TWO

EVOLUTIONARY APPROACHES TO CONFLICT
AND ITS RESOLUTION

9

Evolutionary Models in Economics and Law

Cooperation versus Conflict Strategies

Jack Hirshleifer

Background of this Chapter

This article is the only one in the volume for which the original essay has not been reproduced in full. Only a relatively brief extract has been selected for reprinting.

The full article addressed a huge topic: the interface among the three major fields of economics, evolutionary biology, and law. The essay served as the centerpiece of a day-long seminar on evolutionary theory in law and economics held in May 1980 at the Law and Economics Center at the University of Miami under the leadership of Henry S. Manne. Comments on the presentation were provided by several distinguished discussants: Charles Fried, Robert S. Summers, Gordon Tullock, and Kenneth J. Arrow. The full article and the reviewers' comments were published together in the journal *Research in Law and Economics (RLE)* along with my reply and a transcript of the ensuing exchanges and debates among the conference participants (Rubin, Paul H., ed. (1982), "Evolutionary Models in Economics and Law," *Research in Law and Economics,* 4). That issue of the *RLE* also contains a valuable preface by Richard O. Zerbe, Jr., and an introduction by Paul H. Rubin.

Fortunately, there is considerable overlap between the sections of the article not reproduced here and topics addressed elsewhere in this volume. The brief extract that is reproduced, comprising the introductory sections of the paper, raises fundamental issues about the nature of evolution, of economic efficiency, and of law and social order.

The analysis offered in the original essay was discussed in a later article by E. Donald Elliott (1985, "The Evolutionary Tradition in Jurisprudence," *Columbia Law Review,* 85) along with several other evolutionary approaches to the law.

Attempting to address the combined topics of economics, law, and evolution in a single paper is hubris indeed. All the more so, as I will

Reprinted from J. Hirshleifer, "Evolutionary Models in Economics and Law: Cooperation versus Conflict Strategies," *Research in Law and Economics,* Vol. 4, 1–60, Copyright © 1982, with permission from Elsevier Science.

be adopting very broad interpretations of what we might mean by both economics and law. Economics, as understood here, is *not* limited to selfish, rational "economic man" interacting with his fellows only through impersonal market relationships. For my purposes, all human motivations and interactions constitute the subject matter of economics, so long as they respond to the pervasive fact of resource scarcity. As for law, I shall take that term as covering essentially all modes of *coercive social control* of behavior, thus including much of what might conventionally be considered under the headings of politics or sociology. However, the evolutionary standpoint sets some bound upon the field of discussion. Also, I will be considering only one aspect of interpersonal interactions – though that is perhaps the most important of all – to wit, the determinants of *cooperation versus conflict* in human affairs.

ECONO-LEGAL THINKING AND THE MISSING TREND TOWARD HARMONY

In recent years there has been growing intellectual interchange between legal and economic scholars. The dominant influence, it seems fair to say, has been economics, in the sense that economic propositions have been borrowed or applied to provide new or more fundamental explanations of certain legal phenomena.[1] The influential economic ideas in question, together with their seeming legal implications, can be stated rather baldly (shorn of needed qualifications and possible adornments) as follows:

1. *Smith's Theorem* (11), Book I, ch. 2. Voluntary exchange is mutually advantageous for participants. Implication: The law ought, presumptively at least, to promote trade – negatively, by removing artificial legal barriers, affirmatively, by facilitating and enforcing private exchange agreements.

2. *Coase's Theorem* (4). All available mutually advantageous exchanges will be voluntarily undertaken by the parties involved. Even where individuals impose what are said to be "external" injuries upon others, as when an upstream user of water degrades the quality of the flow to a downstream user, a resolution of the conflict will tend to take place through the exchange process. This conclusion does not depend upon the initial assignment of property rights, provided the entitlements are well defined. If the upstream user has the legal right to degrade quality, the downstream

---

[1] Professionals in both fields, most notably the double-threat economist-legist Posner [see especially (9)], have contributed to these developments.

party can offer him compensation for not doing so. If on the other hand the downstream user has a legal right to unimpaired quality, the upstream party can purchase the other's tolerance of damage. Either way, the upstream use will continue to take place if and only if it can pay its way in comparison with the downstream damage. Given such an assignment of property rights, and if there are no transaction costs, the final outcome will be *efficient* (in a sense to be made more precise below). Implication: In addition to removing artificial barriers to transactions, the law ought to assign well-defined property rights to all resources of economic value. And if transaction costs (barriers to exchange) are absent, the law need not otherwise concern itself with regulating external damage.

3. *Posner's Theorem* (9).[2] Where unavoidable transaction costs (that is, barriers other than those due to the law itself) preclude achievement of a fully efficient result by private negotiation, some particular initial assignments of property rights may constitute or lead to more nearly efficient outcomes than others. Implication: Recognizing the presence of unavoidable transaction costs, the law ought to choose the most efficient of the possible assignments of property rights.

I have in each case stated the seeming legal implication in *normative* terms, the operative phrase being: "The law ought to. . . ." An alternative *positive* interpretation would be indicated by the assertion: "The law will in fact tend to. . . ." In its normative version, this entire line of econo-legal thinking might be summarized: "Market transactions among individuals operate in the direction of economic efficiency, and the law *ought to* aid and where necessary supplement this trend." The positive version would be: "Market interactions tend toward economic efficiency, and the law *will in fact tend to* assist and supplement this tendency."

On either interpretation, a generally Panglossian aura surrounds the entire discussion. In the positive version, it would seem, we scholars need only chronicle the unfolding harmonious progress of law and economy toward the best (most efficient) of all possible worlds. The normative version of the argument, while it suggests some doubt as to the matter (why else concern ourselves with what *ought* to be done?), has the offsetting advantage of providing a more muscular role for savants like us. Whatever blemishes may mar its present complexion, the law can

---

[2] See also Calabresi (3).

be improved, and we are the ones who know how to do so! Indeed, it seems reasonable to suppose, as scholarly understanding advances and as education of the public broadens and deepens over time, the various mistaken ideas that have in the past interfered with sound econo-legal thinking should have decreasing sway.

I have injected a note of sarcasm, for we know that there must be something seriously wrong with this picture. On the most fundamental matter, the rule of law has always fallen short of universal coverage of mankind. The potential mutual gains from cooperation have not abolished war, crime, or politics. Turning to less cataclysmic though still momentous issues, the advanced systems of law that are the proud possessions of Western nations have in fact been changing for at least a century in directions that are on the whole pernicious from the viewpoint of economic efficiency. Rather than being increasingly supportive of property and exchange, the trend has clearly been in the direction of harassment, increasing uncertainty, and even confiscation. Parallel developments taking place in other aspects of life – rising crime rates, increasingly grave race-class conflicts, growing political polarization – suggest that these pernicious legal trends are due not simply to errors in the design of laws, but rather to deeper social realities. The forces promoting harmonious reciprocal exchanges among individuals and leading toward legal structures supporting and facilitating such exchanges are evidently weaker than recent econo-legal thinking might have led us to suppose. The central thrust of this paper will be an attempt to see how far this unfortunate fact is explained by evolutionary theory.

Evolutionary ideas are relevant to our question of the scope of harmonious interaction among men in two main ways. *First*, regarding the nature of man. What capacities for cooperation or for conflict lie innate within members of the human species, either as universal tendencies of life or as the particular results of the evolution of mankind? In short, are we humans essentially fighters or lovers? *Second*, regarding social institutions. Whatever the intrinsic pattern of individual human drives may be, the overall outcome is also a function of the social constraints regulating personal interactions. Adam Smith's [(11), Book IV, ch. 2] principle of the Invisible Hand has shown us how even selfish individuals may be led by appropriate social institutions to cooperate to their mutual advantage. Conversely, even selfless generosity may sometimes be subverted for lack of supportive social arrangements. The first element, our innate make-up, constitutes a background which has been largely constant over the evolutionarily brief span represented by the historical experience of mankind. Furthermore, it is also largely uni-form over the human species. The second element, the institutional or cultural foreground, is in contrast highly volatile over historical time and amazingly varied among different human societies. Both elements are essential for understanding the prospects for and limits upon cooperative versus conflictual interactions among men.

EFFICIENCY

It is time to address the problem of "efficiency," to ask whether this concept is robust enough to bear the weight placed upon it in recent econo-legal thinking.

The root idea is *Pareto-preference*. A social configuration Γ is said to be Pareto-preferred to another social configuration Ω if no affected member of the society prefers Ω to Γ, and at least one member actually prefers Γ. (As we shall see, the proper interpretation to be placed upon "affected" raises difficulties, but let us set this problem aside for the moment.) Any *voluntary transaction*, if the participants can be assumed to be rational, leads to a Pareto-preferred outcome. In particular, since an act of voluntary exchange is mutually beneficial (the Smith Theorem), its outcome is Pareto-preferred to the pre-exchange situation – provided no other members of the society are adversely "affected" thereby. Further-more, rational decision makers will eventually execute *all* mutually ad-vantageous transactions available to them. The final outcome, when there are no further opportunities for mutual gain, is called *Pareto-efficient*. Note that only a small subset of the outcomes that are Pareto-preferred to some initial situation are Pareto-efficient (that is, leave no room for further improvement in the way of mutual gain). Conversely, there will generally be Pareto-*efficient* configurations that are not Pareto-*preferred* to some particular initial situation. That is, there may be outcomes which could not be improved upon (in terms of mutual gain) once arrived at, but which are not achievable by mutually advantageous transactions from a given specified starting point. Nevertheless, the Coase Theorem asserts, any starting point will eventually lead to *some* Pareto-efficient outcome – if existence of property rights and absence of transaction costs permit unrestricted exchange.

Practically all important social issues, however, involve comparisons among situations that cannot be ranked by Pareto-preference consider-ations. That is, almost always, social changes make some parties better off but others worse off. This even holds for "voluntary" exchange, since in general third parties will be affected. Suppose that women were previously barred from some line of employment, and now the barrier has been removed. The females who enter that line of employment gain from the increased scope of exchange, as do their employers. But the previously protected (male) employees will be adversely affected, yet do not have any legal entitlement to retain their old terms of employment. It is a standard proposition of economics that such pecuniary externalities balance out in aggregate value terms. The loss to the male workers (of receiving a lower wage) is exactly counterbalanced by the gain to their employers (in not having to pay a higher wage). Nevertheless, absent compensation it remains true that some parties are now worse off; removal of an artificial barrier to trade is thus *not* in general a strictly Pareto-preferred change.

To get around this difficulty, the concept of "potentially Pareto-preferred" (PPP) social changes has been proposed.[3] Suppose everyone's well-being could simply be scaled in terms of the amount of pie he consumes. Then any way of increasing the overall size of society's aggregate pie meets the PPP criterion. For a larger pie can *potentially* be redivided so that everybody gains (or, at least, so that some gain while nobody loses). Put more generally, the PPP criterion is satisfied by any change such that the gainers could (even *if they do not*) compensate the losers. Any such change is, in the modern econo-legal literature, called a movement in the direction of "efficiency." A final position in which no such PPP changes remain to be made is called simply "efficient."

In terms of changes from an arbitrary initial position, not every potentially Pareto-preferred change (movement in the direction of efficiency) will generally be strictly Pareto-preferred. In particular, the PPP criterion would (subject to some qualifications to be mentioned below) give a favorable response to our example of removing barriers to employment of women, where the strict Pareto criterion does not. Since the losses to the male employees are exactly counterbalanced by the gains to their employers, with a further net gain flowing to the new female workers and their employers, clearly the losers from the change could be compensated. The PPP criterion, if we accept it, thus justifies exchange even where pecuniary externalities are imposed on other parties (as almost always they will be).

Our discussion has suggested that there are a number of ethical or ideological problems associated with efficiency criteria, and it is time to mention three of these explicitly.

---

[3] Also known as the "Kaldor criterion" [Kaldor (6)].

1. *Voluntarism:* The key issue in approving only strictly Pareto-preferred (SPP) changes versus approving all potentially Pareto-preferred (PPP) changes is voluntarism. The PPP criterion overrides dissent. There is an irony in the history of thought here. Proponents of the market process usually contend that it is a way of achieving economic efficiency without compulsion or dictation, yet we have seen that market transactions will be unambiguous movements in the direction of efficiency only if we depart from a strictly voluntaristic interpretation of what "efficiency" means. Indeed, excessive emphasis upon the saliency of the efficiency criterion, in the nonvoluntaristic PPP sense, would seem to open the gates even to rather brutal social processes that might conceivably still operate in accordance with a PPP rule.

2. *Enshrining the status quo:* Matters may appear in a somewhat different light, however, once we appreciate that voluntary changes are necessarily relative to some starting point. Why should the starting point, the initial distribution of wealth and talents, be given such a privileged position in our social thinking? This objection holds with greatest force against the strict Pareto criterion. The PPP criterion is somewhat less bound to the status quo, as it allows some non-unanimistic departures therefrom. Nevertheless, even what is only potentially Pareto-preferred may still depend upon the initial position.

   One example which has received some attention is the so-called reversal paradox [Scitovsky (10)]. Consider an initial social configuration Γ, with its vector of produced goods and associated income distribution. It may be that a change to some other configuration Ω with a different vector of produced goods and income distribution is PPP-indicated, in that compensating payments *could* make everybody better off in comparison with Γ. That is, Ω makes possible some other configuration Ω' which *would* be strictly Pareto-preferred to Γ. But it might also be the case that Γ meets the PPP criterion relative to Ω! That is, there might be a Γ' that is strictly Pareto-preferred to Ω. (It is the change in income distribution, shifting the market weights assigned to individuals' preferences, that makes this possible.) Probably a much more significant phenomenon is the paradox put in inverted form: starting at Γ a change to Ω may be ruled out as a PPP-inferior movement, yet starting at Ω the move to Γ may also be PPP-inferior! A nontrivial example: an enslaved person might not be able to afford buying his freedom from his master, yet were he free to begin with he might not be willing to sell himself into slavery at any price the master would pay. Which configuration is then the more efficient?

3. *Meddlesome preferences:* Suppose that some individuals have preferences that are not "self-regarding." For example, lowering the barriers to female employment in coal mines might be found disturbing by some third parties even though the latter are unaffected in material terms. Ought such preferences to be taken into account, under either the strict Pareto (SPP) or potential Pareto (PPP) criterion? Assuming that individuals are actually willing to pay (to sacrifice their own resources or potential consumption) in order to further such "meddlesome" goals, I see no basis for excluding them from consideration. However, when non-self-regarding tastes are taken into account, it no longer follows that voluntary exchange necessarily leads to efficiency even in the PPP sense.

What is the upshot of this discussion? If you now find yourself less than fully confident as to the normative validity of efficiency (either in the SPP sense or the PPP sense) as a criterion for social policy, you are in agreement with me. And notice that I have nowhere diverged from the premises of utilitarian individualism – the idea that the proper social goal can be expressed entirely in terms of the achievement of individual desires, rather than (for example) the pursuit of abstract ideals like justice or service to God – though in fact I do have reservations about strict utilitarianism. Nor have I attempted to bring in paternalistic arguments – to the effect that some individuals (or all individuals at some times) do not really know their true desires or are not able to choose what is best for them – and I would not entirely reject paternalism either. For all these reasons efficiency criteria fall short of being fully attractive. This is less threatening a thought for those of us who are doubtful in any case about the prospects of purposive social reconstruction in the pursuit of efficiency (or indeed in pursuit of any social goal); a doubt which is, for reasons that will become clear at the end of the next section, more or less consistent with an evolutionary approach to societal phenomena. But, as a matter of *positive analysis*, the difficulties that have been revealed may partially explain the seeming recalcitrance of the politically influential public to the efficiency argument of modern econo-legal thinkers.

Finally, one underemphasized aspect of the efficiency criterion is crucial for our purposes: efficiency is always relative to the boundaries of the society or group envisaged. An act of voluntary reciprocal exchange is beneficial for the "society" comprised by the two participants; it is when we consider third parties that questions begin to arise. If competing merchants were to form a cartel the move would be efficient from their point of view, though not so when consumers are taken into account. Or consider theft. If we set aside long-term effects upon the incentive to produce, theft as such would be purely redistributive. It is only the resources consumed in defenses erected against theft, and the consequent increased costs of thieving, that reduce the aggregate size of society's pie. Would it then be PPP-efficient to ban defenses against theft? Presumably, the answer would be yes (apart from the aforesaid long-run problems) if the thieves are considered numbers of the society, but no, if as *outlaws* they have placed themselves outside the social unit. (I myself prefer the latter answer!) In a broader context, outcomes efficient for our nation as a whole may be adverse to the well-being of other nations; even gains for the whole human species may be achieved at the expense of other species. My point is that no one, probably, favors efficiency in a totally universalistic sense. We all draw the line somewhere, at the boundary of "us" versus "them." *Efficiency thus is ultimately a concept relating to group advantage over other competing groups.*

ELEMENTS OF EVOLUTIONARY MODELS

The word "evolution" primarily suggests to us the biological succession of living types, but the underlying concept is of course much broader. Stars evolve: initially a localized concentration of gases in space, a star goes through several stages as it burns its nuclear fuel, ending up eventually as a white dwarf or black hole. According to current cosmological theories the universe as a whole is evolving, under the sway of the second law of thermodynamics, to an eventual steady state of maximum entropy – a uniform distribution of energy throughout space. On the human level we know also that languages evolve, though following what course I am not prepared to suggest. Thus it is by no means illegitimate to argue that patterns of economic interaction and legal structures may evolve. Yet, I want to say, not everything that changes can usefully be said to *evolve*. Evolution represents a particular type or pattern of change.

1. *Evolution versus randomness:* Evolution is not random variation (totally inexplicable change). The outcomes of successive spins of a roulette wheel vary, but do not evolve. Yet random change on a micro or component level may be an element of evolutionary

change at the level of a larger entity or collection. In biology genetic mutations occur randomly, yet they contribute to the evolutionary development of species.

2. *Evolution versus cyclicity:* Regular cyclical change, which plays a role in certain theories of social processes, is best not regarded as evolution. Cyclicity is a kind of generalized stationarity. Put another way, evolutionary changes have an *irreversible* element, so that things are never quite the same afterward [Lotka (7), ch. 2].

3. *Evolution versus revolution:* In evolutionary models, transitions on the macro level result from the accumulation of small changes in microelements over time. Species evolve through the gradual working of forces contributing to variations in the characters of individual organisms, and to differential multiplication thereof. Stars evolve via a multitude of infinitesimal changes operating over the eons on their atomic or subatomic constituent particles. Where custom is the dominant element, law tends to follow an evolutionary course: the law emerges from a host of small transactions. But a Moses or a Solon hands down the law from above, all at once as a *revolutionary* change. Similarly, in earlier times the economic system changed mainly through the gradual discovery and slow diffusion of new techniques and new social relationships. In modern times, it seems, revolutionary economic transformations are occurring with increasing frequency, often (though not necessarily) imposed from above.

   Whether a change is revolutionary or evolutionary is sometimes a matter of relevant time span or scope of unit. Fusion of a pair of hydrogen atoms within a star is a revolutionary change for the specific atoms involved, but only a tiny component of the evolutionary process for the star. In primitive times, within a small human band the invention of the bow, or the promulgation of a successful new law, may have been revolutionary. But among the larger group of related bands comprising what we now perceive as a single culture, the change may have progressed only at an evolutionary pace, perhaps being repeatedly reinvented or slowly diffusing before becoming characteristic of that culture.

4. *Evolution versus design:* When we speak of evolutionary changes in human affairs, we generally have in mind "unintended" ones. Once again, we must distinguish different levels of analysis. Purposive planning by individuals, or by small groups, might be consistent with unintended evolutionary change on a macro level.

The inventor of the bow had an intention, but it was only to help himself or his band; the spread of a new technique of hunting, not to mention the more remote social consequences following upon that spread, was surely beyond his purpose. Or, modern statute writers may intend some purposive redesign of the social order – but, since "legislation is based on folk notions of causality" [Moore (8), p. 7], the result may be very different from that planned.

One of the inferences I draw from this discussion is that the applicability of evolutionary models ought not be oversold; evolution is not the sole important pattern of social change. In particular, with the increasing connectivity of the human world-system – due mainly to advances in communication and to the development of technology with worldwide impact (most notably, military technology) – "revolutionary" and "designed" changes are playing larger and larger roles. Nevertheless, models of evolutionary change have not lost all relevance. First, many areas of life continue to be subject to evolutionary principles. Language, custom, the sphere of private economic activity, and the common law can still be said to evolve. Second, the *present-day* starting point, even for revolutionary or designed change, is in large part the product of *past* genetic and cultural evolution. The social evolution of the human species places constraints upon the nature and pace of planned future change.

Evolutionary models share certain properties. First of all, they concern populations. Even where we seem to be speaking of single entities, if the course of change is evolutionary it can be described in terms of changing populations of micro-units. Thus, the evolutionary course of a disease within a single human body is a function of the relations among populations of bacteria, antibodies, cells, and so on. Or the evolution of a single nation's economy is the result of changing relations among populations of individuals, trading units, and the like.

Evolutionary models represent a combination of constancy ("inheritance") and variation. There must be an unchanging as well as a changing element, and even the changing element itself must be heritable if a system can be said to evolve. In biological evolution, the emphasis is upon differential survival and reproduction of organismic types or characters from one generation to the next. Here the constancy is due to Mendelian inheritance of permanent patterns of coded genetic instructions (genes). Variation stems from a number of forces, including internal mutations of these instructions (genetic copying errors), recombination of genes in sexual reproduction, and the external pressure of natural selection. Socioeconomic evolution mainly concerns the differential growth and survival of patterns of social organization. The main "inheritance" element is the deadweight of social inertia, supported by intentionally taught tradition. As for variation, there are analogs to mutations ("copying errors" as we learn traditions). Also, natural selection is still effective. Finally, *imitation* and *rational thought* constitute additional nongenetic sources of socioeconomic variation.

Biologists have been much interested in the question of the "direction" of evolution. The main principle recognized is *adaptation*. That is, organisms and their lines of descent over the generations tend to fit themselves into niches of viability offered by their environments. They do so mainly under the pressure of selective competition from other organisms and species, all of which have an irrepressible Malthusian tendency[4] to multiply so as to fill any unsaturated places in the environment.

A number of philosophers have perceived a directional trend toward "complexity" in biological, cultural, and even cosmological evolution. I believe this is mistaken. If complexity is adaptive, the trend of development will be in that direction, but often the direction of adaptation may be toward simplicity. We see movement toward complexity when, for example, a few "founders" enter and proliferate within a new environment that contains many different yet-unfilled niches. We see movement toward simplicity, on the other hand, whenever homogenization of the environment reduces the number of distinct niches available.

The adaptation principle suggests that the external environmental determinants must ultimately govern in the evolutionary process.[5] But biological evolution is opportunistic, and must work with the internal materials at hand. The available internal materials – the genetically coded instructions – will have been shaped by a variety of past irreversible transformations. These transformations were perhaps responsive in their own day to then-current environmental requirements, but persisting today they remain more or less recalcitrant constraints upon adaptive change. Despite this, there are extraordinary examples of parallel evolution in Nature, for example, where traits usually associated with fishes have been independently evolved by quite different biological taxa moving into aquatic environments, among them the mammals (seals, whales), birds (penguins), and lizards (sea-going iguanas). There are also failures

---

[4] As is well known, reading Malthus' *Essay on Population* played a key role in the shaping of Darwin's thought.

[5] As emphasized, for example, by Alexander (1), ch. 4.

of parallel evolution, however. Nothing like the kangaroo has evolved outside Australia, despite large geographical regions where kangaroo-like qualities would seem to be highly adaptive.

The second qualification of the adaptation principle is of greater interest for our purposes. What is adaptive for the individual organism (and its descendants) may or may not be adaptive for the species. Fleetness of foot helps the gazelle escape the lion, but the gain to being exceptionally fleet may largely be that some other gazelle is eaten instead. If the gazelles were making a cooperative group adaptation, presumably somewhat less fleetness than what has actually evolved would be optimal. A different type of imperfect species adaptation is illustrated by the peacock. The enormous tail pleases the female's fancy and so its bearer sires more offspring, yet a heavy price is paid. As a group adaptation, it seems that the peacocks ought to have found a mode of sexual competition involving less energy loss and vulnerability to predators. In economic terms we would say that these forms of biological competition impose *adverse externalities* upon other members of (what we perceive as) a larger potentially cooperating group – in this case, the species.

Group adaptation remains imperfect in such cases because the biological payoff in reproductive competition depends mainly upon *relative* achievement. An organism can get ahead in evolutionary terms either by pulling itself up or by pushing its competitors down:

It is crucial to understanding the behavior of organisms, including ourselves, that in evolutionary terms success in reproduction is always *relative*; hence, the striving of organisms is in relation to one another and not toward some otherwise quantifiable goal or optimum. [Alexander (1), p. 17]

The evolutionary emphasis upon *relative* reproductive competition has important implications for the question of efficiency discussed in the second section. If it were strictly true that only relative status counted, the efficiency concept would be meaningless. If one party's advance automatically means that other parties lose, there is no scope for *mutual* gain, actual or potential [see Becker (2), pp. 1089–1090, and Hirshleifer (5), pp. 329–330]. In the case of the peacock, other males' reproductive survival is not even a neutral but probably on balance a harmful consideration; the descendants of other cocks will use up resources and multiply to the disadvantage of its own descendants.[6]

---

[6] This is somewhat of an oversimplification. For one thing, descendants of other cocks would provide less-inbred mates for one's own descendants.

At the end of the section on efficiency it was argued that efficiency must be interpreted as relative to the boundaries of the group. We can now see that for group efficiency to be economically meaningful as a criterion, the group must be one within which individuals do *not* compete mainly in terms of relative achievement. In nature, *species are mainly fields of relative reproductive competition*. This is why, so often, adaptations tend to be selected that are harmful to the species as a whole.

Nevertheless, truly cooperating groups within species[7] are also often evolved by Nature. Among the more evident examples are families, packs, and insect communities, extending on the human level to tribes and nations. What is happening here, insofar as evolutionary reproductive competition is controlling, is that some individuals have allied to achieve a mutual gain *relative to* other members of their species.

That intragroup cooperation and mutual gain typically take place within a larger context of intergroup competition and conflict is essential to keep in mind in speaking of efficiency. Failure to appreciate this fact is an important weakness of modern econo-legal thinking, which the evolutionary approach has exposed. Even within an actual or potential alliance there remain, however, mixed motives – individual advantage is generally not wholly consistent with group advantage.
[END OF EXTRACT]

REFERENCES

1. Alexander, Richard D. (1979) *Darwinism and Human Affairs*, Seattle, University of Washington Press.
2. Becker, Gary. (November/December 1971) "A Theory of Social Interactions," *Journal of Political Economy*, Vol. 82(6):1063–1093.
3. Calabresi, Guido. (1961) "Some Thoughts on Risk Distribution and the Law of Torts," *Yale Law Journal*, Vol. 70:499.
4. Coase, Ronald H. (October 1960) "The Problem of Social Cost," *Journal of Law and Economics*, Vol. 3:1–45.
5. Hirshleifer, Jack. (October 1978) "Natural Economy versus Political Economy," *Journal of Social and Biological Structures*, Vol. 1:319–338.
6. Kaldor, Nicholas. (1939) "Welfare Propositions in Economics and Interpersonal Comparisons of Utility," *Economic Journal*, Vol. 49:549–552.
7. Lotka, Alfred J. (1956) *Elements of Mathematical Biology*, New York, Dover Publications.

---

[7] There are also many fascinating examples of across-species cooperation, but these are only means whereby individual members of both species compete more effectively against their own conspecifics.

8. Moore, Sally Falk. (1978) *Law as Process: An Anthropological Approach*, London, Routledge & Kegan Paul.
9. Posner, Richard A. (1977) *Economic Analysis of Law*, 2nd ed., Boston, Little, Brown.
10. Scitovsky, Tibor. (1941) "A Note on Welfare Propositions in Economics," *Review of Economic Studies*, Vol. 9:77–89.
11. Smith, Adam. (1937) *The Wealth of Nations*, New York, Random House (original publication 1776).

10

On the Emotions as Guarantors of Threats and Promises

Jack Hirshleifer

Background of this Chapter

This article was one of the first attempts in the economic literature to deal systematically with the "nonrational" phenomenon represented by human emotions. It was prepared for a conference on evolution and information held at Stanford University in 1985. The proceedings appeared as a 1987 volume, edited by John Dupré, under the title *The Latest on the Best: Essays in Evolution and Optimality*.

Despite their violation of rationality, I contended, emotions such as anger and gratitude have been *evolutionarily* selected because they facilitate eliciting cooperation from targeted parties. And in particular, they do so by serving as guarantors of commitments to carry out threats and promises. By coincidence, essentially the same idea was independently developed in a book by Robert H. Frank (1988, *Passions within Reason: The Strategic Role of the Emotions*, New York: W.W. Norton & Co.) that has deservedly received a great deal of attention. A survey article by Jon Elster (1998, "Emotions and Economic Theory", *Journal of Economic Literature*, 36: 47–74) contains some discussion and criticisms of this evolutionary approach along with a more general analysis of recent work on emotions by economists and noneconomists. In a 1993 article in *Rationality and Society* ("The Affections and the Passions: Their Economic Logic," *Rationality and Society* 5: 185–202), I investigated in more detail the likely evolutionary survival of emotional behavior.

The role of the passions or emotions in supporting civil society has been discussed by social theorists and moral philosophers since earliest times. Adam Smith, in particular, whose name is more usually associated with the claim that an economic system may function effectively even when men act only in accordance with calculated self-interest, was actually

Reprinted from J. Hirshleifer, "On the Emotions as Guarantors of Threats and Promises" in John Dupré, ed., *The Latest on the Best: Essays on Evolution and Optimality*, Chap. 14, 307–26, Copyright © 1987, with permission from The MIT Press.

very concerned with aspects of human nature that set limits upon the pursuit of self-interest: "Nature, when she formed man for society, endowed him with an original desire to please, and an original aversion to offend his brethren. She taught him to feel pleasure in their favourable, and pain in their unfavourable regard. She rendered their approbation most flattering and most agreeable to him for its own sake; and their disapprobation most mortifying and most offensive."[1] More intriguing than his appreciation of the force of "positive" emotions like benevolence and sympathy are Smith's insights into how even the more dubious passions – pride, vanity, and ambition – may promote the interests of society.[2] This point had of course already been made by Mandeville in *The Fable of the Bees* (1714). But Smith comes closer to my theme here in his argument that these "negative" sentiments can be most socially useful precisely when they drive people to undertake activities *beyond the bounds of pragmatic self-interest*. Thus, of a "poor man's son ... visited with ambition" Adam Smith says,

For this purpose he makes his court to all mankind; he serves those whom he hates, and is obsequious to those whom he despises. Through the whole of his life he pursues the idea of a certain artificial and elegant repose which he may never arrive at, for which he sacrifices a real tranquillity that is at all times in his power, and which, if in the extremity of old age he should at last attain to it, he will find to be in no respect preferable to that humble security and contentment which he had abandoned for it.[3]

And it is well that nature imposes upon us in this manner. It is this deception which arouses and keeps in continual motion the industry of mankind. It is this which first prompted them to cultivate the ground, to build houses, to found cities and common-wealths, and to invent and improve all the sciences and arts, which ennoble and embellish human life.[4,5]

The point I shall be making is somewhat different, however. The emotions, positive or negative, can indeed be socially useful in driving a person to act beyond the bounds of pragmatic self-interest. But paradoxically the consequence is not necessarily adverse for himself. A person can sometimes best further his self-interest by *not* intending to pursue it. Methodologically speaking also, I shall be advancing

---

[1] Smith, *Moral Sentiments*, p. 212.
[2] On this, see especially Coase (1976), pp. 536, 542–543.
[3] *Moral Sentiments*, p. 300.
[4] Ibid., p. 303.
[5] Compare also the Talmudic argument that even the evil impulse instilled by God in man is "very good": "Were it not for that impulse, a man would not build a house, marry a wife, beget children or conduct business affairs" (Cohen, 1949).

somewhat beyond the classical discussions referred to above, in providing a systematic *analysis* of the precise ways in which different emotional sets may promote or subvert socially advantageous arrangements. My discussion follows a lead by Becker (1976), who demonstrated how "altruism" can, in effect, force cooperation upon a completely selfish partner (the "Rotten-Kid Theorem"). I shall try to show more generally here how, and up to what limits, positive or negative emotions can serve a constructive role as guarantors of *threats* or *promises* in social interactions.

If a mutually desired objective is to be achieved, it is often necessary that one or more of the parties forgo the opportunity to reap a self-interested gain. Intelligence permits reasoning beings to "look around the corner," to visualize the advantages of *not* pursuing immediate self-interest. But the problem of securing the necessary coordination of actions remains. A meeting of the minds – a contract, to use that term in its broadest sense – does not generally suffice; some method of *enforcing* (or otherwise guaranteeing) performance is generally required.[6]

The most obvious method of enforcement is through the legal-judicial system. But it has long been appreciated that in some cases contracts may be self-enforcing (Macaulay, 1963), the key point being that fear of losing profitable future business with a trading partner may suffice to deter defection here and now. This topic has recently been studied by Telser (1980), using the analytical model of the repeated-play Prisoners' Dilemma ("supergame" theory, in the standard jargon). The difficulty is the well-known incentive to defect at the last round of play. This obstacle can be overcome, so that the contract becomes self-enforcing, when the number of rounds is infinite or at least if there is a sufficiently high probability of play always continuing for another round (see also Luce and Raiffa, 1957, p. 102).

In contrast with this line of discussion, I shall be dealing solely with single-round games. But my analysis will not be limited to Prisoners' Dilemma, which is only one of a number of distinct payoff environments combining a mutual gain from cooperation with a self-interested motive to defect. In the situations to be considered the possibility of enforcement stems from an assumed asymmetric game protocol, such that one of the players "has the last word" (Hirshleifer, 1977) and thus is potentially

---

[6] Sometimes a meeting of the minds can suffice, as in adoption of a convention that no one has any incentive to violate. Agreeing to drive on the right (left), or to meet under the clock at Grand Central Station, are possible examples (on this see Schelling, 1978a. Chap. 3). I have shown that such coordination tends automatically to emerge under particular types of social environments (Hirshleifer, 1982, p. 14).

in a position to confer reward or punishment. Since offers of reward or punishment are contingent strategies, we are in the realm of "metagames" in the jargon of the trade (Howard, 1971; Thompson and Faith, 1981).

In what follows I shall first briefly discuss the nature of threats versus promises in different payoff environments. Then I shall provide an explicit analysis for several different categories of emotions. Finally, I shall speculate upon the possible reasons why emotions, and other limitations upon "rationality," have survived as part of the human constitution.

1

An individual who makes a threat or promise is pledging to respond in a contingent way to another's actions, with the goal of influencing the other party's choice. The intended effect would presumably always be to the pledger's advantage, though not necessarily to the other's disadvantage. The only other point worthy of special note is that a promise or threat must be *to do something that the individual would not otherwise be motivated to do.* That is what distinguishes these pledges from mere forecasts, however informative, of one's likely responses to another's actions (see also Schelling, 1960, chapter 2).

Matrix 10.1 illustrates a Prisoners' Dilemma payoff environment, where 4 represents the highest and 1 the lowest of the ordinally ranked returns to each of the players (see Figure 10.1). Here and throughout, unless indicated to the contrary, the Column player moves first so that it is the Row player who "has the last word." It is then possible to define *contingent* strategies for Row. Let the two elementary strategies available to each player be LOYAL and DEFECT. Row's additional contingent

Matrix 10.1		
Prisoners' Dilemma		
	LOYAL	DEFECT
LOYAL	3,3#	1,4
DEFECT	4,1	2,2*

Matrix 10.1A		
Expanded Prisoners' Dilemma		
	LOYAL	DEFECT
LOYAL	3,3	1,4
DEFECT	4,1	2,2
TIT FOR TAT	3,3	2,2
REVERSAL	4,1	1,4

Matrix 10.2		
Chicken		
	DOVE	HAWK
DOVE	3,3#	2,4*
HAWK	4,2**	1,1

Figure 10.1.

strategies can be termed TIT FOR TAT (play LOYAL in response to LOYAL, and DEFECT in response to DEFECT) and REVERSAL (play DEFECT in response to LOYAL, and LOYAL in response to DEFECT). It is standard to represent these contingent strategies by additional rows in the game's normal form, as in the "expanded" Matrix 10.1A. However, for my purposes it suffices to deal directly with the underlying Matrix 10.1, where it is easy enough to visualize the effects of threats or promises on the part of the Row player.

With Column having the first move, suppose that Row – even though he may contemplate or even intend a contingent strategy like TIT FOR TAT – cannot *guarantee* to Column that he will be following it. Then, returning to Matrix 10.1, Column will surely choose DEFECT. (For, his choice of LOYAL would be responded to by Row's DEFECT, leaving Column with his worst payoff of 1.) Row will of course answer Column's DEFECT with his own DEFECT. Thus the parties end up at the cell of Matrix 10.1 marked with a star; the payoffs are 2 each – their next-to-worst outcomes in each case.[7] This is of course the traditional "trap" equilibrium of Prisoners' Dilemma,[8] a seemingly paradoxical result since, by cooperation, the parties could have reaped their next-to-best payoff of 3 each.

This Pareto-superior 3,3 outcome (marked with a # in Matrix 10.1) would indeed be achieved if Row could guarantee abiding by a *promise* to play LOYAL in response to LOYAL on Column's part. Column, if he could rely upon that promise, then would play LOYAL on the first move. What makes Row's utterance a promise (rather than a forecast) is that he offers *not to do* what he is in fact motivated to do when his turn comes up. In promising LOYAL, Row engages himself to confer a benefit upon Column, at a cost to himself, should the latter first choose LOYAL himself. But that Row will play DEFECT in response to DEFECT is only a forecast and not a threat, since Row would be doing that anyway.

---

[7] It might be thought that this analysis is over-elaborate in that DEFECT is by inspection a "dominant" strategy for each player given the payoffs of Matrix 1. But dominance arguments must be used with great care in sequential-play protocols. It is easy to demonstrate underlying payoff matrices where the *first* mover would want to emply a "dominated" strategy, since he can thereby influence the other player's responding choice. Schelling (1978b) provides a number of illustrations: for example, to keep you from kidnapping my children I may give away all my wealth.

[8] The starred cell is also the unique "Nash equilibrium" of the usual (simultaneous move) Prisoners' Dilemma. However, we are dealing here with a sequential-move rather than a simultaneous-move game. It would be possible, using the appropriate expanded matrix in each case, to expand the Nash equilibrium idea to cover sequential-move games, but I shall not in fact be using that solution concept.

To illustrate an actual *threat*, consider the almost equally famous pay-off environment known as the game of Chicken (Matrix 10.2). Holding to the ornithological metaphor, the two strategies can be called HAWK and DOVE. If Row cannot guarantee performance of a contingent strategy, then Column, having the first move, must inspect Row's response to each of his choices. Evidently, Column's best first move is the "less cooperative" HAWK strategy, leading to an asymmetrical 2,4 outcome in his favor (starred in the matrix). In order to influence Column to change his strategy, Row would have to guarantee execution of a *threat* to play HAWK in response to HAWK. Once again, that is an engagement to do something at a cost to himself, but now the action imposes a *loss* on Column. If Column bows to the threat and plays DOVE instead, Row now plays HAWK leading to the reversed payoff outcome 4,2 in Row's favor (double-starred in the matrix).

On the other hand, Row might sweeten the deal by issuing a *threat-and-promise*. That is, in addition to the aforesaid threat to play HAWK in response to HAWK, he could promise to forgo part of his gain and respond to DOVE with DOVE. Then, the parties could achieve the symmetrical 3,3 outcome (marked # in Matrix 2). It might seem puzzling that, if Row's threat is solid enough to work, he would ever choose to reduce his gain by combining a threat and a promise. But throughout this paper we are contemplating the possibility that parties might, owing to emotional limits upon self-interested rationality, *not* necessarily do what it is in their material advantage to do. In such circumstances, threat-and-promise might conceivably trigger a less hostile response than threat alone.

2

In this section I shall examine the consequences of two different scaled classes of emotion: (1) the malevolence/benevolence spectrum and (2) the anger/gratitude spectrum. The first category is *action-independent*, the second is *action-dependent*. I shall continue to employ the assumption throughout that one player always has the first move; in fact, let us call him First. The other player, Second, is therefore the one who may be in a position to confer reward or punishment.

Benevolence/Malevolence

Figures 10.2(a) and 10.2(b) illustrate benevolence and malevolence *on the part of the last mover*, Second. Thus it is Second's indifference curves that are being pictured, on axes representing the two parties' material

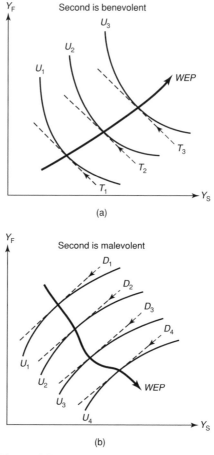

(a)

(b)

Figure 10.2. Benevolence versus malevolence.

incomes Y_S and Y_F. In Figure 10.2(a) Y_S and Y_F are both *goods* for a benevolent Second, so his indifference curves have the familiar negative slope. In Figure 10.2(b) his own income Y_S remains of course a good for Second, but now Y_F is a *bad* from his point of view. Hence the abnormal indifference curve map in Figure 10.2(b).

I shall also be assuming that Second always has the power to transfer income to First, or else to deprive her of income, if he chooses – in each case, at a cost to himself. Specifically, in the transfer mode Second can increase First's income Y_F by giving up his own income Y_S on a 1 : 1 basis. (Note the dashed 135° "transfer lines" TT in Figure 10.2(a), where the arrows attached indicate the direction of movement.) In the deprivation mode, Second can reduce First's income but again only by incurring an assumed equal cost himself – indicated by the dashed 45° "deprivation lines" DD in Figure 10.2(b). (Once again, the arrows indicate the possible direction of movement.)

In Figure 10.2(a) the *WEP* curve (a "Wealth Expansion Path") connects all the tangencies of Second's benevolent indifference curves with the 135° transfer lines. It follows immediately that, provided the starting position is to the *southeast* of the *WEP* curve (that is, provided he is relatively well off and First relatively poorly off to begin with), Second will always transfer exactly that amount of income leading him to a final solution along *WEP.* Similarly, in Figure 10.2(b) the *WEP* curve connects all the tangencies of Second's malevolent indifference curves with the 45° deprivation lines. Here Second will always impose enough deprivation to end up along *WEP,* provided the starting position is to the *northeast.* (That is, provided both parties are relatively well endowed with income to begin with.) Second must be reasonably wealthy in order to afford the cost of inflicting the deprivation, while First must be well off to begin with, else the initial situation would not be intolerable to a malevolent Second.

Another property of the *WEP* curves will be important in what follows. In Figure 10.2(a) *WEP* has positive slope throughout. This indicates that, as a benevolent Second grows wealthier, he will want to choose positions involving greater Y_S and greater Y_F *both.* That is, as he becomes richer, he wants to end up with more income for himself and more income for the object of his benevolence. This represents a special, though reasonable, assumption that Y_S and Y_F are both "superior" goods from Second's point of view.[9] By a corresponding argument, in Figure 10.2(b) the curve *WEP* has negative slope. As Second becomes richer, he prefers to so arrange matters as to have more income himself while leaving the target of his malevolence worse off.

Now we turn to the decisions available to the first mover. It will be assumed that a joint productive opportunity boundary like QQ' in Figure 10.3 always exists, and that First has the sole choice of the productive

---

[9] While superior goods are the normal pattern, standard economic models allow for the possibility of "inferior" goods – i.e., goods of which less is chosen as the consumer becomes richer. This possibility can, however, be excluded here. Note that if Y_F were an inferior good for Second, then First would be motivated to impoverish her benefactor! Even if this were infeasible, First would also be motivated to impoverish herself. If First throws away $10, Second would then rationally compensate her by more than the $10 lost. If Y_F were inferior over any range, this process would continue until Y_F entered a range where it was no longer inferior, unless Second became bankrupt before this point was reached (see Becker, 1981, Chapter 8).

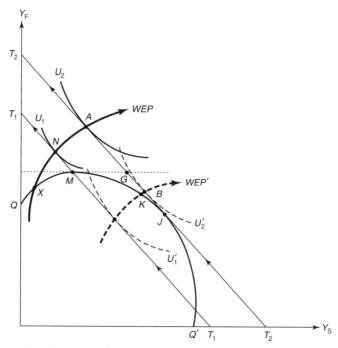

Figure 10.3. The rotten-kid theorem – benevolence as guarantor of a promise.

arrangements to be made – i.e., she determines the point to be chosen along QQ'. Furthermore, for simplicity First is assumed throughout to be merely self-interested, neither benevolent nor malevolent.[10] It then follows that, in the absence of any anticipated reaction from Second, First would always simply prefer the most northerly position along QQ' – point M in the diagram. As it happens, the joint productive arrangements represented by point M do generate some income for Second as well, but this is a merely incidental fact from First's selfish point of view.

But now note the position of Second's (solid) Wealth Expansion Path *WEP* in Figure 10.3. This indicates that, beyond point X, where *WEP* cuts QQ', Second regards himself as wealthy enough to display some benevolence toward First. Thus, First, should she choose her short-sightedly selfish optimum, M, would end up doing better than this – since Second would benevolently transfer enough income to her along the transfer line $T_1 T_1$ to end up at point N that lies to the north of M. But that is

---

[10] The proposition of this section can easily be extended to cover a benevolent or malevolent First. In particular, there can be instances where Second's benevolence can induce cooperation even from a malevolent First, to their mutual gain.

still not the best that a *far-sightedly* selfish First could achieve. In fact, it will be evident from the diagram that First should choose point J, where QQ' is tangent to the highest attainable 135° transfer line T_2T_2. True, in the short run, First will have sacrificed income on behalf of Second. But the latter will then benevolently transfer enough of his enlarged income to First so as to achieve a final indifference-curve tangency at point A. From the selfish First player's point of view, A is better than (north of) N. In fact, A represents the largest income attainable by First under the conditions assumed.

That, however, is not the surprising part of this result. The real point is, not only does "enlightened self-interest" lead the selfish first mover to a better outcome thanks to a predictable benefit from Second's benevolence, but the latter gains as well! And the gain to Second is not merely in terms of his psychic satisfaction from seeing First better off. Even in the crassly material sense, the benevolent second mover himself has gained from his generosity. His own material income Y_S is greater at point A than it would have been otherwise, i.e., had the selfish First player chosen point M along QQ'.

What has happened here is that Second's benevolence guaranteed an implicit "promise" to reward First, a necessary condition for securing cooperation from a merely self-interested individual. The second mover's "hard-core altruism" has served to elicit the first mover's pragmatic or "soft-core altruism."[11]

Another aspect of the constructive role played by benevolence is brought out if we look at the alternative (dashed) Wealth Expansion Path WEP' in Figure 10.3. This curve is associated with a different possible set of preferences for Second, suggested by the dashed indifference curves U'. These alternative preferences are *qualitatively* similar in that they also represent benevolent tastes, but now to a *quantitatively* lesser degree. In these altered circumstances, if First were to choose the jointly cooperative position J along QQ' as before, Second would then transfer a smaller amount to her – so that the parties would end up at position B along WEP' rather than at A along WEP. But, for the selfish First player, position B is inferior to her short-sightedly selfish optimum, M. The conclusion: far-sighted or enlightened self-interest

---

[11] The terminology is due to E. O. Wilson (1978). However, the point made here diverges from Wilson's. He was concerned to contrast the weakness of "hard-core altruism" (benevolence) *compared* to "soft-core altruism" (enlightened self-interest) as organizers of cooperation in large social units. The analysis here indicates that the two factors may sometimes *complement* one another in a socially useful way.

may not suffice to achieve mutual improvement, in the absence of a *sufficiently strong degree* of benevolence on the part of the player having the last move.

Of course, in the latter situation Second could still *promise* to provide First with a sufficient reward to induce cooperation – say, by pledging to choose position *A* if First selects *J* along *QQ′*. But by assumption there is nothing to guarantee Second's promise – save his own benevolence, which is here inadequate. In fact, there is a critical threshold degree of benevolence on the part of Second needed to elicit cooperation from First. To wit, to provide enough inducement for a far-sightedly selfish First to choose point *J*, Second's benevolent Wealth Expansion Path must cut the transfer line T_2T_2 north of its intersection with the dotted line through *M*. Thus, lots of love may do the trick, where a little love achieves nothing at all!

If benevolence can serve as guarantor of a *promise* by the party having the last word, can malevolence serve as a guarantor of a *threat*? It surely can, but the overall effect is not to elicit cooperation, if we hold to the assumption that the *WEP* curve in Figure 10.4 (compare Figure 10.2(b))

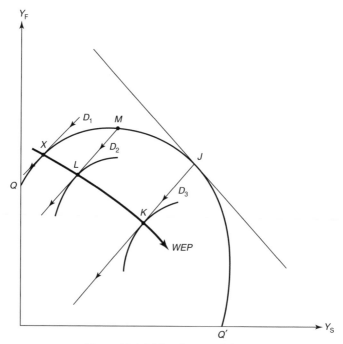

Figure 10.4. Malevolence and threat.

has negative slope throughout. (That is, the richer Second gets, the more he can afford to and want to spend on depriving First.) In Figure 10.4 then, should the first mover short-sightedly choose the most northerly position M along QQ', she will have empowered a malevolent Second to impoverish her to the degree represented by the final position L. If First were instead to choose the efficient productive point J, she would end up still worse off at K. Evidently a selfish First does best to choose point X, where she is initially poorer but where Second is also so poor that he cannot afford (or at least does not care) to incur costs to impose any further deprivation upon her. Thus malevolence guarantees execution of a threat, but the consequence is that *both* parties are worse off – in terms of psychic satisfaction and in terms of material income as well.

Gratitude/Anger

I now turn to the *action-dependent* emotional scale ranging from gratitude at the positive end to anger at the negative end of the spectrum. The question as before will be whether these emotions can guarantee execution of threats or promises and thereby promote achievement of mutually beneficial solutions.

Allowing for the possibility of malevolence and benevolence represented a departure from the economist's standard assumption of self-interested behavior, but did not otherwise do violence to the picture of economic man as a rational utilitarian calculator. An individual who values other people's income (positively or negatively) as well as his own can nevertheless coolly go about his business of calculating a preferred final outcome in the light of his given preferences and opportunities. [12] But I am now introducing a much more serious departure from the standard assumptions of the economist – to wit, the idea that an individual can be *passionate*, in the sense of "losing control" and doing what he does not really want to do (on this see Schelling, 1980). Or an alternative (and my preferred) interpretation would be that what he wants to do need not depend only upon the final outcome in the utilitarian sense (i.e., strictly upon the ultimate distribution of incomes between the two parties), but rather may be *action-dependent*. An income distribution that could be tolerable as an accidental or random event, for example, might lead to violent revolt if seen to be the result of conscious choice on

---

[12] Such models of interpersonal consumption preferences have been employed by a number of economists, including Boulding (1962, Chap. 2), and Becker (1971).

the part of another economic agent. Common observation tells us that, whatever the textbooks assume, such behavior is in fact very important in the makeup of normal human beings. I shall be showing that, at least in certain circumstances, such nonutilitarian behavior[13] makes ultimate utilitarian sense!

Since preferences are now assumed action-dependent, we can no longer postulate a fixed preference map defined simply over the parties' incomes Y_F and Y_S. Nevertheless, it is possible to place plausible restrictions upon how a second mover influenced by anger/gratitude motivations would respond to choices by a first mover. (By analogy with the foregoing, I assume here that only Second is subject to anger/gratitude emotions, First remaining throughout coolly calculating and self-interested.) In Figure 14.5, Second's responses to First's choice along QQ' are summarized diagrammatically by his Anger/Gratitude Response (AGR) curve. This curve might take on a number of possible shapes, subject to the restrictions that (1) increasing wealth empowers Second to spend more either on transferring income to or else withdrawing income from First, but (2) the more "cooperative" is First's behavior (i.e., the more her choice along QQ' approaches point J), the less is Second's anger and/or the greater is Second's gratitude – with the obvious implication for his willingness to confer benefit or injury upon the other.[14]

In Figure 10.5 the "effective anger" region of Second's AGR curve extends from point X to point M along the opportunity boundary QQ'. (If First were to choose any point to the west of X along QQ', Second might be even angrier still, but too impoverished to do anything about it.) As First's choice hypothetically shifts to the east of X so as to provide Second with more income, the latter can *increasingly afford to* react in an angry way but becomes *decreasingly inclined* to do so. Beyond the crossover at M, Second enters his "effective gratitude"

---

[13] It would be possible, by a somewhat forced twist of terminology, to interpret passionate behavior as rational choice – for example, by having the individual's preferences (as to benevolence or malevolence) be responsive to the other's actions. But passionate behavior, the essential character of which involves loss of control and heedlessness of consequences, cannot be fitted smoothly into the utilitarian mold.

[14] While there is some diagrammatic similarity between the *AGR* and the previous *WEP* curves, they stand logically on quite a different footing. An *AGR* curve *could* also be interpreted as a locus of tangencies of transfer lines (or deprivation lines) with the second mover's indifference curves. But, the crucial point is, owing to the emotional action-dependent effects, Second's entire indifference curve map changes in response to First's choice along QQ'.

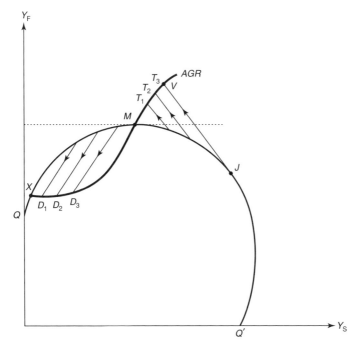

Figure 10.5. The anger/gratitude response (AGR) curve – threat and promise.

region. Here as his income grows thanks to First's making a more co-operative productive decision, Second is increasingly more able to react (now in a positive grateful way) and is also increasingly inclined to do so. Thus in the effective anger region, between X and M, the gap be-tween QQ' and AGR first widens and then narrows. But in the effective gratitude region beyond the crossover at M the gap increasingly widens as Second's income increases. This type of situation, it may be noted, corresponds to the *threat-and-promise* contingent behavior mentioned in Section 1.[15]

The outcome of the pattern pictured in Figure 10.5 is at point V. The efficient productive solution is achieved (at J on QQ') plus a redistribu-tion thereafter in such a way that both parties are better off in comparison with First's simple selfish solution at point M. But this is only one of quite a number of possible consequences of an anger-gratitude scaled reaction pattern.

---

[15] Of course a person capable *only* of anger can only guarantee execution of threats; a person capable only of gratitude is similarly restricted to promises. Having such a narrow repertoire of behaviors may be less costly, but restricts the contingent strategies available.

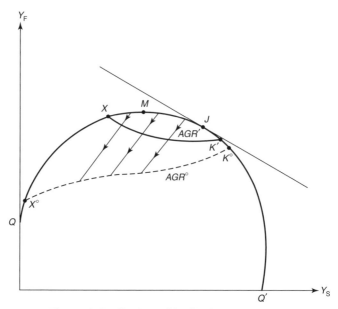

Figure 10.6. Effective and ineffective *AGR* curves.

Two other possibilities are pictured in Figure 10.6. Here, in contrast to Figure 10.5, anger is the dominant emotion influencing Second's
behavior. However, this can have very different implications, as illustrated by the alternative *AGR* curves pictured – the (dashed) *AGR*° versus
the (solid) *AGR'*. In each case, by assumption here the crossover point
along *QQ'* lies to the east of the efficient productive solution *J*; Second
does not give up his wrath until he is very well treated indeed. If Second's
emotional set corresponds to *AGR*°, the best choice for First along *X*°*K*°
is at point *K*°. Second's threat has worked so effectively as to force First
to make a big sacrifice – going not merely beyond First's simple selfish
optimum, *M*, but even beyond the jointly efficient outcome. If Second's
AGR' curve is applicable, on the other hand, First will prefer point *X*.
Second's threat does not work at all. Or rather it works *to the disadvantage* of both parties, in view of the steps First will take to escape the
threat. *X* is inferior for both, not merely in comparison with what could
have been achieved by Second's making a transfer after First chooses the
jointly efficient outcome *J*, but even in comparison with First's simple
selfish outcome *M*.

What is the difference between the two cases? *AGR'* represents a
relatively "small" threat in comparison with *AGR*° – it does not take

hold at all until point X rather than $X°$, and it inflicts smaller punishment throughout the relevant range. This feature is not the essential, however. The important feature is the overall *slope* of the AGR curve. That is, no matter whether the magnitude of the threat is large or small, its effectiveness depends upon the "appeasing" effect of each increment of compliance. A sufficient appeasing effect would be reflected by a positively sloped AGR curve, like $AGR°$ in Figure 10.6. Here a coolly calculating First can always do better by complying, up to the limit of feasibility at point $K°$. But if Second's anger is never sufficiently appeased, as reflected by the negatively sloped AGR' in the diagram, First can minimize the loss to herself by non-compliance – to the disadvantage of Second as well.

While many other pictures can be drawn illustrating interesting possibilities, the following points summarize the key considerations:

1. The rationally selfish first mover will want and (assuming that she has the relevant information) be able to achieve the most northerly point along the AGR curve that represents Second's scaled emotional response to her behavior.

2. Second's AGR curve will typically take off at some interior point X *along* QQ', where he begins to have income enough to be able to indulge his anger. The AGR curve may have positive or negative slope, but will eventually cross QQ' again at a point where First's move has become generous enough to appease Second's anger.

3. If *anger* is Second's dominating emotion, reflected by an AGR curve that does not cut QQ' until some point K to the east of the efficient point J, then the solution for First – the most northerly point along AGR (unless M is higher still) – will tend to be toward one extreme or the other, depending upon whether the slope of the AGR curve is predominantly positive or negative. If the slope is predominantly positive, there are typically positive *marginal* payoffs to First of appeasement, of bowing to the threat. It does not matter how heavy a punishment Second might impose in aggregate, but only how he reacts, on the margin, to First's concessions. A positively sloped AGR function thus tends toward an excellent outcome for Second, with First appeasing her heavily. If, on the other hand, the slope of the AGR curve is predominantly negative, First typically suffers negative marginal payoffs from making concessions. Here the typical outcome is toward the other extreme,

at point X where Second is left too poor to inflict punishment. Of course, here First will end up poor as well.

4. But if *gratitude* is Second's dominating emotion, reflected by an AGR crossing QQ' to the west of point J, the efficient solution tends to be achieved – provided again that the AGR curve has positive slope. Both parties then end up better off than at First's simple selfish optimum.

3

Biologists and anthropologists have been long concerned with explaining the great gap between human intellectual capacities and those of the nonhuman primates, an advance that appears to go beyond the adaptive environmental requirements of primitive man (Washburn, 1960; Rose, 1980; Staddon, 1981). But equally mysterious, perhaps, is the survival of those *limitations* upon self-interested rationality we term the passions or emotions. In *The Expression of the Emotions* (1872), Charles Darwin emphasized the universality of these emotions over the human species, and also their continuity with behaviors visible among animals. Of course, there would be no special need to explain survival of the passions if they are only "imperfections." Since the development of any trait involves some energetic cost, or at least some opportunity cost in terms of other capacities that have to be sacrificed, we do not need to explain why all living beings are not unlimitedly fecund, powerful beyond measure, or as speedy as light. But we ought not prejudge the question as to whether the observed limitations upon the human ability to pursue self-interested rationality are really no more than imperfections – might not these seeming disabilities actually be functional?

The thrust of the argument here has been that certain patterns of environmental payoffs to interpersonal cooperative opportunities can make retention of a capacity for emotion materially profitable. In this paper I distinguished between *action-independent* preferences versus *action-dependent* passions. The first category was illustrated by non-selfinterested motivations (the malevolence/benevolence spectrum), the second by impairment of the ability to calculate owing to reactive "loss of control" (the anger/gratitude spectrum). Given that one party in a social interaction is a selfish and perfectly rational calculator, it turns out that there are circumstances in which it is indeed profitable for the other to diverge from self-interested rationality – in accordance with one or both of these emotional scales.

As a related point, evolutionary biologists have also been concerned to explain the survival of "altruism" on the one hand and "spite" on the other. Despite the psychological connotations of these terms, the interpretation in the standard literature has been entirely operational rather than motivational: "altruism" is taken to mean acting so as to help another organism, at a cost to oneself, while "spite" refers to incurring a cost so as to injure another. Since evolutionary success is a selfish criterion,[16] the biological literature has attempted to explore the different patterns by which proximate sacrifice, the cost incurred to benefit or to injure another organism, can ultimately pay off through some indirect route [for example, in the case of "altruism," if one's beneficiaries are kin (Hamilton, 1964) or if an other-benefiting act leads to adequate reciprocation (Trivers, 1971)]. This paper, in contrast, directly attacks the problem of motivation. (Hence it is not applicable to lower organisms lacking the capacity for emotions.) What it examines are possible mechanisms whereby individuals may be led to supply the reward or punishment (the positive or negative reciprocation) that make certain forms of social cooperation possible. The vague terms "altruism" and "spite" are inadequate to describe the subtly different forms that these reciprocations may take.

In summary, the models analyzed here represent a special but illuminating case. It was assumed that, in a given payoff environment, a merely self-interested and accurately calculating party has the first move, after which a possibly emotion-influenced agent makes his choice in response. When it comes to the action-independent emotions – the malevolence/benevolence spectrum – *benevolence* can serve to guarantee a promise, but *malevolence* is not generally effective in guaranteeing execution of a threat. (A curious yet important point is that just a little benevolence may not work either – a generosity threshold must be overcome.) As for the action-dependent reactions, the anger/gratitude scale, *gratitude* has effects rather parallel with benevolence, but *anger* tends to be more effective than malevolence in securing cooperation. The key reason for the difference is that malevolence becomes a more powerful force as the responding party's wealth increases, a factor that strongly inhibits any desire on the part of the first mover to enrich the other by cooperation. But anger tends to erode as the first mover's choice

---

[16] "Natural selection will never produce in a being any structure more injurious than beneficial to that being, for natural selection acts solely by and for the good of each" (Darwin, *Origin of Species*, Chap. 6).

shifts toward cooperation, and hence may provide the needed induce-ment for achieving a mutually beneficial arrangement. The most general and interesting conclusions are that (i) absence of self-interest can pay off *even measured in terms of material selfish gain*, and, a parallel but quite distinct point, (ii) the loss of control that makes calculated behavior impossible can be more profitable than calculated optimization. (It fol-lows that a coolly calculating individual might more or less successfully *pretend* to be driven by passion-dominated responses. Furthermore, in this pretense he need not be seeking a merely selfish goal!)

Analytically, this paper demonstrates the not-so-paradoxical fact that it is possible to analyze, in terms of effects upon rationally calculated self-interest, the consequences of non-self-interested motivations and of limitations upon the ability to calculate. The economist must go beyond the assumption of "economic man" precisely because of the economic advantage of *not* behaving like economic man – an advantage that pre-sumably explains why the world is not populated solely by economic men.

I would like also to indicate some of the limitations of the analysis, which suggest directions for generalization:

1. The analysis here does not pretend to explain *all* the behaviors and attitudes we think of as emotions, but only certain of these, which are alleged to help guarantee the execution of contracts. Other types of emotions also serve important functions – for example, fear, which makes us flee danger, or romantic love, which helps us win mates – but are not relevant to the purpose at hand. Coming closer to the topic here, there are still other sentiments that bear upon the kinds of interpersonal transactions a group of individuals can arrive at, but which I have not studied – envy, pride, and shame are among them.

2. I have dealt only with one-time interactions. There is already a con-siderable body of literature dealing with repeated interactions, in which refusal to continue a business relationship with a defecting trading partner may alone suffice to enforce a contract. Neverthe-less, I suspect the anger/gratitude response pattern is an important additional factor, providing a degree of extra support where mere refusal of future business cannot carry all the weight of maintain-ing a social relationship.

3. The postulated division of responsibility, whereby the first mover has free choice of productive arrangements while the second

mover can only react by a reward or deprivation response, is of course a special assumption. But I do not believe it is unduly restrictive. We could equally well imagine the first mover as making some preliminary choice that narrows down the productive or other options available, after which the second mover makes a "finalizing" decision, possibly including productive aspects as well. The assumed special shapes of the functions could also be easily generalized. If the productive opportunity locus were to become less concave-downward (i.e., if QQ' in the diagrams were to approach a linear or even a convex-downward shape), the potential mutual gain via productive coordination would be reduced. Cooperation will then, other things being equal, become less likely.[17] And similarly, one could allow for different "exchange rates" in the second mover's ability to transfer or to deprive the other party, with predictable consequences for the efficacy of the second mover's ability to exert influence upon the other.

4. I considered only interactions between a self-interested coolly calculating party on the one hand, and an emotion-driven individual on the other, where the latter has the last move. If the time sequence were reversed, what I have called "threat" and "promise" would evidently not be successful.

5. Finally, the analysis here hints at a more daring suggestion. *Leadership* involves to a significant extent the function of conferring reward or punishment upon other members of the society, i.e., serving as second mover in many social interactions. While the role of leader is often simply seized by the strongest and/or cleverest, there also is commonly some degree of popular consent involved. Might it not be the case that the "inspirational" or "charismatic" quality that we look for in leaders is an extraordinary capacity to transcend self-interested motivations, to be passionately driven by action-dependent, non-utilitarian goals? There are of course merely self-interested, calculating princes who would follow Machiavelli's advice: "Therefore, a prudent ruler ought not to keep faith when by so doing it would be against his interest, and when the reasons which made him bind himself no longer exist" (*The Prince*, XVIII). But such a ruler would likely find it difficult to elicit from citizens that extra measure of devoted cooperation upon which the survival of his regime may depend. So,

---

[17] See Friedman (1980).

even the most Machiavellian of princes is likely at least to *simulate* the possession of genuine action-independent or action-dependent passions – what Boulding (1969) has called the heroic ethic.

REFERENCES

Becker, Gary S. (1971). A Theory of Social Interactions. *J. Polit. Econ.* 82:1063–1093.

Becker, Gary S. (1976). Altruism, Egoism, and Genetic Fitness: Economics and Sociobiology. *J. Econ. Lit.* 14:817–828.

Becker, Gary S. (1981). *A Treatise on the Family*. Cambridge, MA: Harvard University Press.

Boulding, Kenneth E. (1962). *Conflict and Defense*. New York: Harper & Row.

Boulding, Kenneth E. (1969). Economics as a Moral Science. *Am. Econ. Rev.* 59.

Coase, R. H. (1976). Adam Smith's View of Man. *J. Law & Econ.* 19.

Cohen, A. (1949). *Everyman's Talmud*, New American ed. New York: E. P. Dutton.

Darwin, Charles (1872/1859). *The Origin of Species by Means of Natural Selection*, 6th ed. (1st ed., 1859).

Darwin, Charles (1872). *The Expression of the Emotions in Man and Animals*.

Friedman, David (1980). Many, Few, One: Social Harmony and the Shrunken Choice Set. *Am. Econ. Rev.* 70.

Hamilton, W. D. (1964). The Genetical Evolution of Social Behavior. I. *J. Theor. Biol.* 7:1–17.

Hirshleifer, J. (1977). Shakespeare vs. Becker on Altruism: The Importance of Having the Last Word. *J. Econ. Lit.* 15:500–502.

Hirshleifer, J. (1982). Evolutionary Models in Economics and Law: Cooperation versus Conflict strategies. *Res. in Law & Econ.* 4:1–60.

Howard, Nigel (1971). *Paradoxes of Rationality*. Cambridge, MA: MIT Press.

Luce, R. Duncan, and Howard Raiffa (1957). *Games and Decisions*. New York: Wiley.

Macaulay, Stewart (1963). Non-Contractual Relations in Business. *Am. Sociol. Rev.* 28:55–67.

Rose, Michael (1980). The Mental Arms Race Amplifier. *Human Ecology* 8:285–293.

Schelling, Thomas C. (1960). *The Strategy of Conflict*. London: Oxford University Press.

Schelling, Thomas C. (1978a). *Micromotives and Macrobehavior*. New York: Norton.

Schelling, Thomas C. (1978b). Altruism, Meanness, and Other Potentially Strategic Behaviors. *American Economic Review* 68:229–230.

Schelling, Thomas C. (1980). The Intimate Contest for Self-Command. *The Public Interest* 60.

Smith, Adam (1969). *The Theory of Moral Sentiments*, ed. E. G. West. Indianapolis: Liberty Classics.

Staddon, J. E. R. (1981). On a Possible Relation between Cultural Transmission and Genetical Evolution. In P. P. G. Bateson and P. H. Klopfer (eds.), *Advantages of Diversity*, vol. 4, New York: Plenum, pp. 135–145.

Telser, L. G. (1980). A Theory of Self-Enforcing Agreements. *J. of Bus.* 53:27–45.

Thompson, Earl A., and Roger L. Faith (1981). A Pure Theory of Strategic Behavior and Social Institutions. *Am. Econ. Rev.* 71: 366–380.

Trivers, Robert L. (1971). The Evolution of Reciprocal Altruism. *Quart. Rev. Biol.* 46:35–58.

Washburn, S. L. (1960). Tools and Human Evolution. *Sc. Am.* 203:63–75.

Wilson, Edward O. (1978). Altruism. *Harvard Mag.* 81:23–28.

11

What Strategies Can Support the Evolutionary Emergence of Cooperation?

Jack Hirshleifer and Juan Carlos Martinez Coll

Background of this Chapter

In *The Evolution of Cooperation* (1984), the political scientist Robert Axelrod contended that the simple reciprocity behavior known as "Tit for Tat" is an individually optimal strategy in social contexts generally, and thereby constitutes the major source of societal cooperation. These rather sweeping claims were widely accepted, perhaps more so by evolutionary theorists than by social scientists. Actually, more balanced accounts of the evolutionary strengths of reciprocity strategies, *and of their limitations*, had been previously offered in contributions by many authors. Among other examples, the efficacy of reciprocity strategies was evaluated in my "Evolutionary Models in Economics and Law" (1982, *Research in Law and Economics,* 4: 1–60), though not in the extract reprinted in this volume. I have returned to this topic in another article reprinted in this volume, "There Are Many Evolutionary Pathways to Cooperation" (1999, *Journal of Bioeconomics* 1: 73–93).

The present article analyzes, both theoretically and in terms of evolutionary simulations, the competition between Tit for Tat and several other strategies. The analysis reveals that only under a relatively narrow window of assumptions is Tit for Tat reliably successful in generating cooperation. Juan Carlos Martinez Coll and I have since extended the analysis in two additional coauthored articles, one of which appears as another chapter in this volume.

AUTHORS' NOTE: Jack Hirshleifer would like to thank the Ford Foundation and Juan Carlos Martinez Coll would like to thank the Hispano-American Joint Committee and the Fulbright Program for partial support of this research. An earlier version of this article appeared in the Working Paper series of the Center for International and Strategic Affairs, UCLA. Valuable comments and criticisms were provided by Daniel Klein, Barton L. Lipman, John Maynard Smith, Craig McCann, Eric Alden Smith, Gordon Tullock, Heinrich Ursprung, and Donald Wittman, and we thank Robert Axelrod for earlier correspondence. (Reprinted from J. Hirshleifer and J. C. Martinez Coll, "What Strategies Can Support the Evolutionary Emergence of Cooperation," *Journal of Conflict Resolution*, Vol. 32, No. 2, 367–98, Copyright © 1988, with permission from Sage Publications, Inc.)

Anatol Rapoport, one of the most creative early game theorists and the "inventor" of the Tit for Tat strategy, published a valuable comment on this article that appeared with it when initially published in the *Journal of Conflict Resolution* (1988, "Editorial Comments in the article by Hirshleifer and Martinez Coll," 32: 399–401).

I thank Juan Carlos Martinez Coll for allowing reprinting of this jointly authored article.

Abstract

Axelrod found TIT-FOR-TAT to be a highly successful strategy in the Prisoners' Dilemma payoff environment. He concluded that a natural selection process in favor of TIT-FOR-TAT explains the evolutionary emergence of cooperation. This article shows that, contrary to Axelrod, TIT-FOR-TAT does not approach 100% fixation in the population. More generally, TIT-FOR-TAT is not a robustly successful strategy if Axelrod's exact assumptions do not apply – for example, if there is a cost of complexity or a probability of error, or when players compete in an elimination contest rather than a round-robin tournament. In fact, it is unreasonable to expect any single strategy to win out in evolutionary competition. Constructively, we show that the presence of a PUNISHER strategy typically generates, consistent with observation, an interior equilibrium in which more and less cooperative strategies simultaneously coexist.

Social scientists have recently been devoting increasing attention to evolutionary models for the emergence of cooperation, thanks especially to the seminal works of the biologist John Maynard Smith (1976, 1978, 1982). The best known applications are due to the political scientist Robert Axelrod (see Axelrod and Hamilton, 1981; Axelrod, 1981, 1984). A number of other writers, including the present authors (Hirshleifer, 1982; Martinez Coll, 1986), have also analyzed a variety of evolutionary or selectional models of social competition and cooperation. Such models are characterized by the feature that, over time, more successful strategies grow while less successful strategies shrink in representation within the general population. Ultimately, a final equilibrium may be reached, though it is also possible to have a variety of cycling or chaotic outcomes.

The choice of equilibrium concept for evolutionary models is not without problems. The best-known such concept was introduced by Maynard Smith and named by him the "evolutionarily stable strategy" (ESS). More generally, equilibrium may be characterized not by universal adoption of a *single* strategy but rather by a *set* of strategies, so ESS should be taken to mean the "evolutionarily stable strategy set." Going beyond terminology to substance, it has been found that Maynard Smith's definition of the ESS may fail to designate the actual

The Dark Side of the Force

stable state to which the population proportions ultimately converge.[1] The latter, evidently, is what is really meant when people speak of evolutionary equilibrium. Consequently, in encountering references to the ESS, one can never be certain whether what is being alluded to is Maynard Smith's definition or the true evolutionary equilibrium. In this article, in speaking of the ESS we will always be referring to Maynard Smith's original definition; when we mean the ultimate stable proportions to which an evolutionarily changing population converges (if such exist), we will speak more precisely of the "evolutionary equilibrium" (EE).[2]

Quite famous by now are the two computer round-robin tournaments conducted by Axelrod (1984, Chap. 2) in which strategies proposed by various experts competed against one another in a simulated struggle for "survival of the fittest" in a Prisoners' Dilemma payoff environment. In the first tournament, each of 15 different strategies was pitted against every other (and against a clone of itself) in 200-round interactions. In the second tournament there were 62 entries; this time, instead of each pairwise interaction lasting a prespecified 200 rounds, a fixed probability of continuation was chosen that worked out to make the average contest length 151 rounds.

Both tournaments were "won" by the conditional-cooperation strategy known as TIT-FOR-TAT. (This strategy was proposed by the game theorist Anatol Rapoport.) Against any opponent in a Prisoners' Dilemma interaction, the TIT-FOR-TAT player initially acts cooperatively but thereafter simply mirrors his opponent's behavior in the previous round. Thus an opponent who "defects" at any point is punished, but in a proportionate eye-for-an-eye way that leaves open the possibility of later reversion toward more cooperative play. The success of TIT-FOR-TAT in the tournaments was due primarily to its robustness. Even though TIT-FOR-TAT never outscored any single opponent strategy in a one-on-one encounter, it piled up points by never losing very badly and by achieving mutually high scores when paired against opponents able to revert to cooperative play. (And, in particular, TIT-FOR-TAT will always do very well when paired against itself.)

---

[1] See Taylor and Jonker (1978) and Zeeman (1981). Our interpretation of this divergence is that Maynard Smith's ESS is a purely "static" specification of conditions for equilibrium, defined solely in terms of the elements of the payoff matrix. But the actual course of evolutionary change will also depend upon the specific *dynamic process* postulated. Different equations for defining how the population proportions change over time will in general lead to differing terminal situations, even for the same payoff matrix.

[2] The EE terminology was used in Riley (1979) and Hirshleifer (1982).

Going beyond the tournaments, in his book Axelrod develops an extended "ecological" approach to the competition among the different strategies. In a computer simulation of hypothetical future rounds of interaction, the contending strategies were imagined to increase or decrease in relative representation in the population in accordance with their greater or lesser competitive success (survival of the fittest). He found that TIT-FOR-TAT continued to thrive and thus to increase in representation through some 1,000 "generations."[3]

It has been claimed, on the basis of these results, that mutually profitable adoption of TIT-FOR-TAT is *the* explanation for the evolution of cooperation.[4] Social cooperation emerges, supposedly, because populations initially pursuing a variety of strategies tend toward an evolutionary equilibrium (EE) in which everyone ultimately plays TIT-FOR-TAT.[5] But models leading to the result that any single strategy will become universal prove too much. Real populations typically display a considerable variety of behaviors. Apart from testing the claims made on behalf of TIT-FOR-TAT, therefore, our goal is to search for EEs characterized by stable *mixtures* of strategies that at least roughly characterize some aspects of the distribution of choices observed in human populations.

Turning from result to method, Axelrod's tournaments had a number of rather special, idiosyncratic features that ought to make analysts cautious about drawing very sweeping conclusions:

(1) Prisoners' Dilemma is only one of a vast number of mixed-incentive payoff environments in which cooperation might or might not emerge. Prisoners' Dilemma does correspond to important real-world social contexts, for example, to the famous "free-rider" problem in the provision of public goods. But there

---

[3] We should make clear that our use of words like *ecology* or *generation* does not necessarily imply that we believe all choice of strategies to be biologically determined or genetically inherited. These strategies can just as well be culturally evolved rules of behavior such as those considered in Nelson and Winter (1982) or Boyd and Richerson (1985).

[4] Qualifying statements do appear from time to time in Axelrod's works. But the dramatic image of the tournaments, in which TIT-FOR-TAT as David slew assorted Goliaths, apparently caught the fancy of a number of commentators who went on to make rather extreme claims on behalf of TIT-FOR-TAT as the sole or main source of social cooperation.

[5] "Simulated future rounds of the tournament suggested that TIT-FOR-TAT would continue to thrive, and that eventually it might be used by virtually everyone" (Axelrod, 1984: 55).

are a host of other significant classes of mixed-motive interaction patterns. Even within the very special category of two-person games with two strategy options per player, a number of other patterns – such as Chicken[6] (which the biologists call Hawk-Dove) and Battle of the Sexes – are almost as famous as Prisoners' Dilemma itself. Other mixed-incentive payoff patterns have been described by various authors under such titles as Hero and Leader (Rapoport, 1967), Deadlock, Called Buff, Bully, and Protector (Snyder and Diesing, 1977: 45ff), and Tender Trap (Hirshleifer, 1982). And the range of distinguishable payoff environments increases without bound when we allow either *the number of strategy options per player* or the *number of interacting players* to grow from 2 to 3 to 4 (and so on).

(2) The tournaments made no provision for even the most elemental social structure or stratification. Instead, members of an anonymous homogeneous population were imagined to interact with one another entirely at random. Allowing for social stratification – in which, for example, males might interact only or preferentially with females and vice versa – would drastically change the nature of the model.[7]

(3) The victories of TIT-FOR-TAT were achieved by amassing high scores in *round-robin* tournaments with cumulated payoffs. But not all social struggles take this form. A very important alternative is the *elimination* tournament. TIT-FOR-TAT does poorly in elimination contests, as it is essentially never able to defeat any competing strategy in a one-on-one encounter.

(4) The tournaments were necessarily limited to the particular set of strategies put forward by the various experts (though Axelrod attempted to provide a more general formal analysis in an appendix to his book).[8]

We will, apart from occasional remarks, also be holding here to the first two of these limiting features: Our analysis will be conducted solely

---

[6] Axelrod's approach has recently been extended to the game of Chicken in Lipman (1986).

[7] Axelrod (1984, Chaps. 3, 8) does analyze one aspect of social structure in his book, the consequences for evolutionary equilibrium if "invasions" by *clusters* as well as by atomic individuals are permitted.

[8] In a somewhat analogous development in the biological literature, Maynard Smith and Price (1973) studied the interaction of a number of competing strategies within an underlying payoff framework that corresponds to the game of Chicken.

within an underlying Prisoners' Dilemma payoff environment, and we will be assuming a homogeneous, unstructured population of individuals. But we will be diverging from the other two special features of Axelrod's tournaments. With regard to the menu of competing strategies (Number 4 above), Axelrod emphasized that TIT-FOR-TAT as "winner" was the simplest of the candidate strategies submitted by the various experts. But there are two other strategies, not entered into his contests, that are simpler still. These are the archetypical Prisoners' Dilemma options: *Always play COOPERATE* and *Always play DEFECT*.[9] It turns out that there are important circumstances in which one or the other of these "archetype" strategies can defeat TIT-FOR-TAT and displace it in evolutionary competition. Furthermore, as will be seen below, even the simplest triads of strategies – COOPERATE, DEFECT, plus TIT-FOR-TAT or some other third option – generate a rich assortment of permutations that cast light upon the evolutionary viability of alternative modes of cooperation. As to Number 3 above, we will be devoting some attention to *elimination tournaments.*

To complete the preliminaries, Table 11.1 shows a number of the payoff patterns used in the analyses that follow. Each such pattern is a bimatrix containing elements of the form (a_{ij}, b_{ij}), where there is a symmetry such that $a_{ij} = b_{ji}$. Matrices I and II show the basic Prisoners' Dilemma environment (which is defined in terms of the two archetype strategies, COOPERATE and DEFECT) in two different ways. Matrix I displays the "ordinal" or ranked payoffs to each player on a scale from 1 (lowest) to 4 (highest). The characteristic defining Prisoners' Dilemma is that, for each player, the COOPERATE strategy (C) is strictly dominated by the DEFECT strategy (D) – that is, DEFECT yields a higher payoff regardless of what the opponent does. In view of the symmetry of the payoff pattern, the mathematical condition for a Prisoners' Dilemma can be stated solely in terms of the a_{ij}, to wit: $a_{DC} > a_{CC}$ and $a_{DD} > a_{CD}$. As for Matrix II, this is the particular "cardinal" or numerical instance of Prisoners' Dilemma employed in Axelrod's studies.

In what follows, except as needed to illustrate particular points, our menu of strategies will always include the two archetypes – COOPERATE and DEFECT. We will be entering this basic pair into competition with TIT-FOR-TAT, but also with several alternative third strategies of the same order of complexity as TIT-FOR-TAT.

---

[9] Axelrod's formal analysis in Appendix B (see Axelrod, 1984) does consider the COOPERATE and DEFECT strategies. (Further discussion of his analysis is provided in a note below.)

The Dark Side of the Force

Table 11.1.

Matrix I				Matrix II		
Prisoners' Dilemma (ordinal form)				Prisoners' Dilemma (numerical form)		
	C	D			C	D
C	3, 3	1, 4		C	3, 3	0, 5
D	4, 1	2, 2		D	5, 0	1, 1

Matrix III				Matrix IV			
DEFECT versus TIT-FOR-TAT				Prisoners' Dilemma + TIT-FOR-TAT			
	D	T			C	D	T
D	1, 1	1, 1		C	3, 3	0, 5	3, 3
T	1, 1	3, 3		D	5, 0	1, 1	1, 1
				T	3, 3	1, 1	3, 3

Matrix V				Matrix VI			
PD + T with COC = .5				PD + T with POE = .1			
	C	D	T		C	D	T
C	3, 3	0, 5	3, 2.5	C	3, 3	0, 5	2.7, 3.2
D	5, 0	1, 1	1, .5	D	5, 0	1, 1	1.4, .9
T	2.5, 3	.5, 1	2.5, 2.5	T	3.2, 2.7	.9, 1.4	2.89, 2.89

In contrast with Axelrod, we will be using a special interpretation of TIT-FOR-TAT (and other "reactive" strategies) permitting us to make the vastly simplifying assumption of *one-time* rather than *repeated* pairwise interactions. Despite the simplification involved, this interpretation will allow us to replicate, either exactly or to a very close approximation, the evolutionary results of the repeated interactions postulated in Axelrod's "ecological" analysis. Put another way, our analysis is *single-round* but *multi-generation*.

TIT-FOR-TAT AS THIRD STRATEGY
IN THE PRISONERS' DILEMMA

We will be employing an explicit dynamic formula that is standard in models of this type (see, e.g., Zeeman, 1981), though by no means the only one conceivable. This formula determines Δp_s – the change in any single time-period or "generation" in the proportion p_s following strategy s – in terms of underlying variables and parameters:[10]

$$\Delta p_s = k p_s (Y_s - M). \tag{1}$$

[10] There is another possible interpretation, which postulates that instead of a *mixed population* there is a uniform population following a *mixed strategy*. Then p_s would represent the probability attaching to strategy s in the strategy mixture at any moment of time.

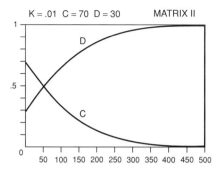

Figure 11.1. Prisoners' Dilemma, historical diagram.

The Y_s represent the respective average payoff yields, defined for any strategy s as:

$$Y_s = \sum_j p_j a_{sj} \qquad [2]$$

where, as before, a_{ij} is the payoff to Row strategy i played against Column strategy j. M is the overall or societal mean of these yields:

$$M = \sum_s p_s Y_s \qquad [3]$$

And, finally, k is a constant representing the "sensitivity" or speed of response.[11]

For background, let us start with the simple Prisoners' Dilemma, in which the archetype strategies COOPERATE and DEFECT are the only ones in contention. Figure 11.1 illustrates a possible evolutionary or "historical" progression of the corresponding population proportions p_C and p_D over 500 generations. The situation pictured is based upon the payoffs of Matrix II (Axelrod's matrix) and an initial population distribution of $p_C = .7$ and $p_D = .3$. As can be seen, COOPERATE, despite its initial preponderance, is being driven to inevitable extinction – or, in biological terminology, DEFECT is approaching fixation. In terms of population proportions, the evolutionary equilibrium (EE) being asymptotically[12]

---

[11] This is of course a discrete-generation model, as was also employed by Axelrod. In a continuous model, the left-hand-side of equation 1 would be the time-derivative $\dot{p}_s$. In some cases, the discrete and continuous models could have significantly different implications. (See the following note.)

[12] If equation 1 were expressed in continuous form, absolute extinction could essentially never occur (since the derivative is going to zero with the same order of rapidity as p_s itself). For the discrete formulation employed here, however, literal extinction can occur – so it is not strictly correct to say that the EE is being approached *asymptotically*. To avoid awkward circumlocutions, we will permit ourselves this slightly imprecise language. (In our simulations, we have taken care to avoid "accidental" extinctions due to the discreteness of Δp_s.)

approached here is $(p_C, p_D) = (0,1)$. This is, of course, an evolutionary version of the standard result with Prisoners' Dilemma: While there is a mutual advantage from cooperation, at any play of the game those choosing DEFECT will do better and thus become steadily more numerous in the population.

Someone who always plays COOPERATE (C) is behaving in accordance with the *Golden Rule* of social interaction. Someone who plays TIT-FOR-TAT (T) may be said to be following a kind of *Silver Rule*: Be nice to begin with and respond to niceness with niceness, but answer meanness with meanness. To complete the metallic metaphor, a DEFECT (D) player can be regarded as a follower of the *Brass Rule*: always be nasty!

As defined by Axelrod, TIT-FOR-TAT is applicable only when there are multiple rounds of play in each interaction, since the T player mirrors his opponent's previous move. Within a single-round model it is not possible to replicate exactly Axelrod's TIT-FOR-TAT strategy. But we can approximate it, in a way that slightly stacks the deck in favor of TIT-FOR-TAT. To be specific, our T players are assumed to have the capacity to recognize *instantaneously* the characteristic moves of the COOPERATE and of the DEFECT players – "nice" and "mean," respectively – in each encounter and to respond to each *immediately* in accordance with the TIT-FOR-TAT principle. Thus our T players cannot be exploited by DEFECT players, even in the very first encounter. And finally, we assume that the T players are also able to recognize and respond appropriately to the initially "nice" moves of fellow-T's. This instant-recognition, immediate-response assumption is somewhat unrealistic and will be reconsidered in our analysis that follows. But there is actually very little quantitative disparity between Axelrod's version of TIT-FOR-TAT and ours. In the payoff environment of Matrix II, Axelrod's T player can be exploited by a DEFECT player only in the very first of some 150 to 200 rounds of play, both parties' behavior thereafter being mutually "mean." Allowing the mutual meanness to start at the first round instead of the second round makes no big difference when the payoffs are aggregated over 150 or 200 rounds. (However, as will shortly be seen, there is a *qualitative* difference that sometimes may affect the equilibrium attained.)

With the basic Prisoners' Dilemma payoffs of Matrix II, where only the "archetype" COOPERATE and DEFECT strategies are in play, we have seen that DEFECT drives COOPERATE to extinction. What happens when TIT-FOR-TAT (Silver Rule) replaces COOPERATE (Golden

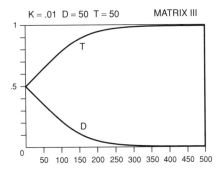

Figure 11.2. DEFECT versus TIT-FOR-TAT historical diagram.

Rule) in this struggle for survival? Matrix III shows the associated payoffs, derived from Matrix II using the instant-recognition assumption for TIT-FOR-TAT. Figure 11.2 is the associated "historical" diagram, with the initial proportions arbitrarily set at .5 each. We can see that the tables have been turned; now it is the uncooperative DEFECT strategy that is being driven to extinction. Consistent with Axelrod's argument, the Old Testament eye-for-an-eye ethic seems to work, whereas the New Testament turn-the-other-cheek ethic does not, in supporting the evolutionary emergence of cooperation.

Our slight stacking of the deck in favor of TIT-FOR-TAT has only a minor quantitative effect upon the evolutionary result. Suppose that the T player could react only in the *second* of 200 rounds. Then Matrix III would have to be modified: The D,T (upper right) element would be (1.02,.995) and the T, D element (lower left) would correspondingly be (.995,1.02). This small change suffices to assure that if the population consists initially almost entirely of D players, it will converge toward an all-DEFECT evolutionary equilibrium. So under Axelrod's strict assumptions, both all-T and all-D are possible EEs when DEFECT and TIT-FOR-TAT are the only strategies in contention.[13] (However, the all-D outcome occurs only for a very narrow range of initial conditions.)

Following the basic procedure outlined above, we now suppose that COOPERATE and DEFECT (as archetypes of the Prisoners' Dilemma interaction) enter into evolutionary competition with alternative third strategies, in this case represented by TIT-FOR-TAT. Matrix IV shows the payoffs for this three-way competition. A typical "historical" development is pictured in Figure 11.3, which shows the evolution of the respective population proportions over 500 generations. (In this picture

[13] Axelrod (1984, Appendix B) recognizes that all-D is always a possible equilibrium.

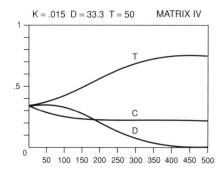

Figure 11.3. Prisoners' Dilemma + TIT-FOR-TAT, historical diagram.

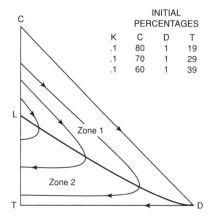

Figure 11.4. Prisoners' Dilemma + TIT-FOR-TAT, phase diagram.

the proportions following the different strategies were set initially at one-third each.) Notice that while DEFECT is being driven to extinction, TIT-FOR-TAT does not seem to be approaching fixation. Instead, it appears that the evolutionary equilibrium EE here will be a mixture of COOPERATE and TIT-FOR-TAT.[14]

The processes at work can be visualized with more generality and precision if we shift from the "historical" illustration of Figure 11.3 to the "phase diagram" picture of Figure 11.4. In such a diagram any point of the triangle represents a distribution of the population over the three strategy options. The vertical coordinate indicates the proportion p_C choosing COOPERATE, the horizontal coordinate shows the

---

[14] Once again, had we refrained from stacking the deck and adopted the strict definition of TIT-FOR-TAT instead, then if the initial population proportions were very nearly 100% DEFECT, the population would converge toward the all-DEFECT solution. From now on we will not take the trouble to repeat this minor qualification.

proportion p_D choosing DEFECT, and finally the remaining proportion p_T choosing TIT-FOR-TAT is measured by the horizontal (or, equivalently, the vertical) distance from the point to the hypotenuse HK. Thus the vertices represent positions where the population consists *exclusively* of individuals playing the corresponding strategy.[15]

It will be useful at this point to provide in Table 11.2 a *partial* listing of the conditions for various types of evolutionary equilibria (EEs) in the 3×3 case. (A full listing of the necessary and sufficient conditions would require quite a lengthy and abstract discussion, which would be out of place here; we will be limiting ourselves to some of the more easily specified relevant conditions.) There are three general types of EEs, to wit: (i) at a vertex (i.e., only one strategy is present in the EE), (ii) along an edge (i.e., two strategies are present), and (iii) in the interior (i.e., all three strategies are present). The conditions are stated with only minimal explanation here, as verification is not at all difficult.

Let us return to the DEFECT-COOPERATE-TIT-FOR-TAT interaction tabulated in Matrix IV. As illustrated in Figure 11.3 and 11.4, DEFECT is becoming extinct. But, contrary to Axelrod's assertion, TIT-FOR-TAT is *not* tending toward universality in the population. Instead, a particular ratio between TIT-FOR-TAT and COOPERATE is being approached as the EE. In fact, we have here an instance of the type of EE specified by condition B.3 in Table 11.2.[16] At vertex T (the origin in Figure 11.4), and also at vertex C, the payoffs to C and T are equal – so that D defeats both of them at vertex C, but is defeated by both of them at vertex T. In Matrix IV, as the D strategy approaches extinction the payoffs to C and T are becoming identical, hence there is no basis

---

[15] Since equation 1 provides no way for a strategy to recover from extinction, we will always be dealing with interior *initial* positions. Such positions put all three strategies in competition, at least initially.

[16] In his text, Axelrod (1984: 59–60, Appendix B) attempts to prove that TIT-FOR-TAT is "collectively stable" – a condition essentially equivalent to what we would call a vertex EE at all-T. (While his proof refers to a repeated-round situation, our instant-recognition assumption is equivalent to making his *w*, the discount parameter, necessarily "large enough" in his terminology.) Our analysis shows that, as a very special case, all-TIT-FOR-TAT could indeed be the EE – but only if there were no COOPERATE players initially in the population! The flaw in Axelrod's proof is his assumption that a vertex equilibrium "cannot be invaded" so long as its payoff at that vertex is *greater than or equal to* the payoff of other strategies at that vertex. As Table 11.2 shows, this is indeed a necessary but not a sufficient condition for a vertex EE. And in particular here, COOPERATE is as profitable as TIT-FOR-TAT at the all-TIT-FOR-TAT vertex. Thus there is a range of possible equilibrium mixtures of COOPERATE and TIT-FOR-TAT – the particular EE arrived at being dependent upon the initial proportions in the population.

for evolutionary selection between COOPERATE and TIT-FOR-TAT in the absence of DEFECT. But as it is the TIT-FOR-TAT players who bear the burden of penalizing those following the DEFECT strategy, the COOPERATE (Golden Rule) players may be regarded as *parasitic* upon those playing TIT-FOR-TAT (Silver Rule). The presence of players

Table 11.2. Conditions for 3 × 3 Evolutionary Equilibrium (Partial)

(A) *EE at vertex I*

    (1) A *necessary* condition is:

$$a_{ii} \geq a_{ji}, a_{ki}$$

    In a condensed notation, we can write this as:

$$I : i \geq j, k$$

    In words: For an evolutionary equilibrium at vertex I, strategy i must do at least as well as any other strategy when the population is all-i.

    (2) A *sufficient* condition is (using the condensed notation):

$$I : i > j, k$$

    It follows immediately from A.2 that a given payoff matrix may be associated with 1, 2, or 3 possible vertex EEs.

    (3) A different *sufficient* condition is:

$$I : i = j > k$$

$$J : i > j$$

(B) *EE along edge IJ*

    (1) A *necessary* condition is:

$$I : j \geq i$$

$$J : i \geq j$$

    and $i, j > k$ at either I or J or both.

    (2) A *sufficient* condition is:

$$I : j > i > k$$

$$j : i > j > k$$

    This condition leads to a unique EE somewhere along the edge, not at a vertex.

    (3) A different *sufficient* condition is:

$$I : i = j > k$$

$$J : i = j$$

    In contrast with B.2, this condition leads to a continuum of possible EEs along a portion of the edge. The portion will be the entire IJ edge if $J : i = j \geq k$. But if $J : k > i = j$, the EEs will lie along a range beginning at the I vertex but extending only partway to the J vertex.

Table 11.2. (Continued)

(C)	*EE in the interior*

A *necessary* condition is:

$I : j$ or $k > i$

$J : i$ or $k > j$

$K : i$ or $j > k$

(D)   Finally, it is quite possible that *no* evolutionary equilibrium EE exists.

Note: Since all the conditions here are defined in terms of the payoffs only, with no explicit provisions for dynamics, these should be regarded as conditions for Maynard Smith's ESS (Evolutionarily Stable Strategy) concept rather than for the EE (Evolutionary Equilibrium), properly speaking. There are ESSs that cannot be attained under some dynamics, and there are dynamics that may lead to EEs that are not ESSs. The "sufficient" conditions shown in the table represent equilibria that are attainable under dynamic equation 1, at least if the Δp_s are kept sufficiently small by choice of a low k.

following the eye-for-an-eye ethic provides a shelter in which those following turn-the-other-cheek can survive. In this case, the parasitism does not destroy the mutually cooperative nature of the EE, since both C and T players engage in "nice" behavior. Still, we might fear, are there perhaps environments in which the presence of parasitic Golden Rule players subverts the possibility of *either* COOPERATE or TIT-FOR-TAT surviving? (For the moment, we will reserve the answer to this question.)

Figure 11.4 is divided into two zones by the curve LD. In zone 1, as indicated by the arrows, the population tends to evolve in a southeasterly direction, that is, p_C tends to decrease and p_D to increase (with the effect upon p_T depending upon whether the movement takes the population proportions closer to or farther from the hypotenuse CD). What is happening here is that, since COOPERATE players are relatively numerous in the population, the DEFECT strategy that exploits them is very profitable, so that the latter grows at the expense of the former. However, all the paths in zone 1 lead eventually into zone 2, where the movement is in a southwesterly direction, that is, TIT-FOR-TAT is increasing at the expense of both COOPERATE and DEFECT. Here, COOPERATE players having become rare, the DEFECT strategy suffers for lack of victims to exploit. In a population consisting mainly of DEFECT and TIT-FOR-TAT players, the latter do relatively better, since they rack up points by cooperating with one another.

The dividing curve expresses the condition that strategy D is neither increasing nor decreasing, so that, from equation 1:

$$Y_D = M.$$

Using the payoffs of Matrix IV this becomes

$$2p_D^2 + 3p_C p_D - 4p_D - 4p_C + 2 = 0$$

The upshot is that the population will eventually attain an EE along the portion of the TC edge falling within zone 2, the exact terminus in this range being dependent upon the initial distribution of the proportions following the various strategies.

This discussion can be summarized by the following propositions:

> *Proposition 1*: In a triadic interaction among COOPERATE, DE-
> FECT, and TIT-FOR-TAT (as defined here, assuming instant recog-
> nition and immediate response), the evolutionary equilibrium EE
> is characterized by the ultimate extinction of DEFECT and a stable
> division of the population between COOPERATE and TIT-FOR-
> TAT.

> *Proposition 2*: The proportion of COOPERATE in the EE, p_C^*, can-
> not exceed a certain critical fraction $\bar{p}_C$ corresponding to the lo-
> cation of point L in Figure 11.4.[17] Furthermore, the larger the
> *initial* proportion p_C° the smaller will be the ultimate *equilibrium*
> proportion p_C^*.[18]

But this otherwise attractive model for the emergence of cooperation – with its EE including a fraction of TIT-FOR-TAT (Silver Rule) players, the remainder being pure COOPERATE (Golden Rule) players – has a very serious flaw. Ability to play TIT-FOR-TAT requires more complex capacities than either of the simple archetype strategies. The TIT-FOR-TAT player has to be able to distinguish between the "nice" and "mean"

---

[17] Numerically, $\bar{p}_C$, the *maximum possible* proportion of COOPERATE in the EE, is determined by the elements of the underlying Prisoners' Dilemma payoff matrix. To find $\bar{p}_C$, we set equal the payoffs to D and T along the TC edge (where $p_D = 0$):

$$a_{DC}\bar{p}_C + a_{DT}(1 - \bar{p}_C) = a_{TC}\bar{p}_C + a_{TT}(1 - \bar{p}_C)$$

For the numbers in Matrix IV, $p_C = .5$ as indicated by the location of point L in the diagram.

[18] When COOPERATE is very numerous to begin with, DEFECT temporarily becomes a large "predator" population that drives down the numbers of its COOPERATE "prey."

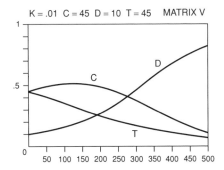

Figure 11.5. PD + T with COC = .5, historical diagram.

moves that the various strategy-types will initially offer, and must possess in his or her behavioral repertory the appropriate maneuvers for responding to each.

There are a number of ways in which this difficulty might be modeled. We shall examine two possible approaches here, which turn out to have remarkably different results for the evolutionary equilibrium achieved – a difference that suggests the fragility rather than alleged robustness of EEs involving the TIT-FOR-TAT strategy.

Our first adjustment for the more sophisticated capacities that TIT-FOR-TAT requires takes the form of a *cost of complexity* penalty (COC). This is assumed to be a fixed burden upon the T player, to be deducted from all his or her payoffs. Specifically here, Matrix V is a modification of Matrix IV in which each TIT-FOR-TAT payoff has been reduced by .5 units.

With TIT-FOR-TAT subject to a COC penalty as in Matrix V, the result is disastrous for the evolution of cooperation. Figure 11.5 pictures a typical evolutionary history. Starting with the initial distribution $(p_C, p_D, p_T, = .45, .1, .45)$, COOPERATE initially grows in representation, but to no ultimate avail, since as TIT-FOR-TAT fades away nothing can prevent DEFECT from moving toward fixation. Figure 11.6 is the corresponding phase diagram, showing how all time paths lead to the D vertex. So, answering the question posed above, given a positive cost of complexity the parasitic behavior implied by the Golden Rule ethic can indeed totally destroy the evolutionary prospects for cooperation.

An alternative way of adjusting for the extra requirements that TIT-FOR-TAT imposes is to allow for a *probability of error* (POE). A certain percent of the time, we now assume, the T player will mistake the opening nice behavior of a C player (or of another T player) for a mean move – and the reverse if a D player is encountered – leading in each case

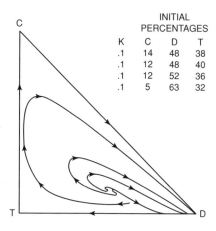

INITIAL
PERCENTAGES

K	C	D	T
.1	14	48	38
.1	12	48	40
.1	12	52	36
.1	5	63	32

Figure 11.6. PD + T with COC = .5, phase diagram.

to an inappropriate response. Matrix VI shows the payoffs when the probability of error[19] is POE = .1.[20]

In comparison with cost of complexity (COC), which as we have seen leads inevitably to all-DEFECT as the sole evolutionary equilibrium, probability of error (POE) has more varied consequences. Using rule A.2 of Table 11.2, we can see from Matrix VI that all-D and all-T are *both* vertex EEs. Which of the two is attained will depend upon the initial population proportions. Figure 11.7 shows a typical historical pattern leading ultimately to an all-TIT-FOR-TAT equilibrium. The basins leading to all-T and all-D outcomes are pictured in Figure 11.8. (As it happens, with the numerical payoffs assumed here the basin for the all-DEFECT solution is quite small, being limited to a thin silver near

---

[19] More generally, we might want to allow for different probabilities of error depending upon whether the opponent encountered is a C, a D, or another T player. But for simplicity, a uniform POE is assumed.

[20] The returns to the T player, in encountering the various types of opponents, are calculated as follows:

T vs. C: The T player will make the correct "nice" response .9 of the time and the incorrect "mean" response .1 of the time, so his or her average payoff for such encounters will be .9(3) + .1(5) = 3.2. By similar reasoning, the C player will receive .9(3) + .1(0) = 2.7.

T vs. D: The average payoff to the T player will be .9(1) + .1(0) = .9, while the D player will receive .9(1) + .1(5) = 1.4.

T vs. T: The assumption here is that both T players initiate "nice" moves, but that *either or both* may make the incorrect interpretation thereof. Then there is a .81 chance that both make the correct moves, a .09 chance that only one (and another .09 chance that only the other) makes an error, and a .01 chance that they both make the mistake. The average payoff for each is then .81(3) + .09(5) + .09(0) + .01(1) = 2.89.

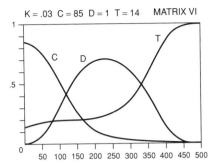

Figure 11.7. PD + T with POE = .1, historical diagram.

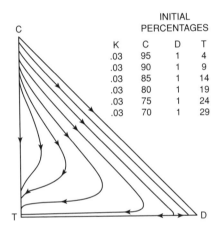

Figure 11.8. PD + T with POE = .1, phase diagram.

	INITIAL PERCENTAGES		
K	C	D	T
.03	95	1	4
.03	90	1	9
.03	85	1	14
.03	80	1	19
.03	75	1	24
.03	70	1	29

the hypotenuse. That is, all-DEFECT will be the EE only if the initial proportion of T players is very low.)

Interestingly, allowing for a probability of error POE can improve the evolutionary prospects of TIT-FOR-TAT – making it possible or even likely that an all-T evolutionary equilibrium will be attained (instead of the C, T mixture otherwise attained). The reason is that such mistakes provide a way of limiting the success of the "parasitic" COOPERATE strategy.

We can summarize these results with two additional propositions:

Proposition 3: When TIT-FOR-TAT is penalized with a positive cost of complexity (COC), however small, both COOPERATE and TIT-FOR-TAT inevitably go extinct. Only DEFECT survives in the evolutionary equilibrium.

Proposition 4: When TIT-FOR-TAT is subject to a positive probability of error (POE), there are two possible vertex EEs, all-DEFECT and all-TIT-FOR-TAT – one or the other being attained, depending upon the initial population distribution.

The implications of the analysis for Pareto-efficiency are rather evident and can be summarized briefly. The basic Prisoners' Dilemma interaction (C versus D) leads of course to the inefficient all-D outcome. The addition of TIT-FOR-TAT, in its ideal costless and errorless form, makes the outcome a C, T mixture that is Pareto-efficient. TIT-FOR-TAT with a positive COC, however, leads back to the inefficient all-D outcome. And TIT-FOR-TAT with a positive POE can lead either to the efficient all-T or the inefficient all-D outcome.

BULLY AS THIRD STRATEGY

We now turn away from TIT-FOR-TAT to consider the consequences of adjoining alternative third strategies to the COOPERATE and DEFECT archetypes that define the Prisoners' Dilemma.

The first such alternative – called BULLY here – is a simple reactive strategy like TIT-FOR-TAT, but reversed. As can be seen in Matrix VII in Table 11.3, BULLY plays like COOPERATE against DEFECT, and like DEFECT against COOPERATE. (We are again assuming an instant recognition capability.) What about BULLY versus BULLY? Our reasoning here is that, since BULLY players are initially mean, the one moving first will behave like DEFECT while the other gives way and is exploited like COOPERATE. Since each player can expect to find him- or herself in either role about half the time (assuming random encounters), the average payoff to each is $.5(5) + .5(0) = 2.5$ as shown in Matrix VII.

The BULLY strategy does not succeed here, however. In Matrix VII, once COOPERATE has been eliminated the payoffs to BULLY are strictly dominated by those to DEFECT. Thus both DEFECT and BULLY will initially combine to drive COOPERATE to extinction – after which DEFECT will have no difficulty disposing of BULLY. And this result holds even without allowing for any complications, like cost of complexity or probability of error, associated with the extra capacities that reactive policies like BULLY impose upon their players. Thus we can summarize briefly:

Proposition 5: The BULLY strategy cannot survive in evolutionary equilibrium, nor will it prevent the extinction of COOPERATE. As in the standard Prisoners' Dilemma, the EE will be all-DEFECT.

Table 11.3.

	Matrix VII PD + BULLY		
	C	D	B
C	3, 3	0, 5	0, 5
D	5, 0	1, 1	5, 0
B	5, 0	0, 5	2.5, 2.5

	Matrix VIII PD + PUNISHER		
	C	D	P
C	3, 3	0, 5	3, 2
D	5, 0	1, 1	0, 3
P	2, 3	3, 0	2, 2

	Matrix IX PD + T – Elimination Payoff Matrix		
	C	D	T
C	.5, .5	0, 1	.5, .5
D	1, 0	.5, .5	.5, .5
T	.5, .5	.5, .5	.5, .5

PUNISHER AS THIRD STRATEGY

None of the interactions considered to this point serve to capture one crucial feature of the real world: to wit, that many different strategies manage to survive in the very mixed pattern that constitutes human behavior. Something more than the simple archetype strategies (COOP-ERATE and DEFECT) or simple reactive strategies (BULLY and TIT-FOR-TAT) seems needed if we are to make progress in this direction.

As a new class of third strategy in Prisoners' Dilemma payoff environments, we propose what will be termed PUNISHER behavior. A PUNISHER (P) player corresponds to what would be called in biological contexts a "superpredator," that is, an organism that preys on lower-level predators, or, in human terms, a bounty hunter. In the Prisoners' Dilemma context, PUNISHER as superpredator would exploit the exploitive DEFECT players but be nice to those choosing COOPERATE.

The Dark Side of the Force

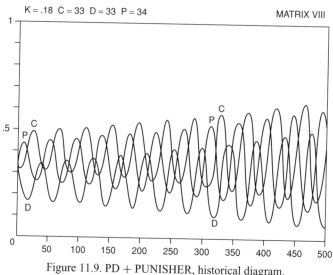

Figure 11.9. PD + PUNISHER, historical diagram.

Matrix VIII represents a possible set of payoffs when a PUNISHER strategy is adjoined to the two archetype strategies. We have chosen numbers such that P is never very profitable (in effect, we have already allowed for a considerable "cost of complexity" penalty), but it does achieve its greatest return when encountering DEFECT. Thus the C, D, P interaction is rather like the children's game of Rock-Paper-Scissors: When the population is at the all-C vertex, the D strategy is most profitable; when it is at all-D, the P strategy yields the biggest return; and at all-P, it is best to be a C player.

As can be seen from Matrix VIII, condition C of Table 11.2 (which is necessary, but *not* sufficient for an interior EE) is met here. The historical diagram in Figure 11.9 reveals, what is perhaps implicit in the Rock-Paper-Scissors analogy, that the population proportions will be changing in a repeated cyclical way. Notice that the oscillations here are explosive. Thus *there is no evolutionary equilibrium*. The corresponding phase diagram is Figure 11.10, where the paths all spiral outward from the "hurricane's eye" at $(p_C, p_D, p_T, = (.40, .25, .35)$. In the long run, the population at any moment of time would be essentially a mixture of just two strategies (the third being practically excluded) – but which strategy is the excluded one would itself be changing over time in a repeating cycle that grows ever more extreme. (For any discrete dynamic model, of course, an edge would ultimately be hit; i.e., one of the strategies will go extinct.) However, whether the oscillations are ultimately damped,

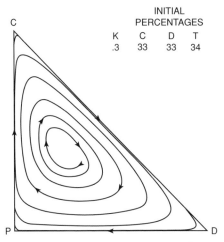

Figure 11.10. PD + PUNISHER, phase diagram.

constant, or explosive depends upon the "sensitivity" parameter k in equation 1. Figure 11.10 was generated with $k = .3$. In contrast, a much smaller $k = .05$ leads to a convergent interior EE as shown in Figure 11.11 – the paths all spiral inward in a whirlpool pattern.[21] And, finally, there is a critical sensitivity, $k = .1425$, approximately, which lead to constant cycling as in Figure 11.12

Summarizing these results we have:

Proposition 6: With PUNISHER as the third strategy, a cyclic pattern develops. If the cycle is convergent, there will be a single interior EE. If divergent, the population will be very close to one edge or another practically all the time, but following a regular succession over time. There is also the possibility of a stable limit cycle, which could be asymptotically approached from within or without.

ELIMINATION TOURNAMENTS

The round-robin tournament is only one type of contest interaction. An obvious alternative is the elimination tournament. The question posed

---

[21] Since the continuous-time dynamic can be regarded as the limiting case as k becomes very small in equation 1, this development suggests that explosive oscillations will occur only in a discrete-generation dynamic. In other words, an interior ESS is necessarily an EE for the continuous analog of equation 1. This is in fact the case. (Personal communication from Daniel Friedman.)

The Dark Side of the Force

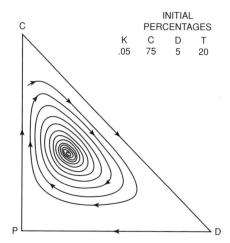

Figure 11.11. PD + PUNISHER, phase diagram.

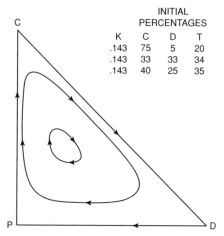

Figure 11.12. PD + PUNISHER, phase diagram.

in this section is how TIT-FOR-TAT fares in this alternative form of competition.[22]

Dealing with elimination tournaments in an evolutionary context requires revision of both the payoff matrix and the dynamic equation. A player following strategy i will eliminate an opponent playing j whenever, in the original matrix, $a_{ij} > b_{ij}$ – or, equivalently, whenever

---

[22] In a somewhat parallel analysis, Behr (1981) raises the question of changing players' goals from maximizing average absolute (numerical) payoff to *outscoring* opponents instead. In elimination contests, survival depends upon relative, not absolute, success, which is the same as outscoring opponents.

$a_{ij} > a_{ji}$. When this occurs, the *elimination payoff matrix* will show $c_{ij} = 1$ and $c_{ji} = 0$. (For a tie, the value .5 is assigned to each party.) The interpretation, of course, is that a player defeated in any one-on-one encounter disappears, a winning player survives, while tying contestants each survive with 50% probability. Matrix IX is the elimination-contest analog of Matrix IV for the C-D-T triad. (Since the elimination matrix for any interaction can be determined easily by inspection of the corresponding numerical matrix, we will save space by not showing the other cases explicitly here.)

Turning to the dynamic equation, elimination contests will of course steadily erode the aggregate population numbers over time. This is an irrelevant fact for our purposes, since we are interested only in the population *proportions* following the various strategies. Our dynamic equation has to allow for this feature. Let us symbolize as h_s the fraction of those following strategy s who survive in any generation. Letting j be an index running over all strategies:

$$h_s = \sum_j p_j c_{sj} \qquad [5]$$

It follows immediately that p'_s, the next-generation or revised proportion of the surviving population following strategy s, is given by:

$$p'_s = h_s p_s / \sum_j h_j p_j \qquad [6]$$

Furthermore, since exactly half the contestants will survive any round of an elimination tournament, the denominator on the right hand side of equation 6 necessarily equals .5. Therefore:

$$p'_s / p_s = 2h_s \qquad [7]$$

Thus, the proportion of the population playing strategy s will rise or fall in any generation, depending upon the extent to which its fractional survival in that generation (h_s) exceeds or falls short of one half. Characteristic results for elimination tournaments are shown in Figures 11.13 through 11.15. In the first of these, for the basic C-D-T triad we see that DEFECT rapidly displaces COOPERATE, while TIT-FOR-TAT exactly maintains its initial proportion in the population. A moment's reflection reveals that the latter condition must necessarily hold. Since instant-recognition TIT-FOR-TAT always ties any C, D, or T opponent, its h_s will always be .5 – so that, in equation 7, $p'_T / p_T = 1$ in each and every generation. Notice that, whereas in the corresponding round-robin

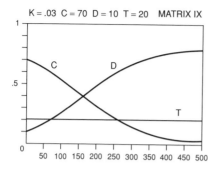

K = .03   C = 70   D = 10   T = 20   MATRIX IX

Figure 11.13. PD + T, elimination tournament, historical diagram.

tournament (as pictured in Figures 11.3 and 11.4) the outcome was a mixture of COOPERATE and TIT-FOR-TAT, here it is a mixture of DEFECT and TIT-FOR-TAT. But TIT-FOR-TAT's survival against DE-FECT in an elimination contest is due solely to the instant-recognition power we have postulated on its behalf. Had we instead used Axelrod's assumption, in which someone following TIT-FOR-TAT can recognize a DEFECT player only by losing to him in the first round, tying thereafter (and so being outscored in total), TIT-FOR-TAT would have been rapidly eliminated.

It follows a fortiori that TIT-FOR-TAT will surely be eliminated if any cost of complexity (COC) penalty is levied against it – leading once again to the inevitable fixation of DEFECT in the population. Somewhat more interesting to explore is the effect of allowing for some proba-bility of error (POE). We saw above that in round-robin tournaments

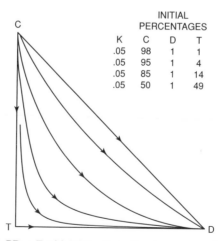

| | INITIAL PERCENTAGES | | |
K	C	D	T
.05	98	1	1
.05	95	1	4
.05	85	1	14
.05	50	1	49

Figure 11.14. PD + T with POE, elimination tournament phase diagram.

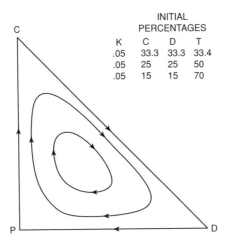

Figure 11.15. PD + PUNISHER, elimination tournament, phase diagram.

TIT-FOR-TAT with a POE sometimes actually survives better, since occasional errors tend to limit the success of the free-riding COOPER-ATE strategy. More specifically, as shown in Figure 11.8, depending upon the initial situation, TFT with POE could lead either to an EE with all-DEFECT or to one representing a mixture of COOPERATE and TIT-FOR-TAT. Once again, however, the elimination tournament is a more onerous environment for TIT-FOR-TAT, in comparison with the round-robin tournament. Figure 11.14 illustrates that any POE (like any cost of complexity COC) leads to the elimination of both TIT-FOR-TAT and COOPERATE, with all-DEFECT becoming the sole EE.

Finally, what of PUNISHER? We saw above that the C-D-P triad tended to lead to cyclic solutions. This also holds true for elimination contests; a divergent case is illustrated in Figure 11.15.

Summarizing the results for elimination tournaments, we have:

Proposition 7: In an elimination contest, the proportionate representation of instant-recognition TIT-FOR-TAT must necessarily always remain at its initial level. Since COOPERATE will always be
driven to extinction, DEFECT will account for the remainder of the
population at the evolutionary equilibrium. However, if any cost of
complexity (COC) or probability of error (POE) is attached to TIT-
FOR-TAT, only DEFECT survives at the EE. Delayed-recognition
TIT-FOR-TAT will surely go extinct, even without any COC or
POE penalty.

Proposition 8: The interaction of COOPERATE, DEFECT, and PUN-ISHER in an elimination contest, as in a round-robin contest, leads to cycling among the three strategies.

DISCUSSION AND SUMMARY

The success of TIT-FOR-TAT, were it reliably and robustly successful, would have significant implications for ethics and political ideology.[23] TIT-FOR-TAT corresponds to the eye-for-an-eye or Silver Rule Old Testament ethic. Since its key feature is restrained retaliation – *no more than* an eye for an eye – the Silver Rule can be regarded as a moderate and educational corrective, one that leaves open the possibility of future cooperation among the parties. Looking at it from another point of view, TIT-FOR-TAT corresponds to the behavior of the frontier hero celebrated in American folklore. Only when an evil-doer absolutely insists on initiating trouble does the hero respond – and then never with excessive, though still with infallibly effective, force.

There is much to be said for such an ethic, with its appealing libertarian/anarchist ideological implications: that in order to support cooperation among humans, little more is needed than for citizens to be willing to follow such a TIT-FOR-TAT strategy.[24] Still, scientific accuracy demands that we not claim too much, even on behalf of our favorite ideologies. And specifically here, we have been concerned to inquire as to the generality of the circumstances in which TIT-FOR-TAT reliably supports the evolutionary emergence of cooperation.

In studying the interactions of TIT-FOR-TAT with the archetypical COOPERATE and DEFECT strategies in the repeated-play Prisoners' Dilemma, we showed how the multiple-round model could be converted into a single-play game – in a way that slightly stacks the deck in favor of TIT-FOR-TAT by granting the latter an instant-recognition, immediate-response capability. Thus, under our assumptions, DEFECT cannot gain even a momentary advantage over TIT-FOR-TAT. Our system of analysis was to retain the archetype strategies, COOPERATE and DEFECT, in all the interactions considered but successively to enter alternative third strategies into the evolutionary competition. As third strategies we

---

[23] Axelrod (1984) discusses these issues at several points (e.g., pp. 136–139, 189–191).
[24] "A community using strategies based upon reciprocity can actually police itself" (Axelrod, 1984: 138).

considered several variants of TIT-FOR-TAT, the reversed reactive strategy that we called BULLY, and also a new class of strategies we termed PUNISHER.

The results, broadly speaking, reveal that TIT-FOR-TAT is *not* very robust when the exact conditions of Axelrod's model do not apply. Suppressing a number of technicalities and qualifications, among our specific conclusions are the following:

1. TIT-FOR-TAT in a two-strategy competition with DEFECT does indeed drive the latter to extinction. But when COOPERATE is also entered in a triadic C-D-T competition, the evolutionary equilibrium (EE) is a *mixture* of COOPERATE and TIT-FOR-TAT. In effect, COOPERATE or Golden Rule players are parasites upon the TIT-FOR-TAT or Silver Rule players.

2. This parasitism becomes far more serious when a cost of complexity (COC) adjustment is imposed on the TIT-FOR-TAT payoffs to correct for the additional capacities required to employ that strategy. In fact, with any positive COC it turns out that in the triadic C-D-T competition only DEFECT survives in the evolutionary equilibrium. We also considered another way of adjusting for the extra capacities required of the TIT-FOR-TAT player, to wit, allowing for a probability of error (POE) in identification or reaction. A positive POE generates a two-vertex EE: Depending upon the initial population proportions, the evolutionary equilibrium may either be all-DEFECT or all-TIT-FOR-TAT.

3. BULLY, we found, being strictly dominated by DEFECT, does not help to support cooperation.

4. The PUNISHER strategy corresponds to a biological superpredator. In this case, the payoff to PUNISHER is the highest against DEFECT – rather like a bounty hunter of the Old West. The triadic C-D-P interaction leads to cycling of the population proportions, which (for certain parameter values) can lead to a stable interior EE in which all three strategies remain viable.

5. We also studied the effect of changing the form of the competitive contest, to wit, by considering elimination tournaments in place of Axelrod's round-robin tournaments. When the (non-penalized) TIT-FOR-TAT is entered into an elimination tournament in a triadic C-D-T interaction, it necessarily maintains its initial proportion in the population (since TIT-FOR-TAT ties against

all contenders). But whereas in the EE under the round-robin tournament the remainder of the population were COOPERATE players, in an elimination context the remainder are DEFECT players. Furthermore, when any COC or POE adjustment is levied to allow for the extra capacities required of TIT-FOR-TAT, only DEFECT will survive at the evolutionary equilibrium.

In our investigations we have been able to relax a number of Axelrod's special assumptions, with the very mixed results summarized above. Thus it seems that, even in a Prisoners' Dilemma context, no strong claims for the robustness of TIT-FOR-TAT are warranted; its success in supporting the evolutionary emergence of cooperation is highly situation-dependent. And in fact, Axelrod's suggestion that an all-TIT-FOR-TAT population will eventuate from evolutionary competition[25] is an unreasonable expectation in the light of the complex and ever-changing strategy mixes actually observed in human life. Constructively, we have shown that what we call PUNISHER strategies can help to maintain a mixed population in which more and less cooperative forms of play remain simultaneously viable – in either a stable evolutionary equilibrium or else in a pattern of temporal cycling. The interpretation is that, despite the libertarian ideological appeal of TIT-FOR-TAT, in many or most Prisoners' Dilemma environments something more is needed. PUNISHER players, being in effect specialized enforcers of cooperation, provide the extra support needed to keep cooperation viable. Using our Wild West metaphor, it is generally not enough for each person to stand up for his or her own rights. Sheriffs and bounty hunters will still be needed.

This entire line of analysis involves a number of limiting assumptions. Two of them were mentioned above. First, all social structure is absent – there are no distinctions among individuals by type (as between male and female), nor any provision for grouping or collective action. Second, Prisoners' Dilemma is only one of a number of important qualitatively distinct payoff environments. It must be immediately evident that going beyond either of these limiting assumptions will have drastic implications for almost all the questions addressed. To mention just one, it turns out that if the Prisoner's Dilemma payoffs are replaced by those associated with the game known as Chicken or Hawk-Dove, the BULLY strategy – so unsuccessful here – can serve very usefully in supporting the viability of cooperation.

[25] See note 5.

A number of other limitations, mentioned scarcely or not at all up to this point, suggest ways in which the analysis might profitably be extended:

(i) No provision has been made for *diminishing returns*. It seems reasonable to assume that the payoffs to any strategy might shift in a favorable direction as that strategy becomes scarce in the population – since each strategy may have a comparative advantage in exploiting some resource or occupying some niche in the environment. Allowing for diminishing returns would tend to generate the interior solutions that better describe real-world populations.

(ii) In dealing with concepts like cost of complexity and probability of error, very simple constancy assumptions were employed here. More generally, these might well be functions of the population fractions. For instance, a higher probability of error is likely in identifying a player following a rare strategy.

(iii) While the possibility of alternative dynamics was mentioned in the text, we employed only the standard form of equation 1, in which the *proportionate* change in the population fractions was a function of differences in the payoffs. An alternative interesting dynamic makes the *absolute* change in the fractions a function of these differences.

(iv) Allowing for "mutations" in which players spontaneously change from one strategy to another might have significant effects upon equilibrium outcomes.

Finally, one feature of all these models, the nonrational character of the choice of strategies, is disturbing to us as economists. Of course, evolutionary natural selection in effect *simulates* rationality, since survival is a kind of ex-post proof of the wisdom of the strategy selected. But we would have preferred models that incorporate rationality of process as well as rationality of outcome. In this connection, our dynamic equation 1 has an interesting rationalistic implication in terms of the alternative interpretation of the proportions p_s, mentioned in the text – as probabilities in a mixed strategy rather than as fractions of the population pursuing simple strategies. Here the changes in the p_s would be interpreted as a kind of adaptive *learning* in which players change their strategies in response to the payoff differentials.[26]

[26] We thank Peter Bernholz for suggesting this point.

REFERENCES

Axelrod, R. (1981) "The emergence of cooperation among egoists." Amer. Pol. Sci. Rev. 75 (June).

Axelrod, R. (1984) The Evolution of Cooperation. New York: Basic Books.

Axelrod, R. and W. D. Hamilton (1981) "The evolution of cooperation." Science 211 (27 March).

Behr, R. L. (1981) "Nice guys finish last – sometimes." J. of Conflict Resolution 25 (June).

Boyd, R. and P. J. Richerson (1985) Culture and the Evolutionary Process. Chicago: Univ. of Chicago Press.

Hirshleifer, J. (1982) "Evolutionary models in economics and law: cooperation vs. conflict strategies." Research in Law and Economics 4.

Lipman, B. L. (1986) "Cooperation among egoists in Prisoners' Dilemma and Chicken games." Public Choice 51.

Martinez Coll, J. C. (1986) "A bioeconomical model of Hobbes" State of nature."' Social Sci. Information 25 (2).

Maynard Smith, J. (1976) "Evolution and the theory of games." Amer. Scientist 64 (January–February).

Maynard Smith, J. (1978) "The evolution of behavior." Scientific Amer. 239 (September): 176–192.

Maynard Smith, J. (1982) Evolution and the Theory of Games. Cambridge: Cambridge Univ. Press.

Maynard Smith, J. and G. R. Price (1973) "The logic of animal conflict." Nature 246 (November 2).

Nelson, R. R. and S. G. Winter (1982) An Evolutionary Theory of Economic Change. Cambridge, MA: Harvard Univ. Press.

Rapoport, A. (1967) "Exploiter, leader, hero, and martyr: the four archetypes of the 2 × 2 game." Behavioral Science 12.

Riley, J. G. (1979) "Evolutionary equilibrium strategies." J. of Theoretical Biology 76: 109–123.

Snyder, G. H. and P. Diesing (1977) Conflict among Nations: Bargaining, Decision Making, and System Structure in International Crises. Princeton, NJ: Princeton Univ. Press.

Taylor, P. D. and L. B. Jonker (1978) "Evolutionarily stable strategies and game dynamics." Mathematical Biosciences 40: 145–156.

Zeeman, E. C. (1981) "Dynamics of the evolution of animal conflicts." J. of Theoretical Biology 89: 249–270.

12

Selection, Mutation, and the Preservation of Diversity in Evolutionary Games[1]

Jack Hirshleifer and Juan Carlos Martínez Coll

Background of this Chapter

My colleague Juan Carlos Martinez Coll and I have coauthored three published articles on reciprocity strategies. The preceding chapter reprinted the first of these articles to appear; the article reproduced as this chapter is the third. The intervening article, "The Limits of Reciprocity" in *Rationality and Society* (1991, Vol. 3, 35–64), has been omitted owing to space limitations. That paper extended the article reproduced as Chapter 11 to take account of the Chicken environment as well as Prisoners' Dilemma, and also to consider other variant strategies.

A theme common to all three papers is that the search for a single "best" strategy, whether Tit for Tat or any other, is fundamentally misguided. One thing we surely know is that, in the actual world, a coexisting mixture of strategies – some more cooperative, some less – manage to maintain themselves. That theme is the core idea of the present essay, as indicated by the phrase "the preservation of diversity" in the title. One unusual aspect of the article is the attention devoted to out-of-equilibrium states, which turn out to display patterns and structure warranting more attention from evolutionary game theorists.

Of the huge number of books and articles in the literature discussing the evolution of cooperation, I will cite here only two papers, one by Robert Boyd and Jeffrey P. Lorberbaum (1987, "No Pure Strategy Is Evolutionarily Stable in the Repeated Prisoner's Dilemma Game," *Nature* 327: 58–9) and one by Bjorn Lomborg (1996, "Nucleus and Shield: The Evolution of Social Structure in the Iterated Prisoner's Dilemma," *American Sociological Review*, 61: 278–307) that also deal with the diversity theme emphasized here.

Reprinted from J. Hirshleifer and J. C. Martinez Coll, "Selection, Mutation and the Preservation of Diversity in Evolutionary Games," *Revista Española de Economía*, Vol. 9, No. 2, 251–73, Copyright © 1992, with permission from *Ministerio de Hacienda* (Spain)

[1] The authors are grateful to John Nachbar, David A. Hirshleifer, and an anonymous referee of this journal for very helpful comments and suggestions.

Resumen

*No pueden ser considerados satisfactorios los modelos evolutivos que sug-
ieren que en situaciones con motivaciones complejas, sólo una única
estrategia o un único tipo de comportamiento prevalecerán en última in-
stancia. Entre las fuerzas que impulsan la diversidad de estrategias y comportamientos están: (i) equilibrios evolutivos múltiples y/o mixtos, (ii) la
presión mutacional, y (iii) procesos dinámicos transitorios. Este artículo
estudia la interacción de las estrategias arquetípicas COOPERAR frente a
DEFRAUDAR en el Dilema del Prisionero, y COBARDE frente a ATREV-
IDO en el Halcón-Paloma, con dos estrategias reactivas alternativas, OJO
POR OJO y TORITO. Sólo en casos límite excepcionales una única estrategia o una única forma de comportamiento consiguen extinguir a todas las
demás. OJO POR OJO tiende a apoyar el predominio de comportamientos
"amables" en el Dilema del Prisionero (pero no en el Halcón-Paloma),
mientras que TORITO tiende a apoyar generalmente el predominio de los
comportamientos "perversos."*

Abstract

*Evolutionary models suggesting that in mixed-motive situations only a sin-
gle strategy, or only a single type of behavior, will ultimately prevail cannot
be regarded as satisfactory. Among the forces supporting diversity of strategies and of behaviors are: (i) multiple and/or mixed evolutionary equilibria, (ii) mutation pressure, and (iii) transient dynamic processes. This paper studies the interaction of the archetype strategies COOPERATE versus
DEFECT in Prisoners' Dilemma, and COWARD versus DAREDEVIL in
Chicken, with two alternative reactive strategies TIT FOR TAT and BULLY.
Only in exceptional limiting cases does a single strategy or a single form
of behavior come to extinguish all others. TIT FOR TAT tends to support the predominance of "nice" behaviors in Prisoners' Dilemma (but
not Chicken), while BULLY tends to support a predominance of "mean"
behaviors generally.*

In mixed-motive situations combining elements of mutuality as well as
opposition of interests, human behaviors and the underlying strategies
are highly varied. Some people show a conciliatory talent, some are
belligerent, others give the impression of being aggressive without actually acting violently, while still others may appear pacific yet respond
forcefully to attack.

Despite this observed diversity, a rather contrasting claim has gained
some acceptance in recent years: that, at least in long-run evolutionary
competition, a single optimal strategy does exist – to wit, the simple
reactive strategy known as *TIT FOR TAT.*[2] The well-received book of
Robert Axelrod [Axelrod (1984)] argued forcefully for the optimality

---

[2] Marimon (1988) translates *TIT FOR TAT* as *OJO POR OJO.*

and superior survivability of *TIT FOR TAT* in evolutionary competition.[3] And while Axelrod's own work was limited to the Prisoners' Dilemma payoff environment, somewhat parallel claims have been made for *TIT FOR TAT* in the Chicken and other payoff environments as well [Lipman (1986)].

The present authors have shown earlier that contentions as to the evolutionary superiority of *TIT FOR TAT* are valid only under a very narrow "window" of assumptions [Hirshleifer and Martínez Coll (1988), Martínez Coll and Hirshleifer (1991)].[4] As just one example, *TIT FOR TAT* has very little survival value when the evolutionary competition takes the form of an elimination tournament rather than a round-robin tournament. The purpose of the present paper is not to offer further criticisms of the sometimes excessive claims made on behalf of *TIT FOR TAT*, but instead to provide a more systematic analysis of the different strategic elements tending to generate and maintain diversity in evolutionary games.

It is important to distinguish diversity in *strategies* from diversity in *behaviors*. Anyone following a "reactive" strategy like *TIT FOR TAT* must have the capability of engaging in different behaviors: in the Prisoners' Dilemma environment, for example, he must be able to make either a *DEFECT* move or a *COOPERATE* move. Conversely, followers of different strategies may find themselves engaging in the same behavior, as when *TIT FOR TAT* players interact with *ALWAYS-COOPERATE* players in the Prisoners' Dilemma environment. The evolutionary survival of diversity in both strategies and behaviors will be explored in the analysis that follows.

The two archetype strategies that define Prisoners' Dilemma are the "nice" strategy *ALWAYS-COOPERATE (C)* and the "mean" strategy *ALWAYS-DEFECT (D)*. (Henceforth we will drop the *ALWAYS* except for purpose of emphasis.) This paper will place these archetype strategies in competition with each of two simple reactive strategies: *TIT FOR TAT* and a less friendly one called *BULLY*. We then do the same

---

[3] Axelrod did indicate several of the necessary qualifications. For one thing, if *TIT FOR TAT* is to be an equilibrium evolutionary outcome the "shadow of the future" must be sufficiently great, that is, the discounting of future payoffs cannot be too severe. Also, in his analyses the *ALWAYS-DEFECT* strategy always remained an alternative possible evolutionary outcome [Axelrod (1984), Appendix B].

[4] Molander (1985), Boyd and Lorberbaum (1987), Mueller (1987), Nachbar (1992), and other authors have also pointed to the non-robustness of *TIT FOR TAT* as a purportedly optimal strategy in evolutionary competitions.

for the payoff environment of Chicken (also known as Hawk-Dove).[5] In Chicken the "nice" archetype strategy will be called *COWARD*, the "mean" archetype *DAREDEVIL* (thus retaining the convenient C and D abbreviations).[6]

The analysis concentrates on three elements tending to generate or to maintain diversity in evolutionary processes:

(i) *Multiple equilibria:* Two distinct types of multiple equilibria will be of importance in what follows. (a) It may be that, within some zone of initial population distributions over strategies, under the dynamic process considered all the distributions will ultimately be attracted to a single determinate terminal state – to what we call an Evolutionary Equilibrium Point (*EEP*) – but there may be other "basins of attraction" leading to different terminal *EEP*'s. (b) Or, it may be that the dynamic trajectories are never attracted to any single *EEP* but are attracted to what we call an Evolutionary Equilibrium Region (*EER*), within which the population distribution may drift without ever settling down to a unique outcome.

(ii) *Mutation pressure:* In the context here, mutations are small shifts in the population distribution over the various strategies, occurring with specified frequency independently of selectional (profitability) considerations. Whereas selectional pressure over the generations tends to destroy variety, mutation pressure acts to preserve variety.[7]

---

[5] The evolutionary equilibrium application to Chicken, under the alternative name Hawk-Dove [Maynard Smith (1976)], actually preceded Axelrod's work on Prisoners' Dilemma. An early contrast of evolutionary outcomes under Chicken and Prisoners' Dilemma was provided in Hirshleifer (1982). Lipman (1986) is a more recent comparison.

[6] While this paper examines only 3-way competitions, elsewhere we have explored 4-way competitions in which both reactive strategies, *TIT FOR TAT* and *BULLY*, are simultaneously in play against the two archetype strategies [Martínez Coll and Hirshleifer (1991)].

[7] Mutation has no close connection with another type of chance variation known as "trembling hand" – in which a player, while intending to follow some particular strategy, with some small probability accidentally behaves in a way consistent with a different strategy. In mutation the random variation has the player *permanently* changing his type; in trembling hand, the player's type remains the same but the actual executed move is subject to variation. The latter comes closer to, though still is not quite the same as, the "probability of error" *(POE)* considered in Hirshleifer and Martínez Coll (1988). The latter concept, applicable only to reactive strategies, referred to recognition errors rather than to execution "trembles."

(iii) *Transient vs. equilibrium states:* In this paper we will be devoting attention not only to final equilibrium but also to the dynamic trajectories of change. Even if variety is destined ultimately to be extinguished, it persists longer when the rate of dynamic change is slow. And before equilibrium is reached, as will be seen, certain patterns of diversity turn out to be more likely than others ("probability clouds").[8]

GAMES AND STRATEGIES

Prisoners' Dilemma and Chicken are best thought of as different pay-off environments within which a variety of different strategies may be employed. The two environments have very similar structures. Matrices 1 and 2 show the respective payoffs from 1 (lowest) to 4 (highest). In the *definitions* of Prisoners' Dilemma and Chicken, these payoffs can be merely ordinal rankings, but our analysis treats them as actual cardinal payoffs. Nevertheless, subject to certain qualifications, in a qualitative sense the results are representative of the entire class of outcomes in the Prisoners' Dilemma or Chicken environments, as the case may be.

In the basic 2×2 games involving the archetype strategies only, each player chooses between a *nice* strategy C (*COOPERATE* in Prisoners' Dilemma, *COWARD* in Chicken) and a *mean* strategy D (*DEFECT* in Prisoners' Dilemma, *DAREDEVIL* in Chicken). The crucial difference between the two environments is that in Prisoners' Dilemma the worst outcome (payoff of 1) is suffered by someone playing nice against mean (*COOPERATE* against *DEFECT*), while in Chicken the worst outcome is incurred when the contenders both play mean (both choose *DARE-DEVIL*). So in Chicken the two players have a stronger mutual interest in avoiding the *D–D* behavior combination.

Turning now to non-archetype strategies, as already indicated only two very simple reactive strategies – *TIT FOR TAT* and *BULLY* – are considered in this paper. Even so, certain modelling options remain to be specified. While evolutionary analysis necessarily deals with *multiple generations* – that is, with the changes that selectional and mutational forces bring about between one generation and the next – whether or not

---

[8] In a more general model, still other sources of variety could be introduced. Members of a single population might be interacting simultaneously in several distinct games, or a single game could be played by interacting populations (buyers encountering sellers, say). Or, additional strategy choices could be permitted for either the Prisoners' Dilemma or Chicken environment [as in the famous tournaments discussed in Axelrod (1984)].

Table 12.1. Prisoners' Dilemma and
Chicken – Basic and Expanded Matrices

Prisoners' Dilemma			Chicken		
Matrix 1			**Matrix 2**		
	C	*D*		*C*	*D*
C	3,3	1,4	*C*	3,3	2,4
D	4,1	2,2	*D*	4,2	1,1
Matrix 3			**Matrix 4**		
	C	*D*	*T*		*C*	*D*	*T*
C	3,3	1,4	3,3	*C*	3,3	2,4	3,3
D	4,1	2,2	2,2	*D*	4,2	1,1	1,1
T	3,3	2,2	3,3	*T*	3,3	1,1	3,3
Matrix 5			**Matrix 6**		
	C	*D*	*B*		*C*	*D*	*B*
C	3,3	1,4	1,4	*C*	3,3	2,4	2,4
D	4,1	2,2	4,1	*D*	4,2	1,1	4,2
B	4,1	1,4	2.5, 2.5	*B*	4,2	2,4	3,3

to assume *multiple rounds of play* in any given one-on-one encounter remains an open question.

Consider first *TIT FOR TAT*. On the more usual interpretation in the literature, a *TIT FOR TAT* player makes a nice move in the opening round and then, observing what the opponent does, in each following round mirrors the latter's *previous choice* – replying nice to nice and mean to mean. Correspondingly, a *BULLY* player would open initially with a mean move and then respond in each following round with the reverse of the opponent's previous choice.[9] This usual assumption, that reaction can be effectuated only in the following round of play, we call "deferred recognition and response" (*DRR*). In contrast, under the alternative assumption employed here, reactive players have the capacity of "immediate recognition and response" (*IRR*). The *TIT FOR TAT* and *BULLY* players are assumed able to detect immediately whether the opponent is opening with a mean or a nice move, in time for making the appropriate *reply in the very same round*.

Neither *DRR* or *IRR* is right or wrong of itself; whether one or the other is the correct assumption to make depends upon the situation

---

[9] There are actually four rather than only two elementary reactive strategies, since a double dichotomy is involved: (i) the initial move can be "nice" or "mean," and (ii) the reactive reply can either *mirror* or *reverse* the opponent's move. *TIT FOR TAT* combines a nice opening with a mirroring reply while *BULLY* combines a mean opening with a reversing reply. The other two possible combinations do not lack interest, but for reasons of space are not considered here. See Martínez Coll (1986) and Nachbar (1992).

investigated. Someone playing *DEFECT* in Prisoners' Dilemma or *DAREDEVIL* in Chicken would of course always prefer to do so *covertly*, thus getting away with a mean move for at least one round before the reactive player can respond. And if the actual real-world situation permits such disguise, *DRR* would be the appropriate assumption. But sometimes disguise is impossible, or easy to penetrate, so that a mean move must be *overt*. Wolves may wear sheep's clothing, but more often the claws and fangs are quite visible. In the latter case, absent any recognition problem the reactive player can respond at once. (If on the other hand *covert* mean moves were actually feasible, a reactive player might have to observe behavior in several successive rounds before being able to definitely learn the opponent's type. Thus, the usual *DRR* assumption, that exactly one round is both necessary and sufficient, is a very special one that could be either too optimistic or too pessimistic.).[10]

Our *IRR* interpretation permits a much simpler analysis, in which only single-round rather than multiple-round play need be considered. There is no need to be concerned about the "shadow of the future," since a reactive player is in a position to make the correct response here and now. On the other hand, this simplicity is purchased at a cost, as it precludes analysis of strategies involving what might be called round-dependent behaviors.[11]

One other consideration is worth mentioning. *IRR*, as compared with *DRR*, works to the advantage of *TIT FOR TAT*. If only a deferred response is possible, a *TIT FOR TAT* player's opening nice move necessarily leaves him open to exploitation in the first round by *D* (DEFECT or DAREDEVIL) players. In consequence, even when the real-world situation would be more accurately described by the *DRR* assumption, the *IRR* model can be used for purposes of *a fortiori* argumentation. And

---

[10] Interestingly, the biologist John Maynard Smith, who may be regarded as the founder of evolutionary game theory, employed the *DRR* assumption in one of his earliest articles [Maynard Smith and Price (1973)] but in later papers has more usually used the equivalent of our *IRR* assumption. In particular, the *RETALIATOR* strategy in Maynard Smith (1976) is the equivalent of *TIT FOR TAT* with our *IRR* assumption; each round lasts long enough for effective recognition and response to influence the payoff in that same round.

[11] Thus our model does not permit analysis of strategies like "*COOPERATE* for the first two rounds, then *DEFECT* one time, and return to *COOPERATE* thereafter." Note that this limitation is not due to the *IRR* assumption *per se;* there is no logical inconsistency between *IRR* and round-dependent behaviors. The limitation is due only to the advantage we took in employing the *IRR* assumption in such a way as to reduce each archetype-versus-reactive encounter to a single-round interaction. With a less restricted strategy set, this simplification would not have been possible even under *IRR*.

specifically, whenever *TIT FOR TAT* loses out against *overt* mean play under our *IRR* interpretation, we can be sure it would do even worse against *covert* mean play under the *DRR* assumption.

Employing the *IRR* interpretation, so that *TIT FOR TAT* players react appropriately to *C* or *D* players in the very same round, the payoffs in Matrices 3 and 4 show the effect of adding *TIT FOR TAT* to the underlying Prisoners' Dilemma and Chicken games, respectively. The only new element needed is the payoff combination when two *TIT FOR TAT* players encounter one another. It might at first seem puzzling how two such players can simultaneously be reacting to one another. The easiest interpretation is that the two reactive players in such an encounter do not literally move simultaneously; rather, each has the first move with 50% probability. Then, following the definition of *TIT FOR TAT*, whoever goes first will make an opening nice move, to which the other will immediately respond in kind.[12] Thus, as shown, the payoff-pair is (3,3) in each case.

Matrices 5 and 6 show the corresponding payoffs when *BULLY* is the reactive strategy considered. Again, the only new element to be determined is the *BULLY-BULLY* payoff combination. Using the same interpretation as before, and following the definition of *BULLY*, whichever player goes first will open with a mean move, to which the opponent will instantly respond with the reverse nice move. Since each player can expect to have the opening move just half the time, the *BULLY-BULLY* payoffs are calculated as the average of the outcomes of playing nice against mean and mean against nice. Specifically, in Matrix 5 for Prisoners' Dilemma the *BULLY-BULLY* payoffs are calculated as $(4 + 1)/2 = 2.5$ for each player. In Matrix 6 for Chicken the corresponding calculation yields $(4 + 2)/2 = 3$ for each.

THE MODEL

Dynamics

The essence of evolutionary dynamics is that more profitable strategies gain increased prevalence over time while less profitable ones suffer diminished representation in the population.

---

[12] An alternative interpretation is that the encounter takes place over an extended period, in a continuing interaction permitting the players to gradually learn what the opponent is doing. Something like this occurred, for example, in the battleship construction race between Britain and Imperial Germany before World War I. In such a context, what was really a very complex game over many rounds can plausibly be reduced to a single round in "slow time." Some such interpretation appears also to underlie the analysis of the *RETALIATOR* strategy in Maynard Smith (1976).

Denote as a_{ij} the payoff obtained from playing strategy I in an encounter with strategy J. The expected return Y_i to a player of strategy I will be weighted by the proportions p_j of the population actually playing all the different possible strategies[13]:

$$Y_i \equiv \Sigma_j \, p_j a_{ij} \tag{1}$$

It will also be useful to define the global expected return Y for a population distributed over the different strategies:

$$Y \equiv \Sigma_i \, p_i Y_i \tag{2}$$

Let F_i signify the relative "fitness" of strategy I, that is to say, the difference between its return and the global expected return:

$$F_i \equiv Y_i - Y \tag{3}$$

Evidently, the expected fitness averaged over the population as a whole must be zero.

When the force of *selection* is considered alone, in each generation the change in the fractional representation of strategy I is given by:

$$\Delta^{\text{SEL}} \, p_i = k p_i F_i = k p_i (Y_i - Y) \tag{4}$$

Here k is a parameter that reflects the sensitivity of the dynamic process; the higher is k, the more rapid the change in the population proportions. Thus, in each generation the change in p_i due to the force of selection alone will be proportional to the sensitivity parameter k, to the current level of p_i, and to the relative fitness of strategy I (the *difference* between its expected return and the global expected return in the population).[14] It is easy to verify that [4] implies the logically necessary property that,

---

[13] We are assuming that only pure strategies are ever employed.

[14] There are other ways of formulating the selectional equation. One well-known version, sometimes called "replicator dynamics," has the form:

$$\Delta^{\text{SEL}} \, p_i = p_i (Y_i - Y)/Y$$

A disadvantage of this version is its sensitivity to "inessential" alterations of payoffs. For example, adding an arbitrary constant to each and every element of the payoff matrices would modify the dynamic characteristics of the evolutionary system [Nachbar (1990)]. Our equation [4], in contrast, would not be affected. Equation [4] can also cope easily with an arbitrary multiplication (for example, that involved in measuring the payoffs in cents rather than dollars), simply by making an offsetting adjustment of the sensitivity parameter k.

over the population as a whole, the sum of the increments must be zero. In general, [4] will be a cubic equation in the p_i.[15]

However, the evolution of the population proportions can also be affected by the force of *mutation*. Let m_{ij} denote the rate at which an individual playing strategy I changes to strategy J in any time-period. Let N be the number of distinct strategies available. If $N = 3$, for example, then the change in the representation of strategy 1 due to mutation, $\Delta^{MUT} p_1$, will be the algebraic sum of those who shift away from 1 and toward 2 or 3 and those who move toward 1 and away from 2 or 3. Thus:

$$\Delta^{MUT} p_1 = -(m_{12} + m_{13})p_1 + m_{21}p_2 + m_{31}p_3 \qquad [5]$$

There are of course corresponding equations for the changes in p_2 and p_3.[16]

We will be using throughout the simplifying assumption that all the m_{ij} are equal to a common mutation rate m. So equation [5] reduces to:

$$\Delta^{MUT} p_1 = m(1 - 3p_1) \qquad [5a]$$

Generalizing, an equation valid for any strategy I, when there are N distinct strategies, is:

$$\Delta^{MUT} p_i = m(1 - Np_i) \qquad [5b]$$

Mutation acts as a centripetal force, pulling the population distribution toward interior solutions. Given that all the $m_{ij} = m$, then $\Delta^{MUT} p_i$ will be positive whenever p_i is less than $1/N$ and negative when $p_i > 1/N$.

Summing the effects of selection and mutation, the proportionate representation of strategy I in the following generation, symbolized as p_i', will be given by:

$$p_i' = p_i + \Delta^{SEL} p_i + \Delta^{MUT} p_i = p_i + kp_i F_i + m(1 - Np_i) \qquad [6]$$

[15] In equation [4] the step size $\Delta^{SEL} p_i$ approaches zero as p_i approaches extinction (goes to zero) or as p_i approaches fixation (goes to unity). Nevertheless, in any such discrete dynamic formulation the possibility remains of a too-big step that would take p_i outside the allowable range between zero and one. In our simulations, we took care to keep the sensitivity parameter k sufficiently small to avoid such an eventuality. Alternatively, it would have been possible to employ a continuous rather than a discrete dynamic equation, replacing Δp_i with the time-derivative dp_i/dt.

[16] While the individual mutations are probabilistic, equation [5] is expressed in deterministic form. This is equivalent to assuming a population of infinite size.

Equilibrium Concepts

Several different concepts of evolutionary equilibrium have to be distinguished, Rather than attempt a rigorous development and comparison, we limit this discussion to an intuitive interpretation of the fundamental ideas.

Any possible state of the population – that is, any vector $p \equiv (p_1, p_2, \cdots, p_N)$, where $\Sigma_j p_j = 1$ – must be one of three types:

Vertex: if only one strategy is represented, that is, $p_i = 1$ for some strategy I, the proportions p_j for all other strategies being zero.

Edge: if more than one strategy, but not all, have positive representation (so that $p_j = 0$ for at least one strategy J).

Interior: if all strategies have positive representation.

A necessary though by no means sufficient condition for a state of the population to be an evolutionary equilibrium is that the proportions p_i are stationary under the dynamic process considered. A vector meeting this condition is called a Critical Point (*CP*):

$$p_i' = p_i, \text{ for all } I \quad \text{Definition of } CP \qquad [7]$$

Or, combining [6] and [7]:

$$kp_i F_i + m(1 - Np_i) = 0, \text{ for all } I \quad \text{Condition for } CP \qquad [8]$$

It follows trivially that:

- If only the force of selection is operative, so that $m = 0$, the condition for a *CP* reduces to:

$$p_i F_i = 0, \text{ for all } I \quad CP \text{ under selection alone} \qquad [8a]$$

  Thus, when only the force of selection is operative, all vertex states of the population are *CP*'s, while edge or interior states might or might not satisfy the condition for a *CP*.
- If only the force of mutation is operative, so that $k = 0$, the condition becomes:

$$p_i = 1/N, \text{ for all } I \quad CP \text{ under mutation alone} \qquad [8b]$$

Thus, under mutation alone there is only a single interior *CP*.

Since the force of mutation enters additively into the general form [8], when selection and mutation are both operative all the *CP*'s must lie in the interior. The exact locations will depend upon the ratio k/m, that is to say, upon the relative weights of the selectional and mutational forces.

As already indicated, not all *CP*'s are actually evolutionary equilibria. Evolutionary equilibria are points, or sets of points, which are the stable termini of the dynamic evolutionary process considered. An evolutionary equilibrium must be an *attractor* for all trajectories in its (sufficiently small) neighborhood. In more formal language, for a Critical Point (*CP*) to be an *Evolutionary Equilibrium Point* (*EEP*) it must have a convergency zone or basin of attraction – a set of points from which all the dynamic trajectories lead into it – that covers *all* the points in some (sufficiently small) neighborhood. Thus, an *EEP* is immune to (sufficiently small) shocks: if the population proportions were arbitrarily displaced in any direction, the dynamic process would work to restore the population to the equilibrium state.[17]

There is also a second type of evolutionary equilibrium, an *Evolutionary Equilibrium Region* (*EER*). Such a region is a set of *CP*'s no one of which is an *EEP*, but the region as a whole attracts all sufficiently nearby trajectories.

Two other classes of equilibria have been discussed extensively in the literature:

Nash Equilibrium (NE): A Nash Equilibrium in pure strategies (we do not consider mixed strategies) exists when, at some cell in the payoff matrix, neither player can gain by deviating. Such an *NE* is *strict* if a player who deviates actually loses thereby, or *weak* if the deviator merely does no worse.

Considering only the symmetrical *NE*'s (corresponding to the cells along the main diagonal of the payoff matrix), the *NE* condition can be expressed as:

$$F_s(S) \geq F_j(S) \quad \text{Condition for symmetrical } NE \qquad [9]$$

This means that when all the population is following strategy S, that strategy must have *no less* fitness than any other strategy J.

Only a partial listing of the relationships between this *NE* condition and our other equilibrium concepts will be relevant for us here: (i) A *strict NE* along the main diagonal of the payoff matrix, i.e., if the strict inequality in [9] holds, corresponds to a *vertex*

---

[17] *Mutations* are not arbitrary displacements in this sense. Rather, mutations represent a systematic dynamic force.

EEP. Only the single strategy associated with that row and column of the matrix is represented in the population. (ii) A *weak NE* along the main diagonal may or may not be an *EEP*, or the end-point of an *EER*. (iii) If there is no *NE* along the main diagonal, any *NE* must correspond to an edge or an interior state in which more than one of the pure strategies are represented in the population. Any such edge or interior *NE* might or might not be an *EEP.*[18]

Evolutionarily Stable Strategy (ESS): The Evolutionarily Stable Strategy concept [Maynard Smith (1976)] is a strengthening of the *NE* condition. Considering once again only symmetrical states (vertex equilibria), the condition for an *ESS* is:

Condition for symmetrical *ESS*:

$$F_s(S) > F_j(S)$$
$$or \qquad\qquad [10]$$
$$F_s(S) = F_j(S) \text{ and } F_s(J) > F_j(J)$$

That is, strategy *S* must have *strictly* superior fitness when the population is all-*S*, *or*, if an equality with some other strategy *J* holds there, then *S* must be strictly superior when the population is all-*J*.

For our purposes the essential equilibrium concepts are the Evolutionary Equilibrium Point (*EEP*) and Region (*EER*). But locating these equilibria requires close attention to the dynamic pattern. While generally insufficient to determine a "true" evolutionary equilibrium, the *NE* and *ESS* concepts are useful quick rules for locating possible candidates.

Graphical Representation

In the 3-strategy case it is convenient to represent the possible states of the population as points associated with an equilateral triangle. In Figure 12.1, the vertex *C* represents a population distribution in which $p_c = 1$, that is, all the individuals are following the archetype nice strategy *C* (*COOPERATE* in Prisoners' Dilemma, *COWARD* in Chicken). Vertex *D* similarly corresponds to $p_D = 1$, where everyone plays the mean strategy *D* (*DEFECT* in Prisoners' Dilemma, *DAREDEVIL* in Chicken).

---

[18] Subject to some reinterpretation, equation [9] is applicable to non-symmetrical *NE*'s as well. First, the *S* within the parentheses describing the state of the population could be an edge or interior population distribution as well as a vertex. $F_s(S)$ would then represent the fitness of any strategy with positive representation at the candidate equilibrium, and $F_j(S)$ the fitness of any other strategy.

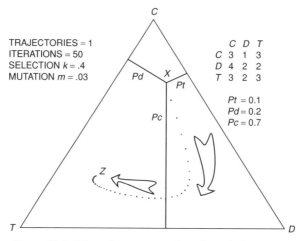

Figure 12.1. Triangular representation of population states.

Vertex T corresponds to $p_T = 1$, representing a population all of whom are playing the reactive *TIT FOR TAT* strategy. (When *BULLY* is substituted for *TIT FOR TAT* as the reactive strategy considered, the third vertex will be labelled B.) For the state represented by any point in the triangle, the proportion p_C is shown by the distance from that point to the opposite side DT, and similarly for the other proportions p_D and p_T. At the specific point X in Figure 12.1, the associated distribution is $(p_C, p_D, p_T) = (.7, .2, .1)$.[19]

Starting from any given point, the dynamic represented by equation [6] generates a series of points or *trajectory*, whose course and direction depend solely upon the associated payoff matrix and the values of the parameters k and m – representing the sensitivities to the forces of selection and mutation, respectively. Figure 12.1 pictures a trajectory starting at point X and ending at point Z. In each simulation to be described, 200 evolutionary trajectories are pictured (beginning from initial positions spaced randomly throughout the triangle). Every trajectory is represented by 50 points, corresponding to 50 iterations of equation [6]. Arrows are used to suggest the general direction of the trajectories within regions.

For given k and m, the separations between successive points along a trajectory depend only upon the profitability differences among the

---

[19] This representation makes use of the geometrical proposition that, for any equilateral triangle, the sum of the orthogonal distances from any point to the three sides equals a constant – the altitude. By setting the altitude equal to l, the three distances become the population proportions.

strategies considered. For the trajectory in Figure 12.1 the points are widely separated to begin with, but as the final point Z is approached the distances from one point to the next normally diminish, since the profitability differences are becoming smaller. Of course, as k and m become larger, other things equal the dynamic rates of change and therefore the separations between points increase.

Relatively dense concentrations of points or "probability clouds" appear in certain regions of the diagrams. Those are regions attracting and retaining, at least for a while, a large number of the trajectories passing nearby. Such clouds tend to appear in the neighborhood of any Evolutionary Equilibrium Point (*EEP*) or Evolutionary Equilibrium Region (*EER*). But even a Critical Point that is not an *EEP* or part of an *EER* may have a probability cloud nearby, owing to the stationarity property of equation [7] that defines a *CP*.

PRISONERS' DILEMMA

In this section we picture and analyze the evolutionary survival of diversity in the Prisoners' Dilemma (*PD*) payoff environment. The available strategies include the archetype strategies COOPERATE (*C*) and DEFECT (*D*) plus one or the other of the reactive strategies *TIT FOR TAT* and *BULLY*. The section following provides a corresponding analysis for the Chicken environment.

TIT FOR TAT as Reactive Strategy in *PD* – under Selection Alone

Figure 12.2 suggests the nature of the evolutionary process in the Prisoners' Dilemma environment, when *TIT FOR TAT (T)* is the reactive strategy considered and only the force of selection is operative. (The mutation coefficient is $m = 0$.) The value $k = .4$ was employed for the selection coefficient. The payoffs are as shown in Matrix 3.

The curve *LD* in Figure 12.2 connects those points where $F_d = 0$, that is, where the relative fitness of *DEFECT (D)* is zero. Its equation, using the payoffs of Matrix 3, is:

$$p_c = \left(2p_d - p_d^2 - 1\right)/(p_d - 2) \qquad [11]$$

where $0 \le p_c$, $p_d \le 1$ and of course $p_c = 1 - p_s - p_d$. In the region above *LD*, the relative fitness of *D* is positive; p_d is increasing, and all the trajectories progress toward vertex *D*. Below the curve, F_d is negative and all the trajectories move away from *D*.

The Dark Side of the Force

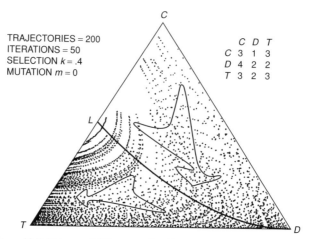

Figure 12.2. Prisoners' Dilemma plus *TIT FOR TAT* – selection alone.

The diagram suggests that there is no interior Critical Point. From equations [6] and [7], such a *CP* would require that all the fitnesses F_i equal zero. But it is easily seen from the payoff matrix that the curves corresponding to $F_c = 0$ and $F_t = 0$ would lie along the side *TC* of the triangle. In other words, when there are no *DEFECT (D)* players in the population, *COOPERATE (C)* and *TIT FOR TAT (T)* have equal fitness. And of course, these relative fitnesses must be zero since they equal the population average. It follows that point *L* where F_d also equals zero, which is located at $(p_c, p_d, p_t) = (.5, 0, .5)$, is an edge Critical Point. But a moment's further reflection reveals that each and every point along the *TC* edge is also *a CP* – since, even where F_d differs from zero along this edge, condition [8a] is still met because $p_d = 0$. So the *CP*'s in Figure 12.2 are the three vertices and the entire side *TC*.

Let us now consider the evolutionary equilibria. Along the side *TC*, looking first at the *upper* range *LC* where the proportion of *TIT FOR TAT* players is relatively small, the diagram shows that all the trajectories are moving away in the direction of vertex *D*. Thus this upper range does not appear to contain any evolutionary equilibria. In fact, the *DEFECT* strategy has positive fitness in this range – lying as it does above the curve *LD* – while *COOPERATE* and *TIT FOR TAT* have negative fitness. The reason is that a *DEFECT* player has a relatively large chance of encountering and exploiting a *COOPERATE* player and only a small risk of suffering punishment from an encounter with a *TIT FOR TAT* player.

In the *lower* range *TL* along the side *TC*, the reverse holds true. *DE-FECT* faces a large chance of encountering *TIT FOR TAT* players, and so tends to be driven out of the population. Thus the range *TL* does represent a set of terminal points of the evolutionary process. However, as the diagram suggests, every point in the range *TL* has a convergency zone consisting only of one single curve (trajectory) leading to that point as terminus. Consequently, *no single point within the range TL is an Evolutionary Equilibrium Point (EEP), but the range as a whole is an Evolutionary Equilibrium Region (EER).*[20] And, as would be expected, there is a somewhat diffuse "probability cloud" in the neighborhood of the *EER* represented by the range *TL*

Near the *CP* at vertex *D*, representing an *all-DEFECT* population, there is also a faint probability cloud, particularly below the curve *LD*. Nevertheless, vertex *D* is not an Evolutionary Equilibrium Point. As has been seen, while above *LD* all the trajectories are moving toward *D*, below that curve they are all heading away. More formally, an *EEP* must have a convergency zone that consists of *all* the points in its (sufficiently small) neighborhood. Starting from *D*, a finite displacement of radius *f*, no matter how small, would have some chance of falling below the curve *LD* – thus initiating a trajectory leading away from rather than back toward vertex *D*. What generates the denser concentration below curve *LD* is that, whereas the trajectories above that curve approach vertex *D* from a wide spread of directions, those departing the close neighborhood of *D* are all funneled into a narrow "channel of high probability" below.

Digression on "evolutionary equilibrium" versus "collective stability": In view of the wide attention his work has received, at this point we digress to explain briefly why certain of Axelrod's results for the Prisoners' Dilemma plus *TIT FOR TAT* context [Axelrod (1984, Appendix B)] differ from ours. Axelrod contends that *DEFECT* (the *D* vertex) and *TIT FOR TAT* (the *T* vertex) are both evolutionary equilibria – more specifically, in his terminology, they are "collectively stable" – whereas in our analysis *neither* is an *EEP* (although the *T* vertex is the end-point of an *EER*).

First, as to the claim that the *T* vertex is an Evolutionary Equilibrium Point (*EEP*). Here the source of the discrepancy is Axelrod's inappropriate formal definition of what he calls "collective stability." (While a definition cannot be said to be incorrect, it is inappropriate if it fails to describe the intended referent.) From his non-technical discussion and

---

[20] The *EER* includes all the edge points of *TL* and also the vertex *T*, but not point *L* – since points arbitrarily close to *L*, in the direction of vertex *C*, are attracted toward *C* rather than toward *L*.

interpretations, it is evident that the evolutionary equilibrium concept Axelrod had in mind was the same as ours: a strategy or distribution of strategies that is an attractor and thus secure from invasions, i.e., is stable as against sufficiently small shocks. However, his formal treatment defined a strategy S as "collectively stable" whenever no other strategy S' has *strictly* higher payoff in an all-S population. This corresponds to equation [9] above, which is the condition for a symmetrical Nash Equilibrium (*NE*). But, we have seen, [9] is not strong enough to define an evolutionary equilibrium. (It is true that a *strict NE* along the main diagonal is always a vertex *EEP*. But a *weak NE*, while still "collectively stable" on Axelrod's definition, need not be an *EEP*.) So Axelrod's "collective stability" condition is not sufficient for an *EEP*.[21]

Specifically here, the key feature is that once *DEFECT* has been driven out, *COOPERATE* can invade *TIT FOR TAT*. The *T–T* strategy-pair in Matrix 3 is only a weak *NE*, such that C and T do equally well played against T. Thus, starting from an *all-TIT FOR TAT* population, any arbitrary shock introducing *COOPERATE* players will *not* (since C and T are then equally profitable) set in motion forces leading back toward the T vertex. (In fact, as can be seen in Figure 12.2, vertex T has a convergency zone that consists only of one single trajectory.)

Next, as to the claim that the D vertex is an *EEP*. Here the difference between our result and Axelrod's is due to the different implications of *IRR* versus *DRR*. Under his *DRR* (deferred recognition and response) assumption, Axelrod is quite correct in claiming that all-D is an *EEP*: there is a neighborhood of D in which arbitrary small shocks would indeed initiate trajectories leading back toward D. Under *DRR*, in an *all-DEFECT* environment a *TIT FOR TAT* player would lose out in the very first round of every encounter and would tie D in all later rounds. In contrast, as seen above, under our *IRR* (immediate recognition and response) assumption *DEFECT* and *TIT FOR TAT* would always tie in an *all-DEFECT* environment, and the dynamic analysis has shown that the convergency zone for the D vertex fails to cover *all* the points in its neighborhood.

TIT FOR TAT as Reactive Strategy in *PD* – Selection and Mutation

The evolutionary outcome in Prisoners' Dilemma + *TIT FOR TAT*, under the *IRR* assumption and where only selectional forces are operative, is

---

[21] And, comparing it with equations [10], we see that it is not sufficient for an *ESS* either.

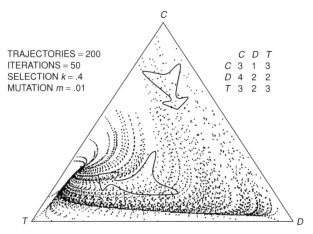

Figure 12.3. Prisoners' Dilemma plus *TIT FOR TAT* – selection and mutation ($m = .01$).

therefore a range of population mixtures of *COOPERATE* and *TIT FOR TAT*. As this is an edge solution (or set of edge solutions) rather than a vertex solution proper, in equilibrium there is *diversity* in *strategies*. But there is no *diversity* in *behavior*, since the two surviving strategies are both "nice": only cooperative moves will actually be observed in equilibrium. To model the survival of both nice and mean behaviors, in a previous paper we expanded the underlying payoff environment to allow a strategy called *PUNISHER*.[22] Here, in contrast, an interior equilibrium is brought about by *mutation pressure*.

Figure 12.3 shows the effect of allowing mutation as well as selection, the mutation coefficient being $m = .01$ while the selection coefficient remains $k = .4$ as before. As follows from equation [6], if $p_s = 0$ in any generation for any strategy S, then in the next generation $p'_s = m$. Thus the edges of the triangle "reject" any nearby trajectory. The darker probability clouds of Figure 12.2, in the neighborhoods of the previous Critical Point at vertex D and of the Evolutionary Equilibrium Region TL along the vertical axis, here have both been displaced somewhat into the interior and converted into a single *channel of high probability*. The vertex at D is no longer even a Critical Point, and the Evolutionary

---

[22] Rather like bounty-hunters in the Old West, *PUNISHER* players make a living from profitable encounters with *DEFECT* players (criminals). Thus, in an *all-COOPERATE* population, *DEFECT* is most profitable; in an *all-DEFECT* population, *PUNISHER* is most profitable; in an *all-PUNISHER* population, *COOPERATE* is most profitable. (Note the analogy with the children's game of Rock-Paper-Scissors.) It follows that when the *PUNISHER* strategy becomes available in the Prisoners' Dilemma environment, only interior solutions can maintain themselves even under selection alone.

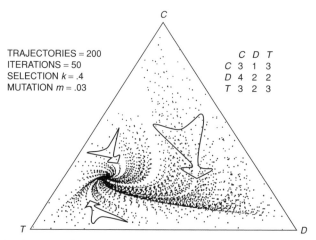

Figure 12.4. Prisoners' Dilemma plus *TIT FOR TAT – selection and mutation* ($m = .03$).

Equilibrium Region has disappeared. And in fact, in Figure 12.3 there is only a single Evolutionary Equilibrium Point, in the interior, located approximately at $(p_c, p_d, p_t) = (.268, .056, .676)$.[23]

The exact position of the *EEP* will depend upon the numerical values in the payoff matrix, and also upon the ratio m/k which reflects the relative strength of the mutational and selective forces. As the mutation rate m increases relative to the selection rate k, the *EEP* will shift inward toward the center of the triangle. This is pictured in Figure 12.4 where m has been increased to .03 (with $k = .4$ remaining unchanged). Here the trajectories are forming a definite "whirlpool" in the neighborhood of the *EEP* located approximately at $(p_c, p_d, p_t) = (.254, .164, .580)$.

BULLY as Reactive Strategy in PD

Building on the previous discussion, a more compact treatment will suffice when *BULLY* replaces *TIT FOR TAT* as the reactive strategy played against the two archetype strategies of Prisoners' Dilemma.

After replacing the T vertex by the B (*all-BULLY*) vertex, Figure 12.5 is like Figure 12.2 in representing *selectional forces alone* ($m = 0$ while $k = .2$). The probability cloud in Figure 12.5 is dense only in the

---

[23] As an important qualification, the posibility of an *EEP* depends also upon the values of k and m. If k were sufficiently large relative to m, all the trajectories might be spiraling *outward* rather than *inward*, and no *EEP* would exist. In this paper we will always be assuming, as pictured in the simulation diagrams, that whenever an evolutionary equilibrium is otherwise possible the dynamic parameters will be such as to permit its existence.

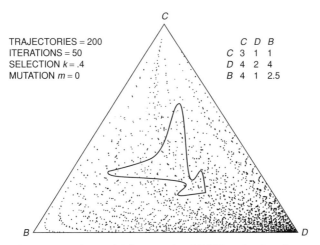

Figure 12.5. Prisoners' Dilemma plus *BULLY* – selection alone.

neighborhood of the *all-DEFECT* vertex. Indeed, it is easy to verify that *all-DEFECT* is now the sole Critical Point *CP* and sole Evolutionary Equilibrium Point *EEP*. That *BULLY* does so poorly is not surprising when we notice that, once *COOPERATE* has been driven out, *BULLY* is dominated by *DEFECT* in Matrix 5. Figure 12.6 shows the effect of introducing a *mutational* element ($m = .02$) into the simulation, with the anticipated consequence of shifting the probability cloud and the *EEP* somewhat into the interior. The single *EEP* here is at the vector $(p_c, p_d, p_d) = (.077, .832, .092)$.

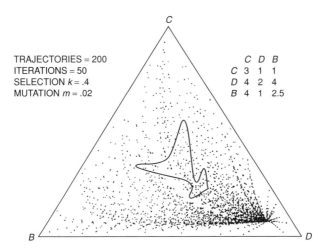

Figure 12.6. Prisoners' Dilemma plus *BULLY* – selection and mutation ($m = .02$).

Summarizing for the Prisoners' Dilemma payoff environment: 1) With *TIT FOR TAT* as reactive strategy, under selection pressure alone, despite contentions to the contrary an *all-TIT FOR TAT* population is not an Evolutionary Equilibrium Point (*EEP*). (Nor is *all-DEFECT* an *EEP* under our *IRR* assumption, though it is an *EEP* under *DRR*.) But an Evolutionary Equilibrium Region (*EER*) exists, representing a range of mixtures of *TIT FOR TAT* with (not too large a fraction of) *COOPERATE*. So there is strategy diversity but no behavior diversity. When mutation pressure is introduced, a single *EEP* does emerge, displaced somewhat into the interior from the *EER* under selection alone. Thus mutation pressure generates a degree of behavioral diversity as well as strategy diversity. 2) With *BULLY* as reactive strategy, under selection alone there is only an *all-DEFECT EEP*. Neither strategy diversity nor behavior diversity persists in equilibrium. Introducing mutations displaces this equilibrium somewhat into the interior, generating as before some diversity of both types. 3) Apart from the diversity that persists in equilibrium, the transient non-equilibrium diversity displays significant systematic patterns: probability clouds near the various *EEP*'s or *EER*'s and, with the introduction of mutation pressure, channels of high probability that tend to attract all nearby trajectories in the course of their dynamic progress.

CHICKEN

Figure 12.7 is the analog of Figure 12.2 for the Chicken environment, portraying *selectional forces alone* with *TIT FOR TAT* serving as the

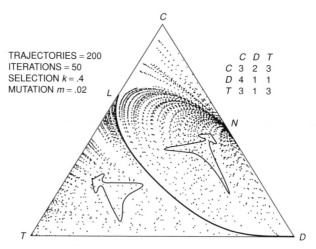

TRAJECTORIES = 200
ITERATIONS = 50
SELECTION $k = .4$
MUTATION $m = .02$

	C	D	T
C	3	2	3
D	4	1	1
T	3	1	3

Figure 12.7. Chicken plus *TIT FOR TAT* – selection alone.

reactive strategy (Matrix 4). Like Figure 12.2, Figure 12.7 contains a curve *LD*. However, since there are now two basins of attraction, *LD* in Figure 12.7 is a separatrix. Like Figure 12.2 again, the trajectories in Figure 12.7 suggest the existence of an Evolutionary Equilibrium Region (*EER*) running along the side *TC* from vertex *T* to point *L* – located at $(p_c, p_d, p_t) = (.667, 0, .333)$, and surrounded by a loose probability cloud. However, what looks very different from Figure 12.2 is the second, denser probability cloud in the region near point *N*, at the population proportions $(p_c, p_d, p_t) = (.5, .5, 0)$ representing a mixture of the archetype strategies *COWARD* and *DAREDEVIL*. The directions shown for the trajectories correctly suggest that the range *TL* is indeed an *EER* comparable to that in Figure 12.2, while point *N* represents an *EEP* with no counterpart in Figure 12.2. Which of these multiple equilibria is actually attained will depend upon the initial state of the population.

When mutations are introduced, we see in Figure 12.8 that (as in the corresponding Figures 12.3 and 12.4 for Prisoners' Dilemma) only a single interior *CP* survives, and it may be verified that this is also an *EEP*. The numerical solution is $(p_c, p_d, p_t) = (.532, .357, .111)$. What is rather remarkable is the difference between the fates of the two selection-alone equilibria after mutation pressure is introduced. The *EEP* at point *N* in Figure 12.7 (representing a mixture of *COWARD* and *DAREDEVIL*) is displaced in Figure 12.8 only slightly into the interior. In contrast, the former *EER* in Figure 12.7 (representing "nice"-behavior mixtures of *COWARD* and *TIT FOR TAT* along the *TC* edge) disappears entirely in Figure 12.8, having been converted into an interior *channel*

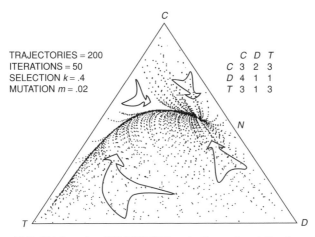

Figure 12.8. Chicken plus *TIT FOR TAT* – selection and mutation ($m = .02$).

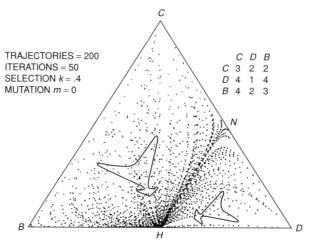

Figure 12.9. Chicken plus *BULLY* – selection alone.

of high probability that leads inexorably to the *EEP* near point *N*. Thus the selection-alone *EEP* at *N* is "resilient" to mutation pressure, while the *EER* along the *TC* edge is not; the former bends a bit, the latter falls apart entirely.[24]

Turning to *BULLY* as the reactive strategy in the Chicken environment (Matrix 6), the picture in Figure 12.9 *under selection alone* (using $k = .4$) leads to a unique edge *EEP* at point *H* located at $(p_c, p_d, p_b) = (0, .5, .5)$. This equilibrium is a mixture of *BULLY* and *DAREDEVIL*, both involving "mean" behaviors! In this case, introducing mutations ($m = .02$) leads only to the expected minor change as shown in Figure 12.10, in which the single *EEP* is displaced somewhat into the interior of the triangle, the solution being $(p_c, p_d, p_b) = (.077, .461, .461)$.

Summarizing for the Chicken environment: 1) With *TIT FOR TAT* as reactive strategy, under selection alone there is an Evolutionary Equilibrium Region *EER* representing a range of mixtures of *TIT FOR TAT* and *COWARD* (paralleling the Prisoners' Dilemma *EER* involving *TIT FOR TAT* and *COOPERATE*) and an alternative Evolutionary Equilibrium Point *EEP* representing a unique specific mixture of *COWARD* and *DAREDEVIL* players. So there are two types of edge equilibria, one

---

[24] The *resilient EEP* at point *N* in Figure 12.7 appears to correspond to what Boylan (1991) terms an "evolutionary equilibrium resistant to mutation," while the range *TL* as *EER* fails this test. In contrast, in Figure 12.2 for Prisoners' Dilemma the range *TL* survives mutation pressure, though compressed into a single point as shown in Figures 12.3 and 12.4.

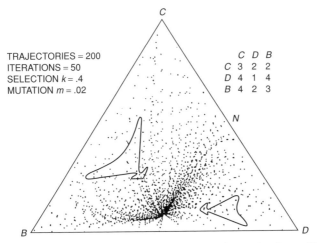

Figure 12.10. Chicken plus *BULLY* – selection and mutation ($m = .02$).

involving uniformly nice behavior and the other both nice and mean behaviors. However, under mutational pressure the first of these equilibria
proves not to be resilient; there is a unique *EEP* quite close to the second
equilibrium (in which *TIT FOR TAT* is unrepresented). So, in Chicken,
TIT FOR TAT tends to be driven out by a mixture of the two archetype
strategies. 2) With *BULLY* as reactive strategy, under selection alone
there is a single *EEP* mixture of *BULLY* and *DEFECT* (both involving
mean behaviors); introducing mutations leads only to a small shift of
this equilibrium into the interior. 3) As before, the dynamic process generates probability clouds near the evolutionary equilibria and channels
of high probability that attract the dynamic trajectories before ultimate
equilibrium is attained.

Comparing the evolutionary outcomes, in the Chicken environment
TIT FOR TAT does not do nearly so well as in Prisoners' Dilemma, while
BULLY does better. Also, in Chicken the reactive strategies are noticeably
less effective in eliciting or supporting survival of nice behavior.

SUMMARY AND DISCUSSION

1. In the actual world a wide diversity of strategies and behaviors
   persist. Our central aim has been to explore several factors that
   can support this diversity, even in narrowly specified environments
   like Prisoners' Dilemma or Chicken and with restricted menus of
   strategies. Special attention was paid to three sources of diversity: (i) multiple equilibria and/or equilibria involving mixtures

of strategies and behaviors; (ii) random mutations, and (iii) the fact that equilibrium may be approached only slowly, so that high probability may attach to some states or sets of states that are not absolutely stable.

2. In both Prisoners' Dilemma and Chicken there is a nice strategy *C (COOPERATE* in Prisoners' Dilemma, *COWARD* in Chicken) and a mean strategy *D (DEFECT* in Prisoners' Dilemma, *DARE-DEVIL* in Chicken). As against these two archetype strategies in each environment, we considered two reactive strategies: *TIT FOR TAT*, and a less friendly one termed *BULLY*. In contrast with most recent analyses, we allowed reactive players the capacity of "immediate recognition and response" (*IRR*). This worked to the advantage particularly of *TIT FOR TAT*, since under *IRR* a *TIT FOR TAT* player cannot be exploited by a *D* player even in the very first round.

3. For a state of the population to be an Evolutionary Equilibrium Point (*EEP*), under the dynamic process considered it must be a stationary state or Critical Point (*CP*) possessing a convergency zone covering *all* the points in its (sufficiently small) neighborhood. Intuitively, all nearby trajectories must lead into it. We also defined an Evolutionary Equilibrium Region (*EER*), for which the convergency condition is satisfied by the region as a whole though not for any single point within it.

4. Without recapitulating the detailed results, *TIT FOR TAT* in the *Prisoners' Dilemma* environment, while not as successful as has sometimes been claimed, does support a tendency toward the predominance of nice behaviors. *BULLY*, in contrast, survives only thanks to mutation pressure and otherwise has little influence upon the outcome. In the *Chicken* environment, the picture is somewhat reversed: *TIT FOR TAT* has little survival value, at least in the presence of mutation pressure, while *BULLY* survives and supports a tendency of mean behaviors to predominate.

5. When transient as well as equilibrium states are considered, the possible diversity is of course greater. Transient diversity is not merely random, and a number of systematic patterns can be observed. Most evident are the "probability clouds" in the neighborhood of the various equilibria. Perhaps more interesting, the dynamic process tends to generate "channels of high probability" attracting the trajectories along which the population distributions progress on the way to equilibrium. Transient as against

equilibrium states take on enhanced importance if we think of a higher-level process that extinguishes and regenerates populations as a whole at random moments of time. If so, then our probabilistic diagrams can be regarded as snapshots showing how the "population of populations" will be distributed over transient and equilibrium states.

6. Apart from the sources of diversity considered here, in the world at large wider menus of strategies are available in both Prisoners' Dilemma and Chicken environments. Even more important, strategies are chosen and behaviors take place not only under these payoff conditions but simultaneously under many other payoff conditions as well. Thus there is no reason to expect any single strategy like *TIT FOR TAT* to emerge as universally superior. Rather, our models and simulations predict (as is in fact observed) a great variety of strategies and behaviors coexisting, each doing relatively well in some environmental contexts but not in others.

REFERENCES

Axelrod, Robert (1984): *The Evolution of Cooperation* (New York: Basic Books).

Boyd, Robert and Lorberbaum, Jeffrey P. (1987): No pure strategy is evolutionarily stable in the repeated Prisoner's Dilemma Game, *Nature*, v. 327 (7 May), pp. 58–59.

Boylan, Richard T. (1991): Evolutionary equilibria resistant to mutation, Washington Univ., Olin School of Business (June).

Hirshleifer, Jack (1982): Evolutionary models in economics and law: Cooperation versus conflict strategies, *Research in Law and Economics*, v. 4, pp. 1–60.

Hirshleifer, Jack and Martinez Coll, Juan Carlos (1988): What strategies can support the evolutionary emergence of cooperation? *Journal of Conflict Resolution*, v. 32 (June), pp. 367–38.

Lipman, Barton L. (1986): Cooperation among egoists in Prisoners' Dilemma and Chicken games, *Public Choice*, v. 51, pp. 315–331.

Marimon, R. (1988): Introduction a los juegos dinamicos, *Cuadernos Economicos del ICE*, v. 40.

Martinez Coll, Juan Carlos (1986): *Bioeconomia*, Secretariado de Publicaciones de la Universidad de Malaga.

Martinez Coll, Juan Carlos and Hirshleifer, Jack (1991): The limits of reciprocity, *Rationality and Society*, v. 3 (Jan.), pp. 35–64.

Maynard Smith, J. (1976): Evolution and the theory of games, *American Scientist*, v. 64 (Jan.–Feb.), pp. 41–45.

Maynard Smith, J. and Price, G. R. (1973): The logic of animal conflict, *Nature*, v. 246 (Nov. 2), pp. 15–18.

Molander, Per (1985): The optimal level of generosity in a selfish, uncertain environment, *Journal of Conflict Resolution*, v. 29 (Dec.), pp. 611–618.

Mueller, Ulrich (1987): Optimal retaliation for optimal cooperation, *Journal of Conflict Resolution*, v. 31 (Dec.), pp. 692–724.

Nachbar, John H. (1990): "Evolutionary" selection dynamics in games: Convergence and limit properties, *International Journal of Game Theory*, v. 19, pp. 59–89.

Nachbar, John H. (1992): Evolution in the repeated Prisoner's Dilemma, *Journal of Economic Behavior and Organization*, v. 19, pp. 307–326.

13

There Are Many Evolutionary Pathways to Cooperation

Jack Hirshleifer

Background of this Chapter

The causes of war and conflict are essentially the same as the causes of peace and cooperation – it's just the point of view. Thus, this last chapter of Part Two has much the same subject as the first chapter of Part One. But the method of analysis is entirely different. "The Bioeconomic Causes of War" in Part One explained historical warfare proximately in terms of economic categories such as preferences and opportunities and then ultimately in terms of evolutionary competition. This chapter is a game-theoretic analysis exploring the extent to which cooperation can be expected to emerge from two alternative processes: negotiations among rational economic agents versus blind natural selection. The comparison takes account of several different environments (typified by the payoff matrices of Prisoners' Dilemma, Chicken, and so forth) and also of different protocols of play ("rules of the game") within each environment.

The article appeared in the opening issue of the new *Journal of Bioeconomics*.

Abstract

Current sociobiological discussions attribute the evolution of cooperation to only two main influences: kinship and reciprocity. As a baseline, the paper analyzes the extent of incidental cooperation achieved in three important 2×2 payoff environments (Prisoners' Dilemma, Chicken, and Tender Trap) and the two simplest 'rules of the game' or protocols of play (single-round simultaneous-move and single-round sequential move). Kinship promotes cooperation beyond these base levels by modifying payoffs of selfish versus unselfish behaviors. Reciprocity may also promote cooperation, but its expression requires protocols that widen available strategy sets (in comparison with the basic strategies in the underlying 2×2 payoff matrices). Once payoff modifications and/or more elaborate protocols are allowed, many other

Reprinted from J. Hirshleifer, "There Are Many Evolutionary Pathways to Cooperation," *Journal of Bioeconomics*, Vol. 1, 73–93, Copyright © 1999, with permission from Kluwer Academic Publishers.

pathways to cooperation are opened up. Among them are punishment options, complementary strategy mixes, recognition effects, coordination using external clues, and group selection.

KEY WORDS • evolution of cooperation • payoff environments • protocols of play

INTRODUCTION

A key question for all the social sciences is why cooperation occurs in some contexts but not in others. Cooperation poses an especially pressing challenge for sociobiology, founded as it is upon the central principle of the selfish gene – that the elements of our genetic heritage have been selected solely for strictly self-interested reproductive survival. The issue is, how can unselfish genes outcompete selfish ones? Or put another way, how can selfish genes translate into unselfish organisms?[1]

A somewhat impoverished view of this profoundly complex problem has become current in the sociobiological literature. To wit, that genetically driven cooperation stems, almost entirely, from only two sources: kinship and reciprocity (see, e.g., Ridley (1996)).[2] Although most sociobiological expositors limit their attention to this very narrow list of influences [Tooby and Cosmides (1996) is a praiseworthy exception], social scientists in other disciplines recognize a far wider range of bases for prosocial behaviors.[3] My intention here is to indicate the richness of the factors influencing the evolution of cooperation among living beings. First, I provide an interpretation of how evolutionary selection leads to subtly different kinds and degrees of cooperation in a variety of different payoff environments and under differing protocols or 'rules of the game'. In doing so I will compare evolutionary selection with self-interested rational choice as an alternative process that also might conduce to mutually helpful behavior.[4] Next I review the extent to which kinship and reciprocity may contribute to the evolution of cooperation.

---

[1] Classic treatments include Dawkins (1976) and Trivers (1985). A valuable recent discussion is Ridley (1996).

[2] A third force, parental manipulation, has also received some attention. Parents, aiming at their own evolutionary advantage, may manipulate offspring to act unselfishly toward one another (Alexander 1974, West Eberhard 1975, Trivers 1985, chapter 7). Parental manipulation is however only a very special kind of kinship effect.

[3] One attempt to connect these up with sociobiological considerations is Hirshleifer (1982).

[4] It might be thought that, since the realms of evolutionary selection and rational choice do not ordinarily overlap, no actual choice can be exercised between them. Still, in certain contexts – for example, software design – researchers have at times employed a kind of artificial evolutionary selection as an alternative to explicit optimization.

Table 13.1. Three Payoff Environments (Numerical Illustrations)

	C_1	C_2
Prisoners' Dilemma (PD)		
R_1	3, 3	0, 5
R_2	5, 0	1, 1
Chicken (CH)		
R_1	3, 3	1, 5
R_2	5, 1	0, 0
Tender Trap (TT)		
R_1	5, 5	0, 1
R_2	1, 0	3, 3

Finally, without attempting an overview of all possible pathways, I shall describe just a few of the many routes to cooperation that need not involve kinship or reciprocity.

COOPERATION AND HELPING IN ALTERNATIVE SOCIAL CONTEXTS

On the level of unilateral action, the kind of behavior that needs to be explained is best described by the psychologically neutral word helping. A pattern of mutual helping among two or more parties constitutes cooperation. (An unfortunate rhetorical tradition in the sociobiological literature confounds *helping*, an action, with *altruism*, which properly speaking refers to motivation. A person can have altruistic motives without engaging in helpful acts, owing perhaps to their high cost or insufficient effectiveness. Conversely, aid might be conferred for any number of reasons apart from friendly feeling.) Of course a great deal of the helping that occurs, whether unilateral or reciprocal, turns out to be merely incidental to self-interested behavior. The analytic difficulty arises only in connection with assistance to others that is actually costly to the donor. It might seem that costly helping necessarily requires altruistic motivation. But, as will be seen, this is not always the case.

The matrices in Table 13.1 are numerical instances[5] of social contexts in which greater or lesser degrees of cooperation might be achieved. Two familiar payoff patterns appear, Prisoners' Dilemma (PD) and Chicken

---

[5] The specific numbers in the Prisoners' Dilemma matrix are those used in the famous tournaments conducted by Robert Axelrod (Axelrod 1984, p. 8). The numbers in the other two matrices have been designed to correspond.

(CH), together with one other called Tender Trap (TT).[6] Letting a_{ij} and b_{ij} be the Row and Column players' payoff elements in the cell located at the ith row and jth column, these matrices display a pattern of symmetry such that $a_{ij} = b_{ji}$. Thus the Row and Column roles can be transposed.

The three matrices illustrate characteristic social problems. Prisoners' Dilemma hardly needs explanation: it represents situations where the players could choose helpful behaviors to their mutual advantage, yet, in terms of unilateral decisions, each is motivated to defect. In the Chicken environment the parties can cooperate by coordinating on different actions, a kind of complementary division of labor, but the payoff from doing so is asymmetrical. In the hope of getting the better of the bargain each side is tempted to behave aggressively, yet to some extent is deterred by the severe penalties suffered when both sides are too assertive. In Tender Trap, cooperation requires adopting the *same* action. Here interests are pretty much in harmony, yet unilateral decisions in ignorance of one another's choices may not achieve the needed coordination.[7]

Figure 13.1 illustrates the associated opportunity sets. In each diagram the four labeled nodes correspond to the cells of the associated payoff matrix, that is, to the pure-strategy outcomes. The convex hull bounding the nodes indicates the expanded set of outcomes attainable when mixed strategies are also considered.

Full cooperation can be regarded as attaining one or more of the Pareto-efficient outcomes, shown diagrammatically by the northeast boundary of the convex hull. There will always be a unique symmetrical

---

[6] Tender Trap (Hirshleifer 1982, p. 14) somewhat resembles other payoff patterns known as the Assurance Game and Stag Hunt.

[7] Many more payoff environments exist than the very few considered here. Even counting only the matrices with four distinct levels of payoff to each player – i.e., excluding ties – there are 78 essentially distinct 2 × 2 patterns (Rapoport & Guyer 1966). Allowing for ties increases the number substantially, and the range of possibilities becomes mind-boggling when more strategy options are allowed (e.g., 3 × 3 matrices). And of course all this is within the context of two-party games; with three or more players the number of possible situation increases almost unimaginably. ('Parental manipulation,' as described in an earlier footnote, is an example of an interaction involving at least three parties: one parent and two offspring.)

Within the set of two-person 2 × 2 matrices, the symmetry restriction reduces the number of possibilities. On this basis, and ruling out certain other patterns as well, Heckathorn (1996) boils down the number of patterns to just five – essentially our three, plus two others that could not be covered here. (In contrast, when it comes to explicit game-theoretic modeling, with a few important exceptions the sociobiological literature deals only with the Prisoners' Dilemma environment.)

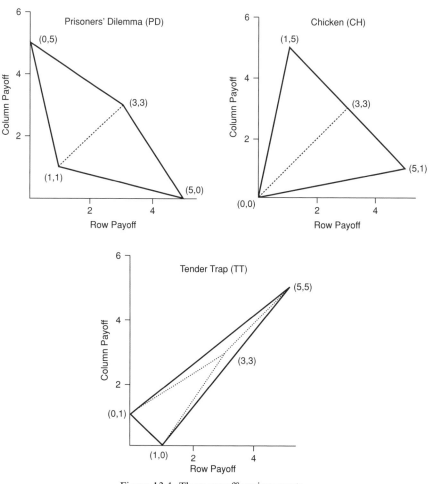

Figure 13.1. Three payoff environments.

'most cooperative' outcome, for example, the (5, 5) payoff point in the TT diagram.

As for helping, in Prisoners' Dilemma Row's first strategy R_1 is always 'more helpful' to his opponent than R_2 – since, whatever her strategy might be, Column does better when Row chooses R_1 rather than R_2 – and similarly Column's C_1 is 'more helpful' to the Row player than C_2. This nice separation holds also for Chicken, but not for Tender Trap. In TT when Column is playing her first strategy C_1, Row's R_1 is 'more helpful' than R_2 – but when Column is playing C_2 the reverse is true. The matrices of Table 13.1 have been set up so as to make the move-pair $[R_1, C_1]$ be the symmetrical 'most cooperative' choices in each case.

So, even avoiding the unfortunate term 'altruism', the psychologically neutral concepts of helping and cooperation remain somewhat soft around the edges. Still, the meanings are clear enough in many important contexts, and in others they retain at least suggestive validity. I will therefore continue to use these terms, indeed one could hardly do without them, but keeping the possible ambiguities in mind.

OPTIMIZATION VERSUS SELECTION: ONE-ROUND SIMULTANEOUS-MOVE PROTOCOL

Can evolutionary selection simulate, replace, or surpass self-interested rational optimization in leading to cooperative outcomes? Despite their limited mental powers, 'lower' animals often display impressive patterns of teamwork. And perhaps the cooperation observed among humans may stem more from evolutionary selection for instinctive behaviors than from calculated rational choices. I will be emphasizing that the relative efficacy of rationality and selection varies depending upon the environmental context (the pattern of payoffs) and also upon the operative 'rules of the game' (the protocol).

Starting with the evolutionary mechanism, think of populations of self-interested players randomly encountering one another in alternative payoff environments represented by some one of the PD, CH, and TT matrices in Table 13.1. And suppose that, in each one-on-one meeting, the protocol of interaction dictates single-round simultaneous-move choices by the Row and Column players. (Other possible protocols will be considered later on.) The basic principle of evolutionary selection is that more successful strategies multiply, while less successful ones suffer reduced representation within the population. An evolutionary equilibrium (EE) is achieved when, for a given strategy or combination of strategies (the 'incumbents'), no other strategies (the 'mutants') can successfully invade.[8]

For each matrix of Table 13.1, let α be the average payoff over all the individuals following the first strategy and β be the corresponding average payoff for the second strategy. Also, let p be the fraction of the population following the first strategy. The first strategy will tend to

---

[8] What is here termed evolutionary equilibrium is often referred to by biologists as an Evolutionarily Stable Strategy or ESS (Maynard Smith 1982), where the strategy can be pure or mixed. (Unless indicated to the contrary, only pure strategies will be dealt with in this paper.) The EE terminology is preferable, since only in special cases does the equilibrium take the form of a single strategy engaged in by all members of the population.

Table 13.2. Rationality Versus Selection in Three Payoff Environments (Simultaneous-Move Protocol)

	Evolutionary Equilibrium (EE)		Nash Equilibrium (NE)	
	Proportion Cooperating (p^*)	Payoffs	Strategy-Pair	Payoffs
PD	0	1	[R2, C2]	(1, 1)
CH	1/3	5/3	(i) [R2, C1]	(5, 1)
			(ii) [R1, C2]	(1, 5)
			(iii) mixed-strategy	(5/3, 5/3)
			($\pi = 1/3$)	
TT	(i) 1	5	(i) [R1, C1]	(5, 5)
	(ii) 0	3	(ii) [R2, C2]	(3, 3)
			(iii) mixed-strategy	(15/7, 15/7)
			($\pi = 3/7$)	

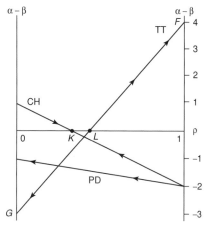

Figure 13.2. Progress toward cooperation in three evolutionary environments.

proliferate within the population when $\alpha - \beta > 0$, where:[9]

$$\alpha \equiv pa_{11} + (1 - p)a_{12}$$
$$\beta \equiv pa_{21} + (1 - p)a_{22} \tag{1}$$

For the numerical matrices of Table 13.1, the associated courses of evolutionary development are pictured in Figure 13.2. The arrows indicate the direction of movement from any momentarily given level of p. The evolutionary equilibria pictured in Figure 13.2 are summarized in the first columns of Table 13.2.

---

[9] The symmetry assumption permits us to employ only the a_{ij} parameters in these equations, omitting Column's b_{ij} payoff elements.

In Prisoners' Dilemma $\alpha - \beta$ is always negative, hence (as indicated by the arrows) the population inevitably progresses toward an EE at $p = 0$ – the familiar PD 'trap' – regardless of the starting point. In each interaction the players end up at the move-pair $[R_2, C_2]$, so the mean payoff is 1. Thus, under the assumed protocol, the evolutionary equilibrium for PD excludes both cooperation and helping.

For Chicken the 'more cooperative' (first) strategy has higher mean payoff when it is relatively rare (when p is low) while the reverse occurs when it is numerically more common (when p is high). Consequently, as the arrows indicate, regardless of the starting point the progression will be toward an interior evolutionary equilibrium at point K where the two strategies are equally profitable: $\alpha - \beta = 0$. At this EE a fraction p^* of the population will be using the first strategy and the remainder the second strategy. Numerically here, $p^* = 1/3$. The average payoff to each strategy, and therefore for the population as a whole, is $5/3$.[10]

Finally, Tender Trap is the evolutionary reverse of Chicken: now either strategy becomes the more profitable when it is sufficiently popular. The crossover point L occurs numerically at $p = 3/7$. So, as the arrows indicate, there are two possible corner EE's. Depending upon whether the starting point is to the right or the left of L in Figure 13.2, the evolutionary outcome will be the 'more cooperative' $[R_1, C_1]$ strategy combination at point F with payoffs of 5 for each player or the 'less cooperative' combination $[R_2, C_2]$ at point G with payoffs of 3. (Note that the mixed population represented by point L is not an EE.)

To interpret these results in terms of achieved cooperation, it seems reasonable to choose as point of comparison the symmetrical most Pareto-inferior outcome within the opportunity set defined by the convex hull. Measured against this base point, the progress toward cooperation achieved by the evolutionary process under the assumed protocol can be summarized:

For Prisoners' Dilemma – no progress at all:
At the EE the proportion making the more cooperative (first row or first column) move is $p = 0$.

---

[10] If mixed strategies were also considered, there would also be a monomorphic ESS in the form of the mixture involving the more cooperative strategy with probability 1/3 and the other with probability 2/3.

For Chicken – an intermediate degree of progress:
In evolutionary equilibrium the fraction choosing the more cooperative strategy is $p^* = 1/3$. The average payoff to each strategy of
$5/3$ is short of the symmetrical 'fully cooperative' payoff of 3 but
a considerable improvement over the symmetrical 'most Pareto-
inferior' payoff of 0.

For Tender Trap – either full or partial cooperation:
If the initial situation is to the right of the cross-over point in Figure
13.2, in equilibrium everyone uses the first strategy with payoffs of
5 to each; otherwise, at the EE everyone uses the second strategy
with payoffs of 3. In comparison, the 'most Pareto-inferior' symmetrical payoffs are 0.5 to each – midway along the line connecting
the (1, 0) and (0, 1) points in Figure 13.1.

Thus, depending upon the payoff environment, greater or lesser degrees
of cooperation can come about simply by evolutionary selection.

A comparison of these results with what would be achieved under
the alternative 'rationality mechanism' is provided in Table 13.2, taking
the game theorists' Nash equilibrium (NE) as the standard of rational
play.[11] In Prisoners' Dilemma the unique NE is at the 'trap' move-pair
$[R_2, C_2]$, which of course matches the EE at $p^* = 0$. So, in terms of
achieved cooperation, the results are equally unsatisfactory under either
mechanism.

For Chicken there are three NE's. The two solutions in pure strategies –
$[R_1, C_2]$ and $[R_2, C_1]$ – are Pareto-efficient but asymmetrical. Of main
interest to us is the symmetrical but Pareto-inefficient mixed-strategy
NE. For the numerical payoffs of the CH matrix, this mixed strategy
has each player choosing the more cooperative move with probability
$\pi = 1/3$ – numerically the same as the proportion of the population
who cooperate ($p^* = 1/3$) in the corresponding EE solution. (In fact,
for Chicken it is true generally that $p^* = \pi$.)[12] And so once again the

---

[11] At a Nash equilibrium, each player's choice is a 'best response' to the opponent's
strategy. I pass over some subtle intellectual issues about the nature of rationality
and how it relates to the Nash equilibrium concept. One approach to the NE, in fact,
justifies it not so much as the 'eductive' outcome of rational play but rather as the
'evolutive' consequence of a trial-and-error process (Binmore 1992).

[12] In Chicken, at the cross-over proportion p^* the two strategies have equal payoffs. And
it is a feature of all mixed-strategy Nash equilibria that each element of a player's
mixture yields the same payoff – else he would shift out of the mixture to whichever
element thereof had highest payoff.

two mechanisms arrive at essentially equivalent levels of cooperation, in this case intermediate between full cooperation and none. For Tender Trap the two symmetrical NE's in pure strategies evidently match up with the corresponding EE's in Table 13.2. But whereas the 'evolutionary mixture' corresponding to point L in Figure 13.2 was not an EE, the corresponding symmetrical mixed strategy is an NE with $\pi = 3/7$, the level of efficiency being lower than at either of the two pure-strategy solutions. It appears that here again the evolutionary process seems to do at least as well as the kind of rationality associated with the Nash equilibrium concept in game theory.

So, under the single-round simultaneous-move protocol, the two mechanisms – rational optimization and evolutionary selection – do about equally well in the PD and CH payoff contexts, while selection has perhaps an edge in the TT environment.

KINSHIP EFFECTS

As has just been seen, a substantial amount of cooperation may – the Prisoners' Dilemma apart – emerge simply as a consequence of incidental helping. The next question is the degree to which kinship and/or reciprocity effects can induce even higher levels of mutual aid. Kinship will be examined in this section, and reciprocity in the next. Since we are concerned here with the possible evolutionary emergence of additional helping, for any given payoff environment it is natural to take the evolutionary equilibrium EE of the previous section as base point. That leaves some residual ambiguity in the Chicken and Tender Trap environments, where the EEs may be mixed or non-unique. So let us start with Prisoners' Dilemma, where (at least for the simultaneous-move protocol) the EE is not only unique but represents a zero level of helping.

One of the key concepts of sociobiology is inclusive fitness (Hamilton 1964). As usually expressed, the evolutionary payoff of any trait or behavior should be evaluated not in terms of its contribution to the organism's own reproductive survival alone. Instead, the contribution to the reproductive survival of relatives should also be counted, weighted by the degree of relatedness (50% for full siblings, 25% for half-sibs, etc.). So any fitness advantage conferred on a sibling would be added, with weight of 50%, to the direct own-fitness gain associated with that gene. (It is important to appreciate, since there has been some confusion on this score, that this adjustment is not valid for the purpose of showing or predicting how an organism would or should count

**Table 13.3. Effect of Kinship in
Prisoners' Dilemma**

	C_1	C_2
Original PD matrix		
R_1	3, 3	0, 5
R_2	5, 0	1, 1
Adjusted for relatedness ($r = 1/2$)		
R_1	4.5, 4.5	2.5, 5
R_2	5, 2.5	1.5, 1.5

benefits conferred on relatives in any and all contexts. It is only valid for determining the stability of an evolutionary equilibrium EE involving such benefits.)[13]

In Table 13.3 the first matrix repeats the PD matrix of Table 13.1. The new matrix in Table 13.3 illustrates the kinship adjustment for interaction between siblings. In the upper-left cell the old (3, 3) payoff have become (4.5, 4.5), with the other cells adjusted accordingly. Inspection of the new matrix reveals the crucial point: it is no longer a Prisoners' Dilemma! In fact, it is in the form of the Chicken (CH) matrix of Table 13.1. As was pictured in Figure 13.2, for the Chicken environment there is evolutionary convergence toward an interior solution, in which part (but not all) of the population now adopts the more cooperative strategy. For the numerical example here, at equilibrium 77.8% of the population will be doing so. Thus, we have seen how kinship may bring about some partial escape from the PD trap.

More generally, it has been shown (Bergstrom and Stark 1993, Bergstrom 1995) that, starting from the non-cooperative 'trap' PD

---

[13] Consider a sexual haploid. (Sexual diploids have two genes at each locus, one inherited from the father and one from the mother. A sexual haploid has only one gene at each locus, equally likely to have been inherited from father or mother. Thinking in terms of the latter avoids complications associated with dominant versus recessive genes.) Starting with a hypothetical non-helping EE, imagine a mutation in the form of a new help-your-sibling gene. In the interaction between two offspring of a mutant organism, if one sibling bears the new gene, there is a 50% chance that the other does so as well. Hence, from the point of view of the gene, any benefit conferred on the recipient sibling would be counted, to the extent of 50%, in calculating the fitness of the mutant helping gene in comparison with the incumbent non-helping gene at that locus. (If the helping gene were not initially rare, there would be a more than 50% chance that the second sibling carries it, having possibly inherited it from the other parent. But it is only the 'rare gene' case that is relevant in determining when the mutant helping gene can invade a previous non-helping EE.) I thank T. C. Bergstrom for clarifying my thinking on this score.

solution, allowing for sibling relatedness opens up four possible classes of solutions: (1) a monomorphic cooperative EE (upper-left cell of the matrix); (2) a monomorphic non-helping equilibrium (lower-right cell); (3) EE's at either of the above, depending upon the initial starting-point; and (4) no monomorphic EE at all (so that the population converges to an interior equilibrium in which the more and the less cooperative strategies both survive in the population). Which type of EE comes about depends upon the specific numerical parameters assumed for the PD matrix. The numbers employed in Table 13.3 are associated with an equilibrium of type (4) above. Had we started with somewhat different numbers in the source PD, any of the other three classes of solutions might have been obtained.

That interacting with one's kin tends to improve the prospects for achieving a cooperative outcome is of course not very surprising. But the analysis here does tend to indicate the various provisos and limitations under which this kinship effect operates in Prisoners' Dilemma environments. (Somewhat parallel results would apply also in Chicken and Tender Trap environments, but will not be covered here.)

The remainder of this section is devoted to the special class of Prisoners' Dilemma matrices illustrated in Table 13.4. Matrix 1 is a generic payoff table in 'cost-benefit form,' where b stands for benefit and c for cost. As in all PD matrices, the lower-right cell (adoption of the less cooperative strategies on each side) is the Nash equilibrium NE and evolutionary equilibrium EE as well. The cost-benefit form sets these payoffs at $(0, 0)$. If Row were to shift unilaterally to his more cooperative strategy, he would incur cost c while conferring benefit b upon Column. So the payoffs in the upper-right cell are $(-c, b)$. The diagonally opposite cell is defined correspondingly. Finally, if both sides cooperate,

Table 13.4. Prisoners' Dilemma in Cost-Benefit Form

	C_1	C_2
General cost-benefit PD matrix		
R_1	$b - c, b - c$	$-c, b$
R_2	$b, -c$	$0, 0$
Numerical illustration ($b = 3, c = 1$)		
R_1	$2, 2$	$-1, 3$
R_2	$3, -1$	$0, 0$

the payoffs in the upper-left cell become $(b - c, b - c)$. Matrix 2 is a specific numerical instance where $b = 3$ and $c = 1$.[14]

PD matrices in cost-benefit form permit a more intuitive answer to the question of when a 'gene for helping' H would win out in evolutionary competition against the 'gene for not-helping' NH. Let W_H and W_{NH} represent the 'fitnesses' of the two genes, and define two new parameters: N is the population size, and m is the 'discrimination factor' (that is, the proportion of helping acts received by fellow-helpers). Then, for the condition $W_H > W_{NH}$ to be met, it must be that:[15]

$$-c + \frac{bmNp}{Np} > \frac{b(1 - m)Np}{N(1 - p)} \qquad (2)$$

On the left-hand side, $-c$ is the fitness loss or cost to the helper (assuming one helping act per unit of time). In the second term on the left, the numerator $bmNp$ represents the aggregate benefit of helping acts per time-period that are directed at fellow-helpers, while the denominator Np is the number of helpers in the population. The ratio of the two then shows the average per-helper benefit of helping acts, in fitness units per time-period. The right-hand side similarly shows the average per-non-helper benefit of having helpers in the population. Simplifying, inequality (3) reduces to:

$$\frac{c}{b} < \frac{m - p}{1 - p} \qquad (3)$$

As a corollary, for costly helping to evolve, at least the condition $m > p$ must be met: fellow-helpers must receive helping acts in bigger proportion than their representation in the population. Kin selection is a way of achieving this. For siblings, and assuming that H is a new mutation in the parent, initially p is effectively zero in the population. If so, the probability that one's sibling also bears the H gene is one-half. As p goes to unity, m must also approach unity, in accordance with the algebraic

---

[14] It is important to note that PD matrices cannot always be put into cost-benefit form, because the costs and benefits of helping may depend on what the recipient is doing as well. In the PD matrix of Table 13.1, for example, the cost to Row of moving from lower-right to upper-right is not the same as the cost to him of moving from lower-left to upper-left. (I thank an anonymous referee of this journal for this point.)

[15] This discussion, applying once again to sexual haploids, is adapted from a development in Hirshleifer (1978) based upon Charnov (1977).

relation:

$$m = \frac{1+p}{2} \tag{4}$$

Making this substitution in (4) leads directly to:

$$\frac{c}{b} < \frac{1}{2} \tag{5}$$

This is Hamilton's Rule (Hamilton 1964) for siblings. Generalizing for any level of relatedness r:

$$\frac{c}{b} < r \tag{6}$$

Thus, if the c/b ratio is less than the degree of relatedness, the NH gene will eventually be swamped by organisms carrying the H gene.

It will be of interest to bring in one other important factor: competition. The cost and benefit parameters c and b (and the payoff patterns from which they were derived) have so far been taken as constants independent of population size. But any fitness gain due to mutual helping would presumably lead to population growth, implying increased pressure upon resources. The consequent intensification of rivalry could then be expected to affect the cost-benefit calculations. The influence of competition can be explored using a generalized helping/hurting rule (following West-Eberhard 1975):

$$\sum_{\text{losers}(i)} r_{i\text{D}}c_i < \sum_{\text{gainers}(j)} r_{j\text{D}}b_j \tag{7}$$

That is, a donor D will be motivated to take any action on the margin for which the relatedness-weighted sum of benefits exceeds the corresponding sum of costs, where i is an index running over all the losers whereas j is an index running over all the gainers. (The donor will count himself, with a relatedness of unity, on whichever side of the inequality is appropriate.)

Turning now to the constraints upon the costs and benefits dictated by pressure on resources, as an extreme *absolute competition* could be defined by the condition (Hirshleifer 1978):

$$\sum_i c_i = \sum_j b_j \tag{8}$$

That is, the individuals are playing a constant-sum game.

In two-party absolute competition the ratio c_i/b_j is necessarily unity, so in such an environment we would not expect to observe costly helping even toward close kin. In fact, extreme sibling hostility has been known to evolve – for example, in bird species for whom within-nest competition is severe – and possible human analogs come to mind. Rewriting the generalized helping/hurting rule (7), where $\bar{r}$ is the average relatedness of members of the population to the donor:

$$\sum_i c_i(r_{i\,\mathrm{D}} - \bar{r}) < \sum_j b_j(r_{j\,\mathrm{D}} - \bar{r}) \tag{9}$$

So, under absolute competition, it is not simple relatedness but relatedness greater or less than the average in the population that serves as the factor weighting costs and benefits. Paraphrasing Hamilton (1970): 'Anyone is your enemy who is less closely related to you than the average in the population'. In sum, relatedness does certainly tend to promote cooperation. But as competition intensifies, the effect weakens and it may actually become selectively advantageous to injure not only strangers but even one's kin.

RECIPROCITY AND OTHER SEQUENTIAL STRATEGIES

The discussion so far has analyzed three important payoff patterns, each representing a possible environment in which one-on-one interactions might take place, but under only a single protocol: single-round simultaneous-move play. Under that protocol there was no way for reciprocative behavior to express itself. In this section I will consider two (among an indefinitely large number of) alternative 'rules of the game' that allow reciprocity to play a role.[16] The first to be considered is the simplest possible sequential arrangement: a single round, but now the players move in turn. Then the later-mover can adapt his choice in response to the opponent's earlier move in the same round. The other protocol to be examined involves simultaneous moves in any given round, but allows for an indefinitely large number of rounds. In that case a player's subsequent-round choices could be conditioned upon what the opponent has done in prior rounds.[17]

---

[16] Comparative studies of different protocols are quite rare in the game-theoretic literature. One important exception is Brams (1993).

[17] Reciprocity brings to mind the institutions of contract and market exchange. These forms of interaction involve a variety of possible negotiation protocols too complex to be examined here. In addition, owing to the need for enforcement, contract and market exchange typically constitute games with three or more players and so are beyond the scope of the present paper. (Some further comments on negotiation and exchange will be offered below.)

Single-Round Sequential Protocol

The change from single-round simultaneous play to single-round sequential play opens up a surprising range of strategy choices. The earlier-mover still has only two options: (1) the 'more helpful' R_1 or (2) the 'less helpful' R_2. (It will be assumed that the Row player has the earlier move.) The later-mover has four reactive options:

(i)   Respond to R_1 with C_1 and to R_2 with C_1 (always follow with the more helpful C_1)
(ii) Respond to R_1 with C_1 and to R_2 with C_2 (echo the opponent's earlier move)
(iii) Respond to R_1 with C_2 and to R_2 with C_1 (reverse the opponent's earlier move)
(iv) Respond to R_1 with C_2 and to R_2 with C_2 (always follow with the less helpful C_2)

Since any individual might either be the earlier-mover or later-mover, there are in all eight possible sequential strategies.

In this context, reciprocity is represented by the strategy 1(ii): pick the 'more helpful' R_1 on the earlier move, and the echoing option ii on the later move.[18] Interacting with one another, reciprocative players would always end up at the move-pair $[R_1, C_1]$ achieving payoffs $(3, 3)$ in PD and CH and payoff $(5, 5)$ in TT. I will be asking here, for the different payoff environments, whether reciprocative behavior is consistent with equilibrium under either the rationality or the evolutionary mechanisms.

The 'rational' game theory solution concept for this sequential protocol is subgame-perfect equilibrium (SGPE). The essential idea is that the player with the earlier move will choose his most profitable option, on the assumption that the reactive later-mover will similarly be choosing whatever is most profitable for herself when her turn comes up. Table 13.5 indicates that, for Prisoners' Dilemma, the SGPE is 2(iv) – in short, never cooperate. Thus the adopted move-pair remains $[R_2, C_2]$ with payoff 1 to each player. (Reciprocity behavior is an available strategy, but it is not consistent with self-interested rational play). Despite the changed protocol, under the rationality mechanism the PD trap still grips as tightly as ever.

For Chicken the SGPE solution is 2(iii): as earlier-mover choose the less helpful option, and as later-mover always reverse the opponent's

---

[18] This form of reciprocity corresponds to the 'Tit for Tat' strategy that has received a great deal of attention in the sociobiological literature (see below).

Table 13.5. Rationality Versus Selection in Three Payoff Environments
(Sequential-Move Protocol)

	Evolutionary Equilibrium (EE)		Subgame-Perfect Equilibrium (SGPE)	
	Is Reciprocity Strategy 1(ii) a Possible EE?	Payoffs	Strategy (See Text) (Earlier-Move, Later-Move)	Payoffs
PD	No	—	2(iv)	(1, 1)
CH	No	—	2(iii)	(3, 3)[a]
TT	Yes[b]	5	1(ii)	(5, 5)

[a] Average of (5, 1) and (1, 5). (Earlier-mover has advantage, but each player has a 50% chance of being the earlier-mover.)
[b] As part of 'drifting equilibrium' with 1(i).

prior choice. In any single run of the game the result is asymmetrical, the earlier-mover having the advantage. But recall that each player is equally likely to be the earlier-mover or later-mover. Then, taking the average of the asymmetrical (5, 1) and (1, 5) payoffs, the mean return is 3 – exactly the same as at the reciprocative outcome. This equivalence is however an accidental result of the specific payoff numbers used in the CH matrix of Table 13.1. If the payoffs in the upper-left cell were changed from (3, 3) to say (2, 2), the game would still be Chicken but the parties would now both do better under self-interested rationality than by following the reciprocity strategy! The opposite would hold if, say, the upper-left payoffs were changed to (4, 4). Finally, for Tender Trap, the SGPE is 1(ii). Here, under the assumed sequential protocol, reciprocity behavior coincides with rational self-interest, and leads to the unique 'most cooperative' outcome with payoff 5.

Now let us turn to the evolutionary process. Having to deal with eight different pure strategies is more than a little troublesome. In addition to a number of more complicated possibilities, the evolutionary equilibrium EE in pure strategies could involve only one strategy surviving, or two, or any number up to the full eight.[19] To keep the problem within bounds, I ask only whether the reciprocity strategy 1(ii) can ever be a single-strategy evolutionary equilibrium.

In the Prisoners' Dilemma environment, 1(ii) cannot be a single-strategy EE. In a population with 1(ii) as sole 'incumbent,' every possible 'mutant' strategy involving C_2 or R_2 – that is, any strategy for which the less cooperative option is chosen on the earlier move or on

---

[19] Up to eight distinct single-strategy EE's might coexist, as many as $8 \times 7/2 = 28$ EE's involving mixtures of two strategies, etc.

the later move or both – will strictly defeat 1(ii) in one-on-one play and thus successfully invade. True, the reciprocative players will be making $[R_1, C_1]$ moves with one another and achieving handsome (3, 3) payoffs. But against these incumbents a mutant choosing the less cooperative R_2 on the earlier move will be earning the higher of the payoff-pair (5, 0), and similarly an entrant choosing the less cooperative C_2 on the later move will receive the higher of (0, 5).

The analysis of Chicken is very similar. If 1(ii) is the incumbent, once again the reciprocative players receive (3, 3) when they interact with one another. But a less cooperative mutant would now earn the higher of (5, 1) on the earlier move and/or the higher of (1, 5) on the later move. For Tender Trap the situation is somewhat trickier. As incumbent, the reciprocative strategy 1(ii) cannot be strictly defeated by any other. However, the Always-Cooperate (AC) strategy 1(i) ties 1(ii) in any one-on-one interaction between them – since both lead to the move-pair $[R_1, C_1]$ with payoffs (5, 5). So we can expect a kind of metastable 'drifting equilibrium' for some range of combinations of 1(i) and 1(ii).

Summarizing, in both the Prisoners' Dilemma and Chicken environments under the single-round sequential protocol, reciprocative behavior does not in general succeed in maintaining itself either as the rational subgame-perfect equilibrium or as an evolutionary equilibrium. However, in Tender Trap the reciprocative strategy is indeed the sole SGPE, and it is an element in a 'drifting' EE in combination with the Always-Cooperate strategy 1(i).

Multiple-Round Simultaneous-Move Protocol

A variety of other 'rules of the game' provide ways for reciprocity behavior to be expressed. Let us suppose here that the players choose simultaneously in any given round, but the interaction is repeated over an indefinite number of rounds. Then a less cooperative move in a prior round could conceivably be penalized by the opponent's refusal to play cooperatively in one or more subsequent rounds. Under the famous Tit-for-Tat (TFT) strategy popularized in the well-known work of Axelrod (1984), initially the player would choose the more helpful option (first row or column in the matrices of Table 13.1), thereafter echoing the opponent's behavior in the previous round. Unhelpful behavior would be punished, but in a proportionate eye-for-an-eye way that leaves open the possibility of later reversion to more cooperative play. In two tournaments conducted by Axelrod using the Prisoners' Dilemma payoffs of

Table 13.1, TFT scored higher than any other of the strategies considered. It has come to be widely believed that TFT is, in a very sweeping sense, the 'best' strategy to follow and constitutes the key to the emergence of cooperation.[20]

A systematic investigation of these issues is out of the question here. Instead, I shall limit myself to a few points bearing specifically upon TFT as one possible reciprocative strategy:

1. Not all social interactions correspond to evolutionary competition. So even if TIT FOR TAT were a universal evolutionary equilibrium, that would not warrant using the TFT strategy in non-evolutionary contexts such as labor-management relations or international policy.[21]

2. For evolutionary processes quite generally, it is unreasonable to expect a 'corner solution' in which only a single strategy such as TFT survives. In almost all real-world contexts a coexisting mix of strategies – more cooperative ones together with less cooperative ones – is observed.[22] (This point will be discussed further under the heading of "complementary strategy mixes" in the next section.)

3. TFT has been discussed almost exclusively in the context of the multiple-round simultaneous-move Prisoners' Dilemma. Even if it were successful under those conditions, that success would not necessarily remain valid for other environments and protocols.

4. But in fact, as has just been seen, although there are a huge number of EE's in the multiple-round simultaneous-move Prisoners' Dilemma, an all-TFT population is not one of them! In parallel with the corresponding result for the single-round sequential-move PD, Tit for Tat as incumbent can never do better than tie with (and thus be subject to invasion by) the Always-Cooperate strategy.

The upshot, then, is that reciprocity, like kinship, can indeed promote cooperation in a number of important specific contexts. But it is no panacea.

---

[20] For a critique of these claims see Martinez Coll and Hirshleifer (1991). Some qualifying statements also appear in Axelrod (1984), pp. 176–177.

[21] Contra occasional suggestions in Axelrod (1984), for example, p. 190.

[22] See, e. g., Dugatkin (1990). For the PD environment and the multiple-round simultaneous-move protocol, Boyd and Lorberbaum (1987) have shown that no single strategy can ever be an EE.

OTHER PATHWAYS

So far the analysis has examined two influences – kinship and reciprocity – that, in certain circumstances, lead to cooperation. These are the forces emphasized in sociobiological summaries and textbook discussions. Yet appearing here and there in the vast literatures of sociobiology, economics, and other social sciences are indications of a great many other possible pathways to cooperation. Kinship promotes cooperation by modifying the payoffs of helpful actions. (Discounted by the degree of relatedness, benefits to others are counted as equivalent to benefits to self.) And reciprocative behavior requires consideration of a number of alternative protocols of play, with a consequent need to deal with extended strategy sets in comparison with the elemental Row and Column strategies of Table 13.1. However, once adjustments of payoffs, protocols, and/or strategy sets are permitted, many other possible routes to cooperation are opened up. A very few of these additional routes are briefly covered in this section.

Punishment Opportunities

Reciprocative strategies such as Tit-for-Tat penalize an opponent's failure to cooperate by reactive non-cooperation. But this is a mild penalty. In some circumstances it may be possible to impose stronger penalties, as exemplified by what has been termed Punisher strategies (Hirshleifer and Martinez Coll 1988). Punisher players gain at the expense of non-cooperators, just as the latter 'make a living' by exploiting cooperators. In the realm of Nature, for example, super-predator species prey upon lower-level predators. In human terms, bounty-hunters specialize in capturing criminals.

When Punisher strategies are available in the PD environment, the typical evolutionary outcome is a mixed population in which the more cooperative, less cooperative, and Punisher strategies are all represented – rather like the continuing survival of ranchers, rustlers, and bounty-hunters in the Old West.[23] Thus, introducing Punisher is a way of modeling the fact that what we observe in the real world is almost never

---

[23] The relation among ranchers, rustlers, and bounty-hunters is somewhat like the children's game of Rock-Paper-Scissors. When ranchers preponderate, it is most profitable to be a rustler. When rustlers are very numerous, it's advantageous to be a bounty-hunter. And when almost everyone is a bounty-hunter, it pays best to be a rancher.

the total victory of any single strategy but rather a co-existing set of differentiated strategies.[24]

Complementary Strategy Mixes

Extending this idea for the Prisoners' Dilemma payoff environment and multiple-round simultaneous-move protocol, Lomborg (1996) generated simulations taking account of all the strategies that can 'remember' and thus react to the opponent's three prior moves. (There are 32,768 such strategies!) Over the evolutionary generations meta-stable (but never fully stable) equilibria[25] emerge. These typically involve a considerable number of mutually supportive strategies, commonly falling into two types labeled 'nucleus' and 'shield'. The nucleus strategies are highly cooperative ones, reacting very little or not at all to opponents' unhelpful moves but scoring well in encounters with other members of the incumbent strategy set. The shield strategies, in contrast, provide protection by reacting adversely to uncooperative deviants.

Despite chaotic periods that show up when an existing meta-equilibrium collapses, the system as a whole spends most of its time at or near the meta-equilibria. Furthermore, these equilibria yield very high average payoffs (high levels of cooperation). In fact, the mean evolutionary payoffs were generally higher than what an all-TFT population would achieve![26]

Recognition and Prompt Response

While ordinarily it is assumed that a TFT player can react to the opponent's prior move in the very next round of play, that is only one of many possibilities. If response delay were greater, the TFT strategy would not do so well. Conversely, however, Tit-for-Tat would do even better than in the standard formulation if a TFT player could recognize and respond to the opponent's choice earlier, perhaps even in the very

[24] On the other hand, for unfavorable values of the parameters an interior solution involving all three strategies might not be viable. If bounty-hunting were too ineffective ever to be profitable, the EE might consist of ranchers and rustlers only.

[25] Meta-stable equilibria are strategy combinations that persist more or less unchanged over a considerable number of generations, but eventually succumb to the invasion of 'mutants' who find a basis for entry.

[26] This was possible because the simulations allowed for 'noise,' that is, for the possibility that a TFT player misperceives and therefore responds incorrectly to the opponent's prior move. Absent noise, in a hypothetical all-TFT world everyone would score 3 per move, and it is not possible to do better. But the all-TFT payoffs decline considerably with even modest levels of noise.

same round. This last could occur if, for example, the situation dictated that the opponent's action, hostile or friendly, had to be overt rather than covert. In the arms race preceding World War I, it was impossible for open societies like Britain or Germany to hide the numbers of battle-ships under construction. So a hostile move by either nation (deciding to build more battleships) could not gain much lead time over the opponent's response. Alternatively, by paying a 'cost of scrutiny' (Frank 1988, pp. 59–63) it might be possible to identify a covertly hostile action in good time – an instance of trading off payoff numbers to gain promptness of response.

Allowing perfect recognition and timely response makes Tit-for-Tat an available strategy even when the protocol is single-round simultaneous-move.[27] Martinez Coll and Hirshleifer (1991) analyzed the Prisoners' Dilemma and Chicken environments under this protocol, with three strategies in contention: TFT, Always-Cooperate (AC), and Never-Cooperate (NC). In such a simple context it was possible to find all the evolutionary equilibria. For PD a 'drifting' EE was found involving TFT and AC, provided the proportion of the latter was not too large. In the Chicken environment there was a similar drifting equilibrium, but also a separate non-drifting EE in which the population ended up with a specific division between AC and NC. (Note the similarity of the latter equilibrium to the EE for Chicken in Figure 13.2.)

Once again, these extended strategy sets allowed the continuing survival of more and less cooperative players in a variety of contexts.

Control

In some circumstances a person might be in a position to 'commit' to a particular strategy, or alternatively to foreclose his ever employing certain other strategies (as in 'burning your bridges behind you'). Commitment or foreclosure can affect the rational equilibrium. If you burn your bridges behind you the enemy knows you can no longer retreat, which might affect his calculation whether or not to attack. However, neither commitment nor foreclosure on the part of an individual can affect the evolutionary equilibrium, since your self-denied strategies still remain available to other players present in the population. Conceivably, however, a player might have the ability to dictate or control the *opponent's* possible actions. Control might be effected by

---

[27] Recall that we have heretofore allowed TFT to play a role only in the single-round sequential-play or the multiple-round simultaneous-play protocols.

physical means like imprisonment,or psychological means like hypnotism or indoctrination.[28] The controlling party would ordinarily incur some cost, yet the trade-off might prove advantageous.

As one example, for Prisoners' Dilemma using the single-round simultaneous-play protocol 'with recognition' (as described just above), Heckathorn (1996) found that the reciprocative Tit for Tat strategy was driven to extinction by a control strategy termed 'hypocritical cooperation'. Under that strategy the player does not cooperate voluntarily, but is willing to incur a cost to force the opponent into a cooperative move. So in a world where such control is not too costly, a great deal of cooperation might emerge, even if unwilling.

Coordination by External Clues

The three payoff contexts of Table 13.1 displayed different types of obstacles hampering mutually advantageous coordination of strategies. Sometimes, however, external clues may provide the basis for harmonizing the players' moves. Starting from the underlying Chicken environment under the single-round simultaneous-move protocol, Maynard Smith (1978) described a strategy termed Bourgeois. The idea is that, in competing for use of a resource, one animal typically arrives earlier and the other later. Using this external clue, the Bourgeois strategy is: As earlier-comer, play aggressively, as later-comer, play submissively. In terms of the CH matrix of Table 13.1 the moves would be $[R_2, C_1]$ with payoffs (4, 2), Row as earlier-comer having the advantage. But on average each animal can expect to be in either situation half the time, so the mean payoff would be 3 – higher than the 5/3 payoff shown in Table 13.2 for the symmetrical EE when only the simpler "more cooperative" and "less cooperative" strategies were available.

Group Selection

Although currently highly controversial among biologists, group selection as a possible force favoring cooperation has a long intellectual history. Darwin suggested that the habit of cooperation, even where disadvantageous to the individual, might be evolutionarily viable owing to its impact upon the differential survival of groups (Darwin 1871 [n.d., 498]). But, at least if we think in terms of environments like the Prisoners' Dilemma matrix of Table 13.1, group selection for cooperative behavior runs against the fact that individual selection favors selfish

---

[28] Parental manipulation, discussed in an earlier endnote, is an example of such control.

actions. And in fact the current standard view among sociobiologists is that individual selection for selfishness must dominate (Williams 1966). The key argument has been that individuals within a population have shorter 'turnover times' (are differentially selected faster) than populations as a whole. So the internal within-group trend toward selfishness will proceed more rapidly than any collective between-group gain from the displacement of less unselfish populations.

But recall that kin selection, whose power no sociobiologist questions, operates essentially by concentrating helping acts upon fellow-carriers of the helping gene. Much the same would hold even for unrelated individuals living in groups characterized by preferential interaction with one another – possibly due simply to propinquity. Group selection is also favored by frequent exterminations of entire clans and tribes, a condition that very likely characterized primal mankind (Alexander 1979, chapter 4). In recent years biological opinion has been swinging back toward assigning a substantial evolutionary role to group selection (Wilson and Sober 1994).

The discussion in this section could do no more than suggest the huge number of pathways to cooperation opened up once we allow for wider ranges of payoff patterns and protocols, and consequently enlarged strategy sets. Sociobiologists have not overlooked these other pathways; indeed, most of the examples in this section derive from the sociobiological literature. What I have tried to critique is the tendency in textbooks and other summary discussions to recognize only kinship and reciprocity as systematic factors tending to produce cooperative evolutionary outcomes.

CONCLUDING THOUGHTS

Cooperation takes many forms and emerges through many channels and pathways. Game-theoretic analyses in the sociobiological literature have concentrated excessively upon just one or a very few payoff environments (notably Prisoners' Dilemma) and similarly only one or a very few of the enormous range of possible protocols of play ('rules of the game'). It is probably owing to this excessive narrowness of viewpoint that usually only kinship and reciprocity have been recognized as systematic influences favoring the rise of cooperation.

As a baseline, this paper first assessed three important payoff environments (Prisoners' Dilemma, Chicken, and Tender Trap) illustrating different types of obstacles hampering the evolution of mutual helping, and using only the two simplest possible protocols (single-round simultaneous-move and single-round sequential move). In these contexts, by and large, comparable levels of cooperation were achieved by the different mechanisms of evolutionary selection and rational self-interested choice. The degree to which kinship and/or reciprocity improved upon these results varied with the specifics of the payoff environment and protocol assumed.

Allowing for kinship and reciprocity already involves a certain widening of horizons in comparison with the baseline conditions. Kinship and reciprocity effects modify the payoffs of cooperative versus uncooperative behaviors and/or require consideration of more complex protocols, the latter implying an extension of the sets of strategies assumed available. Once such alterations of payoffs and protocols are permitted, however, a vast number of other routes to cooperation are opened up. The final main section of the paper summarized a number of these other pathways: punishment opportunities, complementary strategy mixes, recognition effects, techniques of control, coordination with the help of external clues, and group selection.

A few other points relate to limitations of the present analysis. First, not all competition is evolutionary competition. The relations among nations and social classes certainly change over time, but are not usually best modeled as involving large populations of entities subject to evolutionary influences such as inheritance, mutation, multiplication, and selection. Second, the analysis here dealt almost exclusively with symmetrical solutions. But a degree of cooperation is often achieved in asymmetrical ways, for example by systems of dominance and deference that keep internal power struggles within bounds.

As a coda to the main discussion, I will offer a further comment on a secondary theme of the paper: the relative efficacy of evolutionary selection versus rational optimization as mechanisms of competition and cooperation. The second section above suggested there was little to choose between them; if anything, selection had the edge over rationality. But, I now want to argue, the very simple protocols of play postulated in the second section led to an under-estimate of what interacting rational choices can actually achieve in the way of cooperation. In the single-round sequential-move Prisoner' Dilemma, for example, the Subgame-perfect equilibrium associated with rational play offers no escape from the PD 'trap' outcome (Table 13.5). However, rational players can (and are observed to) do much better under quite reasonable though somewhat more complex protocols, in particular one that might be termed the Standard Negotiation Protocol (SNP).[29]

The SNP, while single-round, allows for an indefinite number of negotiation cycles before moves are finalized and payoffs are made. In each cycle players tentatively choose either the more cooperative move (first row or column of the PD matrix in Table 13.1) or the less cooperative move (second row or column). After these tentative choices are revealed at the end of a cycle, either or both players may stand pat or switch. Since any player can always switch away from the exploitative outcome in which he/she would have received zero payoff, there is no reason not to try the cooperative move. The only stable equilibrium involves the mutually advantageous (3, 3) payoffs. So rational players can, given this quite realistic protocol, escape the PD trap after all. More generally, rational players can frequently treat the rules of the game as endogenous, and hence should be able to hit upon a protocol leading to mutually advantageous outcomes. Economists will of course recognize this as a version of the famous 'Coase theorem.'

ACKNOWLEDGMENTS

For helpful comments I especially thank David Hirshleifer, Theodore C. Bergstrom, Michael Ghiselin, and two anonymous referees of this Journal.

REFERENCES

Alexander, Richard D. 1974. The evolution of social behavior. Annual Review of Ecology and Systematics 5:325–383.
Alexander, Richard D. 1979. Darwinism and human affairs. University of Washington Press, Seattle.
Axelrod, Robert. 1984. The evolution of cooperation. Basic Books, New York.
Bergstrom, Theodore C. 1995. On the evolution of altruistic ethical rules for siblings. American Economic Review 85:58–81.
Bergstrom, Theodore C. and Oded Stark. 1993. How altruism can prevail in an evolutionary environment. American Economic Review, Papers and Proceedings 83:149–155.
Binmore, Ken. 1992. Fun and games. D. C. Heath and Co., Lexington.
Boyd, Robert and Jeffrey P. Lorberbaum. 1987. No pure strategy is evolutionarily stable in the repeated Prisoner's Dilemma game. Nature 274:58–59.
Brams, Steven J. 1993. Theory of moves. American Scientist 81:562–570.
Charnov, Eric L. 1977. An elementary treatment of the genetical theory of kin-selection. Journal of Theoretical Biology 66:541–550.

[29] This discussion is an adaptation of a development in Brams (1993).

Darwin, Charles. 1871. The descent of man, and selection in relation to sex. John Murray, London. [Modern Library re-issue of second 1874 edition.]

Dawkins, Richard. 1976. The selfish gene. Oxford University Press, Oxford.

Dugatkin, Lee Alan. 1990. N-person games and the evolution of co-operation: a model based on predator inspection in fish. Journal of Theoretical Biology 142:123–135.

Frank, Robert H. 1988. Passions within reason: the strategic role of the emotions. W. W. Norton, New York.

Hamilton, William D. 1964. The genetical evolution of social behaviour, I. Journal of Theoretical Biology 7:1–16.

Hamilton, William D. 1970. Selfish and spiteful behaviour in an evolutionary model. Nature 228:1218–1220.

Heckathorn, Douglas D. 1996. The dynamics of colletive action. American Sociological Review 61:250–277.

Hirshleifer, Jack. 1978. Natural economy versus political economy. Journal of Social and Biological Structures 1:319–337.

Hirshleifer, Jack. 1982. Evolutionary models in economics and law: cooperation versus conflict strategies. Research in Law and Economics 4:1–60.

Hirshleifer, Jack and Juan Carlos Martinez Coll. 1988. What strategies can support the evolutionary emergence of cooperation? Journal of Conflict Resolution 32:367–398.

Lomborg, Bjorn. 1996. Nucleus and shield: the evolution of social structure in the iterated Prisoner's Dilemma. American Sociological Review 61:278–307.

Martinez Coll, Juan Carlos and Jack Hirshleifer. 1991. The limits of reciprocity. Rationality and Society 3:35–64.

Maynard Smith, John. 1978. The evolution of behavior. Scientific American 239:176–192.

Maynard Smith, John. 1982. Evolution and the theory of games. Cambridge University Press, Cambridge.

Rapoport, Anatol and Melvin Guyer. 1996. A taxonomy of 2×2 games. General Systems 11:203–214.

Ridley, Matt. 1996. The origins of virtue. Penguin Books, New York.

Tooby, John and Leda Cosmides. 1996. Friendship and the banker's paradox: other pathways to the evolution of adaptations for altruism. Proceedings of the British Academy 88:119–143.

Trivers, Robert. 1985. Social evolution. Benjamin/Cummings Publishing Co., Menlo Park.

West Eberhard, Mary Jane. 1975. The evolution of social behavior by kin selection. Quarterly Review of Biology 50:1–32.

Williams, George C. 1966. Adaptation and natural selection: a critique of some current evolutionary thought. Princeton University Press, Princeton.

Wilson, David Sloan and Elliot Sober. 1994. Reintroducing group selection to the human behavioral sciences. The Behavioral and Brain Sciences 17:585–608.

14

The Expanding Domain of Economics

Jack Hirshleifer

Background of this Chapter

At intervals of 3 to 5 years the American Economic Association has customarily published a directory issue. Traditionally, the directory issue also carries a small number of articles – usually only two or three – on topics of wide interest to the profession.

This invited paper in the 1985 Directory explored the prospects for what has been called "imperialist economics." I contended that economics ought not consider itself limited to the analysis of markets nor bound to its usual postulate that the human subject will behave as a rational, self-interested economic man. Instead, economics ought to aggressively investigate any scientific models and make any assumptions about human beings that lead to valid predictions as to how people will behave in a world of scarce resources. The discussion here echoes several of the themes in previous chapters of this volume, especially the significance of conflictual interactions for human behavior and the survival of the emotions as "irrational" yet often effective instruments for attaining one's ends.

I thank Jerome F. Heavey and Allan Persky for finding a logical slip that has been corrected in this reprinted version.

Definitions of economics are legion. Two familiar ones will be particularly appropriate for my purposes:

...ECONOMICS is a study of mankind in the ordinary business of life; it examines that part of individual and social action which is most closely connected with the attainment and with the use of the material requisites of wellbeing.

—Alfred Marshall [1920, p. 1]

* University of California, Los Angeles. (Reprinted from J. Hirshleifer, "The Expanding Domain of Economics," *American Economic Review*, Vol. 75, 53–68, Copyright © 1985, with permission from the American Economic Association.)

Economics is the science which studies human behavior as a relationship between ends and scarce means that have alternative uses.
— Lionel Robbins [1962, p. 16]

As to Marshall, how terribly narrow, dull, bourgeois! Must we economists limit our attention to the ordinary, the crassly material business of
life? While equally prosaic, Robbins' "relationship between ends and
scarce means" does open the door wider. After all, the ends that men
and women seek include not just bread and butter but also reputation,
adventure, sex, status, eternal salvation, the meaning of life, and a good
night's sleep – the means for achieving any of these being, too often,
notably scarce.

In dealing with economics as an expansive imperialist discipline (see
Gerard Radnitzky and Peter Bernholz [1987]), a geopolitical metaphor
may be illuminating. Our heartland is an intellectual territory carved
off by two narrowing conceptions: (1) of *man* as rational, self-interested
decisionmaker, and (2) of *social interaction* as typified by market exchange. However, the logic of ideas irresistibly draws economists beyond
these core areas. Rational self-interested choice plays a role in many domains of life other than markets, for example in politics, warfare, mate
selection, engineering design, and statistical decisions. Conversely, even
within the domain of market behavior, economists can hardly deny that
what people want to buy and sell is influenced by cultural, ethical, and
even "irrational" forces more customarily studied by social psychologists and anthropologists. And how people go about their dealings in the
market touches upon issues also involving law and sociology.

Responding to these intellectual attractions, the rhetoric of an economic imperialist like Gary S. Becker is notably more muscular:

The combined assumptions of maximizing behavior, market equilibrium, and
stable preferences, used relentlessly and unflinchingly, form the heart of the
economic approach. . .

[1976a, p. 4]

It is this approach that has powered the imperialist expansion of economics into the traditional domains of sociology, political science, anthropology, law, and social biology – with more to come.

Space constraints rule out any attempt to review here the detailed
intellectual histories of these various imperialist invasions, or to assess
their overall success or failure. I will have to omit, apart possibly from occasional remarks, a vast array of important and exciting subjects such as:
the substantivist vs. formalist controversy in anthropology; in political

science the design of optimal constitutions, the stability of voting equilibria, and the balance of power among pressure groups; crime and its
deterrence in sociology and law; and a host of interdisciplinary topics
like optimal foraging, the division of labor by sex or age or caste, and
patterns of fertility and marriage.[1] Instead, I shall reverse the emphasis to concentrate upon a necessarily idiosyncratic selection of lessons
that these imperialist forays have for economists about the validity of
our image of economic man and about the relative roles of market vs.
non-market interactions.

I will emphasize two central themes. First, that it is ultimately impossible to carve off a distinct territory for economics, bordering upon
but separated from other social disciplines. Economics interpenetrates
them all, and is reciprocally penetrated by them.[2] *There is only one
social science.* What gives economics its imperialist invasive power is
that our analytical categories – scarcity, cost, preferences, opportunities, etc. – are truly universal in applicability. Even more important is
our structured organization of these concepts into the distinct yet intertwined processes of optimization on the individual decision level and
equilibrium on the social level of analysis. Thus economics really does
constitute the universal grammar of social science. But there is a flip
side to this. While scientific work in anthropology and sociology and
political science and the like will become increasingly indistinguishable
from economics, economists will reciprocally have to become aware of
how constraining has been their tunnel vision about the nature of man
and social interactions. Ultimately, good economics will also have to be
good anthropology and sociology and political science and psychology.

The second underlying theme was succinctly expressed by Marshall:

But economics has no near kinship with any physical science... It is a branch
of biology broadly interpreted.

[1920, p. 772]

That economics is an aspect of a broader biological "economy of nature" would not have seemed strange to Adam Smith who, in the *Moral*

---

[1] A few selected references (the products of economic imperialists, or else "native"
writings with an explicit or implicit economic orientation) are: on the substantivist
vs. formalist controversy, Richard Posner [1980, pp. 2–3]; on optimal constitutions,
James M. Buchanan and Gordon Tullock [1962, Ch. 6], on majority-voting equilibrium Dennis C. Mueller [1979], and on pressure-group equilibrium, Gary S. Becker
[1983]; on optimal foraging, Eric L. Charnov [1976] and Eric Alden Smith [1983];
on the division of labor in insect societies, E. O. Wilson [1978b]; on monogamous vs.
polygamous marriage, Wilson [1975, pp. 327–331] and Amyra Grossbard [1980].

[2] Thus I cannot agree that the other social sciences are, in any useful sense, "contiguous"
to economics as contended by Ronald H. Coase [1978].

Sentiments, sounded a near-Darwinian note:

> The economy of nature is in this respect exactly of a piece with what it is upon many other occasions. ... Thus self-preservation, and the propagation of the species, are the great ends which nature seems to have proposed the formation of all animals. Mankind are endowed with a desire of those ends, and an aversion to the contrary.
>
> [1976 (1759), p. 152]

It is no new idea that the social sciences (including economics) must rest to some degree upon the biological constitution of the human species. But there is a sense in which, I will argue, economics and biology are uniquely intertwined.

ECONOMIC MAN

Economic man is characterized by *self-interested goals* and *rational choice of means*. On both scores, this image of the human animal has been the object of grumbles. After all, men and women do sometimes seek the welfare of others, and they are sometimes led astray by thoughtlessness and confusion. How should our profession respond to these complaints? (1) A kind of answer, one with which I have little patience, is to use a verbal trick so as to redefine all goals as self-interested, and all choice of means as rational. (2) More defensibly, our profession might adopt a self-denying ordinance, setting aside non-self-interested goals and non-rational choice of means as "non-economic." Economists could then modestly claim that the hypothesis of rational self-interested man, though admittedly inaccurate, has proved to have great explanatory power *in the areas where we apply it*.

There is always something to be said for modesty. But the scientific enterprise demands more. When the phenomenon of radioactive decay refuted the principle of conservation of mass, it would have been modest but unproductive for physicists to decide henceforth to limit their investigations to those processes for which mass was indeed conserved. And similarly, if the hypothesis of economic man fails in any field of application, the correct scientific response is not modest retreat but an aggressive attempt to produce a better theory.

The history of imperialist economics illustrates that the model of economic man has indeed been productive, but only up to a point. Each of our expansionist invasions has typically encountered an initial phase of easy successes, where postulating rational self-interested behavior in a new field of application has yielded sudden sharp results. In the field of politics it was like a breath of fresh air when Anthony Downs boldly proposed as "axioms" that men seek office solely for income, prestige, and power and that every political agent acts rationally to achieve goals with minimal use of scarce resources [1957, p. 137]. Or in the field of crime when Gary S. Becker [1968] and Isaac Ehrlich [1973] chose to set aside the possibly "deviant" personalities of criminals and instead treat them as individuals rationally responding to opportunities in the form of punishment and reward. These, and similarly oriented explorations into domains of study such as law, marriage and the family, and war and conflict, have led to a rapid intellectual flowering of exciting results.

But then comes a second phase, when doubts begin to emerge. In the partially conquered new territories some of the evidence persists in remaining intractable, difficult to square with the postulate of rational self-interested behavior. In politics these include the fact of voting, the willingness to provide public goods, the grip of ideology. As to crime, it remains true that faced with the same incentives some people commit offenses while others respect the law. So more than a suspicion remains that, after all, criminals are to a degree "deviant" personalities. In some of the fields of imperialist extension of economics we are still in the first phase, reaping easy results. But my emphasis will be upon the more interesting second stage, and what we can learn from the difficulties encountered.

In what follows I will examine what our imperialist explorations have taught us about the two crucial aspects of economic man – *self-interest* (Sec. II) and *rationality* (Sec. III). I will then take up the topic of *conflict* (Sec. IV) to illustrate what economics can say about this most important of the nonmarket interactions that humans engage in. The final Sec. V analyzes the biological underpinnings of all these patterns.

SELF-INTEREST

Adam Smith, as usual, said it best:

We are not ready to suspect any person of being defective in selfishness.
[1976 (1759), p. 482]

And of course there are his famous lines:

It is not from the benevolence of the butcher, the brewer, or the baker that we expect our dinner, but from their regard to their own interest.
[1937 (1776), p. 14]

From the neoclassical era a characteristically strong statement comes from F.Y. Edgeworth:

The first principle of Economics is that every agent is actuated only by self-interest.

[1881, p. 16]

And finally, a modern quotation from Richard Posner, the celebrated legal scholar who – like the convert more Catholic than the Pope – has become one of the most outstanding of our economic imperialists:

Economics... explores and tests the implications of assuming that man is a rational maximizer of his ends in life, his satisfactions – what we shall call his "self-interest."

[1977, p. 3]

There is a problem here, which Posner promptly raises. Suppose a person's ends in life include the well-being of others. If so, do *their* interests become his "self-interest"? Posner, like many others, answers in the affirmative – an evasion that robs the concept of self-interest of any distinguishable content. But it is not so easy to separate "self-interested" satisfactions from the psychic sensations generated by the experiences of others.

A distinction proposed by Amartya K. Sen illustrates the nature of the difficulty:

If the knowledge of torture of others makes you sick, it is a case of sympathy; if it does not make you feel personally worse off, but you think it is wrong..., it is a case of commitment. ... [B]ehavior based on sympathy is in an important sense egoistic, for one is oneself pleased at others' pleasure and pained at others' pain, and the pursuit of one's own utility may thus be helped by sympathetic action. It is action based on commitment rather than sympathy which would be nonegoistic in this sense.

[1977, p. 327]

Thus Sen would count the emotion of sympathy as self-interested, leaving only an abstract intellectualized moralism as non-egoistic – which does not seem a very appealing categorization. For present purposes, the following commonsense interpretation (consistent, I believe, with David Collard [1978, p. 7]) will serve: someone is non-self-interested to the extent that he or she attaches utility to the impact of events upon the bodies or psyches of other parties. When my mother says, "Drink your milk," that is her benevolent concern for my bodily well-being. And if I drink it only to please her, that is my benevolent concern for her psychic comfort. (Ultimately, as will be seen below, the difficulty can be resolved only in the light of bioeconomic considerations which allow us to separate the *motivational* from the *functional* aspects of self-interest.)

It is important to distinguish motivations, aspects of individuals' utility or preference functions, from *actions*. (Even entirely egoistic individuals, we economists know, may be led to engage in mutually helpful actions by an appropriate set of penalties and rewards.) Self-interested or egoistic motivations represent an intermediate point on a spectrum that has benevolence at one extreme and malevolence at the other.[3]

In what follows I will be showing how imperialist economics has cast light upon the nature and extent of self-interest. In some cases, furthermore, new models and approaches suggested by these explorations promise to be useful even in traditional heartland economics.

Political Behavior and the Split–Smith Model

Can political behavior be explained solely in terms of self-interest? The issue has been debated from the beginnings of political thought. As Roger Masters describes it:

> In ancient Greece, the question was therefore already posed with clarity. The pre-Socratics developed a frankly egoistic or hedonistic theory of human nature. . . . Best known from the speeches of Thrasymachus in Plato's *Republic*, this hedonistic view treats human laws or customs as "restraints" on nature. . . .
>
> Both Plato and Aristotle, following the tradition apparently inaugurated by Socrates, contest this position. For example, when Aristotle asserts that man is by nature a "political animal," he directly challenges the Sophists' assertion that human society rests on contractual or conventional obligations among calculating individuals. Aristotle's view rests on a developmental or evolutionary account of social cooperation.
>
> [1978, pp. 59–60]

The recent irruption of economists into political science has been almost entirely based upon the postulate of self-interest – the Sophist position. This approach, rigorously and unflinchingly pursued, has had its triumphs. But the analytically uncomfortable (though humanly gratifying) fact remains: from the most primitive to the most advanced societies, a higher degree of cooperation takes place than can be explained as

---

[3] The term "benevolence" (from the Latin "to wish well") is less ambiguous than the commonly encountered "altruism". This latter word has become a source of confusion for the very reason mentioned above: while some authors (like Collard [1978]) carefully use it only in its original and proper motivational sense, others loosely characterize as altruistic any *action* which has beneficial effects on others – even if selfishly motivated. Biologists, for example, use the expression "reciprocal altruism" for what is often a merely self-interested *exchange* of benefits.

a merely pragmatic strategy for egoistic man. The social contract seems to maintain itself far better than we have any right to expect, given the agency and free-rider problems involved in enforcing the contract against overt or covert violations. Or putting the emphasis the other way, the workings of the social system appear to be lubricated by individuals who are willing to act voluntarily *pro bono publico*.

Consider voting. Explanations in terms of rational self-interest do carry us a certain distance. As one instance, a self-interested individual would be more likely to incur the costs of going to the polls in a race expected to be close – since his chance of casting the deciding ballot is greater. And larger turnouts have in fact been observed in close elections.[4] Such evidence is consistent with the self-interest assumption in the *comparative* sense: the behavioral response to variations in self-interest parameters is in the direction anticipated. But in *absolute* terms it remains difficult to rationalize self-interested voting at all, so long as there are costs associated with casting a ballot. The chances of any single voter being decisive are usually far too remote to be worth considering.[5]

An even greater "scandal" is the extent of voluntary private provision of public goods. For concreteness, suppose that individual i's utility function is such that at any income level he would devote, if he were the sole contributor, a fraction k of his income to the public good. Then in the specific case where $k = .1$ it turns out that, for a community of N individuals like i, as N rises toward infinity the community in the limit would spend only 10% more *in aggregate* upon the public good than any single member would have spent alone![6] Evidently, individuals' voluntary provisions for public goods go far beyond what can be satisfactorily explained on the self-interest hypothesis.

Howard Margolis [1982] drives home this point with a thought-experiment, of which a modified version is as follows. In the light of his own circumstances and his beliefs as to what others will contribute, Smith has decided to give exactly $50 to a public good – specifically, to the annual United Fund charitable campaign. Just as he is about to make out his check he learns that Jones, from whom no contribution had been anticipated, has in fact just given $50. According to the standard

---

[4] See, for example, Barzel and Silberberg [1973].
[5] Some computations on this score are provided by G. Chamberlain and M. Rothschild [1980], as described in Fred Thompson [1982].
[6] The theorem underlying this remarkable result is apparently due initially to Martin McGuire [1974], but its importance was first recognized by Howard Margolis [1982, p. 21].

analysis, Smith would now drastically scale back his intended donation. For example, if (as in the example used previously) Smith in isolation would have spent 10% of his income on the public good, he should now reduce his own contribution from \$50 to \$5.[7] Everyday observation tells us that this would not happen, that Smith would scale back his own contribution very little if at all.[8] I will use Margolis' proposed resolution of the paradox as my first illustration of new models or approaches arising from the difficulties encountered in the expanded domains of economics.

Let us suppose that within Smith's breast there are really two personalities, Smith$_1$ and Smith$_2$. Smith$_1$ has ordinary selfish motivations; he is concerned only for the well-being of the physical Smith. Smith$_2$ has broader horizons, but he is not exactly unselfish either: Smith$_2$ does derive satisfaction from making contributions, but only via his own "participation utility" rather than through any direct gratification from the actual benefits conferred upon others.

If Smith were *truly* benevolent to some degree, his utility function might take a form like:

$$U^S = U^S(x_S; x_A, x_B, \ldots) \tag{1}$$

where x_S is his own consumption vector and $x_A, x_B, \ldots$ are the consumption vectors of other members of the community (all the marginal utilities being positive).[9] But our Smith's preferences have the form:

$$U^S = U^S(x_S, y_S) \tag{2a}$$

where y_S refers to his own "participation" expenditures. And more specifically, suppose that (2a) can be written:

$$U^S = W u^{S_1}(x_S) + u^{S_2}(y_S) \tag{2b}$$

Here u^{S_1}, the Smith$_1$ utility component, is a function of Smith's consumption while u^{S_2} is a function of Smith's participation expenditures – both

---

[7] Having been in effect enriched by \$50 owing to Jones' contribution, Smith would now like to have \$5 more of the public good than he originally planned, or a total of \$55 worth. But towards this amount Jones has already provided \$50, so Smith need spend only \$5.

[8] But see Russell D. Roberts [1984] for evidence supporting a somewhat opposed view.

[9] Alternatively a benevolent Smith's utility function might take the form:

$$U^S = U^S(x_S; U^A[x_A], U^B[x_B], \ldots)$$

Here Smith takes pleasure in others' *utilities* rather than in their *consumptions of goods*. (The difference is that the text formulation (1) would allow Smith to have "meddlesome" preferences as to his beneficiaries' consumptions.) This distinction will not be pursued here; for further discussion see Collard [1978, pp. 7–8].

components being characterized by positive but diminishing marginal utility. W is a weighting factor, which can be taken as a constant parameter[10] describing the "balance of power" at any moment between the two personalities. We would expect that this internal balance of power would generally differ from person to person and possibly change with age and external circumstances.[11]

Using this model, the public-goods paradox – that Jones' donations, being in traditional theory a near-perfect substitute for Smith's contributions, should displace the latter almost one-for-one (but do not) – can be resolved. For, Jones' contributions are no substitute at all for Smith's *participation expenditures*. Furthermore, if we specify that consumption utility is more easily saturated than participation utility – that u'_1 falls faster than u'_2 – we obtain the additional observed consequence that wealthier individuals will spend relatively more upon such contributions. The model also suggests that investigations into how to measure the weighting factor W, and the interpersonal and circumstantial determinants thereof, may be fruitful. One other point which will have some bearing upon what follows: our human inconsistencies in decisions or occasional seeming "irrationality" may be due to internal switches of command between our $Smith_1$ and $Smith_2$.[12]

Benevolence in the Family and the Rotten-Kid Theorem

In the sphere of politics it may still be possible to argue the thesis of exclusively self-interested motivations. But in the domain of the family no-one can seriously deny that benevolence plays an overwhelming role. Even here, however, economists would expect and have indeed shown that *comparative* predictions can be made on the basis of self-interest. Other things equal, pro-natalist subsidies that reduce parents' cost of child-bearing can be expected to increase the birth rate.[13] And we would expect parents to take children out of school earlier in rural rather than urban environments, since young children can be relatively more helpful on the farm than in the city.

---

[10] Margolis makes W also a function of the ratio x_S/y_S, but this seems a needless complication if (as he assumes) each separate utility component is characterized by diminishing marginal utility.

[11] As discussed in detail by Thomas C. Schelling [1980]. Notice also the affinity with the Freudian tripartite division of the personality among id, ego, and superego.

[12] This point is emphasized in Schelling [1980]. For somewhat parallel discussions see Sen [1977] and Albert O. Hirschman [1984].

[13] See Stephen P. Coelen and Robert J. McIntyre [1978].

Benevolence among family members thus falls short of complete submergence of the individuals' separate interests. Nevertheless, the family typically displays strong cohesive tendencies, as if the benevolence present had a certain "contagious" property. It is this phenomenon that Gary Becker [1976b] explained in terms of the "Rotten-Kid Theorem" – which will serve as my second example of a new model generated to explain the phenomena in the expanded domains of imperialist economics.

In Figure 14.1 the Rotten Kid is self-interested; he simply wants to maximize his material income x_K without regard to Daddy's income x_D. Daddy, however, has a degree of benevolence leading to a normal-looking preference map (as represented by the solid indifference curve U_D) on x_D, x_K axes. Let us suppose that Kid chooses the productive solution along a joint productive opportunity locus QQ, after which Daddy may transfer income on a 1:1 basis to Kid along the 135° line TT. If Kid were *shortsightedly* selfish, he would simply maximize his own income at R^* along QQ. But *enlightened* self-interest would direct Kid to maximize family income at J^* along QQ. He can count on the fact that, starting from J^*, Daddy's benevolent motivations would lead to transfers of income along TT up to position A^* in the diagram. Since x_K is greater at A^* than at R^*, Kid is better off. This alone is not the remarkable result; it has always been known that enlightened self-interest can be more rewarding than shortsighted piggishness. The remarkable part of the theorem is that *Daddy* is better off at A^* than at R^*, even in terms of sheer material income x_D. Thus, it seems, Golden-Rule motivations can be functionally profitable!

I will mention here three conditions that have to be met for this result to hold. *First*, Kid's family-income-maximizing productive choice J^* along QQ must provide Daddy with enough preponderance of income to induce the transfer. *Second*, Daddy's benevolence must surpass a certain threshold. If his benevolence were in fact weaker, as suggested by the dashed indifference curve U_D' in Figure 14.1, the transfers he would make from J^* to B^* would not suffice to induce Kid's cooperation, and so the parties would end up at R^*. *Third*, Daddy has to have the "last word." If Daddy's benevolent transfer had to precede Kid's choice along QQ, Kid would assuredly not make the productive decisions that maximize family income.[14]

---

[14] This discussion and diagrammatic representation are based on Hirshleifer [1977]. See also Gordon Tullock [1977].

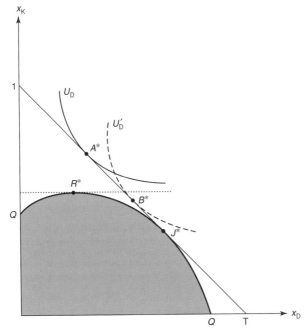

Figure 14.1. The rotten-kid theorem.

The Rotten-Kid Theorem, and the limitations thereon, help us understand a wide variety of phenomena within the family, of which I will mention only one. Outside public assistance to some family members, for example to a handicapped child, has less of an effect upon the beneficiary than might at first be anticipated – because benevolent parents, having already been transferring resources to such a child, would now rationally cut back their own transfers.[15] Finally, the "contagious" property of benevolence, when the conditions for the Rotten-Kid Theorem are met, may help explain the extent of non-self-interested behavior even in domains other than the family.[16]

Gifts, Status, and the "Rat-Race"

The importance of gifts and other "redistribution institutions" in nearly all observed societies may at first suggest widespread benevolence. However, the central tradition of anthropological explanation is in accord with

[15] See Becker [1981, pp. 124–126].
[16] For a discussion of the extent to which government can serve as a big Daddy to induce cooperation among self-interested citizens, see Bruce R. Bolnick [1979].

the model of economic man. Gifts among primitive peoples are interpreted as really a form of social exchange; if not reciprocated, the gift will be revoked (or even severer penalties applied). What appears to be benevolence is but indirect or disguised self-interest. Thus Marcel Mauss contends that such "prestations" are:

> ... in theory voluntary, disinterested and spontaneous, but are in fact obligatory and interested.

> [1954 (1925), p. 1]

But this established tradition[17] leaves open the question: Why go to the trouble of disguising what is really exchange as a gift? There is no point to simulation, absent a real thing to be simulated. So we are led to ask: What is being simulated by these pretended gifts? I will anticipate my biological discussion somewhat to respond along the following lines. In very primitive times, voluntary resource transfers took the form only of sharing within a kin-group (as exemplified by Daddy's transfers in the Rotten-Kid model). The biological basis for such benevolence is immediately evident. With widening scope and extent of interactions, actual kinship among transacting parties diminished. But familial sharing remaining the mental image, as a useful fiction one's trading partners became "adopted" as quasi-kin. This fiction became less and less credible as the social distance among transactors increased – so that, in the limit, truly impersonal exchange among strictly self-interested parties was approximated. Still, a residue of quasi-kinship sentiments aids us even in the "ordinary business of life" (Marshall) of modern times. Some willingness to forego selfish advantage, some element of genuine trust between trading partners or among business associates, almost always remains a necessity in the world of affairs.

In contrast with the foregoing, Friedrich A. Hayek [1979, pp. 153–176] rather paradoxically contends that human social organization could not have advanced beyond the small band to settled communities and civilized life until cultural evolution taught men to *overcome* their biological "innate instincts to pursue common perceived goals." (See also E.O. Wilson [1978a].) At times Hayek appears almost to claim, contra

---

[17] See articles in the *International Encyclopedia of the Social Sciences* [1968] under such titles as "Exchange and Display," "Interaction: Social Exchange," and "Trade, Primitive." A somewhat different point of view is that of Marshall D. Sahlins [1972, Chap. 4–5] who emphasizes the pacifying effect of gift exchange upon parties otherwise likely to war for resources.

Adam Smith, that the natural man is indeed "defective in selfishness."[18] But a fairer interpretation of Hayek's point, I believe, is that the primitive social ethic of kinship sharing had to be replaced by an alternative social ethic – centered upon fair dealing and reciprocity – appropriate to the market order. While Hayek emphasizes that this latter ethic is culturally learned, an ingrained human predisposition may also have evolved to help support reciprocity as a social norm. (I have argued [1980] that social evolution has instilled in man elements of at least three distinct social ethics: one associated with the Golden Rule of sharing, a second with the Silver Rule of private rights and reciprocity, and a third with what might be called the Iron Rule of dominance and subordination.)

Returning to gifts, the economic imperialist Richard Posner [1980] (together with a number of anthropologists) interprets them as essentially a device for mutual insurance. A hunter with a good catch today will help out a less fortunate colleague because he knows that tomorrow the circumstances are likely to be reversed. This explanation cannot be regarded as fully satisfactory, for at least two reasons: (1) Some individuals will be systematically better hunters than others, hence the "insurance" payments and receipts will not balance out over time. (2) In the absence of a formal insurance contract there will be widespread openings for opportunistic behavior: shirking, deferred or slighted repayment, etc.[19]

Nevertheless, to an important extent *reciprocal giving* does approximate self-interested exchange among equals. But what about one-sided or *redistributive giving?* Paradoxically, anthropologists commonly regard the motivation here as not even neutral but often actively hostile – the underlying aim being to enhance or assert status. According to Claude Lévi-Strauss the purpose is:

> . . . to surpass a rival in generosity, to crush him if possible under future obligations which it is hoped he cannot meet, thus taking from him privileges, titles, rank, authority, and prestige.
>
> [1964, p. 85]

---

[18] Starting from a very similar evolutionary orientation, Donald T. Campbell in his Presidential address to the American Psychological Association [1975] argues a position almost the opposite of Hayek's. To wit, that biologically innate selfishness always threatens to subvert the social order, which is defended only by rather fragile culturally evolved moral traditions. Campbell points out that the sins decried by such moral traditions – "selfishness, stinginess, greed, gluttony, envy, theft, lust, and promiscuity" – are in fact behaviors that "come close to biological optimization" [p. 1119].

[19] For evidence on a number of these points see Hillard Kaplan and Kim Hill [1985].

A very well-known example is the "potlatch" institution of certain Pacific Coast Indian societies, in which (allegedly, at least) resources were consumed or even deliberately destroyed in grand feasts designed to shame less affluent rivals.

Rank-oriented motivations are intrinsically malevolent, since one person's rise is another's fall – the process is a zero-sum game. As the desire for status notoriously pervades all human activities,[20] it is quite remarkable that economists up to quite recently have so signally failed to incorporate this phenomenon into their models.[21]

Rank *may* however be only a proximate and not an ultimate concern – for example, if income is generated by a "contest" process with rank-determined payoffs. In a footrace or a war, even if your goal is only to win a material prize you still have to outmatch your opponent. Income-generating processes with highly progressive rank-determined rewards lead to the "superstar" phenomenon recently noticed in the literature (Sherwin Rosen [1981]). But our interest here is where rank enters into the *utility function*, so that:

$$U^i = U^i(x_i, R_i) \tag{3}$$

where x_i is individual i's income and R_i may be interpreted as the percent of the comparison group falling below i on the basis of the status-determining criterion. One interesting implication of (3) is that such a person would be most actively malevolent toward his immediate neighbors along the rank ladder, and be essentially neutral to those far above or below him. Thus, concern for status may be distinguished from sheer *envy* of the well-being of all others.[22]

When status is conferred by conspicuous consumption there is a double payoff to income – greater consumption *plus* higher prestige. From this stems the "rat-race" phenomenon analyzed in the recent book by Robert H. Frank [1985]. As novels about modern suburbia tell us, the

---

[20] One example is provided by surveys of self-reported "happiness." Reported happiness correlates with higher income at any moment of time, as would be expected, but as income has trended upward *over time* there has been no corresponding upward trend in self-estimates of happiness (see Richard Easterlin [1974]). The most natural explanation is that happiness is more powerfully affected by relative income status than by absolute income; the poor are richer than before, but still at the bottom of the heap.

[21] The early discussion by Thorstein Veblen [1953 (1899)] is more satiric than analytical. Models incorporating one of more aspects of the drive for status have been offered by Becker [1971]. Reuven Brenner [1983], and Robert H. Frank [1985].

[22] On envy see Helmut Schoeck [1969 (1966)] and Becker [1971, pp. 1088–1090].

rat-race grows ever worse with increasing levels of income. The reason is that as individuals become richer they attempt to purchase both more consumption and more status. Status being socially in absolutely fixed supply, its marginal desirability relative to consumption steadily rises – inducing ever more intense efforts to achieve it, efforts that in aggregate must fail.[23]

If on the other hand the status-determining condition is distinct from income, the latter can often be traded off against rank. What makes some societies successful may be a suitable rank-determining criterion. A tribe facing fierce enemies is more likely to survive if status is earned by bravery in battle. And redistribution institutions, whereby prestige is earned by liberal generosity, tend to moderate rat-race competitions for income. In such societies high income can be used to support consumption or to generate prestige, but not both.

RATIONALITY

When it comes to rationality, economics as an imperialist discipline finds itself in an unwontedly defensive position. Damaging attacks upon rational man have come from the direction of psychology. But this is all to the good if, as I have maintained, economics must ultimately become coextensive with all of social science. Generalized economics will have to deal with man as he really is – self-interested or not, fully rational or not.

Rationality is an *instrumental* concept. In the light of one's goals (preferences), if the means chosen (actions) are appropriate the individual is rational; if not, irrational. "Appropriate" here refers to *method* rather than *result*. Rational behavior is action calculated on the basis of the rules of logic and other norms of validity. Owing to chance, good method may not always lead to good result.

Few real men and women behave rationally all the time, and many of us scarcely any of the time. How then can economics maintain the postulate of rationality? Several answers can be given, in parallel with the responses offered when the self-interest postulate was challenged: (1) We could redefine all choice as rational. ("If I chose to do X, I must have thought that X was best.") This gets us nowhere. (2) We could retreat to a fallback position, asserting that the rationality postulate yields useful predictions in the field *where economists customarily apply it* – to wit, in

---

[23] *Time* also becomes increasingly scarce, relatively speaking, as income rises. Status and time constraints reinforce one another to help produce the phenomenon of the "harried leisure class" (see Becker [1965] and Staffan B. Linder [1970]).

market decisions. Such modesty, as argued above, is an improper evasion of the scientific challenge.[24] Ultimately we must be ready to abandon the rationality paradigm to the extent that it fails to fit the evidence about human behavior.

Rationality may fail in two quite distinct ways. First, individuals often commit errors in logical inference even when doing their best to reason logically. Second, what is quite a different matter, actions are often "unthinking"; when governed by habit or passion, people do not even attempt rational self-control. (I will be suggesting below that such failures of rationality, like violations of the self-interest postulate, may have proved functionally adaptive in the genetic and cultural evolution of the human species.)

On Lapses of Logic

To reason in accordance with the canons of formal logic is no easy task. I will discuss three different categories of logical lapses.

First are straight violations of the laws of inference. In the following example (adapted from Leda Cosmides [1985]), experimental subjects were instructed somewhat as follows:

Each card has a letter on one side and a number on the other side. There is one rule: "Every card marked with an 'A' on one side should have a '1' on the other." Indicate whether you need to inspect the reverse side of the following cards to detect violation of the rule: (1) A card showing an 'A'; (2) A card showing a 'B'; (3) A card showing a '1'; (4) A card showing a '2'.

In a large preponderance of cases, while the subjects correctly realized the need to inspect the reverse of card #1, they failed to notice that they should do the same for card #4.

What is instructive, however, is that the results were quite different for a formally identical problem presented as follows:

You are the bouncer in a Boston bar, concerned to enforce the following rule: "Anyone who consumes alcohol on the premises must be at least 20 years old." Indicate whether you need more information about any of the following individuals to detect violation of the rule: (1) An individual drinking whisky; (2) An individual drinking Coke; (3) An individual aged 25; (4) An individual aged 16.

---

[24] An interesting issue, however, is why the rationality postulate so often remains a useful social predictor despite its lack of validity on the individual level. One reason is *aggregation:* since rational behavior is systematic and purposive, whereas irrational behavior tends to be random and erratic, after aggregation even a limited degree of rationality tends to dominate the social totals. Another reason is *selection via competition*, to be discussed in more detail below.

Here almost everyone perceived the need for more information about individual #4 as well as individual #1. The author's suggested explanation is biological: however imperfect our mental capacities are at formal logic, Darwinian natural selection has made us efficient at detecting cheating or violations of social norms – a factor entering into the second but not the first experiment.

More familiar to economists is a relatively large literature, most notably associated with the psychologists Amos Tversky and Daniel Kahneman,[25] on errors people make in probability judgments. Tversky and Kahneman indicate that:

> ... people rely on a limited number of heuristic principles which reduce the complex tasks of assessing probabilities... to simpler judgmental operations. In general, these heuristics are quite useful, but sometimes they lead to severe and systematic errors.
>
> [1974, p. 1124]

Among the many examples of such errors are: (1) a tendency to over-estimate on the basis of psychological salience (someone who has seen a house burning down usually assesses a higher probability to such an event than someone who has only read about it), and (2) a tendency to attribute excessive representativeness to small samples (thus, people do not seem to intuitively appreciate that average word lengths in successive lines of a given text vary more than average word lengths in successive pages). As a general conclusion, it appears that the human mind employs rules of thumb that work well most of the time, but which can lead to certain systematic classes of errors.[26]

What psychologists term "cognitive dissonance" has received some attention from economists (see George Akerlof and William T. Dickens [1982]). This phenomenon is not so much a lapse of logical reasoning as its perversion. Suppose someone has chosen an employment generally regarded as excessively risky. To reduce his mental discomfort, he is likely to revise his beliefs and kid himself into thinking that his job is not so risky after all! What is involved here is known in more old-fashioned terminology as *rationalization*. When a person is made aware of a disharmony between his actions and his preferences and beliefs, the economist would expect him to revise his choice of action – but the

---

[25] A useful collection is the volume edited by Kahneman, Paul Slovic and Tversky [1982].

[26] For a related analysis, which emphasizes the strengths rather than weaknesses of commonsense inference, see Harold Kelley [1973].

cognitive dissonance theorist predicts that he is likely instead to modify his preferences or beliefs.

The basic premise here is that a person always tries to present to the world (and to himself) a picture of his own behavior that fits an integrated rational pattern. Observed discrepancies call for correction, but the correction may take either the *rational* or the *rationalizing* form. An elaboration of this idea distinguishes between "underjustification" and "overjustification." Cognitive dissonance is an example of the former. If a subject is made aware of having done something without adequate *extrinsic* justification in the form of reward or constraint, he rationalizes by manufacturing an intrinsic reason (revising his goals or beliefs). "Overjustification" consists of making the subject aware that there is a strong extrinsic reason for his behavior, from which he is likely to infer an *absence* of intrinsic reason. For example, it has been alleged, if children in a classroom are led to expect that reading achievements will be rewarded by gold stars, they are likely to actually reduce their reading activity afterward, when gold stars are no longer offered.[27]

While these processes of belief revision may not always be totally absurd,[28] they tend to violate the reality principle. Suppose a military commander learns that his left flank is dangerously weak. The economist, expecting a *rational* response, predicts that the general will reinforce his left. The cognitive-dissonance theorist rather expects a *rationalizing* response instead, in which the general chooses to believe that the enemy will not attack him on the left. Environmental selection will always be tending to eliminate such inappropriate responses, as will be discussed further below.

On Non-Rational (or "Boundedly Rational") Decision Processes

At least as important as failure to reason correctly is the fact that, in some contexts, people do not even attempt to think rationally at all (or do so only in a very limited way). *Habit* is surely a way of economizing

---

[27] For discussions see Edward L. Deci [1971] and Mark R. Lepper, David Greene, and Richard E. Nisbett [1973]. Notice that "overjustification" is in opposition to the better-known *conditioning* theory, which predicts that patterns of behavior induced by reward (e.g., Pavlov's famous salivating dog) will persist to some extent even after withdrawal of the reward.

[28] A child who observes that a certain activity receives extrinsic social compensation might well infer, for example, that people in general find the activity onerous or distasteful. Since we are all always learning from others, the apparent weight of others' judgments should reasonably have some impact upon our own estimates of what we ought to like or dislike.

on scarce reasoning ability. Indeed, in many contexts habit may be faster and more accurate than thinking; no-one can play the piano or drive a car effectively without engaging in a host of complex unthinking actions. But I am not aware of any studies of the psychoeconomics of habit.

Under the heading of "bounded rationality," Herbert A. Simon [1955, 1959] has contended that a person faced with a complex mental task will not attempt to strictly optimize but will be content instead merely to "satisfice." That is, he aims to find not the best but a good solution – one which achieves a given proximate target or aspiration level. Simon argues that:

> Models of satisficing behavior are richer than models of maximizing behavior, because they treat not only of equilibrium but of the method of reaching it as well... (a) When performance falls short of the level of aspiration, search behavior... is induced. (b) At the same time, the level of aspiration begins to adjust itself downward until goals reach levels that are practically attainable. (c) If the two mechanisms just listed operate too slowly to adapt aspiration to performance, emotional behavior – apathy or aggression, for example – will replace rational adaptive behavior.
>
> [1959, p. 263]

Simon's steps (a) and (b), it might at least be argued, constitute a valid successive-approximation technique for optimization that economizes on humans' limited information and reasoning ability. Only step (c), the emotional response to frustration, seems clearly dysfunctional in terms of rational adaptation. However, it can be shown, even "irrational" emotions may serve a useful adaptive function.

Specifically, an individual's uncontrollable anger/gratitude response[29] to another's hurtful/helpful activity can induce cooperation in much the same way as the Rotten-Kid Theorem. Figure 14.2 is similar to Figure 14.1. But in addition to the "transfer lines" T, T', T'' that describe once again how a grateful Daddy can transfer income to Kid on a 1:1 basis, here there are also "punishment lines" D, D', D''. These indicate that an angry Daddy can deprive Kid of income, but again only on a 1:1 basis – that is, Daddy loses one unit himself for each unit penalty imposed on Kid. (This assumption reflects the fact that anger, like gratitude, can be expressed only at a cost.) Then the rational self-interested first-mover, Kid, in selecting a productive vector along QQ does so in the light of the final positions attainable along Daddy's Anger/Gratitude Response curve (AGR). The pictured shape of the AGR curve reflects

---

[29] This development is based upon Hirshleifer [1984].

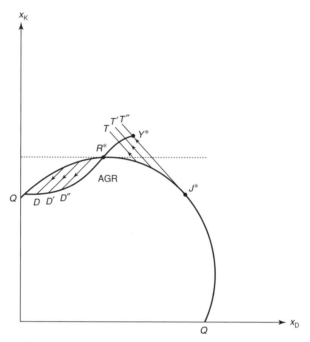

Figure 14.2. The anger/gratitude response (AGR) curve.

the reasonable assumption that Daddy becomes decreasingly grateful (or increasingly angry) the more selfish is Kid's productive choice along QQ. The final Figure 14.2 solution at point V^* is an efficient outcome, quite analogous to the Figure 14.1 solution at point A^*. In Figure 14.1 it was Daddy's benevolence that guaranteed his implicit promise to reward a self-interested Kid for cooperative behavior; in Figure 14.2, the same function is served by Daddy's passionate "loss of control" in response to Kid's good or bad behavior.

The possibility of achieving the efficient outcome through the AGR effect is premised upon a number of special assumptions, very much in parallel with those required for the initial Rotten-Kid model. Once again, Daddy must "have the last word" in the interaction. And the overall result is somewhat dependent upon the specific location and shape of the AGR curve. If Daddy is strongly predisposed to be angry (so that the AGR curve lies almost entirely below QQ), he may even be able to extort income from Kid – i.e., to achieve a distributive gain at Kid's expense. But Daddy's propensity to anger, if carried too far, may lead Kid to settle for a very inefficient productive outcome: one in which both parties are so impoverished that Daddy cannot (or will not want to) inflict further punishment.

I will conclude this discussion of the psychology of rationality on a properly aggressive imperialist note. Economists, for example Akerlof and Dickens [1982] and David Alhadeff [1982], to my mind have been overrespectful of what psychology is supposedly able to tell us. While rich in data, on the theoretical level psychology remains a confusing clamor of competing categories; there is no integrating theoretical structure. I will be so bold as to predict that such a structure, when achieved, will be fundamentally economic – or more specifically bioeconomic – in nature. That is, it will show how mental patterns have evolved as optimizing solutions subject to the constraints of scarcity and competition.[30]

Environmental Selection and "As If" Rationality

Even if individuals commit any or all of the reasoning errors discussed above, to some extent decisions will still be disciplined by competitive selection processes in the economy. Armen A. Alchian [1950] argued that even if a business firm's choices were completely random, the environment would select for survival those decisions that were relatively correct in meeting the minimum standard of viability. Expanding on this, Stephen Enke [1951] argued that competition would ensure that all policies save the truly optimal would in time fail the survival test. As those firms pursuing relatively successful policies expand and (owing to imitation) multiply, a higher and higher standard of achievement becomes the minimum criterion. In the long run, viability dictates optimality. Consequently, for long-run predictive purposes, in competitive situations the analyst is entitled to assume that firms behave "as if" they were truly engaged in rational optimization.

This model has to be inaccurate at least in one respect: in describing the *approach to equilibrium*. Actual economies, though falling short perhaps of the rational ideal, surely avoid the profligate waste (abandonments, bankruptcies, and the like) that would ensue from merely random behavior (see Edith Penrose [1952]). Another serious flaw is that, as shown initially by Sidney G. Winter [1964, 1971], the selectional-evolutionary process will not necessarily always lead to the same long-run equilibrium outcome "as if" firms actually optimized. In this connection Richard R. Nelson and Winter [1982] have explored the consequences of a process wherein boundedly rational firms choose among "organizational routines" while competitive environmental selection is simultaneously operating to change the representation of these

---

[30] A psychology text with such an orientation is J.E.R. Staddon [1983].

alternative routines in the population. And John Conlisk [1980] has examined a process where, with optimization costly relative to mere *imitation*, in general the ultimate "natural selection" equilibrium will be a mixture of the two types. A somewhat parallel analysis, emphasizing that imitation can be regarded as cultural inheritance, appears in Robert Boyd and Peter J. Richerson [1980].

While economists have been working on the environmental selection of firms and their business routines, evolutionary anthropologists have developed strikingly similar models for the natural selection of cultural practices like group size, birth spacing, and land tenure arrangements among primitive peoples.[31] What the anthropologists have been doing here is an instance of a more general (and somewhat controversial) quasi-economic evolutionary modelling principle known as *the adaptationist hypothesis* or *the optimization theory:* that morphology and behavior, on both the individual and social levels, can be explained "as if" chosen to maximize the chances of evolutionary success.[32] Especially on the social level, a number of difficulties have been encountered owing mainly to the fact that what is best for the individual may not be best for the group. Economists could make important contributions here, having already systematically explored the bases for such "fallacies of composition" – e.g., divergent interests, differences of beliefs, and externalities. But I would now like to call attention to another, less familiar yet enormously important reason for disparities between private and social adaptation: the role of *conflict* in determining patterns of social organization.

CONFLICT

Vilfredo Pareto said:

The efforts of men are utilized in two different ways: they are directed to the production or transformation of economic goods, or else to the appropriation of goods produced by others.

[1971 (1927), p. 341]

Pareto is suggesting, as I believe will be proved to be correct, that aggressive behavior aimed at the appropriation of goods will ultimately provide as rich and fruitful a field for the application of economic reasoning as

---

[31] Surveyed in Eric A. Smith [1985]. The anthropologists are analytically ahead of the economists in tying the environmental selection of institutions to more ultimate evolutionary considerations – the reproductive survival of human beings.

[32] The diverging views of evolutionary theorists on this more general issue are illustrated by John Maynard Smith [1978], Richard C. Lewontin [1979], and Richard Dawkins [1982, Chap. 3].

our traditional topics of production and markets. While appropriation can be undertaken to some extent by lawful means, for example via re-distributive politics or what has become known as "rent-seeking,"[33] its most dramatic and indeed characteristic form involves conflict. At any moment of time a rational self-interested person will strike an optimal balance between achieving his ends through production and voluntary exchange on the one hand or through force, extortion, and fraud on the other. In fact, even if he has no intention of using the latter techniques himself, he would be well-advised to devote some of his resources to defense against invasions by others. The final social equilibrium will integrate the destructive and invasive as well as the constructive and co-operative efforts of humans in all of their interactions with one another.

I can briefly allude only to three topics under this vast heading – one concerned with the *causes* of conflict, the second with the *conduct and technology* of conflict, and the last with the social *consequences* of conflict.[34]

On the Causes of Conflict

Involved in a rational decision to engage in conflict, economic reasoning suggests, will be the decision-maker's *preferences*, *opportunities*, and *perceptions*. These three elements correspond to traditional issues debated by historians and political scientists about the "causes of war": Is war mainly due to hatred and ingrained pugnacity (hostile preferences)? Or to the prospects for material gain (opportunities)? Or is war mainly due to mistaken perceptions, on one or both sides, of the other's motives or capacities?

In the simplest dyadic situation, and setting aside complications such as those associated with group choices,[35] Figures 14.3 and 14.4 are alternative illustrations of how preferences, opportunities, and perceptions jointly influence decisions. In each diagram the curve QQ bounds the peaceful possibilities or "settlement opportunity set" – drawn on axes representing Blue's income I_B and Red's income I_R. Points P_B and P_R indicate the parties' respective *perceptions* of the outcome of conflict. And the families of curves labelled U_B and U_R are the familiar utility indifference contours.

---

[33] See Anne O. Krueger [1974].
[34] This discussion is based largely upon Hirshleifer [1987 (forthcoming)].
[35] Some of the problems of group organization in a military context are analyzed in Geoffrey Brennan and Gordon Tullock [1982].

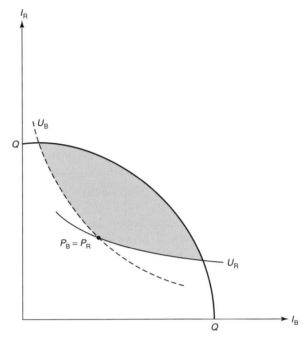

Figure 14.3. Statics of conflict – large potential settlement region.

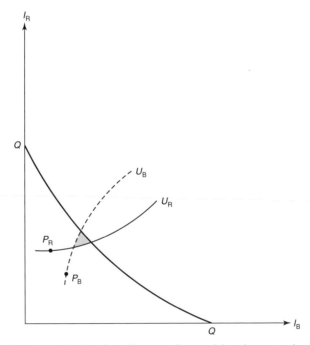

Figure 14.4. Statics of conflict – small potential settlement region.

Figure 14.3 shows a relatively benign situation: settlement opportunities are complementary, preferences display benevolence on each side, and perceptions of returns from conflict are conservative and agreed (P_B and P_R coincide). The "Potential Settlement Region" PSR (shaded area in the diagram), the set of income partitions such that *both* parties regard themselves as doing better by settling than by fighting, is large – which plausibly implies a high probability of coming to an agreement. Figure 14.4 shows a less pleasant situation: antithetical opportunities, mutually malevolent preferences, and divergently optimistic estimates of the returns from conflict. The PSR is therefore small, and the prospects for settlement much poorer.

Such a summary presentation is of course little more than a way of organizing ideas, so as to direct attention to the forces underlying and determining the parties' opportunities, preferences, and perceptions. I can only mention a few specifics here. Whether or not peaceful *opportunities* are harmonious may depend upon Malthusian pressures, upon the economics of increasing returns and the division of labor, and upon the possibility of enforcing agreements. *Preferences* (benevolence or malevolence) may be a function of kinship and shared cultural heritage. And *perceptions* will be influenced by communications, including threats and bluffs, and by each party's demonstrated prowess in past and ongoing hostilities.[36]

But even when these static considerations tend to favor peaceful settlement, the dynamics of the negotiation process may prevent the parties from achieving a mutually beneficial accommodation. In the famous Prisoners' Dilemma, for example, inability to make a binding agreement traps the players in a mutually unsatisfactory outcome.

On the Technology of Conflict

Conflict is a kind of "industry" in which different "firms" compete by attempting to disable opponents. Just as the economist without being a manager or engineer can apply certain broad principles to the processes of industrial production, so, without claiming to replace the military commander he can say something about the principles governing how desired results are "produced" through violence.

Battles typically proceed to a definitive outcome – victory or defeat. *Wars* may be less conclusive, often ending in compromise. These historical generalizations reflect the intertwined working of increasing versus

---

[36] Some of the problems involved in the relation between perceptions and conflict are discussed in Donald Wittman [1979].

decreasing returns applied to the production of violence: (1) Within a sufficiently small geographical region such as a battlefield, increasing returns to military strength apply – a small military superiority is typically translated into a disproportionately favorable outcome. The reason is that, at any moment, the stronger side can inflict a more-than-proportionate loss upon the opponent, thus becoming progressively stronger still (Frederich William Lanchester [1976 (1916)]). (2) But there are decreasing returns in projecting military power away from one's base area, so that it is difficult to achieve superiority over an enemy's entire national territory (see Kenneth E. Boulding [1962], pp. 227–233). The increasing-returns factor explains why there is a "natural monopoly" of military force *within* the nation-state. The diminishing-returns factor explains why a multiplicity of nation-states have remained militarily viable to this date. (However, there is some reason to believe, the technology of attack through long-range weapons has now so come to prevail over the defense that a single world-state is indeed impending.)

Efficiency as Consequence of Conflict

Struggle and conflict are obviously costly, inefficient processes. Yet might it be the case that struggle masks a deeper harmony of interests? Some observers have professed to see, for example, a profound beneficent wisdom underlying conflict in Nature. Thus the leopard is admired for his helpfulness to prey, in controlling their numbers and eliminating the infirm and unfit. And the head-butting of male rams, fighting for sexual access, is said to improve the breed. These arguments, and their analogs on the human level, are to my mind rather fatuous. Conflict, unlike exchange, can rarely benefit all participants.

Somewhat more defensible is the contention that conflict leads, ultimately at least, to *efficiency*. That is, as a consequence of struggle, resources will end up under the control of those parties able to turn them to best use. Such a model has been offered by economic imperialists to explain the evolution of law.

Imagine a situation where mutually advantageous exchanges of entitlements are partially or wholly unfeasible. Then the Coase Theorem (Ronald H. Coase [1960]) does not apply, and the effective assignment of property rights will make a real efficiency difference. The various parties at interest may contend for resources, among other ways, by lawsuits. Then, the proposition is, those individuals and groups for whom a particular entitlement or legal rule is worth more will ultimately win because they can bring more pressure to bear than their opponents. One model of this process, due to Paul H. Rubin [1977], emphasizes *relitigation*. Since precedents are never absolutely binding, attempts will be made repeatedly to overturn an inefficient one. So long as there is a random element in judicial decisions, even apart from any possible learning factor, the efficient rule will eventually be hit upon – and, being efficient, it will be a relatively stable precedent. In an alternative model, those standing to benefit from the more efficient decision can afford to make greater investments (for example, to hire better lawyers) and thus are more likely to win the contest (John C. Goodman [1978]).

Finally, this efficiency-through-strength model is by no means limited to the arena of common-law litigation. With minimal modifications the same logic could be extended to statute law and constitutional interpretation. For that matter, since the process is essentially one of "trial through combat," why not apply it also to civil wars and international conflicts? Clearly the argument that conflict generates efficiency can have only limited validity, but I will have to break off at this interesting point.

ECONOMICS AND BIOLOGY: COMPETING IMPERIALISMS?

While economics has been expanding *horizontally*, so to speak, a simultaneous invasion has been taking place *vertically* as evolutionary biology has asserted a claim to be the foundation of all the social sciences. As argued by Edward O. Wilson:

> For every discipline in its early stages of development there exists an antidiscipline. . . With the word *antidiscipline* I wish to emphasize the special adversary relation that exists initially between the studies of adjacent level of organization. . . . [B]iology has now moved close enough to the social sciences to become their antidiscipline. . . . Many scholars judge this core [of social theory] to be the deep structure of human nature, an essentially biological phenomenon.
>
> [1977, p. 127]

This development, though controversial in some respects,[37] should not disturb economists. The influence of Malthus and of Adam Smith

---

[37] Unfortunately, "sociobiology" has become the object of ideological attack on the part of some scientists and publicists concerned to minimize the genetic as opposed to the cultural sources of social behavior and organization. But no-one can seriously deny that morphology and biochemistry play *some* role in social behavior, just as no "sociobiologist" of repute has ever ruled out the influence of cultural determinants. (Furthermore, the human capacities for culture, of which language is the most notable, are themselves of genetic origin.) While individual sociobiologists may have constructed faulty theories or misread the evidence on particular issues, such errors cannot condemn the entire scientific enterprise of searching for the biological underpinnings of behavior.

upon Charles Darwin's thought is well-known.[38] And whereas Alfred Marshall declared that economics is a branch of biology, the biologist Michael Ghiselin [1978] would make *universal economy* the more general discipline. Under this broad heading, biologists can be regarded as studying *natural economy* while the socially regulated behavior of humans constitutes *political economy*.[39] In short, these two colliding imperialisms can say, with the comic-strip character Pogo, "We have met the enemy, and he is us!"

I could defend this assertion by pointing to fundamental common concepts like competition and specialization, or to terminological pairs like species/industry, mutation/innovation, evolution/progress, etc., or most explicitly by setting up parallel systems of equations describing equilibrium states and paths of change. But I must limit myself to a few specific points that bear upon issues discussed above.

1. As to self-interest, a number of paradoxes are resolved when it is appreciated that in biology *there are two levels of self* – the organism and the gene. The gene is a "selfish gene" (Richard Dawkins [1976]). But sometimes it is profitable for a selfish gene to program its carrier organism to be benevolent (or malevolent) to other organisms. Non-self-interested motivations on the level of the organism may therefore be *functionally* self-interested on the level of the gene.

2. Just as firms and other social groupings are alliances of individuals, so the organism is in a sense an alliance of genes. Certain remarkable phenomena, such as functionless or "parasitic" DNA, reveal that free-riding and other alliance problems occur even within organisms. Thus some of the forces that limit the achievement of social efficiency or harmony also impair the optimal adaptation of individual organisms to their environments.

3. In the game of Darwinian natural selection, *reproductive survival* (RS) or *fitness* can be regarded metaphorically as the "goal" of the gene. But since one's kin have calculable chances of carrying the same gene, it is possible to quantify the degree of benevolence an organism should display toward relatives. In particular, what might be called the first law of bioeconomics (due to W.D. Hamilton [1964]) says that an animal will help another without

---

[38] On this see especially S.S. Schweber [1978].
[39] I have attempted to develop this distinction in Hirshleifer [1978].

reward if and only if:

$$b/c \geq 1/r \qquad (4)$$

Here b is the benefit to the recipient and c the cost to the donor, both in RS units, while r is the degree of relatedness between the parties. An individual should be willing to sacrifice one unit of RS, for example, for two RS units of benefit to a brother or sister (since $r = 1/2$ between full siblings). Translating from RS to income units, and assuming the equivalent of diminishing marginal utility, we can obtain a normally curved benevolent-toward-kin preference map (like Daddy's in Figure 14.1).

4. Of course, Hamilton's formula is valid only in an "other things held equal" sense. As a consequence of generational timing, for example, in RS terms parents are more motivated to help children then children to help parents. More generally, behavior depends not only upon preferences (relatedness) but upon opportunities. In very competitive environments there may be sharp conflict not only between male and female parents but even between parents and offspring, or among siblings competing for parental aid.[40]

5. As Darwin emphasized, natural selection does not choose on the basis of an absolute standard of performance, but rather on how well an organism does in comparison with its closest competitors – for example, in the reproductive competition among males for access to females. This is perhaps the ultimate source of our seemingly ingrained concern for dominance and rank.

6. Darwin argued that, in primitive times, human groups whose members were "courageous, sympathetic, and faithful" would have a selective advantage. But he already appreciated that a free-rider problem would be at work: *individual selection* for effective pursuit of self-interest would tend to subvert *group selection* for benevolent traits. Furthermore, the consensus among biologists has been that individual selection is almost always the more potent. However, many modern biologists follow Darwin in making an exception at least for man. Exceptionally rigorous group selection, especially through conflict and warfare, together with the mental abilities of humans[41] that make it possible to identify and punish subversively selfish behavior, have led to the evolution of a degree of group-oriented benevolence.[42]

---

[40] On these issues see Robert L. Trivers [1972, 1974].

[41] These mental qualities themselves very likely evolved by stringent selection of human strains in warfare (Roger Pitt [1978]).

[42] See, for example, Richard D. Alexander [1979], especially Ch. 4.

7. This development has strongly xenophobic implications. Other things equal an organisms would "treat as 'enemies', harming them when he could, all individuals having less than average relationship" to him (W.D. Hamilton [1970, p. 1219]). Thus the impartial or universalistic benevolence of our moral philosophers finds no counterpart in evolutionary biology.

8. Finally, however, the mental hyperdevelopment of mankind has made us the only species able to "rebel against the tyranny of the selfish replicators" – our genes (Dawkins [1976], p. 215). Recognizing our ingrained behavioral drives, we can train ourselves to oppose them – just as we can amend our bodily shape or internal biochemistry through surgical or medical interventions. While this fact cuts against theories of simplistic genetic determinism, certain ultimate principles like scarcity and opportunity cost, and the universal bioeconomic processes of competition and selection, will always remain valid for analyzing and predicting the course of human behavior and social organization.

I must conclude very briefly. In pursuing their respective imperialist destinies, economics and sociobiology have arrived in different ways at what is ultimately the same master pattern of social theory – one into which the phenomena studied by the various social sciences to some extent already have been, and ultimately will all be, fitted.

REFERENCES

Akerlof, George A. and William T. Dickens, "The Economic Consequences of Cognitive Dissonance," *American Economic Review*, v. 72 (June 1982), 307–19.

Alchian, Armen A., "Uncertainty, Evolution, and Economic Theory," *Journal of Political Economy*, v. 58 (1950).

Alexander, Richard D., *Darwinism and Human Affairs* (Seattle: U. of Washington Press, 1979).

Alhadeff, David, *Microeconomics and Human Behavior: Toward a Synthesis of Economics and Psychology* (Berkeley: U. of California Press, 1982).

Barzel, Yoram and Eugene Silberberg, "Is the Act of Voting Rational?" *Public Choice* v. 16 (Fall 1973).

Becker, Gary S., "A Theory of the Allocation of Time," *Economic Journal*, v. 75 (1965), 493–517.

————, "Crime and Punishment: An Economic Approach," *Journal of Political Economy*, v. 76 (Mar./Apr. 1968), 169–217.

————, "A Theory of Social Interactions," *Journal of Political Economy*, v. 82 (Nov./Dec. 1971), 1063–93.

————, *The Economic Approach to Human Behavior* (Chicago: U. of Chicago Press, 1976a).

————, "Altruism, Egoism, and Genetic Fitness: Economics and Sociobiology," *Journal of Economic Literature*, v. 14 (September 1976b).

————, *Treatise on the Family* (Cambridge, MA: Harvard U.P., 1981).

————, "A Theory of Competition Among Pressure Groups for Political Influence," *Quarterly Journal of Economics*, v. 98 (Aug. 1983), 371–400.

Bolnick, Bruce R., "Government as a Super Becker-altruist," *Public Choice*, v. 34 (1979), 499–504.

Boulding, Kenneth E., *Conflict and Defense: A General Theory* (New York: Harper & Brothers, 1962).

Boyd, Robert and Peter J. Richerson, "Sociobiology, Culture and Economic Theory," *Journal of Economic Behavior and Organization*, v. 1 (June 1980), 97–122.

Brennan, Geoffrey and Gordon Tullock, "An Economic Theory of Military Tactics," *Journal of Economic Behavior and Organization*, v. 3 (1982), 225–42.

Brenner, Reuven, *History – The Human Gamble* (Chicago: U. of Chicago Press, 1983).

Buchanan, James M. and Gordon Tullock, *The Calculus of Consent* (Ann Arbor: U. of Michigan Press, 1962).

Campbell, Donald T., "On the Conflicts Between Biological and Social Evolution and Between Psychology and Moral Tradition," *American Psychologist*, v. 30 (Dec. 1975), 1103–22.

Chamberlain, G. and M. Rothschild, "A Note on the Probability of Casting a Decisive Vote," Social Systems Research Institute, U. of Wisconsin-Madison (1980).

Charnov, Eric L., "Optimal Foraging: The Marginal Value Theorem," *Theoretical Population Biology*, v. 9 (1976), 126–36.

Coase, Ronald H., "The Problem of Social Cost," *Journal of Law and Economics*, v. 3 (Oct. 1960), 1–45.

————, "Economics and Contiguous Disciplines," *Journal of Legal Studies*, v. 7 (June 1978).

Coelen, Stephen P. and Robert J. McIntyre, "An Econometric Model of Pronatalist and Abortion Policies," *Journal of Political Economy*, v. 86 (Dec. 1978), 1077–1101.

Collard, David, *Altruism and Economy* (New York: Oxford U.P., 1978).

Conlisk, John, "Costly Optimizers versus Cheap Imitators," *Journal of Economic Behavior and Organization*, v. 1 (Sept. 1980), 275–93.

Cosmides, Leda, "Deduction or Darwinian Algorithms: An Explanation of the Elusive Content Effect on the Wason Selection Task," unpublished Harvard University Ph.D. thesis (1985).

Dawkins, Richard, *The Selfish Gene* (New York: Oxford U.P., 1976)

————, *The Extended Phenotype* (New York: Oxford U.P., 1982).

Deci, Edward L., "Effects of Externally Mediated Rewards on Intrinsic Motivation," *Journal of Personality and Social Psychology*, v. 18 (1971), 105–15.

Downs, Anthony, "An Economic Theory of Political Action in a Democracy," *Journal of Political Economy*, v. 65 (April 1957), 135–50.

Easterlin, Richard, "Does Economic Growth Improve the Human Lot? Some Empirical Evidence," in Paul David and Melvin Reder, eds., *Nations and Households in Economic Growth: Essays in Honor of Moses Abramovitz* (New York: Academic Press, 1974)

Edgeworth, F.Y., *Mathematical Psychics* (London: C. Kegan Paul & Co., 1881).

Ehrlich, Isaac, "Participation in Illegitimate Activities: A Theoretical and Empirical Investigation," *Journal of Political Economy*, v. 81 (May/June 1973), 521–65.

Enke, Stephen, "On Maximizing Profits: A Distinction Between Chamberlin and Robinson," *American Economic Review*, v. 41 (Sept. 1951), 566–78.

Frank, Robert H., *Choosing the Right Pond* (New York: Oxford U.P., 1985).

Ghiselin, Michael T., "The Economy of the Body," *American Economic Review*, v. 68 (May 1978).

Goodman, John C., "An Economic Theory of the Evolution of the Common Law," *Journal of Legal Studies*, v. 7 (1978), 393–406.

Grossbard, Amyra, "The Economics of Polygamy," in J. Simon and J. DaVanzo, eds., *Research in Population Economics*, v. 2 (Greenwich, CT: JAI Press, 1980).

Hamilton, W.D, "The Genetical Evolution of Social Behavior, I," *Journal of Theoretical Biology*, v. 7 (1964).

―――, "Selfish and Spiteful Behaviour in an Evolutionary Model," *Nature*, v. 228 (Dec. 19, 1970), 1218–20.

Hayek, Friedrich A., *The Political Order of a Free People*, v. 3 of *Law, Legislation, and Liberty* (Chicago: U. of Chicago Press, 1979).

Hirschman, Albert O., "Against Parsimony: Three Easy Ways of Complicating Some Categories of Economic Discourse," *American Economic Review*, v. 74 (2) (May 1984), 89–96.

Hirshleifer, J., "Shakespeare Versus Becker on Altruism: The Importance of Having the Last Word," *Journal of Economic Literature*, v. 15 (June 1977).

―――, "Natural Economy Versus Political Economy," *Journal of Social & Biological Structures*, v. 1 (Oct. 1978).

―――, "Privacy: Its Origin, Function, and Future," *Journal of Legal Studies*, v. 9 (Dec. 1980).

―――, "On the Emotions as Guarantors of Threats and Promises," UCLA Economics Dept. Working Paper #337 (Aug. 1984).

―――, "Conflict and Settlement," in *The New Palgrave; A Dictionary of Economics* (London: Macmillan, 1987).

International Encyclopedia of the Social Sciences, David L. Sills, ed. (New York: Macmillan and Free Press, 1968).

Kahneman, Daniel, Paul Slovic, and Amos Tversky, *Judgment Under Uncertainty: Heuristics and Biases* (Cambridge: Cambridge U.P., 1982).

Kaplan, Hillard and Kim Hill, "Food Sharing Among Aché Foragers: Tests of Explanatory Hypotheses," *Current Anthropology*, v. 26 (1985), 223–46.

Kelley, Harold, "The Processes of Causal Attribution," *American Psychologist*, v. 28 (February 1973), 107–28.

Krueger, Anne O., "The Political Economy of the Rent-Seeking Society," *American Economic Review*, v. 64 (June 1974), 291–304.

Lanchester, Frederick William, *Aircraft in Warfare: The Dawn of the Fourth Arm*, (London: Constable, 1916). Extract reprinted in James R. Newman, ed. *The World of Mathematics*, v. 4 (New York: Simon and Schuster, 1976), 2138–57.

Lepper, Mark R., David Greene, and Richard E. Nisbett, "Undermining Children's Intrinsic Interest with Extrinsic Reward: A Test of the 'Overjustification' Hypothesis," *Journal of Personality and Social Psychology*, v. 28 (1973), 129–37.

Lévi-Strauss, Claude, "The Principle of Reciprocity," in Lewis A. Coser and Bernard Rosenberg, eds., *Sociological Theory* (New York: Macmillan, 1964).

Lewontin, Richard C., "Fitness, Survival, and Optimality," in D.J. Horn, R.D. Mitchell, and G.R. Stairs, eds., *Analysis of Ecological Systems* (Columbus: Ohio State U.P., 1979).

Linder, Staffan B., *The Harried Leisure Class* (New York: Columbia U.P., 1970).

Margolis, Howard, *Selfishness, Altruism, and Rationality* (Cambridge: Cambridge U. Press, 1982).

Marshall, Alfred, *Principles of Economics*, 8th ed. (London: Macmillan, 1920).

Masters, Roger D., "Of Marmots and Men: Animal Behavior and Human Altruism," in Lauren Wispé (ed.), *Altruism, Sympathy, and Helping: Psychological and Sociological Principles* (1978).

Mauss, Marcel, *The Gift: Forms and Functions of Exchange in Archaic Societies* (Free Press, 1954; original French publication, 1925).

Maynard Smith, John, "Optimization Theory in Evolution," *Annual Review of Ecology and Systematics*, v. 9 (1978), 31–56.

McGuire, Martin, "Group Size, Group Homogeneity, and the Aggregate Provision of a Pure Public Good Under Cournot Behavior," *Public Choice*, v. 18 (Summer 1974).

Mueller, Dennis C., *Public Choice* (Cambridge: Cambridge U.P., 1979).

Nelson, Richard R. and Sidney G. Winter, *An Evolutionary Theory of Economic Change* (Cambridge, MA: Harvard U.P., 1982).

Pareto, Vilfredo, *Manual of Political Economy*, tr. Ann S. Schwier (New York: A.M. Kelley, 1971). [Original French publication 1927].

Penrose, Edith T., "Biological Analogies in the Theory of the Firm," *American Economic Review*, v. 42 (1952).

Pitt, Roger, "Warfare and Hominid Brain Evolution," *Journal of Theoretical Biology*, v. 72 (1978), 551–75.

Posner, Richard A., *The Economic Analysis of Law*, 2nd ed. (Boston: Little, Brown and Co., 1977).

———, "A Theory of Primitive Society, with Special Reference to Law," *Journal of Law and Economics*, v. 23 (April 1980), 1–53.

Radnitzky, Gerard and Peter Bernholz, eds., *Economic Imperialism: The Economic Approach Applied Outside the Traditional Areas of Economics* (New York: Paragon House, 1987).

Robbins, Lionel, *The Nature and Significance of Economic Science* (London: Macmillan, 1962).

Roberts, Russell D., "A Positive Model of Private Charity and Public Transfers," *Journal of Political Economy*, v. 92 (Feb. 1984), 136–48.

Rosen, Sherwin, "The Economics of Superstars," *American Economic Review*, v. 70 (1981), 845–58.

Rubin, Paul H., "Why Is the Common Law Efficient?" *Journal of Legal Studies*, v. 6 (1977), 51–63.

Sahlins, Marshall D., *Stone Age Economics* (Chicago: Aldine-Atherton, Inc., 1972).

Schelling, Thomas C., "The Intimate Contest for Self-Command," *Public Interest*, No. 60 (Sept. 1980).

Schoeck, Helmut, *Envy: A Theory of Social Behaviour*, tr. Michael Glenny and Betty Ross (New York: Harcourt, Brace and World, 1969). [Original German publication 1966].

Schweber, S.S., "The Genesis of Natural Selection – 1838: Some Further Insights," *BioScience*, v. 28 (May 1978).

Sen, Amartya K., "Rational Fools: A Critique of the Behavioral Foundations of Economic Theory," *Philosophy and Public Affairs*, v. 6 (1977), 317–44.

Simon, Herbert A., "A Behavioral Model of Rational Choice," *Quarterly Journal of Economics*, v. 69 (Feb. 1955), 99–118.

———, "Theories of Decision-Making in Economics and Behavioral Science," *American Economic Review*, v. 49 (June 1959), 253–83.

Smith, Adam, *The Theory of Moral Sentiments*, E.G. West ed. (Indianapolis: Liberty Classics, 1976). [Original publication 1759].

———, *Wealth of Nations*, Modern Library edition (New York: Random House, 1937). [Original publication 1776].

Smith, Eric Alden, "Anthropological Applications of Optimal Foraging Theory: A Critical Review," *Current Anthropology*, v. 24 (Dec. 1983), 625–51.

———, "Optimization Theory in Anthropology: Applications and Critiques" (April 1985).

Staddon, J.E.R., *Adaptive Behavior and Learning* (Cambridge: Cambridge U.P., 1983).

Thompson, Fred, "Closeness Counts in Horseshoes and Dancing. . . and Elections," *Public Choice*, v. 38 (1982), 305–16.

Trivers, Robert L., "Parental Investment and Sexual Selection," in Bernard G. Campbell, ed., *Sexual Selection and the Descent of Man 1871–1971* (Chicago: Aldine, 1972).

———, "Parent-Offspring Conflict," *American Zoologist*, v. 14 (1974), 249–64.

Tullock, Gordon, "Economics and Sociobiology: A Comment," *Journal of Economic Literature*, v. 15 (June 1977), 502–06.

Tversky, Amos and Daniel Kahneman, "Judgment under Uncertainty: Heuristics and Biases," *Science*, v. 185 (27 Sept. 1974), 1124–1131.

Veblen, Thorstein, *The Theory of the Leisure Class*, rev. ed. (New York: New American Library, 1953). [Original publication 1899].

Wilson, Edward O., *Sociobiology: The New Synthesis* (Cambridge, MA: Harvard U.P., 1975).

———, "Biology and the Social Sciences," *Daedalus* (Fall 1977).

———, "Altruism," *Harvard Magazine*, v. 81 (Nov.–Dec. 1978a).

————, "The Ergonomics of Caste in the Social Insects," *American Economic Review*, v. 68 (December 1978b).

Winter, Sidney G. Jr., "Economic 'Natural Selection' and the Theory of the Firm," *Yale Economic Essays*, v. 4 (1964).

————, "Satisficing, Selection, and the Innovating Remnant," *Quarterly Journal of Economics*, v. 85 (1971).

Wittman, Donald, "How a War Ends: A Rational Model Approach," *Journal of Conflict Resolution*, v. 23 (Dec. 1979).

Name Index

Subject Index

Acquisitiveness instinct, 37n15
Adaptation principle, 194–195
Adaptationist hypothesis, 328
Adaptive strategy, 86, 249
Affiliative instinct, 34
Alliances, 19, 334. *See also*
    Cooperation
Altruism, 200
    benevolence and, 207, 312n3
    bioeconomics and, 32–33, 334–336
    cooperation and. *See* Cooperation
    hard-core, 207, 207n11
    helping and, 281, 284, 334–336
    ideologies and, 40, 310
    kinship and, 32–33, 334–336
    spite and, 215
    See also Benevolence; Self-interest
American rule, 135
Amorphic competition, 103–105,
    125–126
Anarchy
    amorphy and, 103–105, 125–126
    breakdown of, 102–130
    chaos and, 103, 221, 299
    defined, 103
    equilibrium in, 105n5
    hierarchy and, 103
    income inadequacy, 110
    organization and, 126
    overcrowding and, 121n21
    spontaneous social order, 105
    stable solutions in, 105, 123–124
    successors to, 125–126
    territoriality and, 120
    tyranny and, 105
Anger, 209–218, 326

Anger/Gratitude Response curve,
    210–214
Animal instincts, 35–36, 103,
    120–121
Arms races, 65, 125
Art of War, The (Sun Tze), 66
As-if rationality, 327–328
Assurance game, 282n6
Asymmetry
    bias and, 139
    in contests, 94n7
    Cournot equilibrium and, 96, 99
    decisiveness and, 118
    equilibrium and, 95–99
    litigation and, 135
    logistics cost, 117
    in sequential-play game, 167
    strategic, 106
    three types of, 109, 116–117
    See also Stackelberg solution
Auction model, 91n2, 92n3

Battle of the sexes, 224
Battleship race, 258n12
Bayesian theory, 78n10, 79n11, 80n12,
    81n13
Behavior models, 164, 179, 253
Belligerence, 133
Benevolence, 30
    altruism and, 207, 312n3
    bioeconomic sources of, 31–35
    cooperation and, 206n10
    in family, 315–317
    malevolence and, 203–209
    promises and, 215
    See also Altruism; Cooperation